Ethical Problems

Facing the Criminal

Defense Lawyer

PRACTICAL ANSWERS TO TOUGH QUESTIONS

RODNEY J. UPHOFF

Editor

CRIMINAL JUSTICE SECTION

AMERICAN BAR ASSOCIATION

Cover design by Jim Colao.

The materials contained herein represent the opinions of the authors and editors and should not be construed to be the action of either the American Bar Association or the Criminal Justice Section unless adopted pursuant to the bylaws of the Association.

Nothing contained in this book is to be considered as the rendering of legal advice for specific cases, and readers are responsible for obtaining such advice from their own legal counsel. This book and any forms and agreements herein are intended for educational and informational purposes only.

Library of Congress Catalog Card Number 95-075690
ISBN: 1-57073-154-3

Discounts are available for books ordered in bulk. Special consideration is given to state bars, CLE programs, and other bar-related organizations. Inquire at Publications Planning & Marketing, American Bar Association, 750 North Lake Shore Drive, Chicago, Illinois 60611.

99 98 97 96 95   5 4 3 2 1

CONTENTS

ACKNOWLEDGMENTS

In April 1992, Henry Martin, then chair of the Defense Services Committee of the ABA Criminal Justice Section, asked me to chair a subcommittee to review an ongoing Defense Services Committee project—the publication of an ethics manual for public defenders. The subcommittee, which included Vince Aprile, Nick Chiarkas, Rita Fry, Eric Kocher, Robert Spangenberg, and Robert Baum, wholeheartedly endorsed the need for such a publication and decided that the book should contain a series of articles addressing reoccurring ethical dilemmas.

The subcommittee first drafted a series of ethical questions that we believed regularly confounded public defenders. It was decided, however, to expand the project to include ethical quandaries common not only to public defenders but to all defense lawyers. We then contacted prospective authors with considerable experience representing indigent defendants and they, in turn, struggled with their respective ethical question or series of questions. Although the project has taken longer than initially planned, we finally have produced what we believe is a readable, helpful guide to coping with some of the tough ethical issues a defense lawyer invariably will face.

This book represents the culmination of the efforts of many people. The chapter authors, of course, deserve considerable credit for their willingness to participate in this extended project. They have given selflessly of their time and talent to lend guidance to their fellow criminal defense lawyers. Vince Aprile also contributed significantly to the initial development of this book. In addition, Joan Dolby, now with the ACLU Prison Project, started as the ABA staff member on this project. Her assistance was crucial in keeping the project going. Sherrill Klein, Don Gecewicz, and Ken Goldsmith from the ABA also played an important role in the success of this project. Henry Martin, Christopher Stone, who took over as chair of the Defense Services Committee, and Prof. Randolph Stone, who was chair of the ABA Criminal Justice Section in 1994, provided critical support during periods when finishing the book appeared to be a Sisyphean task.

I want to thank the CJS Book Publication Committee, especially Prof. Myrna Raeder and Prof. David Gottlieb, for supporting this publication. Special thanks to my secretary, Lori Ketner, and my research assistant, Koni Johnson, for the countless hours they spent assisting me in preparing the manuscript for publication. Without them, I would still be struggling to finish this project.

My hope is that this book will assist lawyers facing troublesome ethical problems in making prudent, ethical choices without compromising their clients' right to competent, zealous representation. If so, then the struggle was certainly worth it.

FOREWORD

Finally! After several years of deliberation and discussion, the American Bar Association's Criminal Justice Section Defense Services Committee has produced an ethics guide for criminal defense lawyers with particular emphasis on public defenders and appointed counsel representing the indigent. In some ways, the timing and importance of this work is magnified by the recent political hysteria related to crime control. Harsher sentences and increased caseloads concomitant with efforts restricting the constitutional rights of the accused all increase the pressure on defense counsel to provide effective representation.

Issues of professional responsibility affect both civil and criminal practitioners. In fact, ethical questions involving conflicts of interest, attorney-client relationships and discovery problems may be more common in the civil context. As Monroe Freedman has noted, if you want to avoid clients who lie, cheat, steal and murder, stay away from corporate law. Nonetheless, the ethical problems facing those lawyers representing people accused of violent and sometimes repugnant behavior deserve particular attention. The conduct of counsel, required and privileged to zealously advocate on behalf of the unpopular and often despised criminal accused, is subject to heightened scrutiny in a society in which getting tough on crime, protecting victims' rights, and maximizing judicial efficiency are the prevailing watchwords.

The authors of this volume, many of whom have devoted most or all of their legal careers to representing poor people charged with crime, provide an interesting and diverse perspective to the presented ethical questions. The questions they have tackled include some of the most difficult ethical quandaries which will confront the criminal practitioner. Some of the questions overlap and the answers are subject to fact interpretation, but the authors unquestionably provide helpful insight to anyone representing a criminal defendant. While the authors have attempted to provide definitive answers where possible, for the most part, the answers are intended as a starting point and a guide for the criminal defense lawyer.

Oliver Wendell Holmes is said to have noted: "If you aspire to greatness in the profession, involve yourselves in the agonies of the time." By that measure, public defenders and appointed counsel who represent the indigent daily are on the road to greatness. Hopefully, this publication provides a seat belt, air bag, and accurate directions for any lawyer who takes on the task of defending a person accused of a crime.

Randolph N. Stone

ABOUT THE AUTHORS

Robert M. Baum has worked in the Criminal Defense Division of The Legal Aid Society of New York since 1971. His current position is Attorney-in-Charge for New York City. Mr. Baum received his B.A. degree from Brooklyn College in 1968 and his J.D. from Syracuse University College of Law in 1971. He is an active member of several legal associations, including the Association of the Bar of the City of New York, the New York County Lawyers Association, the New York Association of Criminal Defense Lawyers, the American Bar Association, and the National Legal Aid and Defender Association. He has been a featured lecturer for legal organizations, speaking on topics such as trial techniques and defender management.

Marilyn E. Bednarski is a Senior Litigator with the Federal Public Defender's Office in Los Angeles, where she is also responsible for training. She has spent nearly her entire legal career defending clients in criminal cases in state and federal courts in the western United States. Ms. Bednarski began her career as a Deputy Federal Public Defender in 1984. She has since tried approximately sixty-five federal felony jury trials. She also teaches at several trial advocacy colleges around the country, including the National College of Criminal Defense in Macon, Georgia; the Western Trial Advocacy Institute in Laramie, Wyoming; and the Institute for Trial Advocacy in San Diego, California.

George Bisharat is an Assistant Professor of Law at Hastings College of the Law in San Francisco, where he teaches a criminal practice clinic, criminal procedure, and law and social anthropology. Prior to teaching at Hastings, Mr. Bisharat was a Deputy Public Defender for the City and County of San Francisco, where he tried both misdemeanor and felony cases. He has also been a frequent lecturer and writer on legal issues.

Carol A. Brook has been the Deputy Director of the Federal Defender Program for the Northern District of Illinois since 1985. Ms. Brook received her undergraduate degree from the University of Michigan in 1971 and earned her law degree from the University of Illinois College of Law in 1976. She has taught trial advocacy at various law schools, including DePaul College of Law and the University of Chicago Mandel Legal Aid Clinic. Ms. Brook has been an instructor for many years at the Federal Judicial Center's Annual Seminar for Assistant Federal Defenders. She is currently a member of the Federal Defender National Subcommittee on Legislation, the Advisory Panel of the MacArthur Justice Foundation, and the Board of Directors of the Chicago Chapter of the Federal Bar Association. Ms. Brook is a frequent lecturer for numerous legal organizations and has published many articles in books and journals.

Keith N. Bystrom is currently a Professor of Law and Director of Clinical Legal Education at the University of Oklahoma College of Law. Prior to joining the faculty in 1979, he practiced four years as the Lincoln County Public Defender in North Platte, Nebraska. Since joining the faculty, Mr. Bystrom has taught live-client clinics representing civil and criminal clients and assisting inmates at a nearby federal prison. He has served four years as Associate Dean of the College of Law and was appointed Acting Dean in 1988–89. Mr. Bystrom has extensive experience at the trial and appellate level representing people charged with crimes who are unable to afford a lawyer. He earned his undergraduate degree from the University of Nebraska in 1972 and his law degree from Georgetown University Law Center in 1975.

Nicholas L. Chiarkas was appointed Wisconsin State Public Defender in 1988. Prior to his appointment, he was the General Counsel of the United States Architectural and Transportation Barriers Compliance Board; the Deputy Chief Counsel and Research Director for the President's Commission on Organized Crime; and Deputy Chief Counsel of the U.S. Senate Permanent Subcommittee on Investigations. Mr. Chiarkas has also been an Associate Professor of Law and a Professor of Criminology, has been in private practice, and has been a New York City police officer. He has a law degree from Temple University; doctorate and master's degrees in sociology from Columbia University; a master's and bachelor's degree in criminology from the City University of New York; and a postgraduate certificate in computer systems analysis from New York University. Among Mr. Chiarkas's publications are three law books and several articles.

James Clark is an Assistant Professor at the University of Kentucky College of Social Work and a Ph.D. candidate at the University of Chicago. He is affiliated with the University of Kentucky Mental Health Research Center and is a consultant with the Department of Public Advocacy, the Department of Mental Health, and other organizations at state and local levels. Mr. Clark's special research and practice interests involve psycholegal issues, especially violence and mental illness. Mr. Clark's publications include *The Fiend Unmasked: The Mental Health Dimensions of the Defense*, coauthored with Lane Ueltkamp and Ed Monahan, published in the ABA's *Criminal Justice* Vol. 8, No. 2 (1993).

Judy Clarke is the Executive Director of Federal Defenders of Eastern Washington and Idaho. She has been a public defender in the federal courts for almost seventeen years. She served as a trial attorney with Federal Defenders of San Diego, Inc. for five years and Executive Director of that organization for eight years before a one-year stint in private practice. Ms. Clarke returned to the Federal Defender Program in 1992. She has argued twice before the U.S. Supreme Court and has tried a range of federal criminal cases, from white collar to immigration to murder. She has written articles on bail and sentencing; is the co-author of Matthew Bender's *Federal Sentencing Manual;* and is responsible for the *Guideline Grapevine*, a monthly newsletter summary of federal sentencing cases. Ms. Clarke serves on the Board of Regents of the National Criminal Defense College and is the 1994–95 First Vice President of the National Association of Criminal Defense Lawyers.

Janet R. Fink is Assistant Deputy Counsel to the New York State Unified Court System, in charge of family law and family court issues, and served as a child welfare consultant to the New York State Permanent Judicial Commission on Justice for Children. A graduate of Bryn Mawr College and Georgetown University Law Center, she was formerly Senior Counsel to the New York State Assembly Codes Committee. For sixteen years, Ms. Fink was employed by the Juvenile Rights Division of the New York City Legal Aid Society, serving for the last six years as the Division's Assistant Attorney-in-Charge. Starting as a law guardian representing children in the New York City Family Court, she then directed the Juvenile Rights Division's Appeals and Law Reform Unit. Ms. Fink recently completed a four-year term as Chair of the Juvenile Justice Committee of the ABA Criminal Justice Section, is the Vice-Chair of the Editorial Board for ABA's Criminal Justice magazine, and is editing an anthology on juvenile justice for the CJA Book Publications Committee. Ms. Fink is also a member of the Bar of the City of New York, the New York State Bar Association, and the Family Court Advisory Committee of the New York Supreme Court, Appellate Division, First Department.

Monroe H. Freedman is the Howard Lichtenstein Distinguished Professor of Legal Ethics at Hofstra University in Hempstead, New York. One of the nation's leading ethics experts, Freedman has written numerous books and articles on ethical issues including *Understanding Lawyers' Ethics,* published by Matthew Bender in 1990.

Rita Aliese Fry was appointed Public Defender for Cook County (Illinois) in 1992. In this capacity she is Chief Executive of the Office of the Cook County Public Defender. She was previously appointed First Assistant Public Defender for the same office in August 1988. From 1986 to 1988, she was a Senior Attorney Supervisor of the Municipal Prosecutions Divisions for the City of Chicago Law Department. Ms. Fry was an Assistant Public Defender from 1980 through 1986, assigned to the Felony Trial Division and Homicide Task Force. She has been an instructor or faculty member for the National Legal Aid and Defender Association, Illinois Institute for Continuing Legal Education, the Chicago Bar Association's Trial Practice Workshops, Georgia Indigent Defense Council, Harvard Law School Trial Advocacy Workshop, and the ABA Criminal Justice Section. Ms. Fry is a member of numerous legal organizations such as the National Legal Aid and Defenders Association, the Illinois State Bar Association, the American Bar Association, and the Board of Directors of the Illinois Public Defenders Association. She earned her B.A. degree from Loyola University in 1968 and her J.D. from Northwestern University College of Law in 1979.

Phyllis Goldfarb is an Associate Professor at Boston College Law School. She received her J.D. from Yale Law School in 1982 and her LL.M. from Georgetown University in 1985. Since 1986, Ms. Goldfarb has served as Director of Criminal Process, the criminal clinical program at Boston College Law School. She also teaches criminal law and procedures as well as courses in jurisprudence and feminist theory. From 1982 through 1984 she served as an E. Barrett Prettyman Fellow at Georgetown University Law Center and was an attorney and clinical instructor in the Georgetown Criminal Justice Clinic and the Georgetown Juvenile Justice Clinic. In addition to teaching, she is involved in pro bono criminal defense work, including death penalty cases, at the postconviction stage.

David R. Katner is a Professor of Clinical Law at Tulane Law School in New Orleans. He is the Dreyfous Fellow of Juvenile Law at Tulane, and he teaches courses in Professional Responsibility and Advanced Criminal Procedure. Mr. Katner is the Director of Tulane's Juvenile Law

Clinic. Before joining Tulane's faculty, he was in private practice and he litigated both criminal and civil cases. He served as an indigent defender in Jefferson Parish, Louisiana, and concentrated on insanity defenses. Mr. Katner received both his undergraduate and law degrees from Tulane.

Terence F. MacCarthy has been with the Federal Defender Program, U.S. District Court, Northern District of Illinois, since 1966. He is currently Executive Director. Mr. MacCarthy has served on many major federal court committees, including the National Advisory Committee on Criminal Rules (U.S. Supreme Court), and is presently Chair of the Panel Attorney Selection Committee and a member of the Seventh Circuit Court of Appeals Educational Long-Range Planning Committee. He is an active member of the American Bar Association, serving on numerous committees including the Criminal Justice Section Council (1982 to present), Chair 1988–89; Delegate to the House of Delegates (1990 to present); ABA Criminal Justice Liaison to National Association of Criminal Defense Lawyers (1989 to present); and Liaison, ABA Special Committee on the Drug Crisis (Litigation Section). Mr. MacCarthy is also a member of over a dozen other legal organizations including the National Legal Aid and Defender Association and the National College of Criminal Defense. Among his many awards, he received a Distinguished Service Award in 1993 from the National Association of Criminal Defense Lawyers. He earned a B.A. from St. Joseph's College in 1955 and a J.D. from DePaul University College of Law in 1960.

Wallace J. Mlyniec is the Associate Dean for Georgetown University's clinical programs, is Professor of Law, and has been the Director of the Law Center's Juvenile Justice Clinic for twenty years. He has litigated or supervised the litigation of hundreds of cases involving children. He also teaches courses in family law and juvenile justice, and he assists with the training of fellows in the Prettyman Legal Internship Program. Mr. Mlyniec is the author of many books and articles on legal issues. He was the Director of the Judicial Conference Study on ABA Criminal Justice Standards and the Administrator of the Emergency Bail Fund. Mr. Mlyniec served as a consultant to San Jose State University and the University of Maryland schools of social work, the ABA's National Resource Center on Child Abuse and Neglect, and University of Baltimore and Brooklyn law schools. He received a B.S. degree from Northwestern University and his J.D. from Georgetown University.

Ed Monahan has been an Assistant Public Advocate with the Kentucky Department of Public Advocacy (DPA) since 1976 and directs its statewide training program. In his eighteen years of public defender work, Mr. Monahan has been an appellate attorney and chief of the trial services branch. He has been editor of *The Advocate*, DPA's journal of research and education, since 1984. Mr. Monahan is a charter board member of the Kentucky Association of Criminal Defense Lawyers, Past Chair of the Kentucky Bar Association's Criminal Law Section, and Vice-Chair of the National Legal Aid and Defender Association's Training Section. He has given presentations across the country on capital representation, criminal litigation skills, and defense training. Mr. Monahan's publications include "Who Is Killing the Sixth Amendment?" (*Criminal Justice*, American Bar Association, 1991). He is a 1976 graduate of Catholic University of America Law School in Washington, D.C.

Eva S. Nilsen is an Associate Clinical Professor at Boston University School of Law. She received her J.D. from the University of Virginia School of Law in 1977 and her LL.M. from Georgetown University Law Center in 1980, and worked as a public defender in the E. Barrett Prettyman program at Georgetown. Ms. Nilsen has taught in the student defender clinic at Boston University School of Law since 1980. She also assists in teaching ethics to clinical students. In 1987, Ms. Nilsen assisted the Massachusetts Committee for Public Counsel Services in drafting the Performance Guidelines Governing Representation of Indigents in Criminal Cases. She has served on numerous ABA, AALS, and Boston Bar Association committees working on criminal justice and legal education issues. She teaches a nonclinical course in sentencing. Ms. Nilsen's writings are about criminal practice and procedures. She taught trial advocacy for a semester in Lahore, Pakistan, and participated in an evaluation of a legal clinic in Johannesburg, South Africa.

Barbara A. Schwartz has been on the faculty of the University of Iowa since 1977. She teaches in Iowa's clinic program, where she supervises students in misdemeanor defense, state postconviction and federal habeas practice, and prisoners' rights representation. Ms. Schwartz also regularly teaches courses in criminal law and procedure and professional responsibility. She received her B.A. and M.A. in 1967 and 1968, respectively, at the University of Michigan. She received her J.D. from Wayne State University. Before joining the faculty at the University of Iowa, Ms. Schwartz worked at a private criminal defense practice in Detroit for two years.

Nancy Shaw is the Federal Defender for the District of Alaska, where her criminal practice includes Indian law, fish and wildlife law, banking, and tax matters. She was previously in-house counsel to Local 959 of the International Brotherhood of Teamsters.

Abbe Smith is Deputy Director and Clinical Instructor at the Criminal Justice Institute at Harvard Law School. She is also Lecturer on Law for the Trial Advocacy Workshop at Harvard. She was Assistant Defender for the Defender Association of Philadelphia from 1982 through 1987 and from 1989 through 1990. She earned her B.A. degree from Yale University and she received her J.D. degree from New York University School of Law in 1982.

Randolph N. Stone is a Clinical Professor of Law and Director of the Mandel Legal Aid Clinic at the University of Chicago Law School. From 1988 to 1991, he served as the first African-American Public Defender of Cook County, Illinois, and was responsible for the management of a $32 million budget and the leadership of 508 lawyers and 248 support staff members servicing over 200,000 clients per year. Mr. Stone was previously the Deputy Director of the Public Defender Service for the District of Columbia. He has served as a Lecturer on Law at Harvard Law School, was on the faculty for the National Institute for Trial Advocacy and the National Criminal Defense College, and was Adjunct Professor for IIT Chicago-Kent College of Law. From 1980 to 1983, he was a partner in the Chicago firm of Stone & Clark. Mr. Stone is the outgoing Chair of the ABA's Criminal Justice Section, a Defender Committee Member of the National Legal Aid and Defender Association, is on the Board of Directors of the Sentencing Project, Inc., and the Illinois Board of Admissions to the Bar. He has received a number of awards and he writes and lectures on issues related to the legal profession, criminal justice, poverty, and race. Mr. Stone earned a B.A. degree from the University of Wisconsin in 1972 and a J.D. degree from the University of Wisconsin in 1975.

Graham B. Strong is Visiting Professor of Law at Whittier Law School where he teaches evidence, professional responsibilities, and lawyering skills. He received his B.A. degree in 1972 and his J.D. degree in 1975 from University of Virginia. Mr. Strong earned his LL.M. in 1980 from Georgetown University where he was a Prettyman Fellow. He has taught and trained law students in criminal practice at the University of Virginia, Cornell, and U.C.L.A.

William Talley, Jr., has been a Clinical Instructor for the Criminal Justice Institute at Harvard Law School since 1991. He was an Assistant Public Defender for the Committee for Public Counsel Services in Massachusetts from 1984 through 1990. Mr. Talley earned an A.B. degree from Brown University and received his J.D. degree from Case Western Reserve University in 1983.

Rodney J. Uphoff is presently an Associate Professor and Associate Director of Clinical Legal Education at the University of Oklahoma School of Law. He has B.A. and J.D. degrees from the University of Wisconsin and a Masters Degree from the London School of Economics. In addition to doing criminal defense work as a public defender and a private practitioner, Mr. Uphoff served as Chief Staff Attorney for the Milwaukee Office of the Wisconsin State Public Defender. He directed a criminal defense clinic program at the University of Wisconsin Law School and now directs a similar program at the University of Oklahoma. Mr. Uphoff is a Vice-Chair of the ABA Defense Service Committee and chair of the subcommittee responsible for the organization of this publication. He has written and lectured frequently on ethical issues and the delivery of indigent defense services.

Richard J. Wilson is Professor of Law and Director of the International Human Rights Law Clinic at the Washington College of Law, American University, in Washington, D.C. He worked as public defender in Illinois for eight years before becoming Director of the Defender Division at the National Legal Aid and Defender Association in 1980. Mr. Wilson began teaching at CUNY Law School in 1985, and served as Reporter for the Third Edition of the ABA Standards in Criminal Justice, Providing Defense Services.

INTRODUCTION

In March, 1982, two young part-time public defenders, George and Walter Stenhach, were appointed to represent Richard Buchanan in a first-degree murder case. Based on information provided by Buchanan, an investigator hired by the Stenhach brothers recovered the rifle stock used in the homicide. Despite the objections of their investigator, the Stenhachs retained the rifle stock in their office because their research satisfied them that they had the legal duty to preserve their client's confidential communications and that their retention of the weapon was dictated by the lawyer-client privilege. During Buchanan's murder trial, however, their investigator was compelled, over objection, to answer a question regarding the location of the weapon. The Stenhachs were then ordered to retrieve the rifle stock from their office and hand it over to the prosecutor.

Buchanan was convicted. Although the rifle stock was not used by either the prosecution or the defense at trial, the Stenhach brothers, as a result of withholding the rifle stock, were charged with conspiracy, criminal solicitation, hindering prosecution, and tampering with physical evidence. Each was convicted of three counts and an appeal followed. The appellate court rejected the Stenhachs' contention that their behavior was proper and instead found that they had breached an affirmative duty to deliver the rifle stock to the prosecution. Nonetheless, the court reversed their convictions holding that the statutes prohibiting hindering prosecution and tampering with physical evidence were unconstitutionally overbroad when applied to lawyers representing criminal defendants.[1]

The *Stenhach* case is illustrative for several reasons. First, criminal defense lawyers are called upon to provide zealous representation and to steadfastly champion their clients' rights while at the same time they are required to uphold their responsibilities as officers of the court. Like the Stenhach brothers, however, criminal defense lawyers often find that to fulfill a duty to a client or to the court they must ignore, compromise, or abandon a duty owed to the other. Thus, as experienced criminal defense lawyers are only too aware, lawyers who represent criminal defendants regularly confront confusing, demanding ethical dilemmas growing out of their conflicting responsibilities. Moreover, lawyers grappling with these difficult ethical issues frequently have little time and often only limited access to expert guidance or assistance before having to make extremely tough choices.

In addition, even those lawyers who have the time to research troublesome ethical issues encounter an intimidating task. They must struggle to ascertain the right answer often amid a "morass of conflicting precepts."[2] Indeed, as the Pennsylvania court noted in *Stenhach:*

> [A]ttorneys face a distressing paucity of dispositive precedent to guide them in balancing their duty of zealous representation against their duty as officers of the court. Volumes are filled with other potential sources of guidance, such as ethical codes and comments thereto, both proposed and adopted, advisory opinions by ethics committees and myriad articles in legal periodicals. The plethora of writing exemplifies the profession's concern with the problem, and although they may help to clarify some of the issues, they fail to answer many of the difficult questions in this area of legal practice.

Finally, the consequences of making a "wrong" ethical choice can be devastating. As the *Stenhach* case also illustrates, the criminal defense lawyer who makes a difficult ethical choice may also be subject to criminal prosecution as well as a disciplinary proceeding if someone disagrees with that choice.[3]

The purpose of this book, then, is to give criminal defense lawyers, especially public defenders and lawyers representing indigent defendants, assistance and guidance in making some of the difficult ethical choices they inevitably will face in their practice. Many of the dilemmas that public defenders or assigned counsel encounter are similar to those faced by all criminal defense lawyers. Nevertheless, there are recurring problems that lawyers representing indigent criminal defendants confront that privately retained defense lawyers may never or only rarely face. Although this publication should be of interest and use to anyone practicing criminal law, a number of the ethical problems presented in this book only bedevil lawyers involved in the delivery of indigent defense services.

Of course, all criminal defendants are entitled to zealous representation notwithstanding who is paying for that representation. Although many indigent defendants receive competent and at times, superb representation, numerous studies have confirmed the obvious reality of our underfunded, underresourced criminal justice system: poor defendants all too often do not receive competent representation and are not routinely defended with the same zeal accorded to wealthy defendants.[4] Public defenders frequently must cope not only with inadequate resources and large caseloads but with clients who mistrust them.[5] Thus, the indigent defender-client relationship is affected, often adversely, by the fact that an indigent criminal defendant rarely has little say in selecting counsel and generally lacks the ability to retain new counsel if dissatisfied with defense counsel's performance.[6] Because of the nature of their lawyer-client relationships, a public defender or court-appointed lawyer may at times be in a different, and sometimes more difficult, ethical bind than retained counsel. Moreover, the indigent client's lack of a viable alternative may place a heightened responsibility on a public defender or assigned counsel to ensure that ethical questions are resolved without unduly compromising the indigent defendant's right to an effective, zealous advocate.

Private defense lawyers, retained and court appointed, also face pressures that may impact the resolution of the ethical problems they encounter. As Justice Brennan pointed out:

> A lawyer and his client do not always have the same interests. Even with paying clients, a lawyer may have a strong interest in having judges and prosecutors think well of him, and, if he is working for a flat fee—a common arrangement for criminal defense attorneys—or if his fees for court appointments are lower than he would receive for other work, he has an obvious financial incentive to conclude cases on his criminal docket swiftly. Good lawyers undoubtedly recognize these temptations and resist them, and they endeavor to convince their clients that they will. It would be naive, however, to suggest that they always succeed in either task.[7]

Despite pressures and temptations, most defense lawyers, public and private, struggle to "do the right thing." Unfortunately, in many ethical situations it is often difficult to ascertain what doing the right thing actually entails.

The goal of the ABA Criminal Justice Section Defense Services Committee, which conceived this project, was to provide criminal defense lawyers, particularly those lawyers representing indigent defendants, regardless of the size or location of their office, with a quality reference work to assist them in resolving recurring ethical dilemmas. All of the authors selected for this book have considerable experience in the criminal justice system, most of whom either were or are public defenders. Many of the authors either have managed or presently manage a public defender office or program. Each was asked to tackle a specific ethical dilemma and prepare a readable, reasoned response to the ethical problem presented. Each author has also included a bibliography of additional materials should the reader want to do additional research or explore a related question.

The format of this book, in part, reflects a recognition of the fact that criminal defense lawyers often must make hard choices without time for extended research. Whenever possible, of course, lawyers should anticipate ethical problems far enough in advance so that adequate research can be performed before a decision must be made. Additionally, counsel should seek to avoid putting herself into a position where she must make a hard ethical decision under pressure without the opportunity to conduct adequate research. Ideally, this book will sensitize criminal defense lawyers to difficult issues that they are likely to confront and stimulate thought as well as discussion about those issues before they arise. The book also should provide some concrete guidance in those situations where time is of the essence.

Several caveats are warranted. Every jurisdiction has its own set of rules and regulations governing the conduct of lawyers in that jurisdiction. Generally, states have adopted their own version of the ABA Model Code of Professional Responsibility[8] or the ABA Model Rules of Professional Conduct.[9] Throughout this book, the authors have referred to the ABA Model Code of Professional Responsibility as the ABA Model Code or just Model Code. Similarly, the authors have referred to the ABA Model Rules of Professional Conduct as the ABA Model Rules or the Model Rules. The authors have attempted to point out that an appropriate response to a specific ethical problem may be different in a Model Code jurisdiction as opposed to a Model Rules jurisdiction. But, before relying on any answer in this book, it is absolutely essential that the reader check the specific language of the relevant ethical provisions of the lawyer's own jurisdiction, as well as any case law or ethics opinion in that jurisdiction. It is important to bear in mind that various states made significant changes from the ABA Model Code and ABA Model Rules when crafting their own regulations so that it is critical for any lawyer using this book to determine if the law in his or her state includes comparable provisions to those utilized in the answer being considered.[10]

When working with the ABA Model Code, also remember that the Model Code consists of three different components. As the Preliminary Statement sets forth:

The Canons are statements of axiomatic norms, expressing in general terms the standards of professional conduct expected of lawyers in their relationships with the public, with the legal system, and with the legal profession. They embody the general concepts from which the Ethical Considerations and the Disciplinary Rules are derived.

The Ethical Considerations are aspirational in character and represent the objectives toward which every member of the profession should strive. They constitute a body of principles upon which the lawyer can rely for guidance in many specific situations.

The Disciplinary Rules, unlike the Ethical Considerations, are mandatory in character. The Disciplinary Rules state the minimum level of conduct below which no lawyer can fall without being subject to disciplinary action.[11]

Despite this disclaimer, courts and disciplinary entities often have treated violations of the Ethical Considerations as well as the Disciplinary Rules as the basis for disciplinary action.[12] Be mindful also that the failure to comply with an obligation or prohibition mandated by a Model Rule subjects a lawyer to discipline. Lawyers should be wary, though, of blindly accepting the Comments to the Model Rules as authoritative pronouncements as to what constitutes proper conduct. The Comments to the Model Rules "do not add obligations to the Rules but provide guidance for practicing in compliance with the Rules."[13] Unfortunately, the guidance offered by the Comments to the Model Rules is at times inconsistent with, or even contrary to, the conduct clearly mandated by the Model Rules.[14]

Additional guidance regarding the proper conduct for criminal defense lawyers can be found in a number of excellent sources including the ABA Standards for Criminal Justice; the ABA/BNA Manual for Professional Conduct; and the ABA Annotated Guide to the Model Rules (2d ed. 1992). The authors in this publication frequently looked to the ABA Standards for Criminal Justice Defense Function (generally shortened in the articles to the ABA Standards) for direction in addressing these ethical questions because state and federal courts regularly rely on the ABA Standards. Lawyers also should be aware that the ABA Standing Committee on Ethics and Professional Responsibility issues formal and informal opinions on ethical questions as do many state and local bar associations. Similarly, the National Association of Criminal Defense Lawyers (NACDL) has an Ethics Advisory Committee that issues opinions that deal exclusively with ethical problems that confront criminal defense lawyers.[15] None of these ethics opinions, however, have the force of law until cited with approval by a court. Nevertheless, such opinions provide useful guidance and generally a lawyer who acts in accordance with such an opinion will not be disciplined.[16] Finally, a criminal defense lawyer should enlist the aid of other knowledgeable lawyers in her office or, when appropriate and in a manner consistent with the protection of the client's confidences, the assistance of other experienced criminal defense lawyers in resolving ethical problems.[17]

Unquestionably, there is often more than one right answer or solution to the ethical problems defense counsel may confront. The authors in this book have suggested an answer or answers that make sense to them based on their research and experience. Certainly as facts and circumstances change, the appropriate response to the ethical issues presented in this book also may change. Correspondingly, the proper answer to a particular dilemma may change based on the prevailing law in counsel's jurisdiction. A criminal defense lawyer, like any lawyer, has the right to challenge the ethical opinions in her jurisdiction and to seek to have those controlling opinions reversed or modified as long as the lawyer has a good faith basis for advocating the change. When acting contrary to the established law or ethical opinions in a particular jurisdiction, however, defense counsel must recognize that she faces disciplinary action if the disciplinary authority disagrees with counsel's course of action. Nonetheless, if defense counsel makes a conscientious, well-thought-out decision based on reasonable authority, then counsel is in a better position to avoid a disciplinary sanction than if counsel simply acts without carefully considering the issue.

All criminal defense lawyers owe their clients various duties: to provide competent representation, to work zealously and diligently on behalf of their clients, to avoid conflicts of interests that undermine or appear to undermine counsel's loyalty, and to preserve their client's confidences. In trying to be a zealous advocate, defense counsel frequently finds that counsel's responsibilities as a zealous advocate clash with the interests of the judge, the legal system, third parties, or counsel's own interests. This clash of competing interests generates most of the ethical questions found in this book. Although the chapters in this book will aid defense lawyers in resolving the ethical dilemmas they will confront, counsel's own personal sense of morality and commitment to her clients will, in the final analysis, shape the manner in which counsel responds to ethical problems. In making those tough decisions, remember that:

Our system of justice is inherently contentious, albeit bounded by the rules of professional ethics and decorum, and it demands that the lawyer be inclined toward vigorous advocacy.... Counsel's place in our adversary process of justice requires that counsel be guided constantly by the obligation to pursue the client's interests. Counsel must not be asked to limit his or her zeal in the pursuit of those interests except by definitive standards of professional conduct.[18]

Finally, it should be noted that the answer to any particular ethical question represents the author's own response to the question and not the position of the American Bar Association, the ABA Criminal Justice Section, or the ABA Defense Service Committee.

Notes

1. Commonwealth v. Stenhach, 514 A.2d 114, *appeal denied,* 524 A.2d 769 (Pa. Super. 1987).

2. GEOFFREY C. HAZARD & SUSAN P. KONIAK, THE LAW AND ETHICS OF LAWYERING 254 (1990). For example, on the subject of the lawyer's duty when dealing with client fraud, Hazard and Koniak conclude, "the Code position is almost totally incoherent." *Id.* at 284.

3. Fortunately for the Stenhach brothers, not only was their criminal case dismissed but they were subsequently absolved by the Pennsylvania Disciplinary Board. *See* Office of Disciplinary Council v. Stenhach, 479, slip opinion at 25-27 (Pa. Supr. Ct. Disciplinary Board August 8, 1989) (finding that the brothers had made a good faith effort to balance their duties owed to their client and to the court and their resolution of the issue in favor of their client did not undermine the integrity of the legal system). Nonetheless, in light of the clear holding in the first *Stenhach* case, the next lawyer in Pennsylvania who receives and retains physical possession of material evidence is unlikely to escape discipline.

4. *See, e.g.,* ABA SECTION ON CRIMINAL JUSTICE, CRIMINAL JUSTICE IN CRISIS: A REPORT TO THE AMERICAN PEOPLE AND THE AMERICAN BAR ON CRIMINAL JUSTICE IN THE UNITED STATES (1988); Colloquium, *Effective Assistance of Counsel for the Indigent Criminal Defendant: Has the Promise Been Fulfilled?* 14 N.Y.U. REV. L. & SOC. CHANGE 1–276 (1986).

5. "It is no secret that indigent clients often mistrust the lawyers appointed to represent them." Jones v. Barnes, 463 U.S. 745, 761 (1983) (Brennan, J., dissenting). *See also* Robert Burt, *Conflict and Trust Between Attorney and Client,* 69 GEO. L.J. 1015 (1981).

6. *See* ABA STANDARDS FOR CRIMINAL JUSTICE DEFENSE FUNCTION 4-1.2 and Commentary (3d ed. 1993) (hereinafter ABA STANDARD).

7. Jones v. Barnes, 463 U.S. 745, 761–62 (1983) (Brennan, J., dissenting).

8. The ABA Model Code of Professional Responsibility (1969) was originally adopted by the ABA House of Delegates in 1969. Although virtually all states initially promulgated ethical rules based on this Model Code, only eleven states as of 1994 still have ethical provisions patterned on the Model Code.

9. In 1983, the ABA House of Delegates took action to replace the Model Code by adopting the ABA Model Rules of Professional Conduct (1983). As of 1994, thirty-eight states and the District of Columbia have adopted a version of the Model Rules. California does not follow either the Model Code or the Model Rules.

10. *See, e.g.,* DR 7-102(B)(1), which was amended in 1974 by the ABA by adding the critical phrase "when information is protected as a privileged communication" thereby limiting a lawyer's duty to disclose fraud. Only some states, however, chose to adopt this amendment.

11. ABA MODEL CODE OF PROFESSIONAL RESPONSIBILITY, Preliminary Statement.

12. *See* HAZARD & KONIAK, *supra* note 2, at 13.

13. ABA MODEL RULES OF PROFESSIONAL CONDUCT, Scope.

14. *See, e.g.,* MONROE H. FREEDMAN, UNDERSTANDING LAWYERS' ETHICS 98-102 (1990) (describing the inconsistency between Model Rule 1.6 and its Comments).

15. *See, e.g.,* Nat'l Ass'n of Crim. Defense Lawyers Ethics Advisory Comm., Formal Op. 92-2 (1992), in THE CHAMPION (Mar. 1993) (dealing with client perjury).

16. *See* HAZARD & KONIAK, *supra* note 2, at 15. *See also* CHARLES W. WOLFRAM, MODERN LEGAL ETHICS, at 65–67 (discussing limited value of ethics opinions but noting "a lawyer who has acted in accordance with a recent ethics committee recommendation is ordinarily given the benefit of the doubt in disciplinary proceedings").

17. The NACDL and many local criminal defense lawyer organizations often will direct lawyers to experienced defense lawyers within their organization who will provide assistance. *See also* ABA STANDARD 4-1.5 and Commentary (recommending that every jurisdiction set up an advisory body to assist criminal defense lawyers with ethical problems). Unfortunately, it does not as yet appear that any jurisdiction has formally established such an advisory council.

18. ABA STANDARD 4-1.2, Commentary.

PART I

Defense Counsel's Role and the Allocation of Decision-Making Responsibility

Unquestionably, criminal defense lawyers often find themselves forced to choose between conflicting ethical commands. Although at times defense counsel as zealous advocate will feel pulled to pursue a particular course of action, counsel may recognize that such action violates another ethical norm. Chapter 1, by Randolph Stone, serves to introduce the reader to this common dilemma. Stone provides a useful overview of the limited options available to defense counsel who finds herself in a situation where she believes continued representation is unethical. Stone explores a series of difficult ethical situations and argues that defense counsel must carefully analyze a potential ethical dilemma to ensure, before concluding that continued representation is unethical, that the dilemma indeed demands the drastic step of seeking to withdraw. Stone forcefully reminds defense lawyers—a reminder repeated throughout this book—that defense counsel's fundamental role is to zealously defend one's clients. Nevertheless, the Model Code and Model Rules sometimes demand that defense counsel take action adverse to a client. Certainly many ethical defense lawyers are loath to take any action that would be detrimental to or hurt a client. Many also are willing to risk contempt, discipline, or even prosecution to vindicate their client's rights. As the authors of this book make clear, however, loyalty to one's clients is not unbounded.

1

Abbe Smith surely believes that client loyalty is a trait essential to anyone who purports to be a good criminal defense lawyer. Like Stone, Smith believes that the client's interest should be paramount. But in Chapter 2, Smith also posits that there are a limited number of instances where a public defender should be entitled to "a little autonomy, a little personal dignity." In Smith's view, the conscientious public defender should be permitted to opt out of certain cases when that defender honestly believes, for ideological or moral reasons, that her ability to effectively represent her client will be impaired. Smith challenges conventional wisdom, which dictates that a public defender is required to defend any client regardless of that defender's personal or moral feelings. Certainly a public defender must posses the mental toughness and willingness to tackle unpopular causes and take on the defense of those defendants no one else will defend. But Smith argues that public defender administrators and programs ought to be flexible enough to make room for the committed defender who conscientiously cannot handle a particular type of case. As Smith recognizes, however, her position raises a host of institutional and community issues that are not easily resolved.

In the next five chapters, Rodney Uphoff, David Katner, George Bisharat, Rita Fry, and Keith Bystrom look at different aspects of a recurring problem confronting criminal defense lawyers—the proper allocation of decision-making authority between lawyer and criminal defendant. As these chapters demonstrate, ethical rules and case law allow for rather different views about which decisions ultimately are to be made by the client and which decisions finally rest with defense counsel.

As the authors wrestle with this question of decision-making authority in the context of several different ethical problems, it is clear that even defense lawyers who share a commitment to providing aggressive, zealous representation may disagree sharply as to whether lawyer or client has the final say when there is disagreement over an important strategic decision. The authors struggle to balance the defendant's right of self-determination and Sixth Amendment right to receive effective assistance of counsel with the lawyer's ethical obligation to provide zealous, competent representation.

George Bisharat resolves the balance by adopting the position of the client-centered lawyer who permits the defendant to make strategic choices even though the lawyer ultimately may feel that the client's choice or decision is unwise. Rita Fry, on the other hand, takes a more traditional approach and insists that although consultation is warranted, all strategic decisions are to be made by the lawyer. Certainly Fry would not permit her client to trump a decision she feels belongs to the lawyer—for example, calling a particular witness—when such a decision could compromise success at trial. But to Bisharat, the uncertainty of many strategic decisions coupled with the reality that it is the client who must live with the consequences of poor decisions dictate that the defendant be given the final call on all important decisions, including the filing of a suppression motion or the calling of a particular witness.

This disagreement as to how far a criminal defense lawyer can or should go to protect the best interests of the client surfaces throughout this book. In Chapter 5, Keith Bystrom points out that ethical rules and court opinions give the defense lawyer little room to claim that the lawyer has the authority to determine whether to accept or reject a plea bargain. That decision is clearly the client's, even though the lawyer may feel the client's decision is foolish. But decision-making questions are muddied when the client has a mental condition that impairs his ability to make rational choices. Chapter 3 by Rodney Uphoff and Chapter 4 by David Katner examine the related issues of competency and insanity and defense counsel's role when counsel and the client do not agree on how to proceed. Model Rule 1.14 requires counsel to respect as much as possible the mentally impaired client's right to make decisions. Yet, as Justice Marshall observed, total deference is only proper—if at all—if the client's decisions are based on intelligent and informed understanding.[1] But, of course, that is often the crux of the problem. Both Uphoff and Katner highlight the complexity of the decision-making process and of defense counsel's role when the client is insisting on making irrational decisions seemingly at odds with the client's best interests.

In the final two chapters of Part I, Wallace Mlyniec and Janet Fink examine the lawyer-client relationship and the allocation of decision making in the context of defending juvenile delinquency proceedings. As both chapters demonstrate, defense counsel representing the juvenile often finds herself in a difficult position with pressure to respond to the interests and demands of others concerned about the outcome of the juvenile client's case. Fink and Mlyniec argue that defense counsel's proper role is to function as much as possible as the client's advocate in a traditional sense. Counsel ought not, then, override the juvenile's decisions and substitute counsel's judgment or that of the parent when counsel disagrees with the juvenile's decision. As in the case of the marginally competent defendant, however, defense counsel representing a juvenile may find it difficult to adhere to the client-centered model advocated by George Bisharat. Counsel may be tempted in such instances to adopt the more directive and controlling approach suggested by Rita Fry and others discussed in Chapter 6. This is especially true when the juvenile is very young or is insisting on a course of action that counsel believes is contrary to the client's best interest. Nonetheless, it is clear that if counsel decides to adopt a more directive approach, an approach not favored by Fink or Mlyniec, counsel must ensure that the client's best interests are served—not those of counsel or a third party.

Notes

1. Alvord v. Wainright, 469 U.S. 956, 961 (1984) (Marshall, J., dissenting).

CHAPTER 📖 1

Between a Rock and a Hard Place: Responding to the Judge or Supervisor Demanding Unethical Representation

Randolph N. Stone

May a public defender be found in contempt for refusing to accept a criminal appointment because she believes that she is ethically barred from representing a defendant? What should a public defender do if a judge or her supervisor orders her to proceed or to continue representing a defendant when the defender believes she cannot ethically do so?

In resolving ethical issues a lawyer should consult the prescribed courses of conduct promulgated in her jurisdiction and by the American Bar Association. The ABA adopted the Model Rules of Professional Conduct in 1983, replacing the 1969 Model Code of Professional Responsibility. Although some version of the Model Rules has been adopted in more than half the states, the Model Code remains relevant in many jurisdictions. The ABA Standards for Criminal Justice, The Defense Function, intended as a guide to professional conduct, are also instructive.

In answering the questions that open this chapter, remember that the interests of the client are paramount. ABA Standards for Criminal Justice, The Defense Function, Standard 4-1.2 (b) (3d ed. 1993) states:

> The basic duty defense counsel owes to the administration of justice and as officer of the court is to serve as the accused's counselor and advocate with courage and devotion and to render effective, quality representation.

Thus, when considering how to resolve an ethical conflict it is imperative that the lawyer act in a manner that protects her client's interests.

The term "ethically barred" is vague, inviting a variety of interpretations. In the context of this discussion, it suggests at least the following situations. First, the lawyer may believe a heavy caseload will prevent supplying competent representation to a newly appointed client. Second, "ethically barred" may include avoiding the dangers of a conflict of interest. The lawyer may believe that a conflict of interest would preclude providing effective assistance of counsel and thus feel ethically compelled to remove herself from the case. Third, the lawyer may believe her new client or the alleged crime is so "morally repugnant" that she could not zealously defend the client. Finally, the lawyer may also feel "ethically barred" from representing a client if he believes the client has or is about to commit perjury or fraud upon the court and that by representing the client he would help perpetrate that fraud.

There may be other situations that fall within the meaning of "ethically barred" but the four mentioned above are the ones most likely to be met by a public defender. Since other chapters in this book address these issues in more detail, this chapter will not explore fully the complexities of each situation. Instead, we will examine the impact of each of these situations on the appropriateness of the public defender's withdrawal from the case.

Caseload Pressures
"It's Too Funky In Here"[1]

A careful reading of the Model Code suggests a public defender must withdraw if caseload pressures prevent effective represention of a client. Disciplinary Rule 2-110(B) states the circumstances in which withdrawal is mandatory. DR 2-110 (B)(2) requires withdrawal when a lawyer "knows or it is obvious that his continued employment will result in violation of a Disciplinary Rule." By not withdrawing, an overworked lawyer violates at least two disciplinary rules. DR 6-101 (A)(2) forbids a lawyer from handling a legal matter without adequate legal preparation. DR 6-101(A)(3) bars a lawyer from neglecting a legal matter entrusted to her. Both disciplinary rules reach to the heart of the public defender's concern—that an excessive caseload prevents him from adequately preparing his new client's case.[2]

Although the Model Code compels the public defender to move to withdraw, it does not compel the judge to grant withdrawal. DR 2-110(B) states, "A lawyer representing a client before a tribunal, with its permission if required by its rules, shall withdraw from employment. . . ." (emphasis added).[3] Obviously, the judge, in most jurisdictions, has discretion to grant or deny the lawyer's motion and withdrawal without the court's permission could result in contempt.

The Model Rules also suggest that a lawyer should move to withdraw, but speak less forcefully than the code. Model Rule 1.16(a) provides that, ". . . a lawyer shall not represent a client or, where representation has commenced, shall withdraw from the representation of a client if: (1) the representation will result in violation of the rules of professional conduct or other law. . . ." The lack of adequate preparation inherent in carrying an excessive caseload may violate Model Rule 1.1, which requires a lawyer to provide "competent" representation to a client. The rules define competent as including the "thoroughness and preparation reasonably necessary for the representation." Thus, the public defender should move to withdraw if she believes caseload pressures prevent providing the level of competent representation prescribed by the rule.

The determination of whether the lawyer can meet that prescribed level is left to the judge. According to Model Rule 1.16(c), "When ordered to do so by a tribunal, a lawyer shall continue representation notwithstanding good cause for terminating the representation." The public defender must continue to represent his client if the judge disagrees with the public defender's ethical determination. As under the Model Code, a lawyer who fails to continue representation when ordered by a judge to do so invites sanctions, including contempt.[4]

Some courts have, however, shown a willingness to relieve a public defender of the burdens of an excessive caseload if the public defender can show that a high volume of work prevents her from providing effective assistance of counsel. In *Ligda v. Superior Court*, 5 Cal. App. 3d 811, 827 (1970), the appellate court suggested the following recourse to alleviate the burdens of a voluminous caseload:

> When a public defender reels under a staggering workload, he need not animate the competitive instinct of a trial judge by resistance to or defiance of his orders to the public defender. . . . The public defender should proceed to place the situation before the judge, who upon a satisfactory showing can relieve him, and order the employment of private counsel . . . at public expense.

Similarly, in addressing itself to the Defender Association of Philadelphia's objection that zealous prosecutions under a federal gambling statute had overburdened the association, the district court ruled that ". . . the Defender Association may at any time decline an appointment, and should decline to accept an appointment if the Association is not in a position to properly defend the action." *Iacona v. United States*, 343 F. Supp. 600, 604 (E.D. Pa. 1972).

Caseload pressures are endemic to the delivery of legal services to the indigent. If the situation is intolerable and the institutional leadership is not adequately dealing with the problem, the lawyer should seek support for systemic reform from local and national bar associations and other organizations, including the Criminal Justice Section of the American Bar Association, the National Legal Aid and Defender Association, and the National Association of Criminal Defense Lawyers.[5]

Conflicts of Interest
"Living Double, In a World of Trouble"[6]

The conflict-of-interest scenario is similar to the situation faced by the public defender with an excessive caseload. A lawyer who is aware that representation of the client will be directly adverse to another client, or may be materially limited by the lawyer's responsibilities to another client or third persons, should, under Model Rule 1.16, move to withdraw because the representation violates Model Rule 1.7 (conflict of interest, general rule). A lawyer should also examine the possibility of a breach of Model Rule 1.8 (nonlitigation transactions with the client) and Model Rule 1.9 (current client's interests conflicting with those of a former client). Similarly, in Model Code jurisdictions a lawyer violates Model Code DR 2-110(B)(2) (mandatory withdrawal if the lawyer knows or it is obvious that continued employment will result in violation of a disciplinary rule) because representations that create a conflict of interest violate DR 5-101(A) (acceptance of employment forbidden if the lawyer's business and personal interests will affect his or her professional judgment) or DR 5-105(A) (acceptance of employment forbidden if a prospective client's interests conflict with those of an existing client).

Although a motion to withdraw is mandated under both the Model Code and Model Rules, the judge need not grant it. In *Holloway v. Arkansas*, 435 U.S. 475, 98 S. Ct. 1173, 55 L. Ed. 2d 426 (1978), the Supreme Court ruled that a trial court must investigate defense counsel's timely allegation of a conflict of interest; failure to do so may violate the defendant's Sixth Amendment right to effective assistance of counsel. Of course, even if a conflict of interest exists, substitution of counsel is not always required. For example, in rejecting a motion to withdraw based on an alleged conflict of interest, the Florida Court of Appeals has reiterated:

As long as the trial court has a reasonable basis for believing that the attorney-client relationship has not deteriorated to a point where counsel can no longer give effective aid in the fair presentation of a defense, the court is justified in denying a motion to withdraw. *Boudreau v. Carlisle,* 549 So. 2d 1073, 1079 (1989).

The court stressed that withdrawal should be granted sparingly, for assigning new counsel overloads an already strained system and "severely hampers the administration of justice." *Id.* at 1081.

The public defender can remove the ethical barrier by requesting that her client(s) waive any conflict of interest. Such a waiver must be a fully informed one; the public defender must completely and honestly disclose to her client(s) the nature of the conflict and the potential problems that may arise from her continued representation. It is of paramount importance that the public defender give a frank assessment of her ability to provide minimally adequate legal services. The ABA Standards for Criminal Justice necessitate such candor. According to Defense Function Standard 4-5.1(A), ". . . the lawyer should advise the accused with complete candor concerning all aspects of the case, including a candid estimate of the probable outcome."[7]

The lawyer should only recommend waiver if she honestly feels unable to provide effective and quality representation. The public defender should never see waiver as a convenient means of brushing aside a potential ethical impediment. She must always hold the client's interests above all others and act accordingly. Waiver is appropriate only when the client's interests are protected.

Perjury
"Talkin' Loud & Sayin' Nothing"[8]

A public defender may learn that her client plans on committing perjury on the witness stand, or may learn after the fact that her client has committed perjury. In rare situations the client may pressure the public defender into lying or offering fraudulent evidence to the court. Before moving to withdraw, the public defender should consider several other courses of action that may remove the ethical obstacle to continued representation. First, the lawyer should examine the basis of her "knowledge," exercising restraint in assessing the veracity of her client's statements and remembering that she is the client's advocate, not the client's judge or jury. Such restraint dictates that the public defender has no ethical dilemma except in the clearest of cases, when it is absolutely certain that the planned testimony is perjurious.[9]

Furthermore, a tendency to resolve the issue against the client, absent clear and certain evidence that the testimony is in fact perjury, would undermine the establishment of trust and confidence between the public defender and the accused required by ABA Defense Function Standard 4-3.1(a), which describes the relationship a lawyer should strive to establish with a client. Subsection (a) recommends that "[d]efense counsel should seek to establish a relationship of trust and confidence with the accused. . . ." A lawyer who moves to withdraw because of information the client confides in her violates the trust dictated by this standard, especially if the lawyer reveals to the court the basis for withdrawal.

If, after investigation, the public defender remains convinced that her client plans to present false evidence, she should attempt to persuade the client not to do so. The public defender should advise the client that perjuring himself will not work in his best interests; that both judge and jury are adept at identifying false testimony. A strong "practice" cross-examination of the client by an experienced colleague often convinces the client to abandon a questionable story.

There are times, however, when the lawyer may feel there is no other recourse than to withdraw. Under the Model Rules, withdrawal in these cases, though not mandatory, is permissible. Model Rule 1.16(b) states when a lawyer *may* withdraw from representing a client (emphasis added). (Note that Model Rule 1.16(a), which covers mandatory withdrawals, specifies when "a lawyer shall not represent a client"). Model Rule 1.16(b)(1) allows withdrawal when the "client persists in a course of action involving the lawyer's services that the lawyer reasonably believes is criminal or fraudulent." Model Rule 1.16(b)(2) permits termination of representation when the "client has used the lawyer's services to perpetrate a crime or fraud." Both rules cover the cases of future or past perjury or fraud.

Under the Model Code, withdrawal may be either mandatory or permissive. DR 2-110(B) (mandatory withdrawal) may apply because allowing the use of perjured testimony violates DR 7-102(A)(4) (forbidding a lawyer from knowingly using perjured testimony or false evidence) and DR 7-102 (A)(7) (forbidding a lawyer from counseling or assisting the client in conduct that the lawyer knows to be illegal or fraudulent). DR 2-110 (C) (permissive withdrawal) may also apply if the client insists on committing perjury, since DR 2-110(C)(1)(b) allows withdrawal if a lawyer's client personally seeks to pursue an illegal course of conduct.

In any event, withdrawal in the case of perjury is not the best solution; it is a recognized last resort, but one of dubious value. Consequently, when a judge denies withdrawal the lawyer must continue with her representation. As the District Court of Appeals of Florida warned:

> If withdrawal were allowed every time a lawyer was faced with an ethical disagreement with the accused, the ultimate result could be a perpetual cycle of eleventh-hour motions to withdraw and an unlimited number of continuances for the defendant. In addition, new counsel might fail to recognize the problem of fabricated testimony and false evidence would be presented to the court; or, perhaps the defendant might eventually find an attorney who lacks ethical standards and who would knowingly present and argue false evidence. Neither result is acceptable since fraud is committed upon the court in either case. *Sandborn v. State,* 474 So. 2d 309, 314 (1985).

Although rare in occurrence, the issue of client perjury is the subject of much discussion.[10] As noted earlier, other chapters in this volume focus more specifically on the ramifications of the problem. Of the many proposed solutions, perhaps the most persuasive is the rationale of the Ethics Advisory Committee of the National Association of Criminal Defense Lawyers, Formal Opinion 92-2, which states in pertinent part that:

> If the lawyer is unable to dissuade the client or to withdraw, the lawyer may not assist the client to improve upon the perjury, but must maintain the client's confidences and secrets, examine the client in the ordinary way, and, to the extent tactically desirable, argue the client's testimony to the jury as evidence in the case. . . . [A]ttorney's should proceed carefully, with full knowledge of the applicable rules of the jurisdiction, and with the advice, if possible, of counsel.

Moral Repugnancy
"I Can't Stand Myself"[11]

As with suspected client perjury, the issue of withdrawal because a lawyer feels her client is morally repugnant should occur only in the rarest of cases. Public defenders often represent unpopular people accused of repulsive crimes; it is a privilege. A public defender who refuses to render services because she disapproves of her client or her client's behavior will refuse far more cases than she will accept, placing a serious burden on colleagues. A lawyer whose moral qualms would easily interfere with her ability to represent a client accused of a heinous crime should seek other employment. A public defender should only request withdrawal in the exceptional case where her moral repugnancy runs so deep as to prevent the rendering of competent legal services.

The Model Rules do not speak directly to a lawyer's moral repugnancy to the client and/or the crime, but the Rules do suggest that if the lawyer can no longer provide competent services, she should request to withdraw. Model Rule 1.16(b)(3) permits withdrawal if "the client insists upon pursuing an objective that the lawyer considers repugnant or imprudent." There may be some argument as to whether a public defender's repugnancy to representation falls squarely within the language of the rule, but the lawyer's motion to withdraw surely follows in its spirit. According to the first paragraph of the comment to Model Rule 1.16, "A lawyer should not accept representation in a matter unless it can be performed competently, promptly, without improper conflict of interest and to completion." Only when the public defender's repugnancy to the client and the client's case interferes with the quality of her representation is there legitimate grounds for seeking withdrawal. In addition to Model Rule 1.16(b)(3), the lawyer can make the argument under Model Rule 1.16(b)(6)—"other good cause for withdrawal exists."

The cause for withdrawal under the Model Code is somewhat less compelling. The most relevant provision is an Ethical Consideration, not the more binding Disciplinary Rules. EC 2-30 states: "[e]mployment should not be accepted by a lawyer when he is unable to render competent service. . . ." More specifically, EC 2-30 warns that a lawyer "should decline employment if the intensity of his personal feeling, as distinguished from a community attitude, may impair his effective representation of a prospective client." DR 2-110(C)(6), however, allows permissive withdrawal if the lawyer can show good cause. As under the Model Rules, moral repugnancy that significantly interferes with the lawyer's ability to work with and defend the client should qualify as good cause.

The Judge Denies the Motion to Withdraw
"Cold Sweat"[12]

A problem arises, of course, when the court refuses withdrawal. Courts have the power of contempt to ensure obedience to their orders, and the public defender who refuses to serve as the client's lawyer may face punishment. ABA Standard for Criminal Justice 6-4.1 affirms that "[t]he trial judge has the power to cite and, if necessary, punish summarily anyone who, in the judge's presence in open court, willfully obstructs the course of criminal proceedings." Refusal to continue to represent a client is among the most obvious means by which someone can obstruct the "course of criminal proceedings." Should the public defender defy the court's order? Probably not.[13]

If the court denies the motion to withdraw, the public defender can, in some cases, resolve the ethical dilemma by fully disclosing the matter to her client(s). Both Model Rule 1.7(a)(2), Model Rule 1.7(b)(2), DR 5-101(A), and DR5-105(C) allow the informed consent of a lawyer's client(s) to remove conflict of interest as a barrier to proceeding with the case. Asking for consent, however, requires the lawyer to have made a determination that she either can or cannot, if pressed to do so, competently defend the client. The manner in which the lawyer explains the nature of the conflict and the availability of waiver as a solution will have an enormous impact on a defendant unfamiliar with the legal system. More often than not the client will follow the lawyer's recommendation, relying on the informed, reasoned opinion of a professional.

A lawyer may also consider violating the court's order to continue representation. Most likely the lawyer will be found in contempt and will have to defend her actions in a contempt proceeding. Such was the action taken by a lawyer in *State v. Lennon*, 115 Misc. 2d 738, 454 N.Y.S.2d 621 (1982). Respondent, an assistant public defender, claimed his own professional judgment to protect the constitutional rights of his two clients in a conflict of interest situation took precedence over his obligation to obey the court. He thus argued he was justified in refusing to proceed to trial. *Id.* at 742.

Although the court conceded that justification is a valid defense to the charge of criminal contempt, the threshold is quite high. The *Lennon* court ruled that a lawyer could *successfully* claim the defense of justification only when "the conflict of interest asserted in this case meet[s] the test of immediate, irreparable injury to an obvious and fundamentally valuable right." *Id.* at 745. The court ruled that here, where the public defender's office was defending both the defendant and a witness for the prosecution, the claimed conflict failed to meet the test and the court found the public defender in contempt of court.

In cases where the *Lennon* criteria are met, the trial court should grant the lawyer's motion to withdraw, thus avoiding the possibility of sanctions. But even if the motion to withdraw was not initially granted when immediate, irreparable injury to an obvious and fundamentally valuable right exists, the reviewing court is likely to defer to the judgment of the trial court.

The conflict-of-interest scenario is instructive. In *Holloway v. Arkansas, supra,* the Supreme Court ruled that the trial court, over the objections of defense counsel, improperly ordered a lawyer to represent two defendants in the same trial. Nonetheless, the Court stressed that a lawyer's assertions of a conflict of interest do not bind the trial court's hands. The trial court, after investigation, should determine if a conflict of interest exists. The Court further opined: "Nor does our holding preclude a trial court from exploring the adequacy of the basis of defense counsel's representations regarding a conflict of interests. . . ." *Holloway, supra,* 435 U.S. 475 at 487.

If withdrawal cannot be obtained, the public defender should follow the court's order and continue representing the client, relying on Sixth Amendment challenges on appeal. In *Boudreau,* 549 So. 2d 1073 (1989), the court, citing Florida Rule of Professional Conduct 4-1.16(c), which reads verbatim to Model Rule 1.16(c), stated that the lawyer no longer faces an ethical problem once the trial court denies the motion to withdraw. The lawyer has no choice. *Boudreau* at 1088. Recall the determination in Model Rule 1.16(c) that "[w]hen ordered to do so by a tribunal, a lawyer shall continue representation notwithstanding good cause for terminating the representation." The lawyer has been ordered to continue representation and would violate the Model Rules by refusing to do so.

The public defender should also explore the possibility of an interlocutory appeal. Depending on the jurisdiction, filing a writ of prohibition or mandamus may be an appropriate vehicle for staying the proceedings until the state's highest appellate court has an opportunity to review the issue.

The Supervisor Denies Withdrawal
"The Payback"[14]

The correct approach is more clear-cut if it is the public defender's supervisor who orders her to continue representation. By eliminating the option to withdraw, the supervisor breaches Model Rule 5.1. Model Rule 5.1(b) requires the supervising lawyer to "make reasonable efforts to ensure that the other [supervised] lawyer conforms to the Rules of Professional Conduct." Model Rule 5.1(c)(1) makes the supervising lawyer responsible for the other lawyer's violation of the Rules if the supervising lawyer orders the conduct involved. Thus, the supervisor—not the subordinate lawyer—would be subject to disciplinary sanctions for any violations of the Model Rules or Model Code that result from the public defender's continued representation of the client.

Continued representation at the direction of the supervisor should not usually place the supervised public defender in violation of the Model Rules. Model Rule 5.2(b) states that a subordinate lawyer does not breach the Rule if "that lawyer acts in accordance with a supervisory lawyer's reasonable resolution of an arguable question of professional duty." The subordinate public defender's liability thus hinges upon the reasonableness of the supervisor's order not to withdraw. As the comment to Model Rule 5.2 explains, "If the question can reasonably be answered only one way, the duty of both lawyers is clear and they are equally responsible for fulfilling it." But if the solution is reasonably arguable, authority to answer the question rests with the supervisor and the subordinate lawyer should act as guided, relieved of liability.

The Model Code contains no counterpart to this Rule. Again, it is important that the public defender review the rules of the jurisdiction and consult the local ethics committee.

Conclusion

A public defender faced with representing a client that she feels ethically barred from representing has few options other than withdrawal. Nonetheless, withdrawal is properly an action of last resort, sought only after careful research of the ethical issue to ensure an ethical bar truly exists. Local bar associations and ethics committees can help the lawyer determine the extent of the ethical problem. Other worthy sources of assistance include the American Bar Association Ethics Hotline, the National Legal Aid and Defender Association, the National Association of Criminal Defense Lawyers, ethics professors in the state's law schools, and ethics "experts" in the public defender's office. A public defender should also consult her supervisor. It is possible the public defender's office is already aware of problems of the sort the lawyer is facing and the supervisor may be able to inform the lawyer of systemic or other extrajudicial remedies the office is pursuing.

If a valid ethical bar does in fact exist, the public defender should not move to withdraw until after considering elimination of the dilemma by seeking, if appropriate, the informed waiver of her client. A lawyer should seek consent, however, only when the lawyer feels she can adequately represent the client's interests.

Even though the Model Rules and Model Code permit withdrawal, a judge need not grant it. When ordered by a judge or supervisor to continue representation, the public defender should obey and consider the possibility of interlocutory relief. The lawyer should not invite contempt by defying the order unless she is fairly certain of appellate success and there is internal support from the public defender's office, or outside support from the private bar and/or any of the organizations mentioned earlier in this chapter.

Notes

The author acknowledges the valuable assistance of former clinic student and current assistant public defender, Marc Boxerman.

1. James Brown, "The Godfather of Soul," circa 1972.

2. An oppressive caseload will not shield an attorney from disciplinary action; *see In re* Klipstine, 108 N.M. 481, 483, 775 P.2d 247, 249 (1989), ". . . a failure to keep one's caseload within manageable proportions cannot and does not excuse . . . blatant neglect of cases."

3. *See, e.g.,* Schwarz v. Cianca, 495 So. 2d 1208, 1210 (Fla 4th Dist. Ct. App. 1986), where the court, in granting the public defender's motion to withdraw, noted that "the case law recognizes the authority of the trial court to relieve the public defender from representation because of excessive caseload."

4. *See In re* Sherlock, 37 Ohio App.3rd 204, 525 N.E.2d 512 (1987) where a defender was held in contempt for refusing to try an unprepared case. The appeals court, while vacating the contempt order, noted that counsel disobeys a court at great peril and will only be justified when no other course is reasonably available. *See also* Maness v. Myers, 419 U.S. 449 (1975) suggesting that a more appropriate response is to preserve the issue for appeal.

5. *See, e.g.,* "The Indigent Defense Crisis" (1993) prepared by the Ad Hoc Committee on the Indigent Defense Crisis of the American Bar Association Section of Criminal Justice, which offers recommendations to deal with the current crisis.

6. Lou Rawls, circa 1975.

7. *See also* ABA STANDARDS FOR CRIMINAL JUSTICE DEFENSE FUNCTION 4-3.5(b) (3d ed. 1993) requiring counsel to disclose to the defendant at the earliest feasible opportunity any information reasonably sufficient to permit the client to appreciate the significance of any conflict of interest.

8. James Brown, "The Hardest Working Man in Show Business," circa 1972.

9. *See, e.g., In re* Grievance Committee, 847 F.2d 57 (2d Cir. 1988) and United States v. Long, 857 F.2d 436 (8th Cir. 1988) emphasizing "actual knowledge" and a "firm factual basis" as opposed to a "strong suspicion" regarding perjury.

10. *See, e.g.,* Monroe H. Freedman, *Professional Responsibility of the Criminal Defense Lawyer: The Three Hardest Questions,* 64 MICH. L. REV. 1469 (1966); Norman Lefstein, *Client Perjury in Criminal Cases: Still in Search of an Answer,* 1 GEO. J. LEGAL ETHICS 521 (1988); George Rutherglen, *Dilemmas and Disclosure: A Comment on Client Perjury,* 19 AM. J. CRIM. L. 267 (1992); Wayne D. Brazil, *Unanticipated Client Perjury and the Collision of Rules of Ethics, Evidence, and Con-*

stitutional Law, 44 Mo. L. Rev. 601, (1970); Monroe H. Freedman, *Client Confidence and Client Perjury: Some Unanswered Questions,* 136 Pa. L. Rev. 1939 (1988); Williams, *Client Perjury and the Duty of Candor,* 6 Geo. J. Legal Ethics 1005 (1993).

11. James Brown, "Soul Brother #1," circa 1967.

12. James Brown, "The Sex Machine," circa 1967.

13. The lawyer should make, where feasible, a full and detailed record of the reasons for withdrawal to preserve the issue for appeal. Moreover, the client, after consultation and if practicable, should speak to the record. *See, e.g., Easley v. State,* 334 So. 2d 630 (Fla. 2d Dist. Ct. App. 1976), a trial court denied a private lawyer's motion to withdraw from a case in which the lawyer felt he could not effectively represent the appointed client. After the lawyer informed his client and the client signed an affidavit requesting a new lawyer, on reconsideration the court granted the motion to withdraw but held the lawyer in contempt. In reversing the contempt finding, the court noted that the lawyer had never violated the court's order to represent the client but had instead, "simply informed the defendant *as he should have,* that he felt incompetent to represent him and thereafter filed a motion consistent with the desires of his client." *Id.* at 632 (emphasis added).

14. James Brown, "Mr. Dynamite," circa 1974.

Bibliography

Standards

ABA Model Code of Professional Responsibility, DR 2-110(B), 2-110(B)(2), 2-110(C), 2-110(C)(1)(b), 1-110(C)(6), 5-101(A), 5-105(A), 5-105(C), 6-101(A), 6-101(A)(2), 6 101(A)(3), 7-102(A), 7-102(A)(4), 7-102(A)(7), EC 2-30 (1969).

ABA Model Rules of Professional Conduct, Rules 1.1, 1.7, 1.7(a)(2), 1.7(b)(2), 1.8, 1.9, 1.16, 1.16(a), 1.16(b), 1.16(b)(1), 1.16(b)(2), 1.16(b)(3), 1.16(b)(6), 1.16(C), 5.1, 5.1(b), 5.1(C)(1), 5.2(b) and Cmt. (1983).

ABA Standards for Criminal Justice, 4-1.12(B), 4-3.1(A), 4-3.5(B), 4-5.1(A), 6-4.1 (3d ed. 1993).

Florida Rules of Professional Conduct, Rule, 4-1.16(C) (1994).

Cases

Boudreau v. Carlisle, 549 So. 2d 1073 (1989).

Holloway v. Arkansas, 435 U.S. 475, 98 S. Ct. 1173, 55 L. Ed. 2d 426 (1978).

Iacana v. United States, 343 F. Supp. 600 (E.D. Pa. 1972).

Ligda v. Superior Court, 5 Cal. App. 3d 811 (1970).

Sandborn v. Florida, 474 So. 2d 309 (1985).

State v. Lennon, 115 Misc. 2d 738, 454 N.Y.S.2d 621 (1982).

CHAPTER 📖 2

When Ideology and Duty Conflict

Abbe Smith

Should an individual public defender be permitted to refuse to represent certain categories of clients for moral or ideological reasons? Does the public defender supervisor or agency have the right to limit a defender's ability to "opt out" of certain cases?

Public defenders have a unique duty to represent people accused of crimes who cannot afford to retain their own counsel. Because poor clients lack the power and resources to choose who represents them, they are forced to rely on the professionalism and commitment of public defenders. For individual defenders to choose among clients, whatever the reason, undermines that professionalism and commitment.

An individual public defender should represent all clients assigned to her, no matter who the client is, no matter what crime is alleged, and no matter the moral or ideological conflicts posed by such representation, unless the individual defender simply cannot represent the client with the requisite zeal. Even the most committed defender is likely to encounter the rare case in which she is unable to zealously represent a particular client. No defender should represent a client if she knows that her representation will be measurably compromised by moral or ideological conflict. The focus of the question should at all times be the interests of the client.

While public defender administrators have the "right" to limit the circumstances under which individual defenders may refuse to represent a client, they should do so only after careful reflection. Public defender agencies should not exclude would-be defenders or punish

18

those already on staff because of heartfelt questions about the defender's ability to handle certain kinds of cases. On the other hand, there are valid institutional concerns about the training and experience of new defenders; the undue burden on those defenders taking the cases others refuse; and the message conveyed to the client community when defenders opt out of certain kinds of cases.

The Hard Cases: Representing Alleged Rapists and Racists

A lifelong feminist, who became a public defender out of her commitment to social and criminal justice, her understanding of issues of power and inequality in the criminal system, and her empathy for the underdog, is assigned a rape case. From her examination of the case, there is every reason to believe that the defendant is guilty of a brutal sexual assault, and that this is not the first time the defendant has engaged in such conduct. The feminist defender is a talented, tireless advocate, who has never before refused a case, and sees herself as a career defender. She is deeply ambivalent about taking this case, and would very much like not to take it.

A lifelong civil rights activist, who became a public defender out of a commitment to racial justice and a desire to help poor and oppressed people, is assigned to represent a skinhead accused of committing a racially motivated assault on an African American child. Examination of the case reveals that the defendant is an angry, volatile racist, whose life quest is to assert white peoples' racial superiority through acts of violence against people of color and Jews. The defender is a talented, tireless advocate, who has never before refused a case, and identifies as a career defender. The defender is deeply ambivalent about taking this case, and would very much like not to take it.

Many people are drawn to public defender work out of the kind of personal and political commitment reflected in the above two examples. While not all public defenders are political activists, or even political liberals, there are a number of defenders who come to the work out of a desire for social change.[1] No doubt the women's movement and the civil rights movement spawned many defenders, along with other public interest and poverty lawyers.

These are the defenders and would-be defenders who might have trouble representing "rapists" and "racists" (and other clients who commit crimes of violence against members of oppressed communities) on moral or ideological grounds. These clients are not the ones that drew these lawyers to become defenders. These are the hard cases.

Institutional and Individual Concerns

On an institutional level, surely public defender offices do not want to discourage those with strongly held views about gender and racial equality from applying for defender positions. Many of these would-be defenders are committed individuals with the perspective and stamina to make a career of public criminal defense. These are the defenders with the compassion to go the extra yard for a client. Often such defenders are the lifeblood of offices hit hard by budget cuts and spiraling caseloads. *See* Abbe Smith, *The Public Defender: The Practice of Law in the Shadows of Repute* (book review), 62 Temple L. Rev. 651, 661 (1989).

As a policy matter, public defender offices ought not *force* all defenders to represent all clients, notwithstanding deep personal, political, or moral ambivalence. The absence of an "opt out" or refusal policy for the rare case in which the defender finds either the defendant or the conduct alleged so repugnant as to interfere with her ability to defend the client is likely to have an adverse effect on the quality of representation and staff morale. Both the Model Code and the Model Rules allow lawyers to decline to accept certain cases. *See* Model Code of Professional Responsibility EC 2-26 ("[a] lawyer is under no obligation to act as advisor or advocate for every person who may wish to become his client . . ."); Model Rules of Professional Conduct, Rule 6.2, Comment ("[a] lawyer ordinarily is not obliged to accept a client whose character or cause the lawyer regards as repugnant.").

Admittedly, a policy permitting defenders an "easy out" of troubling cases might generate serious problems of its own. Public defender offices should be careful about broadcasting the message that some staff lawyers are as fainthearted as the general public when it comes to certain kinds of crime or that some individuals accused of crime are simply not worth defending. Defender offices should also be careful not to overburden those defenders willing to take cases that others decline or to perpetuate a meritocracy based on acceptance or rejection of these cases alone.

While every profession may exact costs to individuals, a defender should be able to set limits on personal cost. A defender should have some autonomy, some control, some personal dignity. Must a defender be the "government issue" version of the Sixth Amendment—a warm body, any warm body will do?[2] What harm is done to the quality of the defender's life when detachment is the only allowed response to moral conflict?[3]

Public Defenders as the Embodiment of the Right to Counsel

Public defenders are, in many ways, the embodiment of the right to counsel, the right to due process, and the right to participate fully in the adversary system. Many have noted that the right to counsel is "the most pervasive" of rights, because it affects a client's ability to assert all other rights.[4]

Both individual freedom and any meaningful notion of criminal justice depend on the right to counsel. As the Preamble to the Code of Professional Responsibility pronounces:

> The continued existence of a free and democratic society depends upon the recognition of the concept that justice is based upon the rule of law grounded in respect for the dignity of the individual and his capacity through reason for enlightened self-government. Law so grounded makes justice possible, for only through such law does the dignity of the individual attain respect and protection. Without it, individual rights become subject to unrestrained power, respect for law is destroyed and rational self-government is impossible.

To public defenders and other criminal defense lawyers, the Sixth Amendment is the Exalted One, the one we'd go to the mat for, the one that encompasses the core principles. What remains of the Fourth Amendment follows close behind. While civil libertarians feel that way about the First Amendment, and civil rights and poverty lawyers feel that way about the Fourteenth Amendment, those amendments are simply not our bread and butter.

To public defenders, *Gideon* is God, Anthony Lewis's *Gideon's Trumpet* a defender bible, and Henry Fonda as Clarence Earl Gideon the face we see on those sleepless, eve-of-trial nights (or Fonda in *Twelve Angry Men* on a good night). As Justice Black wrote for the majority in *Gideon*:

> Lawyers to prosecute are everywhere deemed essential to protect the public's interest in an orderly society. Similarly, there are few defendants charged with crime, few indeed, who fail to hire the best lawyers they can get to prepare and present their defenses. That government hires lawyers to prosecute and defendants who have the money hire lawyers to defend are the strongest indications of the widespread belief that lawyers in criminal courts are necessities, not luxuries. The right of one charged with crime to counsel may not be deemed fundamental and essential in some countries, but it is in ours.[5]

The right to counsel and the presumption of innocence, which counsel safeguards, are not merely devices to ensure the smooth administration of justice or the credibility of criminal prosecutions. They are "affirmations of respect for the accused as a human being—affirmations that remind him and the public about the sort of society we want to become and, indeed, about the sort of society we are." Lawrence Tribe, *Trial by Mathematical Precision and Ritual in the Legal Process,* 84 Harv. L. Rev. 1329, 1391–1392 (1971).

Respect for clients is the sine qua non of the public defender. *See* ABA Standards for Criminal Justice, Standard 4-1.1, ("The basic duty the lawyer for the accused owes to the administration of justice is to serve as the accused's counselor and advocate with courage, devotion, and to the utmost of his or her learning and ability and according to law."). The truth is our clients, not unlike most clients (of corporate lawyers, real estate lawyers, tax lawyers, divorce lawyers, personal injury lawyers) are not perfect. Sometimes they do bad things. That is how they become our clients.

Our ability to distinguish "bad people" from "bad things" is what enables public defenders to do the work we do. Our ability to feel compassion instead of condemnation, connection instead of detachment, and understanding instead of judgment, is what draws us to the work. Our ability to identify when the rest of the world stands at a scornful distance is what carries us through.

It is the public defender's particular duty to take unpopular, unpleasant cases from time to time. Though most lawyers do not have to face this task, it is, of course, the duty of all lawyers to take unpopular cases. *See* ABA Standards for Criminal Justice, Standard 4-1.5 ("All qualified trial lawyers should stand ready to undertake the defense of an accused regardless of public hostility toward the accused or personal distaste for the offense charged or the person of the defendant."). The image of Atticus Finch in *To Kill a Mockingbird* comes to mind: he took on the representation of accused rapist Tom Robinson readily and with a sense of honor.[6]

Issues of respect, dignity, and autonomy are especially important to the indigent criminal defendant. In many ways, the poor criminal defendant is a study in the lack of choice. Whether or not the poor criminal defendant truly "chooses" to commit the act for which he becomes involved in the criminal justice system, *see, e.g.,* Richard Delgado, *Rotten Social Background: Should the Criminal Law Recognize a Defense of Severe Environmental Deprivation?* 3 Law & Ineq. J. 9 (1985), the poor criminal defendant doesn't choose to be arrested, doesn't choose to have charges leveled against him, doesn't choose to be locked up in lieu of bail, and doesn't choose a lawyer.

The truth is, the presumption that attaches to criminal defendants is not one of innocence, but one of guilt. Most people working in the criminal system will concede that, notwithstanding the number of principles, protections, and pleas on behalf of criminal defendants, judgment and prejudgment abounds. It just doesn't seem right or fair for public defenders to join the pack. We are supposed to stand between the pack and our clients. Our clients don't need us to judge them or to choose against them. They need us—and the Constitution needs us—to take on their cause, to advocate for them, to believe in them. *See* Arthur Weinberg, ed., *Attorney for the Damned: Clarence Darrow in the Courtroom*, 3–15 (University of Chicago Press, 1989).

On the other hand, clients and defenders sometimes have irreconcilable differences. Though it is largely a matter of judicial discretion, an indigent defendant may fire his defender under certain circumstances. Though most defenders are loath to do so, defenders may withdraw from representing clients who assault them, threaten to assault them, perjure themselves, or involve the lawyer in a continuing crime or fraud. *See* Monroe Freedman, *Understanding Lawyers' Ethics* 92–93, 100–102, 124–25 (1990). Nonetheless, good public defenders rarely seek to withdraw from a case. Simply stated, good defenders aren't quitters.

Of course, the lawyer's decision to take a case raises different questions from the lawyer's decision to withdraw from the case. There are many scholars who find it not only acceptable, but desirable, for lawyers to refuse to take certain cases on moral grounds.[7] But there is also a strong folklore, especially among defenders, that the worse the case, the better. The more repulsive the crime, the more depraved the client, the better. The story is better; the audience more attentive. The victory is sweeter; the odds higher. This is the kind of folklore that goes well with cowboy boots, the preferred defender footwear in many a criminal courtroom.

There is also a principle: It is both moral and essential that lawyers uphold the autonomy of clients, no matter who they are or what they have done. *See generally,* Charles Fried, *The Lawyer as Friend: The Moral Foundations of the Lawyer-Client Relation*, 85 Yale L.J. 1060 (1976). David Dudley Field's response when he was criticized for his choice of clients could be the creed on the mantle of public defender offices everywhere: A lawyer is "bound to represent any person who has any rights to be asserted or defended." Quoted in Andrew Kaufman, *Problems in Professional Responsibility* 258 (1976). Judge George Sharswood put it this way: "The lawyer, who refuses his professional assistance because in his judgment the case is unjust and indefensible, usurps the functions of both judge and jury."[8]

Balancing Strongly Held Convictions

Deeply held moral or ideological convictions may be an insurmountable obstacle for even the most committed public defender. These kinds of convictions may well have led the defender to become a defender in the first instance, as in the above two examples, and may be the kinds of beliefs that make the defender an effective advocate. Why shouldn't defenders be allowed to be people too? Why shouldn't defenders be entitled to a little autonomy, a little personal dignity? There's nothing like a good moral/ideological dilemma. It keeps us on our toes, keeps us thinking, keeps us struggling.

The problem is more institutional than individual. Most big city public defender offices can probably afford to let individual defenders opt out of cases or trade cases among themselves. Institutional flexibility in this regard is good for staff and good for clients. A little sensitivity and respect from the top helps the defenders on the bottom feel a little less on the bottom. A public defender office which takes seriously the concerns of those in the trenches is more likely to be an office of career public defenders.

From the client's perspective, most would prefer to have a defender who doesn't have to struggle so hard to do the job. The client may be more likely to trust a public defender if she knows the defender was given a choice about taking the case. The indigent criminal client has to rely on blind faith that the lawyer assigned to her case gives a damn. The mechanisms other clients have for prying a good performance from a lawyer—money, prestige, good publicity—are often not present. Whenever possible, a client should be encouraged to feel that the assigned defender is happy to be there.

For larger public defender offices, there may be valid questions about the training and experience of defenders. The serious and troubling cases—racially charged crimes, crimes of sexual violence, "hate crimes," and the almost endless list of other repugnant crimes—provide an enormous learning opportunity. These are the cases that are well prosecuted and involve intensive police work. For all of the reasons that the defender may find the task upsetting and difficult, these are the cases that demand the most skill before a judge or a jury.

Even in larger offices there may be a burden on those defenders who are willing to take the "hard cases," which, if assigned without reprieve, can be quite grueling. Perhaps worse, a hierarchy may develop, having nothing to do with ability. The "tough" public defenders, who handle all the hard cases, will rise to the top. The angst-ridden, "politically correct" public defenders will be perceived as less talented and will stay at the bottom.

There is a slippery slope here, of course. If there is a line, where should it be drawn? Perhaps a defender should not be a defender if too many cases pose moral dilemmas, requiring hours of scrutiny, consternation, and self-castigation. Defenders simply do not have the time for all that hand-wringing. How much patience must a defender's supervisor have for a defender who can't represent someone accused of rape, and can't represent someone accused of child molesting, and can't represent someone accused of racially-motivated violence, and can't represent someone accused of selling drugs, and can't represent someone accused of assaulting an elderly person, and certainly can't represent someone who is actually guilty? What message is conveyed to the client community about public defenders?

For smaller offices, the burden issue is a serious one. The bottom line is evident: If you are the only criminal lawyer in town, you take the case. You don't have the luxury of counting on someone else to do it in your stead. The public defender office may be the "only lawyer" in town. The other two staff attorneys have their hands full with other cases. The client needs a lawyer now. The defender does what has to be done to reconcile herself to the task. Would-be defenders applying for positions in smaller offices ought to think hard about potential moral and ideological dilemmas before taking the job.

The question posed here, like so many others in this book, has to be viewed from the perspective of the client's interest. If "client-centered advocacy" means anything, this is it. *See generally* David A. Binder and Susan C. Price, *Legal Interviewing and Counseling: A Client-Centered Approach* (1977). What impact will a lawyer's ambivalence about representing a particular client in a particular case have on the representation? When will the obligation of zealous representation be undermined? *See* Model Code of Professional Responsibility, Canon 7 ("A Lawyer Should Represent a Client Zealously Within the Bounds of Law"). *See also* ABA Canons of Professional Ethics, 15 (1908) (The lawyer has an obligation to give "entire devotion to the interest of the client, warm zeal in the maintenance and defense of his rights and the exertion of [the lawyer's] utmost learning and ability.").

When will the lawyer's *feelings* overwhelm the lawyer's *duty* to seek justice on behalf of a particular client? When will the defender be so torn that she is unable to embrace the words of Lord Brougham:

[A]n advocate, in the discharge of his duty, knows but one person in all the world, and that person is his client. To save that client by all means and expedients, and at all hazards and costs to other persons, and amongst them, to himself, is his first and only duty; and in performing this duty he must not regard the alarm, the torments, the destruction which he may ring upon others. Separating the duty of the patriot from that of an advocate, he must go on reckless of the consequences, though it should be his unhappy fate to involve his country in confusion.[9]

Conclusion

When an individual defender, after critical reflection, has serious questions about her ability to represent a client with the requisite dedication, commitment, and zeal, that defender should decline to represent. The "serious questions" should be the sort that would render the defender incapable of performing the task well. The standard should be high. The question is not whether the defender could do a competent job or an adequate job, the question is whether the client would be proud to have that defender as a lawyer; whether the client will be well-served.

For the lifelong feminist, the issues raised may be both ideological and personal. Both the defender in the trenches and the defender supervisor should acknowledge that, while the structure of the adversary system is essential to protecting the rights of criminal defendants, it creates "intractable problems for the victims of crime." *See* Ellen Yaroshefsky, *Balancing Victim's Rights and Vigorous Advocacy for the Defendant,* 1989 Annual Survey of American Law 135. Especially in a rape case, as the suspect becomes the defendant, the victim becomes suspect. This is the rare case where the sides are almost even: the defendant faces the awesome power of the state and the complainant faces the awesome power of sexism. No other criminal complainant comes to court burdened by the presumption of incredibility borne by the rape complainant.

So many women are victims of physical and sexual violence in this society. Some of these women may even be public defenders. The conflicts raised by the assignment of a rape case, a child sexual abuse case, or a spousal assault case may be deeply personal as well as profoundly political.

The feminist defender ought to ask herself what her feelings are about representing someone accused of rape. She should ask herself why she became a defender, and how, if at all, her feelings about rape and other serious offenses comport within her answer. She should ask herself whether she has any capacity for empathy with the defendant, whether innocent or guilty. She should ask herself whether her over-arching commitment to keeping the state at bay, to making the state prove its case, to protecting the rights of even the most heinous offenders can overcome her ambivalence.

The civil rights activist will have to struggle with similar issues. What feelings come up? Are those feelings entirely inconsistent with zealous representation of the accused? Is there anything that connects the defender and the defendant? Is the defender's empathy for the complainant so strong that it overwhelms the defender's capacity for connection with the client? Can role and duty propel the defender to fight the good fight in principle if the fight doesn't feel so good in the concrete?

If the civil rights activist has herself been the victim of racist violence, or is close to someone who has, this too becomes a deeply personal quandary. Hopefully, defender administrators will recognize that moral and ideological dilemmas are not mere intellectual exercises. For some, ideology and identity go hand in hand.

In the end, the defender must ask herself whether she can fully devote herself to the client, whether her passion and skill will go toward advocacy and not judgment, and whether she can go the distance. Only the individual defender can answer these questions.

Notes

1. *See generally* Abbe Smith, *Rosie O'Neill Goes to Law School: The Clinical Education of a Sensitive, New Age Public Defender,* 28 HARV. C.R.-C.L. L. REV. 1 (1993); Charles J. Ogletree, *Beyond Justifications: Seeking Motivations to Sustain Public Defenders,* 106 HARV. L. REV. 1239 (1993). *See also* Barbara Babcock, *Defending the Guilty,* 32 CLEV. ST. L. REV. 175, 177–779 (1983).

2. *See generally* Michael McConville and Chester Mirsky, *Criminal Defense of the Poor in New York City,* N.Y.U. REV. L. & SOC. CHANGE 581 (1986–87); LISA J. MCINTYRE, THE PUBLIC DEFENDER: THE PRACTICE OF LAW IN THE SHADOWS OF REPUTE 45–61 (1987).

3. *See id.* at 140–43. *See also* JACK RAND, MORAL VISION AND PROFESSIONAL DECISIONS: THE CHANGING VALUES OF WOMEN AND MEN LAWYERS 36–42 (1989); SEYMOUR WISHMAN, CONFESSIONS OF A CRIMINAL LAWYER 4 (1981); JEAN-PAUL SARTRE, EXISTENTIALISM AND HUMANISM (1977); Gerald J. Postema, *Moral Responsibility in Professional Ethics,* 55 N.Y.U. L. REV. 63, 74, 79 (1980).

4. Walter V. Schaefer, *Federalism and State Criminal Procedure,* 70 HARV. L. REV. 1, 8 (1957). *See also* MONROE H. FREEDMAN, UNDERSTANDING LAWYERS' ETHICS 13 (1990); GEOFFREY C. HAZARD, ETHICS IN THE PRACTICE OF LAW 123 (1978).

5. Gideon v. Wainwright, 372 U.S. 335, 344 (1963). *See also* ANTHONY LEWIS, GIDEON'S TRUMPET (1964).

6. Harper Lee, To Kill a Mockingbird (1960). *But see* Monroe H. Freedman, *Atticus Finch, Esq., R.I.P.*, Legal Times, May 18, 1992, p. 20; Monroe H. Freedman, *Finch: The Lawyer Mythologized*, Legal Times, February 24, 1992, p. 20. *Compare* David Margolick, *Chipping at Atticus Finch's Pedestal*, The New York Times, Feb. 28, 1992, p. B1.

7. *See e.g.*, Howard Lesnick, Being a Lawyer: Individual Choice and Responsibility in the Practice of Law 328–405 (1992); Monroe H. Freedman, Understanding Lawyers' Ethics 66–70 (1990); David Luban, Lawyers and Justice 104–47 (1988); Richard Wasserstrom, *Lawyers as Professionals: Some Moral Issues*, 5 Human Rights 1, 2–22 (1975).

8. George Sharswood, *An Essay on Professional Ethics* 83–84 (1854), quoted in David Luban, Lawyers and Justice 10 (1988). *But see* Monroe H. Freedman, Understanding Lawyers' Ethics 68 ("The lawyer's decision to take or to reject a client is a moral decision for which the lawyer can properly be held morally accountable."). *Compare* ABA Model Rules of Professional Conduct 1.2(b) ("A lawyer's representation of a client . . . does not constitute an endorsement of the client's political, economic, social or moral views or activities.").

9. Brougham, Life and Times of Lord Brougham 405–407 (n.d.), quoted in Roy L. Patterson, *Legal Ethics and the Lawyer's Duty of Loyalty*, 29 Emory L.J. 909, 910 n. 3 (1980).

Bibliography

Articles, Reports, and Standards

ABA Canons of Professional Ethics 15 (1908).

ABA Model Code of Professional Responsibility, EC 2-26; Canon 7, Preamble (1980).

ABA Model Rules of Professional Conduct, Rule 1.2(b); 6.2 and Cmt. (1983).

ABA Standards for Criminal Justice, Standard 4-1.1, 4-1.5

Barbara Babcock, *Defending the Guilty*, 32 Clev. St. L. Rev. 175 (1983).

David A. Binder and Susan C. Price, *Legal Interviewing and Counseling: A Client-Centered Approach* (1977).

Richard Delgado, *Rotten Social Background: Should the Criminal Law Recognize a Defense of Severe Environmental Deprivation?* 3 Law & Ineq. J. 9 (1985).

Monroe H. Freedman, *Understanding Lawyers' Ethics* 13 (1990).

Monroe H. Freedman, *Atticus Finch, Esq., R.I.P.*, Legal Times, May 18, 1992.

Monroe H. Freedman, *Finch: The Lawyer Mythologized*, Legal Times, February 24, 1992.

Charles Fried, *The Lawyer as Friend: The Moral Foundations of the Lawyer-Client Relation*, 85 Yale L.J. 1060 (1976).

Geoffrey C. Hazard, *Ethics in the Practice of Law* 123 (1978).

Andrew Kaufman, *Problems in Professional Responsibility* 258 (1976).

Harper Lee, *To Kill a Mockingbird* (1960).

Howard Lesnick, *Being a Lawyer: Individual Choice and Responsibility in the Practice of Law* 328 (1992).

Anthony Lewis, *Gideon's Trumpet* (1964).

David Luban, *Lawyers and Justice* (1988).

Michael McConville and Chester Mirsky, *Criminal Defense of the Poor in New York City*, N.Y.U. Rev. L. & Soc. Change 581 (1986–87).

Lisa J. McIntyre, *The Public Defender: The Practice of Law in the Shadows of Repute* 45 (1987).

David Margolick, *Chipping at Atticus Finch's Pedestal*, The New York Times, February 28, 1992.

Charles J. Ogletree, *Beyond Justifications: Seeking Motivations to Sustain Public Defenders*, 106 Harv. L. Rev. 1239 (1993).

Ray L. Patterson, *Legal Ethics and the Lawyer's Duty of Loyalty*, 29 Emory L.J. 909 (1980).

Gerald J. Postema, *Moral Responsibility in Professional Ethics*, 55 N.Y.U. L. Rev. 63 (1980).

Jack Rand, *Moral Vision and Professional Decisions: The Changing Values of Women and Men Lawyers* 36 (1989).

John-Paul Sartre, *Existentialism and Humanism* (1977).

Walter V. Schaefer, *Federalism and State Criminal Procedure*, 70 Harv. L. Rev. 1 (1957).

Abbe Smith, *The Public Defender: The Practice of Law in the Shadows of Repute*, 62 Temple L. Rev. 651 (1989) (book review).

Abbe Smith, *Rosie O'Neill Goes to Law School: The Clinical Education of a Sensitive, New Age Public Defender*, 28 Harv. C.R.-C.L. L. Rev. 1 (1993).

Lawrence N. Tribe, *Trial by Mathematical Precision and Ritual in the Legal Process*, 84 Harv. L. Rev. 1329 (1971).

Richard Wasserstrom, *Lawyers as Professionals: Some Moral Issues*, 5 Human Rights 1 (1975).

Arthur Weinberg, ed., *Attorney for the Damned: Clarence Darrow in the Courtroom* 3–15 (University of Chicago Press, 1989) (1957).

Seymour Wishman, *Confessions of a Criminal Lawyer* (1981).

Ellen Yaroshefsky, *Balancing Victim's Rights and Vigorous Advocacy for the Defendant*, 1989 Annual Survey of American Law 135.

Cases

Gideon v. Wainwright, 372 U.S. 335 (1963).

CHAPTER 📖 3

The Decision to Challenge the Competency of a Marginally Competent Client: Defense Counsel's Unavoidably Difficult Position

Rodney J. Uphoff

Does defense counsel with doubts about a client's competence have an ethical duty to raise the competency issue even though doing so is contrary to the defendant's best interests or wishes?

Introduction: Assessing a Client's Competency

In every jurisdiction criminal defense lawyers, especially public defenders and assigned counsel, encounter criminal defendants who are mentally impaired. A defendant's mental state not only may determine a defendant's responsibility for the offense with which he is charged, but also may affect the accused's ability to assist counsel in conducting a vigorous defense, his understanding of the proceedings being brought against him, his capacity to make important decisions, and ultimately, his competence to stand trial. Thus, defense counsel must carefully investigate a defendant's mental condition if, at any time during the representation of an accused, the defendant's appearance, statements, conduct, or prior history suggest that the defendant is mentally impaired. *See* ABA STANDARDS FOR CRIMINAL JUSTICE DEFENSE FUNCTION 4-4.1 (3d ed. 1993) (hereinafter ABA STANDARD). Unquestionably, the failure to adequately investigate a defendant's mental condition can lead to deficient representation for the mentally impaired defendant.[1] A defense lawyer, therefore, should carefully screen her clients to determine if they have a history of any mental illness and then obtain pertinent mental health records.

Whenever defense counsel discovers that a defendant's mental impairment is adversely affecting the defendant's ability to communicate, to make decisions, or to understand the proceedings and his legal predicament, counsel must carefully consider the competency issue. Unlike the mental responsibility or insanity issue, which turns on the defendant's mental state at the time of the commission of a crime, a competency inquiry focuses on the defendant's present mental state. To be competent to stand trial, a criminal defendant must possess a "sufficient present ability to consult with his lawyer with a reasonable degree of rational understanding . . . and . . . a rational as well as a factual understanding of the proceeding against him." *Dusky v. United States,* 362 U.S. 402, 402 (1960).[2] A defendant who lacks the mental capacity to understand the nature and object of the legal proceeding he faces, to consult with defense counsel, or to assist counsel in preparing a defense is incompetent and may not be subjected to trial. *Drope v. Missouri,* 420 U.S. 162, 171 (1975).

The competency doctrine is designed primarily to protect a mentally impaired defendant from being unfairly subjected to criminal proceedings when the defendant either is unable to assist counsel in his defense or to understand adequately those proceedings. *Pate v. Robinson,* 383 U.S. 375 (1966). Nonetheless, simply because a defendant exhibits mental problems, even serious ones, does not necessarily mean the defendant is incompetent. Many mentally impaired defendants are legally competent to stand trial.[3] Indeed, the vast majority of defendants referred for competency evaluations are determined to be competent.[4]

According to the American Bar Association Mental Health Standards, "competency is functional in nature, context-dependant and pragmatic in orientation." ABA STANDARD at 7-175. A competency determination generally turns on three distinct findings: a diagnosable mental illness, the impairment of one or more of the defendant's legal abilities, and a causal connection between the mental illness and the legal impairment.[5] Unquestionably, the indefinite, imprecise, context-related nature of the competency test often makes it difficult for defense counsel to determine whether a defendant's mental impairment, in fact, raises a competency question. *Drope v. Missouri,* 420 U.S. 162, 180 (1975); ABA STANDARD at 7-170 to 7-175.

In analyzing the competency issue, therefore, defense counsel should consider the extent to which the defendant's mental condition actually interferes with that person's ability to understand the proceeding or affects the client's capacity to assist counsel. Counsel must assess her client's ability to appreciate his legal predicament and to grasp the basic workings of the adversary system. Moreover, counsel must judge her client's ability to interact with counsel, process information, participate appropriately in court, and make informed decisions.[6]

A zealous defense lawyer should not simply seek a formal competency determination whenever a defendant's mental condition makes communication difficult or the defendant appears mentally ill. Rather, counsel must patiently interview the defendant, review records, and ascertain the extent to which the defendant's mental condition is, in fact, affecting the various functions that a "competent defendant" is expected to perform. Although the Comment to Model Rule 1.14 notes that "to an increasing extent the law recognizes intermediate degrees of competency," courts and commentators often disagree whether differing competency standards should apply depending on the nature of the legal task an impaired criminal defendant is being asked to perform.[7] At a minimum, however, the *Dusky* standard mandates that a defendant must be sufficiently able to communicate with counsel and to render appropriate assistance so that counsel is able to explore and to present an adequate defense. Not surprisingly, it is defense counsel who usually is in the best position to assess the extent to which the defendant's impairment truly limits the defendant's ability to assist counsel or actively participate in his own defense.[8]

In many instances, defense counsel will benefit by obtaining the assistance of a privately retained expert before making the decision to challenge a client's competency. In those jurisdictions where such an expert can be obtained without the need to notify the court or prosecutor, such assistance should be secured. Additionally, counsel must be aware of the workings of the mental health system in her jurisdiction so she can make a competent assessment of the costs and benefits of seeking a formal competency determination. Although raising the competency issue benefits some clients, other defendants suffer significantly.[9] For some clients raising competency actually subjects the defendant to greater punishment than that likely to be imposed for the charged offense.[10] Accordingly, a lawyer should undertake a prudent assessment of the merits of raising competency for that particular client before reaching any decision regarding the competency issue.

In addition, defense counsel must consider the seriousness of the charge lodged against the defendant, the strength of the prosecution's evidence, counsel's ability to raise defenses given the nature of the defendant's condition, and the availability and relative merits of other alternatives. It may be possible, for example, to arrive at a noncriminal disposition that obviates the need to raise competency. An effective lawyer must be sufficiently familiar with the resources in her community so that she can divert her client's case from the criminal justice system when diversion is warranted. *See* ABA STANDARD 4-6.1.

The Decision to Raise the Competency Issue

If counsel determines that her client is mentally impaired, she should strive to ensure that her client receives the same conscientious, zealous representation provided to her other clients. A criminal defense lawyer representing a mentally impaired defendant also should seek to establish or maintain a normal lawyer-client relationship. MODEL RULE 1.14. Although a defendant's mental condition may make communication and decision-making more difficult, many mentally ill defendants are able to adequately discuss their cases, understand legal advice, and make reasonably informed decisions about their cases. MODEL RULE 1.14 Comment. A mentally impaired defendant may well require more of a lawyer's time and patience. Nevertheless, such defendants should be treated with the same dignity and respect afforded to other clients.

Before taking any action regarding the competency issue, defense counsel must take the time to discuss the competency issue as thoroughly as possible with the defendant. *See* MODEL RULE 1.2, 1.4; ABA STANDARD 4-3.8, 4-5.1; and EC 7-7, 7-8. Because invoking the competency process may mean lengthy hospitalization, stigmatization, and a significant delay in the proceedings, it is imperative that the lawyer take the time needed to ensure that her client understands as fully as possible the merits of raising competency and the consequences of not doing so. Mentally ill defendants frequently are capable of making choices and articulating objectives. MODEL RULE 1.14 Comment; ABA STANDARD 4-3.1 Commentary.[11] As with many criminal defendants, the mentally impaired defendant may be confused, inconsistent, and indecisive. As with other defendants, defense counsel ultimately may have to push her mentally impaired client to make a decision. The question becomes, then, whether defense counsel should respect the mentally impaired client's decision regarding raising the competency issue or disclose her doubts about her client's competence to the court regardless of her client's wishes.

According to ABA Standard 7-4.2(c), "[d]efense counsel should move for evaluation of the defendant's competence to stand trial whenever the defense counsel has a good faith doubt as to the defendant's competence." If the client objects, ABA Standard 7-4.2(c) states that the defense lawyer "may" move for evaluation despite that objection. As the Commentary to Standard 7-4.2 acknowledges, such a requirement "resolves the difficult conflict of concerns inherent in such circumstances . . . in favor of counsel's obligation to the court." I disagree with this resolution. Instead, I urge lawyers facing a decision about whether to raise the issue of the competency of a mentally impaired defendant to weigh the client's choice on raising the issue along with the seriousness of the client's mental impairment, the nature of the defendant's case, counsel's ability to raise effective defenses, and the lawyer's assessment of the costs and benefits of various actions.[12] The lawyer's role is clear in any case in which the client and counsel agree that the client's competence should be challenged. Counsel should utilize the appropriate statutory procedures to request a competency determination.

The lawyer's role is also fairly straightforward when the client insists on challenging his own competence even though defense counsel feels that doing so is not in the client's best interest. Except in the very rare case in which a client's decision is extremely detrimental, the client's right to make fundamental case decisions, the value of client autonomy, and the uncertainty of judgments regarding competency mandate that defense counsel provide to the defendant the opportunity to litigate the question of his competence if the defendant so desires, even if counsel believes that the decision is unwise. *See Faretta v. California,* 422 U.S. 806 (1975); *In re Link,* 713 S.W.2d 487 (Mo. 1986). In addition, the client's choice must be honored because the defendant generally has a specific statutory right to challenge his own competency.

Taking "Protective Action" on Behalf of the Incompetent Defendant

There are, however, some mentally impaired defendants who are unable or unwilling to discuss the competency issue, to articulate any goals, or to make any fundamental decisions. Rather than automatically raise the competency issue, defense counsel should undertake an analysis of the merits of raising the issue given the particular circumstances of the defendant's case. Indeed, Model Rule 1.14(b) permits a lawyer to "seek the appointment of a guardian or take other protective action" for an impaired client who the lawyer "reasonably believes . . . cannot adequately act in the client's own interest." For some clients, the most appropriate action the lawyer could take would be to persuade the prosecutor to dismiss the charge, to allow the defendant to be voluntarily admitted to a hospital, or to pursue civil commitment proceedings. Such "protective action" by the lawyer may be warranted when the charges facing the client are minor, the client can be quickly stabilized on medication, or the client has a strong support network. *See* MODEL RULE 1.14; EC 7-12; Winick, *supra* note 8, at 969–79.

In other instances, however, the client's mental condition may be so aggravated that although the charge is fairly minor, defense counsel has no viable recourse but to request a formal competency evaluation.

Similarly, when the client's ability to communicate is severely restricted and the nature of the case is such that the client's account of the incident is crucial to determine the client's involvement in or degree of responsibility for a particular offense, counsel must raise the competency issue. The process of securing a competency evaluation may produce a significant improvement in the defendant's mental condition such that the accused regains the ability to make informed choices about his case. Thus, a lawyer ordinarily will need to seek expert assistance or a formal competency evaluation before subjecting a significantly impaired defendant to a trial or a guilty plea that the client neither wants nor really understands.

Yet, for a few incompetent, uncommunicative clients, defense counsel may identify a course of action, other than raising competency, which would allow her to resolve the case favorably for the defendant. In such a rare case, if the lawyer can secure a favorable result for the client without raising competency, the lawyer may assume a paternalistic role and secure the desired result. *O'Beirne v. Overholser*, 193 F. Supp. 652, 661 (D.C. Cir. 1961), *rev'd on other grounds*, 302 F.2d 852 (D.C. Cir. 1961).[13] Assume, for example, the case of a mentally retarded defendant charged with a minor offense. The prosecutor is unwilling to dismiss the charge or consider any noncriminal disposition but will agree to a sentence of "time served" in exchange for the defendant's guilty plea. If counsel is satisfied that the defendant clearly was involved in the offense and is unlikely to successfully raise an insanity defense, counsel should be permitted to respond to her client's request "to go home" and assist her client in entering a plea so as to secure his requested release, even though counsel has doubts about her client's competence to plead guilty. Rather than raising competency or litigating such a case and thereby needlessly extending the defendant's detention, counsel should be allowed to take "protective action" and attempt to obtain the result apparently consistent with the client's wishes and best interests. MODEL RULE 1.14.[14]

A trial judge, of course, is not to accept a guilty plea absent a knowing and intelligent waiver of the defendant's constitutional rights. *Boykin v. Alabama*, 395 U.S. 238 (1969). But in *Allard v. Helgemoe*, 572 F.2d 1 (1st Cir.), *cert. denied*, 439 U.S. 858 (1978), the court held that a defendant who lacked the capacity to make a "reasoned choice" among alternatives was still competent to enter a plea despite the fact he could not understand the intent element of a burglary charge because he relied on competent counsel's recommendation that a lenient plea bargain was preferable to going to trial. Some trial judges will accept the plea of a mentally impaired defendant represented by competent counsel if the judge is convinced that the defendant's plea serves the defendant's best interest. Under certain circumstances, therefore, a marginally competent defendant assisted by conscientious counsel who has thoroughly investigated the case should be permitted to enter a guilty plea so that the defendant can avail himself of the benefits of a desirable plea bargain.[15]

It is generally not appropriate for a criminal defense lawyer merely to substitute her judgment as to what case disposition is in the client's best interest. Defense counsel should strive to act in accordance with the expressed wishes of her impaired defendant and protect the defendant's right to make all significant case decisions. Nonetheless, for some clients who cannot or do not express their wishes, a defense lawyer should be permitted to use counsel's best judgment and secure a favorable plea bargain for the defendant. In exercising this judgment, defense counsel ordinarily should pursue a plea for her mentally impaired client, only if, based on her investigation, case assessment, and experience with similarly situated clients, counsel is confident the client would choose such action if he were capable of doing so. If lawyers are mindful to use this approach sparingly, the danger of counsel unduly compromising the autonomy or rights of their mentally impaired clients will be minimized.

Deciding Not to Raise Competency: Counsel's "Unavoidably Difficult" Position

Even if counsel declines to request a competency evaluation but chooses to attempt to assist a marginally competent defendant to plead guilty, a criminal defense lawyer may find it necessary to alert the court to the client's mental state in the course of the guilty plea colloquy. This may result in the court sua sponte moving for a competency determination and thereby generating the attendant problems counsel was attempting to avoid. Despite counsel's interest in obtaining a favorable result for her client, counsel may find it impossible to participate in a guilty plea hearing and comply with Model Rule 3.3(a) or DR 7-102(A) without disclosing her concerns to the court. This is particularly so if the defendant's competence is so questionable that the defendant cannot meaningfully discuss the competency issue.

This does not mean, however, that defense counsel must routinely volunteer to the court any doubt counsel may have about her client's competence and that the failure to do so constitutes a violation of Model Rule 3.3(a) or Model Code DR 7-102(A) or (B)(1).[16] Rather, a lawyer's duty to disclose information about her client's mental state to the court at a guilty plea hearing rests on the degree of the client's impairment, the nature as well as the source of the information creating counsel's doubts, and the specifics of the court's inquiries at the hearing. A specific answer to this difficult issue turns primarily on the actual questions directed to the defendant and to defense counsel, and the ethical rules, statutory mandates, and existing case law in a particular jurisdiction. *See Hawkins v. King County,* 602 P.2d 361 (Wash. App. 1979) (defense counsel under no duty to divulge information about client's dangerous mental state at bail hearing but rather under duty to zealously advocate client's position unless clear provision of law required counsel to reveal information detrimental to the client's interest). Model Rule 1.6 and DR 7-102(B) severely limit the extent to which a criminal defense lawyer is obligated to disclose information to the detriment of a client. In light of the broad protection afforded to defendants by these ethical rules, it is difficult to understand why a defense counsel's doubts about a client's competence necessarily must be disclosed when counsel's suspicions regarding perjury, *United States ex rel. Wilcox v. Johnson,* 555 F.2d 115, 122 (3d Cir. 1977), or counsel's knowledge of client fraud need not. *See* Monroe H. Freedman, *Understanding Lawyers' Ethics,* 87–141 (1990). Absent direct questions to counsel regarding her client's competence, counsel may well be able to assist the defendant at a guilty plea without making any false statement of material fact. Nor should nondisclosure of counsel's doubts, without more, constitute assisting in a client's fraud in violation of either DR 7-102 or Model Rule 3.3.[17] Nonetheless, even in those cases in which counsel and the client have agreed not to raise competency, defense counsel's ethical obligations may change as the defendant's guilty plea proceeding unfolds.

In some jurisdictions, moreover, case law or statutory directives specifically obligate defense counsel to bring the competency issue to the court's attention whenever counsel has a reasonable doubt about her client's competence. *See, e.g., Johnson v. State,* 395 N.W.2d 176 (Wis. 1986). Furthermore, in those jurisdictions imposing such a duty, defense counsel must alert the court to her doubts about a client's competency even though doing so works to the disadvantage of the defendant or the client objects. *Jones v. District Court,* 617 P.2d 803 (Colo. 1980). As already noted, ABA Standard 7-4.2(c) recommends that a defense lawyer with a good faith doubt regarding the competency of her client "should" bring that doubt to the attention of the trial court. It is significant that the drafters of ABA Standard 7-4.2(c) chose to use "should" instead of a mandatory directive like "must" or "shall." Even more significant, ABA Standard 7-4.2(c) gives a lawyer discretion to move for an evaluation if the client objects. Thus, despite the language in the Commentary to the ABA Standard 7-4.2(c), the standard does not mandate raising the competency issue over the client's objection.

Moreover, even a criminal defense lawyer in a jurisdiction with specific authority imposing a clear duty upon defense counsel need not automatically raise the competency issue in any case in which her client is mentally impaired. Counsel in these jurisdictions should still make a case-by-case determination of the merits of requesting a competency evaluation and, if raising the issue appears detrimental, seek to obviate the need to raise competency by securing a noncriminal disposition. Alternatively, counsel may secure the opinion of a privately retained expert who may dispel counsel's doubts. Moreover, if a lawyer can satisfy herself that she does not have a good faith doubt about her client's competency, she need not raise the issue.[18] If, however, the defendant's mental state does raise a reasonable doubt about the defendant's competency, a defense lawyer in a jurisdiction such as Wisconsin must alert the trial court to that doubt.

Yet, for lawyers in most jurisdictions, their duty when confronted with a mentally impaired defendant is far from clear. The mentally impaired defendant is entitled to the same zealous representation afforded to any other criminal defendant. Thus, defense counsel should discuss the merits of raising competency with her client after undertaking the analysis described above. Some clients will state unequivocally that they do not want their competency challenged. Despite doubts about a client's competency, counsel should respect the client's choice not to raise competency when counsel agrees that the decision is consistent with the client's best interests. Compelling a criminal defense lawyer to ignore her client's wishes and take adverse action against her client by raising competency forces counsel to betray her client, to compromise the lawyer-client relationship, and to act primarily as an officer of the court instead of as a zealous advocate for her client. Both the Model Code and Model Rules sharply limit the circumstances in which counsel is required to divulge to the court harmful information about a client. Accordingly, as long as there is agreement between counsel and her client on all fundamental case decisions, including the decision not to raise competency, a lawyer should honor her client's choice and go forward with the case without requesting a competency evaluation.[19]

Overriding the Defendant's Decision Regarding Competency

Despite the mentally impaired defendant's choice not to raise competency, defense counsel will be confronted with cases in which counsel feels compelled to override the defendant's choice. The defendant may be acutely psychotic, harmful to himself or others, or insistent on making a fundamental decision that the lawyer deems disastrous and not in the client's best interest. For example, the defendant refuses a prosecutor's offer to reduce a felony to a misdemeanor with a recommendation for credit for "time served" and, in the face overwhelming evidence, insists on a jury trial on the felony charge even though conviction carries a mandatory prison term because the witnesses are agents of Satan. Defense counsel cannot simply plead the client guilty to the misdemeanor because it is clearly the defendant's decision whether to plead guilty. *Jones v. Barnes*, 463 U.S. 745, 751 (1983); MODEL RULE 1.2(a); EC 7-7; ABA STANDARD 4-5.2 and Commentary. Counsel will have to respect the mentally impaired defendant's decision to try the case or else raise the competency issue. Under what circumstances, then, should defense counsel override the client's decision and raise the competency issue over the client's objection?

Defense counsel's decision turns, once again, on the degree of the client's impairment, the nature of the case, and the relative costs or benefits of respecting the defendant's wishes.[20] The "normal" client is afforded the right to make his own decisions, even harmful ones, because society values highly the individual's freedom to choose for himself what constitutes his best interests. *Faretta v. California*, 422 U.S. 806, 834 (1975). Society restricts the mentally impaired person's right to choose because it lacks confidence in that person's capacity to understand alternatives or make a reasoned choice. When a sensitive, empathetic lawyer is unable to ascertain from her impaired client why he is making a seemingly irrational, detrimental decision, or the defendant's reasons are wholly irrational, the lawyer is understandably reluctant to honor that decision. The farther a mentally impaired defendant is from the rational decision-maker or "normal" end of the continuum, the more willing counsel should be to override a defendant's disastrous choice and raise the competency issue.[21]

Model Rule 1.14(b) gives counsel the right to take appropriate "protective action" when the lawyer reasonably believes that the client cannot adequately act in the client's own interest. Despite the broad grant of power provided by Model Rule 1.14(b), the conscientious lawyer should be mindful to exercise this override function so as not to unduly compromise the autonomy of the mentally impaired client. Respect for individual autonomy does not, however, require the defense counsel to rely blindly on the choices of a defendant whose reasoning is suspect. *See, e.g., Thompson v. Wainwright*, 787 F.2d 1447 (11th Cir. 1986); *Brennan v. Blankenship*, 472 F. Supp. 149 (W.D. Va. 1979), *aff'd*, 624 F.2d 1093 (4th Cir. 1980). The lawyer's role will be particularly clear when the client's irrational decision is inconsistent with the client's primary case objective, far removed from the decision of similarly situated clients, or when the decision obviously is disastrous to the client's well-being. The more irrational the client's choice not to raise the competency issue when that choice runs contrary to the client's own stated goals, the easier the lawyer's decision to raise the issue. If the impaired client's irrational choice impinges significantly upon counsel's ability to pursue her strategic means of achieving the client's desired ends, defense counsel may need to seek a competency evaluation.[22] Finally, the seriousness of the charge facing the defendant or the dire consequences of the defendant's proposed decision may preclude defense counsel from respecting the ill-considered choice of a mentally suspect defendant and compel counsel to seek a competency determination.

Conclusion

Defense counsel with doubts about a client's competence must thoroughly investigate the defendant's mental condition and carefully weigh the decision to raise the issue of a defendant's competence to stand trial. Prior to making any decision regarding a client's competence, counsel must discuss the issue fully with the defendant. If the defendant's mental condition precludes any meaningful discussion and counsel doubts the defendant's competence, counsel frequently will be required to raise the competency issue. In some instances, however, even absent the ability to meaningfully consult with the accused, a conscientious lawyer may conclude that raising competency will be highly detrimental to the client's best interests. In certain exceptional cases, therefore, a lawyer may decline to raise the competency issue and attempt to resolve the case consistent with counsel's assessment of the defendant's best interests.

In other cases, a criminal defendant may insist on raising the competency issue despite defense counsel's belief that doing so is strategically unwise or contrary to the client's best interests. Respect for client autonomy, statutory directives, and the relative importance of the competency issue dictate that the defendant's choice to raise competency be respected. It does not follow, however, that a lawyer must routinely honor a defendant's choice not to seek a competency determination. Defense counsel may feel compelled to question a client's competence despite the client's objection. A lawyer's decision to override a client's desire not to raise the competency issue turns on the extent of the client's mental impairment, the seriousness of the charge facing the defendant, the client's stated reasons for not raising the issue, and counsel's assessment of the costs and benefits of challenging the competence of that defendant.

Finally, in those cases in which the defendant and defense counsel agree that raising the competency issue is detrimental to the defendant, counsel usually should decline to raise the issue even though counsel may harbor doubts about the defendant's competence. Nevertheless, a lawyer may be required to bring those doubts to the attention of the trial court at a guilty plea hearing. Moreover, in certain jurisdictions, case law specifically obligates defense counsel to alert the trial court to counsel's good-faith doubts about a defendant's competence despite the counsel's belief that raising the competency issue is harmful to the defendant. Absent clear authority imposing such a duty, however, a zealous defense lawyer will resolve whether to raise the competency issue by conscientiously balancing the defendant's choice with the seriousness of the defendant's mental impairment, the nature of the defendant's case, and counsel's assessment of the costs and benefits of the defendant's alternatives.

Notes

1. *See, e.g.,* Boykins v. Wainwright, 737 F.2d 1539 (11th Cir. 1984), *cert. denied,* 470 U.S. 1059 (1985); State v. Felton, 329 N.W.2d 161 (Wis. 1983). *See also* Richard J. Bonnie, *The Competence of Criminal Defendants with Mental Retardation to Participate in Their Own Defense,* 81 J. Crim. L. & Criminology 419–46 (1990) (criticizing criminal defense lawyers for frequently failing to identify or properly assist mentally retarded individuals.)

2. The *Dusky* standard is substantially followed in all jurisdictions. *See* ABA Standards for Criminal Justice Mental Health 7-4.1 (1984) and Commentary.

3. *See* Gerald T. Bennett, *A Guided Tour Through Selected ABA Standards Relating to Incompetence to Stand Trial,* 53 Geo. Wash. L. Rev. 375, 391 (1985).

4. Bruce J. Winick, *Presumptions and Burdens of Proof in Determining Competency to Stand Trial: An Analysis of* Medina v. California *and the Supreme Court's New Due Process Methodology in Criminal Cases,* 47 U. Miami L. Rev. 817, 847–48 (1993).

5. *See* Sanford L. Drob, Robert H. Berger & Henry C. Weinstein, *Competency to Stand Trial: A Conceptual Model for its Proper Assessment,* 15 Bull. Am. Acad. Psychiatry & L. 85–94 (1987). *But see* ABA Standards 7-175 (noting that under ABA Standard 7-4.1 a finding of incompetence not dependant on a diagnosis of mental illness).

6. Thomas Grisso, Evaluating Competencies: Forensic Assessment and Instruments 76–77 (1986). For additional guidance on the complex task of assessing competency, *see* ABA Standards 7-4.1 and Commentary; Robert D. Miller & Edward J. Germain, *The Specificity of Evaluation of Competency to Proceed,* 14 J. Psychiatry & L. 333–44 (1986); Lipsett, Lelos & McGarry, *Competency*

for Trial: A Screening Instrument, 128 AM. J. PSYCHIATRY 105 (1977). *See also* Rodney J. Uphoff, *The Role of the Criminal Defense Lawyer in Representing the Mentally Impaired Defendant: Zealous Advocate or Officer of the Court?* 1988 WIS. L. REV. 65–109.

7. Unfortunately, the Supreme Court's recent forays into the competency thicket have not provided much guidance to courts or lawyers struggling with competency questions. *See* Godinez v. Moran, 113 S. Ct. 2680 (1993); Medina v. California, 112 S. Ct. 2572 (1992); Riggins v. Nevada, 112 S. Ct. 1810 (1992). In *Godinez*, however, the majority rejected the notion that the competence standard for pleading guilty or waiving the right to counsel should be higher than the competence standard for standing trial set out in *Dusky*. Rather, the court reaffirmed the notion that there is a single standard of competency. *But see* Justice Blackmun, "[t]he majority's monolithic approach to competency is true to neither life nor the law. Competency for one purpose does not necessarily translate to competency for another purpose." *Godinez*, 113 S. Ct. 2680, 2694 (1993) (Blackmun, J., dissenting). Prior to *Godinez*, several courts shared the view of ABA Standard 7-5.1 that a special higher standard ought to govern in guilty plea proceedings to ensure that a defendant entering a plea has made a "reasoned choice." *See, e.g.,* Moran v. Godinez, 972 F.2d 263 (9th Cir. 1992). For an extended discussion of the utility of a functional test focusing on the defendant's "decisional competence," *see* Bonnie, *supra* note 1, at 424–46.

8. *See* Medina v. California, 112 S. Ct. 2572, 2580 (1992). *See also* Richard J. Bonnie, *The Competence of Criminal Defendants: Beyond* Dusky *and* Drope, 47 U. MIAMI L. REV. 539, 564–86 (1993) (arguing that because defense lawyer is in best position to determine if the defendant's impairment actually impedes the defense, defense lawyer should, in some circumstances, be able to function as a surrogate decision-maker without raising the competency issue).

9. ABA STANDARDS at 7-179; Bruce J. Winick, *Restructuring Competency to Stand Trial*, 32 UCLA L. REV. 921, 928–49 (1985).

10. *See, e.g.,* Brown v. Warden, Great Meadow Correctional Facility, 682 F.2d 348, 352–53 (2nd Cir. 1982), *cert. denied*, 459 U.S. 991 (1982). *See also* Winick, *supra* note 9, at 928–49.

11. *See also* Winick, *supra* note 4, at 858–62. *But see* Bonnie, *supra* note 1, at 423 (warning that mentally retarded defendants often conceal their disability, act as if they understand when they do not, and respond as they think their lawyers want them to respond).

12. For a critical look at Standard 7-4.2(c) and the "duty" to disclose doubts about a client's competence, *see generally* Uphoff, *supra* note 6. *See also* Winick, *supra* note 9, at 959–79 (arguing that even under existing case law, defense lawyer should be permitted to waive the competency issue and assist impaired clients to plead guilty when doing so is in the client's best interest); Bonnie, *supra* note 8, at 564–67 (disagrees with Standard 7-4.2(c) and calls for greater reliance on attorney decision-making in deciding whether to seek a competency evaluation); ANTHONY G. AMSTERDAM, TRIAL MANUAL 5 FOR THE DEFENSE OF CRIMINAL CASES, 1-303 to 1-318 (1988) (calling for counsel to make a

careful assessment of the costs and benefits of raising competency without any acknowledgement of a duty to raise the issue if doing so appears contrary to the client's best interests).

13. *See* GEOFFREY C. HAZARD, JR. & WILLIAM W. HODES, THE LAW OF LAW-YERING, 442–51 (2d ed. 1990) (cautioning lawyers for disabled clients not to merely impose their own values on their clients when seeking to take protective action designed to secure the best interests of their clients but offering examples of appropriate paternalistic lawyering).

14. *See also* Winick, *supra* note 9, at 969–79; Uphoff, *supra* note 6, at 107–8. EC 7-12 notes that a lawyer with a disabled client may be compelled "to make decisions for his client" and in doing so "should consider all circumstances then prevailing and act with care to safeguard and advance the interests of the client." But EC 7-12 goes on to warn that "obviously a lawyer cannot perform any act or make any decision which the law requires his client to perform or make, either acting for himself if competent, or by a duly constituted representative if legally incompetent." Although this seemingly limits the ability of defense counsel in a Model Code jurisdiction from acting as a surrogate decision-maker for a marginally competent defendant lacking the capacity to make informed decisions about fundamental case decisions such as the decision to plead guilty, as long as counsel is seeking to advance the best interests of her client she should be permitted to act without securing the appointment of a guardian. HAZARD & HODES, *supra* note 13, at 445–49. *See also* CHARLES W. WOLFRAM, MODERN LEGAL ETHICS, 159–62 (1986).

15. *See* Winick, *supra* note 9, at 954–79. *See also* North Carolina v. Alford, 400 U.S. 25 (1970) (defendant permitted to plead guilty to avail himself of favorable plea bargain despite continued claim of innocence). This approach assumes, of course, that counsel's efforts indeed are directed at obtaining a result in the client's best interests and not a result of counsel's caseload pressure or inadequate investigation. Many of the appellate cases on the competency issue involve an ineffective assistance of counsel claim in which defense counsel failed to recognize, to investigate, or to analyze the competency issue. *See, e.g.,* Speedy v. Wyrick, 702 F.2d 723, 727 (8th Cir. 1983), *cert. denied,* 471 U.S. 1019 (1985); Kilbert v. Peyton, 383 F.2d 566, 568 (4th Cir. 1967). *But see* Bonnie, *supra* note 1, at 419, 423, 443–46 (arguing that because public defenders fail to spend adequate time with retarded clients, lack adequate training and specialization to identify retarded persons, and succumb to pressures to cut corners, a surrogate decision-maker, not the defense lawyer, should be permitted to assent to a guilty plea on behalf of a marginally competent defendant when the surrogate agrees with defense counsel that such a plea is desirable). Although Bonnie's observations may hold true for some defense lawyers and public defenders, especially those in seriously underfunded jurisdictions, a competent, dedicated defense lawyer committed to providing zealous representation should be able to act to secure a result that clearly is in the client's best interest without the need to request the appointment of a guardian or use a surrogate decision-maker. At this point, however, no reported case has explicitly autho-

rized a criminal defense lawyer or other surrogate decision-maker to enter a plea on behalf of an incompetent client.

16. *But see* ABA STANDARD 7-4.2 and Commentary at 7-179 to 7-181 (stating that failure to advise court of a defendant's possible incompetence violates Model Rule 3.3(a)(1)'s prohibition that a lawyer not knowingly make a false statement of material fact to a tribunal) and Gerald T. Bennett, *supra* note 3, at 375–84 (arguing that Model Code EC 7-25 and DR 7-102 require defense counsel to disclose doubts about a client's competency to the court).

17. It is questionable that nondisclosure of counsel's doubts about a client's competence amounts to participating in or perpetrating a fraud on the court. *Compare* Doe v. Federal Grievance Committee, 847 F.2d 57, 64 (2d Cir. 1988) (Van Graafeiland, J., concurring); Great Coastal Express, Inc. v. International Brotherhood of Teamsters, 675 F.2d 1349, 1356 (4th Cir. 1982) (taking a restricted view of "fraud on the court or tribunal") with ABA STANDARD 7-179 to 7-181. *See also* ABA Formal Opinion 341 (1975) and ABA Formal Opinion 84-349 forbidding counsel to disclose information relating to client fraud, bail jumping, or a parole violation. Lawyers in a Model Rule jurisdiction, however, would seemingly be under more pressure to disclose pursuant to Rule 3.3(a) than lawyers bound by DR7-102(B). And yet, the Comment to Model Rule 1.14 recognizes that disclosure of a client's disability could adversely affect the client and concludes that the lawyer's position "is an unavoidably difficult one." By suggesting that counsel could decline to disclose information about a client's disability, the comment clearly implies that nondisclosure is consistent with ethical lawyering. For a more extended discussion of this question, *see* Uphoff, *supra* note 6, at 74, 88–92.

18. *See* Hernandez v. Ylst, 930 F.2d 714 (9th Cir. 1991) (pointing out that "sufficient doubt," "genuine doubt," "bona fide doubt," and "good faith doubt" all describe the same constitutional test, and finding that the defendant's odd statements, bizarre actions, or even psychiatric testimony need not raise a sufficient doubt about the defendant's competence.) As in cases dealing with client perjury, a lawyer should resolve doubts in favor of her client and only if the information raising her doubts is sufficiently clear should she take action she perceives as harmful to her client. *See* United States v. Long, 857 F.2d 436 (8th Cir. 1988). Finally, two of the leading commentators on professional ethics suggest that in close cases under Rule 1.14 "a lawyer cannot be disciplined for any action that has a reasonable basis and arguably is in his client's best interest." HAZARD & HODES, *supra* note 13, at 442.

19. This decision is a fairly easy one when the client and counsel both agree that a trial is in the client's best interests and counsel feels satisfied that despite the client's impairment, the client can "assist" in the defense. *See* Bonnie, *supra* note 8, at 576–82.

20. *See* AMSTERDAM, *supra* note 12, at 1-303 to 1-318 (defense counsel to engage in a "particularized analysis" of advantages or disadvantages of raising a competency claim before making any decision).

21. *See, e.g.,* People v. Bolden, 99 Cal. App. 3d 375, 160 Cal. Rptr. 268 (1979) (public defender permitted to present evidence of client's incompetence despite client's objection because counsel felt client's decision, grounded in his belief that the prosecution's witnesses were from outer space, was not in defendant's best interest).

22. *See,* for example, Lafferty v. Cook, 949 F.2d 1546 (10th Cir. 1991), *cert. denied,* 112 S. Ct. 1942 (1992) where the court rejected the trial judge's view that the defendant was competent to decide to refuse to present a defense when that decision was based on the defendant's paranoid delusional system. Rather, the court found that the defendant was not competent to waive an insanity defense against his lawyer's advice when his mental illness stripped him of the ability "to realistically determine where his best interests lie." *Id.* at 1554–56.

Bibliography

Articles, Reports, and Standards

ABA MODEL CODE OF PROFESSIONAL RESPONSIBILITY, DR 7-102; 7-102(A); 7-102(B); 7-102(B)(1); EC 7-7; 7-8; 7-12; 7-25 (1980).

ABA MODEL RULES OF PROFESSIONAL CONDUCT, Rules, 1.14; 1.14(b); 1.2; 1.2(a); 1.4; 1.6; 3.3(a); 3.3(a)(1) (1983).

ABA STANDARDS FOR CRIMINAL JUSTICE DEFENSE FUNCTION 4-3.1; 4-3.8; 4-4.1; 4-5.1; 4-5.2 (3d ed. 1993).

ABA STANDARDS FOR CRIMINAL JUSTICE MENTAL HEALTH 7-4.1; 7-4.2; 7-4.2(c) and Cmt. (1984).

Anthony G. Amsterdam, *Trial Manual 5 for the Defense of Criminal Cases* (1988).

Gerald T. Bennett, *A Guided Tour Through Selected ABA Standards Relating to Incompetence to Stand Trial,* 53 Geo. Wash. L. Rev. 375 (1985).

Richard J. Bonnie, *The Competence of Criminal Defendants with Mental Retardation to Participate in Their Own Defense,* 81 J. Crim. L. & Criminology 419 (1990).

Richard J. Bonnie, *The Competence of Criminal Defendants: Beyond* Dusky *and* Drope, 47 U. Miami L. Rev. 539 (1993).

Sanford L. Drob, Robert H. Berger & Henry C. Weinstein, *Competency to Stand Trial: A Conceptual Model for its Proper Assessment,* 15 Bull. Am. Acad. Psychiatry & L. 85 (1987).

Monroe H. Freedman, *Understanding Lawyers' Ethics* (1990).

Thomas Grisso, *Evaluating Competencies: Forensic Assessment and Instruments* (1986).

Geoffrey C. Hazard, Jr. & William W. Hodes, *The Law of Lawyering* (2d ed. 1990).

Lipsett, Lelos & McGarry, *Competency for Trial: A Screening Instrument*, 128 Am. J. Psychiatry 105 (1977).

Robert D. Miller & Edward J. Germain, *The Specificity of Evaluation of Competency to Proceed*, 14 J. Psychiatry & L. 333 (1986).

Rodney J. Uphoff, *The Role of the Criminal Defense Lawyer in Representing the Mentally Impaired Defendant: Zealous Advocate or Officer of the Court?* 1988 Wis. L. Rev. 65 (1988).

Bruce J. Winick, *Presumptions and Burdens of Proof in Determining Competency to Stand Trial: An Analysis of* Medina v. California *and the Supreme Court's New Due Process Methodology in Criminal Cases*, 47 U. Miami L. Rev. 817 (1993).

Bruce J. Winick, *Restructuring Competency to Stand Trial*, 32 UCLA L. Rev. 921 (1985).

Charles W. Wolfram, *Modern Legal Ethics* (1986).

Cases

Allard v. Helgemoe, 572 F.2d 1 (1st Cir.), *cert. denied*, 439 U.S. 858 (1978).

Boykin v. Alabama, 395 U.S. 238 (1969).

Boykins v. Wainwright, 737 F.2d 1539 (11th Cir. 1984), *cert. denied*, 470 U.S. 1059 (1985).

Brennan v. Blankenship, 472 F. Supp. 149 (W.D. Va. 1979), *aff'd*, 624 F.2d 1093 (4th Cir. 1980).

Brown v. Warden, Great Meadow Correctional Facility, 682 F.2d 348 (2nd Cir. 1982), *cert. denied*, 459 U.S. 991 (1982).

Doe v. Federal Grievance Committee, 847 F.2d 57 (2d Cir. 1988).

Drope v. Missouri, 420 U.S. 162 (1975).

Dusky v. United States, 362 U.S. 402 (1960).

Faretta v. California, 422 U.S. 806 (1975).

Godinez v. Moran, 113 S. Ct. 2680 (1993).

Great Coastal Express, Inc. v. International Brotherhood of Teamsters, 675 F.2d 1349 (4th Cir. 1982).

Hawkins v. King County, 602 P.2d 361 (Wash. App. 1979).

Hernandez v. Ylst, 930 F.2d 714 (9th Cir. 1991).

Johnson v. State, 395 N.W.2d 176 (Wis. 1986).

Jones v. Barnes, 463 U.S. 745, 751 (1983).

Jones v. District Court, 617 P.2d 803 (Colo. 1980).

Kilbert v. Peyton, 383 F.2d 566 (4th Cir. 1967).

Lafferty v. Cook, 949 F.2d 1546 (10th Cir. 1991), *cert. denied*, 112 S. Ct. 1942 (1992).

In re Link, 713 S.W.2d 487 (Mo. 1986).

Medina v. California, 112 S. Ct. 2572 (1992).

Moran v. Godinez, 972 F.2d 263 (9th Cir. 1992).

North Carolina v. Alford, 400 U.S. 25 (1970).

O'Beirne v. Overholser, 193 F. Supp. 652 (D.C. Cir. 1961), *rev'd on other grounds*, 302 F.2d 852 (D.C. Cir. 1961).

Pate v. Robinson, 383 U.S. 375 (1966).

People v. Bolden, 99 Cal. App. 3d 375, 160 Cal. Rptr. 268 (1979).

Riggins v. Nevada, 112 S. Ct. 1810 (1992).

Speedy v. Wyrick, 702 F.2d 723 (8th Cir. 1983), *cert. denied*, 471 U.S. 1019 (1985).

State v. Felton, 329 N.W.2d 161 (Wis. 1983).

Thompson v. Wainwright, 787 F.2d 1447 (11th Cir. 1986).

United States v. Long, 857 F.2d 436 (8th Cir. 1988).

United States ex rel. Wilcox v. Johnson, 555 F.2d 115 (3d Cir. 1977).

CHAPTER 📖 4

Raising the Insanity Plea

David R. Katner

Does counsel have an ethical duty to disregard the client's wishes and assert the insanity defense when counsel believes that raising the defense is in the client's best interest?

Sources of Regulation

Counsel must look to two essentially different sources of authority to resolve the ethical dilemmas associated with raising or failing to raise the insanity defense.[1] The obvious source of authority is the state ethics codes of professional responsibility. These state codes are divided into roughly three groups: (1) those that continue to follow the ABA Model Code of Professional Responsibility (1969)[2]; (2) those that are based on the ABA Model Rules of Professional Conduct (1983)[3]; and (3) those that follow neither the ABA Model Code nor the ABA Model Rules.[4] The second major source of authority for resolving ethical dilemmas involving the insanity defense is judicial decisions that apply the *Strickland v. Washington*[5] standard of review to Sixth Amendment claims of ineffective assistance of counsel.[6] Arguably, the ABA Standards for Criminal Justice 4-1.1 to 4-8.6 (3d ed. 1993) might constitute a third source of authority for clarifying counsel's role in asserting the insanity defense,[7] but these standards have not been adopted or incorporated into state ethics codes.[8] The ethical dilemmas are moot in those jurisdictions that have eliminated the insanity defense,[9] and are diminished in jurisdictions where verdicts of guilty but mentally ill serve as alternatives to the insanity defense.[10]

State Ethics Rules

Model Code

In those jurisdictions that continue to base their ethics codes on the ABA Model Code, no enforceable Disciplinary Rule authorizes counsel to raise an insanity plea over the client's objection. Nevertheless, the Model Code's Ethical Considerations provide some limited direction for counsel. Only the Disciplinary Rules are mandatory in character, in that their violation would subject counsel to disciplinary action.[11] The Ethical Considerations are aspirational in character and represent objectives that every member of the profession should strive for.[12] The Model Code contains no enforceable Disciplinary Rule that clarifies the lawyer's role in asserting the insanity defense.

Ethical Consideration 7-11 indicates that responsibilities of a lawyer may vary according to the mental condition of a client or the nature of a particular proceeding, including the representation of an incompetent. The Model Code fails to define "incompetent," and fails to explain what responsibilities counsel has when representing such a client.

Ethical Consideration 7-7 states that in a criminal case, *"it is for the client to decide what plea should be entered. . . ."* [Emphasis supplied]. Ethical Consideration 7-12, however, indicates that:

> Any mental or physical condition of a client that renders him incapable of making a considered judgment on his own behalf casts additional responsibilities upon his lawyer. Where an incompetent is acting through a guardian or other legal representative, a lawyer must look to such representative for those decisions which are normally the prerogative of the client to make. If a client under disability has no legal representative, his lawyer may be compelled in court proceedings to make decisions on behalf of the client. If the client is capable of understanding the matter in question or of contributing to the advancement of his interests, regardless of whether he is legally disqualified from performing certain acts, the lawyer should obtain from him all possible aid. If the disability of a client and the lack of a legal representative compel the lawyer to make decisions for this client, the lawyer should consider all circumstances then prevailing and *act with care to safeguard and advance the interests of his client.* But obviously a lawyer cannot perform any act or make any decision which the law requires his client to perform or make, either acting for himself if competent, or by a duly constituted representative if legally incompetent.[13]

Thus, a guardian or other legal representative would be the appropriate individual to decide whether or not to enter an insanity plea if the client is "incompetent." Where the client lacks a guardian, counsel may be compelled to make decisions for the client. Although appearing to vest tremendous autonomy in the lawyer's decision-making, the last sentence of EC 7-12 obfuscates counsel's role. If EC 7-7 *requires* the client to decide what plea should be entered, then counsel could *not* raise an insanity plea over the client's objection. Of course, all of this Model Code language is contained in aspirational yet unenforceable Ethical Considerations. No enforceable Disciplinary Rule of the Model Code authorizes counsel to raise an insanity plea over the client's objection.

Model Rules

The Model Rules of Professional Conduct go further in attempting to define counsel's ethical obligations toward a mentally impaired client. The Model Rules restrict the lawyer's autonomy in selecting the plea to be entered in a criminal case, and no enforceable Model Rule authorizes counsel to raise an insanity plea over the client's objection.

According to Model Rule 1.2(a), "[i]n a criminal case, the lawyer *shall abide by* the *client's decision*, after consultation with the lawyer, *as to a plea to be entered.* . . ." In a case where "the client appears to be suffering mental disability, the lawyer's duty to abide by the client's decisions is to be guided by reference to Rule 1.14."[14]

Model Rule 1.14 mandates that the lawyer who represents a mentally impaired client must maintain "as far as reasonably possible . . . a normal client-lawyer relationship with the client."[15] According to the *ABA/BNA Lawyers' Manual on Professional Conduct*, "[o]rdinarily . . . the lawyer must respect a client's decision whether to . . . assert an incompetency defense, or demand a jury trial where the law permits."[16] The rationale is that "ultimate decisions rest with the disabled client as they do with competent clients."[17] The lawyer's role in the representation of a "mentally impaired" client does not allow counsel to raise an insanity plea over the client's objection.

Following counsel's attempt to maintain a normal client-lawyer relationship, Model Rule 1.14(b) further grants counsel discretion to "seek the appointment of a guardian or take other protective action," but only "when the lawyer reasonably believes that the client cannot adequately act in the client's own interest." Presumably, if the lawyer believes the client is unable to "adequately act in the client's own interest," then the guardian would be called upon to make decisions for the client. The Comments to Model Rule 1.14 concede that where a client has no guardian or legal representative, "the lawyer often must act as de facto guardian." Neither Model Rule 1.14 nor its Comments authorize counsel to disregard the client's wishes as to what plea to enter. The rule fails to explain or discuss what "other protective action" counsel *may* take when the "client cannot adequately act in the client's own interest." It would be difficult to argue, however, that the permissive language in Model Rule 1.14 creates an affirmative duty for counsel to raise an insanity plea over the client's objection.

When deciding whether or not the lawyer should disclose the client's disability, the Comments to Model Rule 1.14 allow counsel to "seek guidance from an appropriate diagnostician." Comment 5 to Model Rule 1.14 recognizes the potential ethical dilemma of seeking to have a guardian appointed where the mere "disclosure of the client's disability can adversely affect the client's interests."

Raising the question of the client's mental condition may lead to proceedings for involuntary commitment.[18] One of the unique problems involved in raising the insanity defense is the prospect that an insanity acquittee may be committed to a psychiatric hospital under some state statutes.[19] Unlike other defense strategies, the client who asserts the insanity defense may be faced with an involuntary hospital commitment even where the defense prevails at trial. "The loss of liberty produced by an involuntary commitment is more than a loss of freedom from confinement." *Vitek v. Jones*, 445 U.S. 480, at 492 (1980).

In addition to the concern over possible involuntary commitment proceedings, counsel should also be aware of the possible effect upon the client of a thirty- or ninety-day pretrial incarceration in a mental institution; the possible rescission of bail or increase of bail because of the client's supposed dangerousness; the possible discouragement of the prosecutor's willingness to negotiate for a noncourt disposition; the stimulation of damaging psychiatric inquiry or evaluations by the prosecution to rebut the defense; and the possible disclosures by the client during an examination initiated by the prosecution after defense counsel has disclosed the client's mental disability.[20]

The Model Rules do not create an ethical duty for counsel to disclose a client's "mental disability." Unless counsel elects to seek the appointment of a guardian to make decisions on behalf of the client, counsel may not wish to disclose the client's disability, let alone disregard the client's decision on whether to raise the insanity plea. The provisions of Model Rule 1.14 do not appear to modify the Model Rule 1.2 mandate that counsel abide by the client's decision on the plea to be entered.

Lawyer's Option to Withdraw from Representation

Clearly both the Model Code and the Model Rules designate the client as the autonomous decision maker when deciding whether to raise the insanity defense. Counsel may feel uneasy in some instances where the client may be legally competent to proceed to trial, but counsel believes the client's judgment is impaired.[21] Although some arguments have been advanced for counsel to adopt a paternalistic role and assert or not assert an insanity plea depending on counsel's own assessment of what is in the client's best interest, this paternalistic role is contrary to the provisions of both sets of ethical codification, the Model Code and the Model Rules. This is not to say that the lawyer is confined to a passive role after the client indicates what plea he seeks to enter. The lawyer may use her best efforts to insure that the client makes a decision only after having been informed of all relevant considerations.[22]

If after advising a legally competent client, the lawyer maintains a belief that the client's decision to assert or not to assert the insanity defense is a poor decision, the lawyer's alternatives may be limited to abiding by the client's decision or attempting to withdraw. Under the Model Code, "[t]he lawyer's refusal to go along with the questionable conduct might well result in his dismissal by the client, but conduct that is arguably legal would not justify the lawyer's outright withdrawal (or threat of withdrawal) from the representation."[23] If counsel does attempt to withdraw under DR 2-110, counsel must obtain permission from the tribunal (if the court rules so require), and take reasonable steps to avoid foreseeable prejudice to the client's rights before seeking to withdraw.[24]

Although a weak argument may be made that the Model Code and Model Rules *mandate* withdrawal when the lawyer strongly disagrees with the client's plea decision, a much stronger argument may be made that both ethical codifications *permit* withdrawal. Under DR 2-110(C)(1)(d), when the client's "other conduct renders it unreasonably difficult for the lawyer to carry out his employment effectively," *permissive* withdrawal is allowed. Additionally, under the Model Code, if counsel believes that the court "will find the existence of other good cause for withdrawal,"[25] then counsel may withdraw. Under Model Rule 1.16(b)(3), permissive withdrawal is allowed when the client insists upon pursuing an objective that the lawyer considers repugnant or imprudent, and under Model Rule 1.16(b)(5) permissive withdrawal is allowed when representation has been rendered unreasonably difficult by the client. Finally, under Model Rule 1.16(b)(6), a lawyer may withdraw where "other good cause for withdrawal exists," unless the court orders counsel to continue the representation.[26]

The courts are very reluctant to embrace lawyer withdrawal as a resolution.[27] The bar ethics committees look with disfavor upon lawyer withdrawl as well.[28] One prominent authority has concluded that "when a disabled client wants a lawyer to act contrary to the client's best interests, withdrawal, even if technically permissible, only solves the lawyer's problem and may belittle the client's interest."[29]

Judicial Decisions on the Client's Sixth Amendment Right to Effective Assistance of Counsel

Lawyer's Duty to Her Client

The state ethics codes may only be enforced against a lawyer who has engaged in misconduct, and the consequences of disregarding the Model Code or the Model Rules may have little or no impact on the outcome of the client's case. However, the second major source of regulation for asserting the insanity defense—judicial decisions interpreting the defendant's Sixth Amendment right to effective assistance of counsel—provides a mechanism for the accused to challenge his conviction. Admittedly, the defendant does not enjoy a high probability that a disagreement with counsel over whether or not to raise the insanity defense will result in a reversal of a conviction.

> Ineffective assistance of counsel is one of the most—if not *the* most—common appeal grounds asserted by convicted criminal defendants as appellants. However, proportionate to its assertion, it is infrequently the stated basis for the reversal of criminal convictions. "An analysis of approximately 4,000 federal and state reported appellate decisions regarding claims of ineffective assistance between 1970 and 1983," for example "showed that only 3.9 percent resulted in a finding of ineffective counsel." Aside from the inherent difficulty of satisfying the constitutional tests for establishing ineffective assistance of counsel set out by the courts, many appellate judges and commentators have expressed the view that there are compelling systemic considerations militating de jure or de facto against post hoc judicial findings of ineffective assistance.[30]

The courts are divided on whether or not counsel has an affirmative obligation to challenge a client's competency. The cases focus on whether or not an accused has been denied effective assistance of counsel when the lawyer had reason to doubt the client's competency, but failed to raise the issue with the trial court. Although requesting a competency hearing is not the same as entering an insanity plea, problems of client-versus-lawyer autonomy are similar. No majority opinion has balanced the Sixth Amendment rights of the accused against the lawyer's ethical obligations.

Unfortunately, the courts frequently apply Sixth Amendment analysis without clearly differentiating between challenging the client's competency to stand trial and raising the insanity defense. In *Enriquez v. Procunier*, 752 F.2d 111 (5th Cir. 1984), *cert. denied*, 471 U.S. 1126 (1985), the Fifth Circuit Court of Appeal rejected a writ of habeas corpus that alleged ineffective representation where court-appointed counsel failed to urge the insanity defense or request a competency hearing. The court reasoned that:

> [d]efense counsel investigated the competency issue and decided, for tactical reasons, that an insanity defense should not be advanced. A measure of investigation leading to a reasonable tactical decision does not fall below the *Strickland v. Washington* threshold. The same reasoning applies to the decision not to request a competency hearing.[31]

In a rare attempt to balance defense counsel's ethical obligations with the defendant's right to effective assistance of counsel, Justice Marshall's dissent in *Alvord v. Wainwright* concluded:

> Thus, regardless of whether the ultimate decision on an insanity defense is that of the attorney or his client, counsel must fully inform himself of the facts and law, make a reasonable investigation into the only plausible line of defense, and share his conclusions with his client. This is the essence of effective assistance of counsel. This conclusion, which I would have thought to have been well ingrained in our Sixth Amendment jurisprudence, is wholly at odds with the view that a lawyer reasonably may assume that his client—no matter what his training or mental capacity—has based his decision on sufficient information and knowledge as to render the lawyers's further effort unnecessary. To my mind, such total deference is only proper, if at all, when counsel has good reason to assume that his client's decisions are based on an intelligent and informed understanding of his situation.[32]

The courts simply have not reconciled counsel's ethical obligations with the mandates of providing effective assistance under the Sixth Amendment. The dilemma is less compelling in Model Code jurisdictions where no enforceable Disciplinary Rules govern counsel's relationship with an impaired client. In Model Code jurisdictions, counsel should comply with the mandates of the Sixth Amendment cases. However, in those jurisdictions that follow the Model Rules, the Sixth Amendment cases have not taken into consideration counsel's ethical obligations as defined in Model Rule 1.14. Under Sixth Amendment analysis, a lawyer may render ineffective assistance by raising an insanity defense,[33] even though Model Rule 1.14 allows counsel to take this "protective action" when counsel "reasonably believes that the client cannot adequately act in the client's own interest."[34]

Asserting the Insanity Defense

In most jurisdictions a competent defendant, and not his lawyer or the court, makes the final decision regarding whether or not to assert an insanity defense at trial.[35]

Traditionally, counsel has retained complete control over tactical and strategic decision making at trial.[36] However, because of the potential consequences of an insanity plea—including mandatory commitment in a mental institution if the defense prevails—the plea decision is of "such fundamental importance" that it should not be taken from the client.[37] Therefore, the affirmative defense of insanity is quite different from all other affirmative defenses.[38]

Many legitimate reasons, including a desire to present a defense on the merits, may compel a defendant to forgo raising the insanity defense.[39] A defendant may not wish to deny the validity of his motives, or may prefer a limited prison term compared to potentially unlimited confinement in a mental institution. He may want to avoid the stigma of being adjudged criminally insane. Perhaps he may want to pressure the jury into acquittal by not providing a compromise verdict or wishes to use the lack of mental responsibility in seeking conviction on a lesser offense. Finally, the defendant may be reluctant to raise an insanity defense simply because he is opposed to psychiatric treatment.[40]

In an erratic series of cases from the District of Columbia,[41] courts were allowed sua sponte to impose the insanity plea over the defendant's objection. Several other jurisdictions have followed the D.C. rationale to resolve disagreements between counsel and client on whether or not to plead insanity.[42]

The test developed in *Frendak v. United States* (subsequently adopted in other jurisdictions) requires the trial court to determine whether the defendant's decision to forgo an insanity defense was intelligent and voluntary.[43] If the trial court is so satisfied, then neither the court nor counsel may intervene and impose the insanity plea over the defendant's objection. The required level of competency for raising the insanity plea may be different from the required level of competency for the accused to stand trial. The court must determine whether the defendant has "sufficient intelligence and judgment to waive the defense."[44]

Considering the two sources of authority that regulate the assertion of an insanity plea—the state ethics codes and the Sixth Amendment cases—counsel should be in a position to formulate an approach that respects the rights of the client while allowing counsel to comply with her ethical obligations. Because these two sources of authority have never been examined jointly in a bar opinion or judicial decision, counsel is often left to grapple with the dilemma with little to no guidance.

In Model Code jurisdictions, because of the lack of enforceable Disciplinary Rules on the subject, counsel need only refer to the Sixth Amendment cases to resolve any dilemmas. In Model Rule jurisdictions, however, counsel must decide whether Model Rule 1.14 authorizes counsel to override the client's decision to enter or forgo an insanity defense. Because the language of Model Rule 1.14 is permissive rather than mandatory, counsel would be wise to follow the dictates of the prevailing Sixth Amendment case law in her jurisdiction. Choosing to withdraw from the representation simply puts the next lawyer in the dilemma, and it will probably delay further the proceedings (meaning the client may be exposed to a longer period of pretrial incarceration). If counsel is convinced that the client's decision in a Model Rule jurisdiction will have catastrophic results, then counsel may opt to petition the court to appoint a guardian under Model Rule 1.14(b). Hopefully, counsel and the guardian will be able to make a rational and intelligent choice on whether or not to assert the insanity defense.

Conclusion

The courts have not concluded that a defendant's Sixth Amendment right to effective assistance of counsel either authorizes or compels counsel to raise an insanity plea over the client's objection. Neither the Model Code nor the Model Rules authorize counsel to plead insanity over the client's objection. Both the Model Code and the Model Rules vest the client with the decision-making authority of pleading insanity.

Notes

1. References to the "insanity defense" will include several tests currently employed: (1) the M'Naghten test—*See* M'Naghten's Case, 10 C. & Fin. 200, 8 Eng. Rep. 718 (1843) where the defendant is presumed to be sane unless he proves that he was suffering from a mental defect or disease that caused a

defect in his ability to reason and resulted in his not understanding the "nature and quality" of his act or not knowing that his act was wrong; (2) the Irresistible Impulse test where the defendant is considered insane if by reason of the duress of such mental disease he had lost the power to choose between right and wrong, and his free agency was destroyed at the time of the act in question; (3) the Durham test where the defendant must prove that his unlawful act was the product of mental disease or defect; and (4) the Model Penal Code—the American Law Institute test—where (a) a person is not responsible for criminal conduct if at the time of such conduct as a result of mental disease or defect he lacks substantial capacity either to appreciate the criminality of his conduct or to conform his conduct to the requirements of law; and (b) as used in this chapter, the terms "mental disease or defect" do not include an abnormality manifested only by repeated criminal or otherwise antisocial conduct. *See* Donald J. Tyrell, *Insanity: A Crazy Defense*, 35 MED. TRIAL TECH. Q. 48, 54–57 (1989).

2. Over one dozen jurisdictions continue to follow the ABA Model Code of Professional Responsibility (hereinafter Model Code), adopted in 1969 and amended through 1981, but no longer endorsed by the ABA. Many of these jurisdictions also incorporate provisions of the Model Rules in their ethics codes. *See, e.g.,* New York, North Carolina, Oregon, and Virginia.

3. As of September 1993, approximately thirty-eight states pattern their ethics codes after the ABA Model Rules of Professional Conduct (hereinafter Model Rules), which replaced the Model Code as the official policy of the ABA in August 1983. *See* ABA/BNA LAWYERS' MANUAL ON PROFESSIONAL CONDUCT, at 01:3, which provides a state-by-state list of jurisdictions that have revised their rules since 1983.

4. *See, e.g.,* California, which adopted the California Rules of Professional Conduct (1988, effective 1989), which embodies neither the Model Rules nor the Model Code. According to MONROE H. FREEDMAN, UNDERSTANDING LAWYERS' ETHICS (1990), several other states have rejected the Model Rules, including Massachusetts, New York, and the District of Columbia. *Id.* at 5, nn. 13–14. This chapter, however, will focus on those jurisdictions that follow the Model Rules or the Model Codes.

5. 466 U.S. 668 (1984). Under *Strickland's* two-prong test, the defendant must show that in light of all the circumstances the identified acts or omissions were outside the wide range of professionally competent assistance, and the defendant must show that there is a reasonable probability that, but for counsel's unprofessional errors, the result of the proceeding would have been different.

6. Counsel is usually not subject to disciplinary action in these Sixth Amendment cases. As the Supreme Court noted in *Nix v. Whiteside:* "[B]reach of an ethical standard does not necessarily make out a denial of the Sixth Amendment guarantee of assistance of counsel. When examining attorney conduct, a court must be careful not to narrow the wide range of conduct acceptable under the Sixth Amendment so restrictively as to constitutionalize particular standards of professional conduct and thereby intrude into the

State's proper authority to define and apply the standards of professional conduct applicable to those it admits to practice in its courts." 475 U.S. 157, 165 (1986).

7. Although "[a] few courts have occasionally given the Standards the kind of unquestioned acceptance usually reserved for statutes or other official enactments . . . the dominant judicial view is that they are neither controlling nor an exhaustive statement of the duties of defense counsel." CHARLES W. WOLFRAM, MODERN LEGAL ETHICS, 589 fn. 35 (1986).

8. The Supreme Court characterized the ABA Standards for Criminal Justice (2d ed. 1980) as mere "guides to determining what is reasonable, but they are only guides." Strickland v. Washington, 466 U.S. 668, 688 (1984).

9. Between 1979 and 1983, three states—Idaho, Montana, and Utah— passed legislation designed to abolish insanity as a separate affirmative defense. *See* IDAHO CODE §18-207 (1990); MONT. CODE ANN. §46-14-102 (1989); UTAH CODE ANN. §76-2-305 (1990). *See also Due Process—Insanity Defense—Idaho Supreme Court Upholds Abolition of Insanity Defense Against State and Federal Constitutional Challenges,* State v. Searcy, *118 Idaho 632, 798 P.2d 914 (1990),* 104 HARV. L. REV. 1132 (1991).

10. Twelve states have adopted as an alternative to the insanity defense, the verdict of guilty but mentally ill ("GBMI"). *See* ALASKA STAT. §§ 12.47.020(c), 12.47.030, 12.47.050 (1989); DEL. CODE ANN. tit. 11 §§ 401(b), 408, 409, 3905 (1987); GA. CODE ANN. § 17-7-131 (Michie Supp. 1989); ILL. ANN. STAT. Ch. 38, Para. 115-3 (Smith-Hurd 1990); IND. CODE ANN. §§ 35-36-1-1 to 35-36-2-5 (Burns 1985 & Supp.); KY. REV. STAT. ANN. §§ 504.120 to 504.130 (Michie/Bobbs-Merrill 1985); Pouncey v. State, 465 A.2d 475 (Md. 1983); MICH. COMP. LAWS ANN. § 768.36 (West 1982); N.M. STAT. ANN. §§ 31-9-3, 31-9-4 (Michie 1984); 18 PA. CONS. STAT. ANN. § 314 (1983); S.D. CODIFIED LAWS ANN. §§ 23A-7-2, 23A-7-16, 23A-26-14, 23A-27-38 (1988); UTAH CODE ANN. § 77-13-1 (1990).

11. ABA MODEL CODE OF PROFESSIONAL RESPONSIBILITY, Preliminary Statement.

12. *Id.*

13. E.C. 7-12.

14. MODEL RULE 1.2, Comment 2.

15. MODEL RULE 1.14(a).

16. ABA/BNA LAWYER'S MANUAL, 31: 603. This multi-volume looseleaf service includes a treatise-like "Manual"; an "Ethics Opinions" volume with state and local bar opinions; and the "Current Reports" volume reporting new developments biweekly.

17. *Id.*

18. MODEL RULE 1.14, Comment 5.

19. Under Addington v. Texas, 441 U.S. 418 (1978), where a state sought to commit an individual to a mental institution in a *civil* proceeding, the due process clause required proof by clear and convincing evidence that the person sought to be committed was mentally ill and that he required hospitalization for his own welfare and the protection of others. However, when an individual charged with a crime is found not guilty by reason of insanity, the state may

commit that person without satisfying the *Addington* requirements, Foucha v. Louisiana, __ U.S. __, 112 S. Ct. 1780, 1783 (1992), and "the acquittee may be held as long as he is both mentally ill and dangerous, but no longer." *Foucha* at 1784.

20. *See* ANTHONY G. AMSTERDAM, TRIAL MANUAL 5 FOR THE DEFENSE OF CRIMINAL CASES, vol. 1, sec. 180 (ALI-ABA 1988).

21. For a discussion of the lawyer's dilemma in representing clients who make self-destructive or antisocial decisions, *see* Jan Ellen Rein, *Clients With Destructive and Socially Harmful Choices—What's an Attorney to Do?: Within and Beyond the Competency Construct*, 62 FORDHAM L. REV. 1101 (1994). Although Rein focuses on representing elderly clients, the discussion of the lawyer's dilemmas under Model Rule 1.14 applies to counsel asserting an insanity defense as well.

22. E.C. 7-8.

23. MONROE H. FREEDMAN, UNDERSTANDING LAWYER'S ETHICS 59 (1990).

24. DR 2-110(A)(1) and (2). Arguably, under DR 2-110(B)(3), if the lawyer's "mental condition" renders it unreasonably difficult to carry out the representation effectively (i.e., the lawyer cannot accept the client's decision to raise or not to raise insanity), after obtaining permission from the tribunal, the lawyer *shall* withdraw. Additionally, EC 2-30 advises that "a lawyer should *decline employment* if the intensity of his personal feeling, as distinguished from a community attitude, may impair his effective representation of a prospective client." [Emphasis supplied]. Nevertheless, EC 2-32 cautions that "[a] decision by a lawyer *to withdraw* should be made only on the basis of compelling circumstances. . . ." A similar argument could be made for mandatory withdrawal under Model Rule 1.16(a)(2), i.e., that the lawyer's "mental condition" materially impairs the lawyer's ability to represent the client.

25. DR 2-110(c)(6).

26. *See* MODEL RULE 1.16(c).

27. *See, e.g.,* People v. Frierson, 39 Cal. 3d 803, 705 P.2d 396 (Cal. 1985), where court-appointed defense counsel was not permitted to withdraw even when the client requested new counsel.

28. *See, e.g.,* Maine Ethics Opinion 84 (1988), where withdrawal was *not* a satisfactory resolution of the dilemma of a lawyer representing a mentally impaired client. Withdrawal would leave the client without much needed advice at a crucial time in the proceeding.

29. CHARLES W. WOLFRAM, MODERN LEGAL ETHICS, 162 (1986).

30. JOHN M. BURKOFF & HOPE L. HUDSON, INEFFECTIVE ASSISTANCE OF COUNSEL, 1–3 (1993).

31. Enriquez v. Procunier, 752 F.2d, at 114.

32. Alvord v. Wainwright, 469 U.S. 956, 961 (1984).

33. *See* Kennedy v. Shillinger, 759 F. Supp. 1554 (D. Wyo. 1991), where the court found ineffective assistance of counsel when the defense lawyer raised an insanity defense, but failed to fully inform the client of the alternatives of defending the case on the merits.

34. MODEL RULE 1.14(b).

35. *See, e.g.*, Treece v. State, 547 A.2d 1054 (Md. 1988); Jacobs v. Commonwealth, 870 S.W.2d 412 (Ky. 1994); United States v. Moody, 763 F. Supp. 589 (M.D. Ga. 1991); Foster v. Marshall, 687 F. Supp. 1174 (S.D. Ohio 1987); People v. Frierson, 705 P.2d 396 (Cal. 1985); People v. Gauze, 542 P.2d 1365 (Cal. 1975); State v. Jones, 664 P.2d 1216 (Wash. 1983); People v. MacDowell, 508 N.Y.S.2d 870 (N.Y. 1986); United States v. Marble, 940 F.2d 1543 (D.C. Cir. 1991).

36. For an explanation of how the notion of counsel's complete control developed, *see Treece*, 547 A.2d, at 1056–58.

37. *See Frierson, supra* note 27, at 402.

38. *Jacobs*, 870 S.W.2d, at 417.

39. *See Treece*, 547 A.2d, at 1057 (client's defense on merits was "hopelessly prejudiced" by counsel's insistence on presenting evidence of insanity).

40. *See The Right and Responsibility of a Court to Impose the Insanity Defense over the Defendant's Objections*, 65 MINN. L. REV. 927, 945 (1981).

41. For a good review of the controversy within the D.C. courts, *see* State v. Jones, 664 P.2d 1216 (Wash. 1983), and Anne C. Singer, *The Imposition of the Insanity Defense on an Unwilling Defendant*, 41 OHIO ST. L.J. 637 (1980).

42. These cases include Whalem v. United States, 346 A.2d 364 (1965), and United States v. Wright, 627 F.2d 1300 (1980). The reasoning behind this line of cases is that a court should not allow conviction of a person who is legally insane, even if he refuses to enter a plea of insanity, because he is morally blameless and, therefore, not criminally responsible. In 1991, United States v. Marble overruled this line of decisions and held that a court must "honor the choice of a competent defendant not to raise the insanity defense." 940 F.2d at 1548 (1991).

43. 408 A.2d 364 (1979).

44. People v. MacDowell, 508 N.Y.S.2d 870 (N.Y. 1986).

Bibliography

Articles, Reports, and Standards

ABA/BNA LAWYERS MANUAL ON PROFESSIONAL CONDUCT, 01:3, 31:603.

ABA MODEL CODE OF PROFESSIONAL RESPONSIBILITY, EC 2-30, 2-32, 7-7, 7-8, 7-12, DR 2-110(A)(1), 2-110(A)(2), 2-110(B)(3), 2-110(C)(l)(d), 2-110(C)(6) (1981).

ABA MODEL RULES OF PROFESSIONAL CONDUCT, 1.2(a) & cmt., 1.14, 1.14(b) & cmt., 1.16(a)(2), 1.16(b)(3), 1.16(b)(5), 1.16(b)(6), 1.16(c) (1983).

ABA STANDARDS FOR CRIMINAL JUSTICE (2d ed. 1980).

ABA STANDARDS FOR CRIMINAL JUSTICE, Standard 4-1.1–4-8.6 (3d ed. 1993).

Anthony G. Amsterdam, *Trial Manual 5 for the Defense of Criminal Cases*, (5th ed. 1988–1989).

Andrew Blum, *Debunking Myths of the Insanity Plea*, Nat'l L. J., April 20, 1992.

John M. Burkoff & Hope L. Hudson, *Ineffective Assistance of Counsel*, (1993).

CALIFORNIA RULES OF PROFESSIONAL CONDUCT (1989).

Due Process—Insanity Defense—Idaho Supreme Court Upholds Abolition of Insanity Defense Against State and Federal Constitutional Challenges, State v. Searcy, 118 Idaho 632, 798 P.2d 914 (1990), 104 Harv. L. Rev. 1132 (1991).

Monroe H. Freedman, *Understanding Lawyers' Ethics*, (1990).

MAINE PROFESSIONAL ETHICS COMMITTEE OF THE STATE'S BOARD OF OVERSEERS OF THE BAR, Op. 84 (1988).

Jan Ellen Rein, *Clients With Destructive and Socially Harmful Choices—What's an Attorney to Do?: Within and Beyond the Competency Construct*, 62 Fordham L. Rev. 1101 (1994).

The Right and Responsibility of a Court to Impose the Insanity Defense Over the Defendant's Objections, 65 Minn. L. Rev. 927 (1981).

Anne C. Singer, *The Imposition of the Insanity Defense on a Unwilling Defendant*, 41 Ohio St. L. J. 637 (1980).

Donald J. Tyrell, *Insanity: A Crazy Defense*, 35 Med. Trial Tech. Q. 48 (1989).

Charles W. Wolfram, *Modern Legal Ethics*, (1986).

Statutes

ALASKA STAT. §§ 12.47.020(C), 12.47.030, 12.47.050 (1989).

DEL. CODE ANN. tit. 11 §§ 401(b), 408, 409, 3905 (1987).

GA. CODE ANN. § 17-7-131 (Michie Supp. 1989).

IDAHO CODE § 18-207 (1990).

ILL. ANN. STAT. Ch. 38, Para. 115-3 (Smith-Hurd 1990).

IND. CODE ANN. §§ 35-36-1-1 to 35-36-2-5 (Burns 1985 & Supp.).

KY. REV. STAT. ANN. §§ 504.120 to 504.130 (Michie/Bobbs-Merrill 1985).

MICH. COMP. LAWS ANN. § 768.36 (West 1982).

MONT. CODE. ANN. § 46-14-102 (1989).

N.M. STAT. ANN. §§ 31-9-3, 31-9-4 (Michie 1984).

18 PA. CONS. STAT. ANN. § 314 (1983).

S.D. CODIFIED LAWS ANN. §§ 23A-7-2, 23A-7-16, 23A-26-14, 23A-27-38 (1988).

UTAH CODE ANN. §§ 76-2-305, 77-13-1 (1990).

Cases

Addington v. Texas, 441 U.S. 418 (1978).

Alvord v. Wainwright, 469 U.S. 956 (1984).

Enriquez v. Procunier, 752 F.2d 111 (5th Cir. 1984), *cert. denied*, 471 U.S. 1126 (1985).

Foster v. Marshall, 687 F. Supp. 1174 (S.D. Ohio 1987).

Foucha v. Louisiana, 112 S. Ct. 1780 (1992).

Frendak v. United States, 408 A.2d 364 (D.C. 1979).

Jacobs v. Commonwealth, 870 S.W.2d 412 (Ky. 1994).

Kennedy v. Shillinger, 759 F. Supp. 1554 (D. Wyo. 1991).

M'Naghten's Case, 10 C. & Fin. 200, 8 Eng. Rep. 718 (1843).

Nix v. Whiteside, 475 U.S. 157 (1986).

People v. Frierson, 705 P.2d 396 (Cal. 1985).

People v. Gauze, 542 P.2d 1365 (Cal. 1975).

People v. MacDowell, 508 N.Y.S.2d 870 (N.Y. 1986).

Pouncey v. State, 465 A.2d 475 (Md. 1983).

State v. Jones, 664 P.2d 1216 (Wash. 1983).

Strickland v. Washington, 466 U.S. 688 (1984).

Treece v. State, 547 A.2d 1054 (Md. 1988).

United States v. Marble, 940 F.2d 1543 (D.C. Cir. 1991).

United States v. Moody, 763 F. Supp. 589 (M.D. Ga. 1991).

United States v. Wright, 627 F.2d 1300 (D.C. 1980).

Vitek v. Jones, 445 U.S. 480 (1980).

Whalem v. United States, 346 F.2d 812 (D.C. 1965).

CHAPTER 📖 5

Pursuing a Questionable Suppression Motion

George E. Bisharat

Is defense counsel obligated to pursue a suppression motion requested by her client if she feels that the motion is strategically damaging to the defendant's case? If counsel wants to pursue a legal issue in a pretrial motion, but defendant does not, may counsel still go forward?

One's approach to questions about the allocation of decision-making responsibility between lawyer and client, such as the questions posed above, is very likely to be influenced, if not determined, by one's ideal model of lawyering. My own model might be considered a variant of what some have called "client-centered" lawyering, based on the fundamental premise that clients are competent, and indeed should be legally entitled, to exercise authority and responsibility over matters affecting their own lives. The lawyer's primary role in this model is to empower clients to choose for themselves the course of their own litigation.[1]

One of the practical advantages of this model (and I will try to point out others below) is that, properly applied, it should greatly aid the lawyer in *avoiding altogether* tactical and strategic disagreements with her client. In my experience, these disagreements most frequently stem not from the client's dissatisfaction with the substance of his lawyer's advice but from the suspicion that this advice is tainted by the lawyer's self-interest—in broad terms, in "not rocking the boat" (the judicial system) in which the lawyer is a regular passenger. Placing ultimate decision-making responsibility in the hands of the client is a very effective method for disarming him, and, paradoxically, for

greatly increasing the probability that the lawyer's advice is actually
followed.

The general principle that the client should be entitled to exercise
authority over the conduct of his case is not without limitations.
Among other things, the lawyer should not promote or participate in
illegal conduct, not only because of the possibilities of criminal liability
and disciplinary action by the bar, but because to do so is morally
wrong. It also seems to me fully legitimate for the lawyer to protect her
independent interests, such as remaining in practice and maintaining
an untarnished professional reputation. Thus, a lawyer properly may
refuse to engage in noncriminal conduct sought by her client that may
yet result in bar discipline or have other, informal repercussions (such
as the loss of professional respect and trust that attends repeated fil-
ings of frivolous motions).[2] Finally, the general assumption of client
competency—and by "competency," I have in mind a nontechnical
definition entailing simply the capacity to rationally understand a
range of legal options and to comprehend their probable consequences—*can be* refuted in specific circumstances.

The thrust of my discussion is that while both constitutional rules
and ethical principles, viewed in the abstract, appear to grant significant authority over pretrial decisions to the lawyer, when viewed in the
context of the actual circumstances where disputes over case direction
tend to arise, it is, in fact, the client to whom deference is largely owed.
Thus, the client-centered model dovetails comfortably with prevailing
law and ethical principles in most cases. This is especially true of the
principles embodied in the 1969 ABA Model Code of Professional Responsibility (Model Code).

In some situations, however, the 1983 ABA Model Rules of Professional Conduct (Model Rules) and the nonbinding though influential third edition of the ABA Standards for Criminal Justice Defense
Functions (ABA Standards) unjustifiably privilege the lawyer at the expense of the client. There are a number of reasons why an lawyer may
decline to exercise this privilege without significant fear of being found
ineffective. To be clear, however, the stance I advocate derives from my
outlook on lawyering, rather than the Model Rules or ABA Standards
themselves. Obviously, one adhering to a different model of lawyering
might advocate a position somewhat different than mine. No matter
how one resolves a dispute with one's client over case direction, it is
imperative that one keep a detailed, confidential record of the dispute,
usually in one's case file.[3]

With these caveats, let me present a brief overview of the framework of constitutional rules and ethical principles in the Model Code,

the Model Rules, and the ABA Standards that bear on the allocation of decision making between lawyer and client. Following that, I will explain how these rules and principles seem likely to play out in the kinds of actual circumstances in which the questions presented might arise, with respect first to the client's request for a motion to suppress opposed by his lawyer, and second, to the lawyer's desire to proceed with motions opposed by her client.

Constitutional rules are a good starting point, of course, as they provide an underpinning common to all jurisdictions. A series of decisions of the U.S. Supreme Court has assigned the right of decision making to the client in specific areas. These include the decisions in *Faretta v. California*, 422 U.S. 806 (1975) (whether to waive counsel); *Boykin v. Alabama*, 395 U.S. 238 (1969) (what plea to enter); *Adams v. United States ex rel. McCain*, 317 U.S. 269 (1942) (whether to waive a jury trial); *Rock v. Arkansas*, 483 U.S. 44 (1987) (whether to testify); and *Fay v. Noia*, 372 U.S. 391 (1963) (whether to pursue an appeal of right). Actions of counsel that impinge on the client's control over these decisions are not only unethical but constitute violations of the client's constitutional rights.

Beyond these fundamental rights vested in the client, the Supreme Court has entrusted the "day-to-day conduct of the defense," including whether and when to object to the admission of evidence, to the lawyer. *Wainwright v. Sykes*, 433 U.S. 72 (1977). Further, the Court has held that defense counsel is under no obligation to raise every non-frivolous issue desired by a petitioner appealing against a criminal conviction. *Jones v. Barnes*, 463 U.S. 745 (1983).

Ethical principles relevant to the allocation of authority between lawyer and client are found in Ethical Considerations (EC) 7-7 and 7-8, and Disciplinary Rule (DR) 7-101 of the Model Code. EC 7-7 declares that: "[I]n certain areas of legal representation not affecting the merits of the cause or substantially prejudicing the rights of the client, a lawyer is entitled to make decisions on his own. But otherwise the authority to make decisions is exclusively that of the client. . . ." EC 7-8 proclaims that ". . . the decision whether to forego legally available objectives or methods because of non-legal factors is ultimately for the client. . . ." DR 7-101, which deals generally with zealous representation of a client, provides in subsection (A)(1) that a lawyer may not intentionally "[F]ail to seek the lawful objectives of his client through reasonably available means. . . ." within the bounds of the law and other disciplinary rules. Subsection (B)(1) of DR 7-101 authorizes a lawyer to "Where permissible, exercise his professional judgment to waive or fail to assert a right or position of his client." DR 7-102, in several subsections, bars a lawyer from assisting or counseling her client in illegal or fraudulent conduct. Generally, it seems to me that the Model Code strikes a balance of authority substantially favoring the client.[4]

The Model Rules address more directly the question of the distribution of authority between lawyer and client, and in so doing strike a somewhat different balance than does the Model Code. Generally speaking, the Model Rules contemplate a "means-ends" division of authority between defense counsel and client: the lawyer holds exclusive authority to determine trial strategy and tactics—the "means"—whereas the client enjoys exclusive authority to define the purposes or objectives—the "ends"—of representation, within the bounds of the law. Hence, Rule 1.2(a) states that "[A] lawyer shall abide by a client's decisions concerning the objectives of representation . . . and shall consult with the client as to the means by which they are to be pursued." As under the Model Code, a lawyer cannot simply follow a client's dictates without limitation. Indeed, Rule 1.2(d) bars a lawyer from counseling or assisting the client in criminal or fraudulent conduct.

The means-ends division is qualified in several ways: (1) the lawyer "should assume responsibility for technical and legal tactical issues, but should defer to the client regarding such questions as the expense to be incurred and concern for third persons who might be adversely affected," as the Comment to Rule 1.2 states; (2) the lawyer has a duty to consult with her client; (3) constitutional rules vest some decisions over means in the client (e.g., the right to demand or waive a jury); and (4) the acknowledgment in the Comment to Rule 1.2 that "[A] clear distinction between objectives and means sometimes cannot be drawn. . . ." The Comment to Rule 1.2 goes on to clarify that in instances where a clear distinction cannot be drawn, the relationship "partakes of a joint undertaking" (a singularly unenlightening observation, one might add). Despite these qualifications, the Model Rules would appear to entrust the lawyer with considerably greater responsibility for decision making than the Model Code.

The Defense Function Standards (a third edition of which was approved by the ABA House of Delegates in 1991) deal with questions of decision-making authority in Standard 4-5.2 "Control and direction of the case." Subsection (a) of that standard states that "[C]ertain decisions relating to the conduct of the case are ultimately for the accused and others are ultimately for defense counsel" and thereafter enumerates the decisions for the client as what plea to enter, whether to accept a plea agreement, whether to waive a jury trial, whether to testify, and whether to appeal. Subsection (b) proclaims that such decisions as what witnesses to call, whether and how to conduct cross-examination, what jurors to accept or strike, what trial motions should be made, and what evidence to introduce should be made by counsel after consultation with the client, "where feasible and appropriate." Standard 4-5.2, therefore, empowers the lawyer in a more detailed fashion than the Model Rules, and in the view of some commentators, establishes a *duty* to control the case.[5]

Under what circumstances might a client request a motion to suppress that his lawyer believes is strategically damaging to his case? The client who demands the filing, not just of a motion to suppress, but of every other motion he has heard of in hours of idle time in the cell block, is probably distressingly familiar. At the extreme, that is, where the client is demanding a groundless motion, the issue, it seems to me, is easily resolved: defense counsel is under no obligation to file frivolous motions. I have hinted at one reason for this—loss of professional credibility. Moreover, counsel is obligated under either Model Code DR 7-102(A)(1,2) or Model Rule 3.1 to avoid asserting a frivolous claim or defense, except that she may put the prosecution to its proof and require it to prove each and every element of the charged offense. Needless to say, at the other extreme, failure to assert a meritorious motion to suppress due to neglect, ignorance, or erroneous judgment constitutes ineffective assistance of counsel. *Kimmelman v. Morrison*, 477 U.S. 365 (1986).

The problem becomes challenging when the motion demanded by the client is *nonfrivolous* and yet, in the estimation of counsel, still strategically damaging. One example might be a colorable motion that is, nonetheless, unlikely to prevail, and the making of which requires testimony that is otherwise harmful to the defense. Another example might be a motion that is a probable winner, but that would suppress evidence that is supportive of a defense at trial. In practice, however, it should be rare that defense counsel, with her professional training and experience, is unable to convince her client of the wisdom of her strategic and tactical recommendations. So we are left with the relatively infrequent situation where lawyer and client are at an impasse over the decision whether or not to file the motion to suppress.

Given my client-centered approach, I am strongly in favor of proceeding with a nonfrivolous motion to suppress if the client insists on it. To repeat: this assumes that counsel has thoroughly discussed with her client the costs and benefits of the motion, as she perceives them, and has tried—with tact, respect, and honesty—to convince her client of the validity of her recommendation, but has failed. Does this resolution comport with the framework of constitutional rules and ethical principles outlined above? For reasons I will explain, in many kinds of circumstances, proceeding with the client's desired motion to suppress may be the *only* permissible route for defense counsel.

Deference to the client is mandated in all jurisdictions in any case in which the failure to proceed with the desired motion would impinge upon the client's *fundamental rights*. Assume a case in which, to effectively litigate the motion to suppress, defense counsel must expose a defense witness unknown to the prosecution (and who the defense would otherwise be under no obligation to reveal in advance of trial), thereby subjecting the witness to investigation and far more effective prosecution impeachment at trial. Of course, foregoing a nonfrivolous motion to suppress is justifiable only if a benefit is realized by the defendant at some later stage of the case. It is conceivable that the strategic damage to the case *might* be the compromising of another, more promising motion, or the weakening of the defendant's position in plea bargaining. However, if the damage to be avoided would only occur at trial—as in the above example—and the defendant could only realize the benefit of avoiding that damage by *going* to trial, then his lawyer, in declining to present the motion to suppress, has gone a long way toward *forcing* her client to plead not guilty and to proceed to trial. This is a completely impermissible infringement of the client's fundamental right to decide how to plea to the charges enshrined in *Boykin v. Alabama*.[6] In practice, it would seem probable that in many circumstances the choice to forego a motion to suppress would be tantamount to a decision to go to trial.

Although the right to decide how to plea is the most likely decision to be infringed by the lawyer's refusal to litigate a motion to suppress, one can surely imagine others. For example, the client's fundamental right to testify, first explicitly recognized by the U.S. Supreme Court only in the 1987 case *Rock v. Arkansas*,[7] might be infringed by the lawyer's refusal to proceed with a motion to suppress that relied on the client's own testimony. This is not certain, as the contours of the right to testify remain to be defined. While the relevant cases all involve the right to testify *at trial*, their language and rationale seem equally applicable to a pretrial context.[8]

Although my claim is that the lawyer is *constitutionally* barred from making this decision, it is worth noting that even the "pro-lawyer" ABA Standard 4-5.2, in the Commentary, recognizes that some seemingly "tactical" decisions (such as deciding to seek a jury instruction on a lesser included offense) directly implicate the fundamental rights of the client, and thus, must be made by the defendant.

A second circumstance compelling compliance with the client's demand for a motion to suppress—although by ethical principles, rather than constitutional rule—is where the motion *in itself* will vindicate some lawful objective of the client. Model Code DR 7-101(A)(1), as we have seen, states that a lawyer may not intentionally "[F]ail to seek the lawful objectives of his client through reasonably available means . . ." and Model Rule 1.2(a) provides that "[A] lawyer shall abide by a client's decisions concerning the objectives of representation. . . ."

Compliance with these ethical directives requires careful and explicit probing of the client's purposes or objectives in a case. In criminal practice it is all too easy to assume that these purposes or objectives will be limited to avoiding conviction or minimizing punishment. Indeed, these may well be the exclusive concerns of the vast majority of defendants. However, more frequently than one might expect, the client may have additional goals—such as vindication of his personal dignity or integrity; protection of his privacy; shielding of others from legal liability or harassment; advancement of a political viewpoint; a speedy, even if otherwise less favorable resolution of the case; or simply "having his day in court"—which the client may seek to optimize even at considerable risk of conviction and/or more severe punishment. The fact that these latter goals are less commonly paramount, and frequently are either unarticulated or even actively concealed from counsel, imposes on counsel an even greater need to be attentive to their existence and to their importance in comparison with other, more obvious or articulated objectives of her client.

The kinds of cases where a motion to suppress might represent or vindicate a client's lawful objective are as diverse as the multitude of interests at stake in criminal cases. One possible scenario: the client is adamant about taking a case to trial (thus eliminating the fundamental-right problem posed above). Although sharing his lawyer's assessment of the risk of strategic damage in a motion to suppress, the client is convinced that he was arrested and searched solely because of his race, and insists the motion be made out of a belief that the police should be held accountable for their misconduct and out of a desire that his account of the arrest be publicly heard. Here, the client has staked out a lawful objective, which might be described as vindication of his personal dignity and right to be free of racial discrimination, that his lawyer is bound to pursue by all legally available means.[9]

The only other alternative—only clearly available under Model Rule 1.16(b)(3)—is for the lawyer to withdraw, if doing so causes no material adverse effect for the client, or if the client is pursuing an objective that is repugnant or imprudent. The closest the Model Code comes to authorizing withdrawal in such circumstances is in DR 2 110(C)(l)(d), which permits withdrawal where the client ". . . renders it unreasonably difficult for the lawyer to carry out his employment effectively." ER 7-8 allows withdrawal when the client insists on a course of conduct that is contrary to the judgment and advice of the lawyer, but it is limited to nonadjudicatory matters and is, therefore, not applicable here.

A third category of cases where a dispute might arise over the advisability of a motion to suppress are those cases where the client, though not seeking to maximize some objective other than avoiding conviction or minimizing punishment, nonetheless disagrees with his lawyer's assessment of the risk in a motion, or is willing to assume that risk, for whatever reason—perhaps simply because he is more of a gambler than his counsel. The Model Code, it seems to me, affirms the primacy of the client's preference in this situation as well. According to EC 7-7, authority over decisions going to the merit of the case or which substantially prejudice the rights of the client ". . . is exclusively that of the client . . . [and that] such decisions are binding on his lawyer." In addition, DR 7 101(A)(l) directs the lawyer to seek the lawful objectives of her client through reasonably available means.

In contrast, the Model Rules, with less stringent restrictions on lawyer authority, would seem to leave the decision in this kind of case to the lawyer. Moreover, there would seem to be no constitutional bar to the lawyer's exercise of discretion in this type of situation (although it may be argued that neither *Wainwright* nor *Jones*, cited above, specifically *endorse* such an exercise of discretion either). As suggested above, some may read in ABA Standard 4 5.2 a *duty* that counsel control direction of the case.[10] Furthermore, there is precedent in some jurisdictions that counsel may be considered ineffective for deferring to a client's wishes.[11]

Given my conception of lawyering, however, there can be no justification for a lawyer substituting her assessment of risk, or willingness to assume risk, for that of a competent, well-informed client. To do so would be unacceptably paternalistic, particularly because it is the client who will always bear the main consequences of the course of action eventually taken. In my view, therefore, the lawyer must file the nonfrivolous motion to suppress requested by her competent client who has been fully apprised of likely strategic damages.

Candidly, my resolution of the problem might involve some risk of an ineffectiveness finding, at least in a Model Rules-influenced jurisdiction. For a variety of reasons, I believe this risk would be minimal. One practical advantage of a "client-centered" model of lawyering is that, as a general rule, people are more likely to accept with grace the consequences of their own decisions than they are decisions imposed upon them by others. This by no means guarantees that lawyers adhering to the model will never be the focus of ineffectiveness claims. Rather, it simply means that they are less likely to be targeted for such claims than lawyers who have overridden their client's expressed desires; clients who, despite their lawyers' best judgment, will not always escape conviction. Another advantage, if the limitations I have discussed are carefully observed—a competent client, well-informed of the likely consequences of the motion to suppress—is that persistent disagreements with the lawyer would tend to reflect that there is some, perhaps even considerable, tactical or strategic merit in the client's preferred action. Given that great deference to informed tactical judgments has been urged by the U.S. Supreme Court in *Strickland v. Washington*, 466 U.S. 668 (1986), a reviewing court would likely have to base a finding of ineffectiveness not on the merits of the tactical choice but on the identity of the decision-maker client rather than the lawyer. Here it pays to recall the U.S. Supreme Court's warning in *Faretta v. California*, 422 U.S. 806 (1975), that a client cannot represent himself and thereafter complain that the quality of his defense amounted to a denial of effective assistance of counsel. I do not think it likely that many courts would view the competent client's informed choice of tactics while represented by counsel in a significantly different light.

Many of the above considerations apply equally in those cases where the lawyer wishes to pursue a pretrial motion opposed by the client. So, for example, the lawyer is unjustified in pursuing a motion against her client's wishes if to do so would significantly trammel her client's decision to go to trial—as she would in the example mentioned above by proceeding with a motion to suppress, revealing the hidden defense witness, and strengthening the prosecution's case at trial.

If disagreements concerning motions to suppress should be rare, they should be even more so where the lawyer is actively *pursuing* motions—complaints about actions *not* taken are far more common than complaints about energetic advocacy. Opposition to well-substantiated and clearly explained prospective motions, where it does occur, should signal counsel to the possibility that the client is harboring lawful objectives that the client senses may not be approved, understood, or respected by counsel, or are too private to be shared with her. As we have seen, if pursuit of the motion would frustrate a lawful objective of the client, defense counsel would be bound by her client's preference. Where counsel can establish that the disagreement merely involves differing assessments of risk or willingness to assume that risk, she is faced with the same situation as above: the Model Rules seem to authorize her to proceed in accord with her best professional judgment. I would advocate, for reasons already adduced, deference to the client.

However, there are additional concerns flowing from the fact that going forward with a motion may involve costs that simply refraining from making a motion does not. For example, while it is hard to imagine any danger of an unconsented disclosure of confidential information in *not* pursuing a motion, it is much easier to imagine this danger where the defendant has the affirmative obligation to present evidence, as he would in many pretrial motions. Client confidences are, of course, protected both under the Model Code (DR 4-101) and the Model Rules (Rule 1.6(a)), and proceeding with a motion that results in unconsented disclosure of confidences is clearly improper. Likewise, although there is some uncertainty concerning the extent of the right to testify, as we have seen above, there is much less uncertainty concerning the right *not* to testify. It is unthinkable that any lawyer could *force* her client to testify against his will in the service of a motion he opposed.

The Model Code and Model Rules both seem to recognize the additional costs involved in action rather than inaction, providing more explicitly for client primacy where action is contemplated. Model Code EC 7-8, for example, states that ". . . the decision whether to forego legally available objectives or methods because of non-legal factors is ultimately for the client . . ." and not for the lawyer. Recall, as well, the qualification noted in the Comment to Model Rule 1.2 that even regarding technical and legal issues, the lawyer "should defer to the client regarding *such questions as* the expense to be incurred and concern for third persons who might be adversely affected. . . ."(emphasis added). As the language I have emphasized suggests, this is not an exhaustive list of "questions" to be decided by the client. The Model Code and Model Rules provisions may in fact be redundant; arguably, the "nonlegal factors" or the "questions" falling within client prerogative are already placed there by the respective Model Code and Model Rules provisions concerning lawful objectives (avoiding expense, for example, though effectively not a concern in appointed cases, can easily be viewed as a lawful objective). These provisions do underscore, I think, the potential additional dangers of proceeding, rather than not proceeding, with pretrial motions in the absence of client approval.

No doubt the reader will have detected several exceptions I have inserted into my client-centered model that might well eviscerate it of meaning. The first relates to the lawyer's powers of persuasion, and the second to the determination of the client's "competency." Of course, the very legitimacy of the legal profession is founded on its supposed monopoly of a specialized knowledge. To the "natural" advantage over the layperson that membership in the profession bestows on the lawyer, may be added advantages of higher social class standing, greater familiarity with the culture of dominant social groups, private knowledge of and personal relations with critical members of the legal system, and a variety of other traits that invest the lawyer's "advice" with the attributes of a functional command.[12] This power of persuasion can easily be abused. I regret that I cannot recommend a fail-safe check against such abuse. The only check I can offer is self-administered, and consists of the lawyer's continual and frank self-interrogation about motives in supplying her client with advice and her identification and nullification of those motives that elevate her interests at the expense of her client's.

The determination of a client's "competency," especially in the broad way I have defined it ("the capacity to rationally understand a range of legal options and to comprehend their probable consequences"), is at least problematic. Even assuming the most honorable of intentions on the part of the lawyer (who else is to make the determination?), recognizing when a person "rationally understands a range of legal options" can itself be a major challenge.[13] Anyone who has explained such a range of legal options to a non-English-speaking client, even with the aid of a highly competent interpreter, only to be met with a combination of superficially appropriate responses and blank look of incomprehension, knows exactly what I mean. What factors should one look to when trying to gauge a client's "competence"? Age? Level of education? Cultural background? Experience with the legal system? Psychiatric history? Certainly at least these factors, if not more. My palliative is the recommendation that the lawyer begin with the assumption of client competence, and of the rationality of his expressed desires, and refuse to surrender this assumption in the absence of unequivocal evidence to the contrary.[14] Only by doing so will the lawyer be fulfilling her ethical responsibility and constitutional obligation to provide assistance, not supremacy, of counsel.

Conclusion

Defense counsel *must* defer to her client's tactical and strategic preferences regarding nonfrivolous pretrial motions whenever they implicate either the client's fundamental rights or the lawful objectives of representation, as these objectives are defined by the client. In all other circumstances, defense counsel *should* follow the directives regarding nonfrivolous pretrial motions of a competent, well-informed client. Under most circumstances, therefore, defense counsel is obligated to pursue a suppression motion requested by her client, notwithstanding potential strategic damage to the case, and may not pursue a legal issue in a pretrial motion absent her client's authorization.

Notes

1. Readers interested in "client-centered lawyering" may wish to examine Stephen Ellmann, *Lawyers and Clients*, 34 UCLA LAW REVIEW 717 (1987), or the group of articles published as part of the symposium *Theoretics of Practice*, 43 HASTINGS L.J. (1992).

2. This position is supported by the Commentary to ABA 4-1.2 (3d ed.).

3. This is mandated by ABA Standard 4-5.2(c) (3d ed. 1993).

4. I share this judgment with Monroe H. Freedman; *see* UNDERSTANDING LAWYERS' ETHICS.

5. *See, e.g.,* JOHN WESLEY HALL, JR., PROFESSIONAL RESPONSIBILITY OF THE CRIMINAL LAWYER.

6. 395 U.S. 238 (1969).

7. 483 U.S. 44 (1987).

8. Timothy O'Neill, *Vindicating the Defendant's Constitutional Right to Testify at a Criminal Trial: The Need for an On-the-Record Waiver*, 4 CRIM. PRACT. L. REV. 133 (1991).

9. For a fascinating description of a case involving just these interests, *see* Clark Cunningham, *Lawyer as Translator, Representation as Text: Toward an Ethnography of Legal Discourse*, 77 CORNELL L. REV. 1298 (1992).

10. *See* HALL, *supra* note 5.

11. These cases have dealt with the failure, at the defendant's bidding, to present mitigating evidence in the penalty phase of capital litigation; *see, e.g.,* People v. Deere, 41 Cal. 3d 353 (1985).

12. *See* Ellmann, *supra* note 1.

13. Readers may find useful Deana Dorman Logan, *Learning to Observe Signs of Mental Impairment*, CALIFORNIA LAWYERS FOR CRIMINAL JUSTICE FORUM, Vol. 19, No. 5-6 (1992), and Rodney J. Uphoff, *The Role of the Criminal Defense Lawyer in Representing the Mentally Impaired Defendant*, 1988 WIS. L. REV. 65.

14. Certainly this seems consistent with Model Rule 1.14's command to maintain normal lawyer-client relationship as far as is reasonably possible.

Bibliography

Books and Articles

Bette Kester Conrad, *Client Control and Rule 1.2: Who Pulls Whose Strings, When, and Why Does it Matter?* 29 Law Office Economics and Management 227 (1988).

Clark Cunningham, *Lawyer as Translator, Representation as Text: Toward an Ethnography of Legal Discourse*, 77 Cornell L. Rev. 1298 (1992).

Stephen Ellmann, *Lawyers and Clients*, 34 UCLA L. Rev. 717 (1987).

John Wesley Hall, Jr., *Professional Responsibility of the Criminal Lawyer*, (1987).

Timothy O'Neill, *Vindicating the Defendant's Constitutional Right to Testify at a Criminal Trial: The Need for an On-the-Record Waiver*, 4 Crim. Pract. L. Rev. 133 (1991).

Marcy Strauss, *Toward a Revised Model of Lawyer-Client Relationship: The Argument for Autonomy*, 65 N.C. L. Rev. 315 (1987).

Cases

Adams v. United States ex rel. McCain, 317 U.S. 269 (1942).

Boykin v. Alabama, 395 U.S. 238 (1969).

Faretta v. California, 422 U.S. 806 (1975).

Fay v. Noia, 372 U.S. 391 (1963).

Jones v. Barnes, 463 U.S. 745 (1983).

People v. Deere, 41 Cal. 3d 353 (1985).

Rimmelman v. Morrison, 477 U.S. 365 (1986).

Rock v. Arkansas, 483 U.S. 44 (1987).

Strickland v. Washington, 466 U.S. 668 (1986).

Wainwright v. Sykes, 433 U.S. 72 (1977).

CHAPTER ⬚ 6

Calling Defense Witnesses: Whose Case Is This Anyway?

Rita A. Fry

Is it ethically proper for defense counsel to call a defense witness to testify, when the defendant insists, if counsel knows the witness will testify falsely?

The Sixth Amendment guarantees each defendant the right to testify in their own behalf, and only the defendant can waive that right. *Wainwright v. Sykes*, 433 U.S. 72 (1977); ABA MODEL RULE 1.2(a) (1992); ABA STANDARDS FOR CRIMINAL JUSTICE 4-5,2(a) (3d ed. 1993). However, a defendant's right to testify does not include the right to commit perjury,[1] and under both the ABA Model Code and the ABA Model Rules, lawyers are prohibited from engaging in or assisting the presentation of perjured testimony. DR 7-102(A)(4), (7) (1983); MODEL RULE 3.3(a)(4), 1.2(d); ABA STANDARDS FOR CRIMINAL JUSTICE, 4-3.7(b), 4-7.5(a).

If a defendant/client refuses to waive the right to testify, and the defense lawyer knows or has made a good faith determination that the client is going to testify falsely, a lawyer is ethically bound to refuse to present perjured testimony and must advise the client that she will not assist in presenting such testimony to the court. MODEL RULE 1.2(e); DR 7-102(B). Therefore, if the defendant refuses to waive his right to testify and the defense lawyer knows or has made a good faith determination that the client is going to testify falsely, defense counsel only has two options:

1. The lawyer must seek to withdraw from the case, DR 2-1110(B), (C); Model Rule 1.16(b)(1), citing reasons to the court that do not breach the lawyer-client privilege. MODEL RULE 1.16(a), Cmt. 3. The client is then free to represent himself as he chooses.

2. If the lawyer is not allowed to withdraw, she can allow the witness/client to testify in a narrative fashion without partici-pating in the presentation of the testimony herself. This ap-proach allows the lawyer to stay on the case and honor the defendant's right to testify, without directly assisting the witness/client in presenting perjured testimony.[2] This strategy has been criticized, however,[3] and has the potential to be highly prejudicial, in that it tends to signal or indicate that the client is committing perjury. Such an approach, therefore, should only be used if defense counsel has no other choice; usually, that means when the court has denied the motion to withdraw, which is often the case when the client is represented by a pub-lic defender.

The lawyer is on solid ground when she refuses to present false testi-mony of a nonclient witness. A witness other than the defendant does not have the same Sixth Amendment right to testify.[4] Thus defense counsel has greater freedom to decide whether or not to call a nonde-fendant witness to the stand, and counsel should not present such a witness to the court under any circumstances.[5] In addition, defense counsel has the "immediate and ultimate responsibility" for decisions related to defense strategy and tactics, such as "deciding if and when to object, which witnesses, if any, to call, and what defenses to de-velop."[6] Refusing to allow a perjurious nonclient witness to testify is a tactical decision within the lawyer's authority to make. MODEL RULE 1.2(a) and Cmt. 1; MODEL RULE 1.3 and Cmt. 1; EC 7-7; DR 7-101(B)(1); DR 2-110(b); ABA CRIMINAL JUSTICE STANDARD 4-5.2(b).

A threshold consideration for an lawyer faced with a potentially perjurious witness, especially a defendant, is the degree to which the lawyer must be certain of the witness' intention to present false testi-mony. Both the ABA Model Rules and Model Code prohibit a lawyer from presenting or facilitating the offer of testimony *known* to be false. MODEL RULE 1.2(d), 3.3(a)(4), 1.16(b)(1); MODEL CODE DR 7-102(A)(4), (7). However, whether a lawyer is considered to "know" when a client or witness intends to testify falsely is subject to varying standards, de-pending on the jurisdiction.[7]

Although different courts and jurisdictions have adopted various degrees of certainty required of a lawyer to act upon the potential per-jury of a witness or client, it is clear that mere suspicion by the lawyer is not enough, while an announced intent to testify falsely is a suffi-cient basis. Between these two extremes, a lawyer should obtain some factual basis to support a good faith conclusion that a client or witness intends to commit perjury before acting upon such suspicions. It is clear, however, that a lawyer in a Model Rules jurisdiction is given more discretion under Rule 3.3(c) in the case of a witness and may refuse to call a witness other than the accused as long as she "reasonably believes" the witness will testify falsely.

Thus, a lawyer is never justified in permitting a defense witness to knowingly present perjured testimony. The ABA Code of Professional Responsibility, the ABA Model Rules, court rules, and public policy all prohibit such conduct. In the case of a nondefendant witness, the lawyer is free to refuse to allow the witness to testify falsely. Despite the rules against presenting false testimony by a defense witness, the lawyer is in a precarious position when the witness is also the defendant/client, but there are a number of strategies at his disposal to address the problem.

> *Is it ethically proper for defense counsel to call a defense witness to testify, when the defendant insists, if counsel believes the witness' testimony will be detrimental to the client's case?*

Defendants have the ultimate authority to make certain fundamental decisions regarding the conduct of their case, including whether to plead guilty, whether to waive trial by jury, whether to appeal, and whether to accept assistance of counsel or represent themselves instead.[8] When the witness in question is not the defendant, however, the determination of defense theory and strategy is the province of the lawyer assigned to the case and defense counsel is not obligated to call witnesses who do not advance the defense simply because the client insists. *Wainwright v. Sykes,* 433 U.S. 72 (1977); MODEL RULE 1.2(a), 1.3; DR 7-101(B)(1). While defense counsel should consult with her client (and in the case of a public defender with her supervisor) when questions or conflicts arise with regard to tactics and strategy, counsel is legally and ethically responsible for the trial of the case, and considerations of providing competent and zealous representation should override the client's wishes when the two conflict.

Although decisions about which witnesses to call fall within the province of the lawyer's authority to make strategic and tactical decisions, there is also a duty to consult with a client about such matters and to discuss any disagreements that may arise regarding such decisions. MODEL RULE 1.4; EC 9-2; EC 5-12, EC 7-3, EC 7-7; ABA CRIMINAL JUSTICE STANDARD 4-5.2(b), (c). Therefore, after defense counsel has thoroughly investigated the case, interviewed the witnesses suggested by the client, and decided which witnesses she will present at trial, it is important that the client be informed of the reasons for defense counsel's decision not to call any of the client's desired witnesses. If the client does not agree with the lawyer's decision, however, it is the ethical responsibility of the lawyer to use her best professional judgment and experience to determine the suitability of using the witness.[9]

On the other hand, defense counsel should be careful not to materially damage a client's cause or defense by refusing to allow a witness to testify who would actually be an important asset to the defendant's case. Failure to call a witness that could have helped the accused or advanced the theory of defense could be considered ineffective assistance of counsel. MODEL RULE 1.1.[10]

If the client asks defense counsel to call a witness who the lawyer believes will be detrimental to the client's case, therefore, the lawyer should not call the witness. However, the lawyer should consult with the client and discuss the reasons for the decision. Prior to making a decision not to call a witness requested by the defendant, counsel must undertake an appropriate investigation.

Is it ethically proper for defense counsel to call a defense witness if counsel believes that the witness' testimony will be helpful, but the client objects to calling that witness?

One view of a defense lawyer's responsibility in the face of a client's wish to call a witness that the lawyer feels will be detrimental to the client's case holds that counsel should bow to the wishes of a client who makes a fully informed decision.[11] This view is based upon the proposition that the Sixth Amendment provides each defendant a personal right to *assistance* of counsel, not submission to counsel.[12] Pursuant to the personal nature of Sixth Amendment rights, the case "belongs" to the client, not the lawyer, according to this view, and the defendant retains the ultimate authority to control his own defense, including tactical decisions.

It should be noted that in some situations, a client's objection to the calling of a witness may be related to certain decisions that are the client's to make. The client has a right to decide not to pursue an insanity defense, for example, and can object to the calling of witnesses whose testimony is designed to establish that defense.[13]

Aside from special cases such as an insanity defense, however, the majority view is that the wishes of the defendant must be subordinated to the lawyer's duty to provide zealous and competent representation in vindicating the client's cause. MODEL RULE 1.1, 1.3; DR 6-101.[14] This view is based upon the necessity of the lawyer to make independent, professional judgments to properly advocate her clients interests based upon her superior knowledge and skill. Once the client initially accepts representation, the lawyer must be able to make binding decisions to effect her obligation to pursue her client's best interests. *Jones v. Barnes,* 463 U.S. 745 (1983); DR 7-101(B)(1) (where permissible, a lawyer can exercise her professional judgment in waiving or asserting a right or position of her client). This latter position is more in accord with the ethical duties of the lawyer as codified in most jurisdictions, and with the reality of a public defender's experience with clients.

If defense counsel believes that a witness' testimony would provide an affirmative defense or mitigation to the client's culpability, the lawyer has the responsibility to advise the client of the necessity of calling the particular witness. The witness should be called over the client's objection, if necessary. The lawyer should keep in mind that a client may often be reacting to fear and emotion, and counsel's job is to do all that is legally, morally, and ethically allowed to vindicate the client's cause. This may often involve saving a client from their own lack of judgment. Where a witness' testimony is not important to advancing the defense, more deference should be given to the wishes of the client. *Strickland,* 466 U.S. at 688; MODEL RULE 1.4; EC 7-8, 9-2; ABA CRIMINAL JUSTICE STANDARD 4-5.2.

In the case of sentencing hearings, for example, if a client has loved ones who wish to testify as to his character, but the client does not want them subjected to the trauma of testifying, defense counsel should defer to any nonlegal considerations that may be the basis of a defendant's decision not to have a certain witness testify as long as the witness in question is not important to the client's defense. EC 7-8; MODEL RULE 1.2(a). However, the lawyer must exercise his right to control strategical and tactical decisions and call any witnesses who are essential to advancing the client's defense, based upon counsel's best professional judgment. Failure to present proper mitigation witnesses can be held to be ineffective assistance of counsel, and possibly unethical conduct.[15]

In short, failing to call a witness whose testimony would advance the defense is not acceptable. Cases in which a client insists that certain witnesses *not* be called to testify, even though their testimony would aid in the client's defense, therefore, pose a unique dilemma for defense counsel. This question should be resolved in favor of providing the defendant with competent and zealous representation, and the client's wishes should be overridden if necessary.

Conclusion

The ethical questions presented here pose challenges for all criminal defense lawyers, especially lawyers representing indigent defendants who often are mistrustful of appointed counsel. As caseloads increase, the pressure for public defenders to push cases through the system also increases. Thus, public defenders and assigned counsel must become more attuned to the need to provide the best defense for each client, and not merely to disposing of cases.

Public defenders and assigned counsel, just as retained counsel, must represent their clients competently and completely. The rules governing ethical conduct of lawyers do not change simply because a lawyer is a public defender, nor is the ethical requirement to provide zealous representation mitigated by excessive caseload. Public defenders and assigned counsel, like other lawyers, are required to use their knowledge, skill, and best professional judgment to advance their clients' defense, even if, after consultation with their client, this may entail derogating a client's wishes in some instances.

Notes

1. Nix v. Whiteside, 475 U.S. 156, 162 (1986); Harris v. New York, 401 U.S. 222 (1971).

2. The narrative approach was initially proposed in a draft ABA Standard 4-7.7. That proposed Standard, however, was never adopted by the ABA. Several courts, however, have approved of the narrative approach. *See, e.g.,* People v. Guzman, 45 Cal. 3d 915, 755 P.2d 917 (1988); People v. Lowery, 52 Ill. App. 3d 44, 366 N.E.2d 155 (1977).

3. ABA Comm. on Ethics and Professional Responsibility, Formal Op. 87-353 (1987) (relying on Model Rule 3.3(a)(2) and *Nix v. Whiteside*, 475 U.S. 156 (1986)). *See also* Rule 3.3, Cmt. 9.

4. Jones v. Barnes, 463 U.S. 745, 749 (1983); Wainwright v. Sykes, 433 U.S. 72, 93 (1977) (Burger, C. J., concurring).

5. People v. Flores, 128 Ill. 2d 66, 538 N.E.2d 481 (1989); State v. Meeker, 143 Ariz. 256, 693 P.2d 911 (1984); People v. Schultheis, 638 P.2d 8 (Colo. 1981) (en banc).

6. *Wainwright, supra* note 4; Estelle v. Williams, 425 U.S. 501 (1976); Henry v. Mississippi, 379 U.S. 443, 451 (1965).

7. Wilcox v. Johnson, 555 F.2d 115, 120-2 (3rd Cir. 1977) (more than "private conjectures" about the guilt or innocence of client necessary to support assertion of client/defendant's intent to testify falsely); United States v. Long, 857 F.2d 436 (8th Cir. 1988) (lawyer required to take steps to establish a "firm factual basis," through an independent investigation, to support the assertion that a defendant intended to testify falsely, absent client's "clearly expressed intent" to do so); *Schultheis, supra* note 5, (mere inconsistencies in a client's or witnesses' stories not enough of a basis to support an assertion of intended perjury); *Flores, supra* note 5, at 106 ("reasonable belief under the circumstances" that an individual's testimony is unreliable or would likely be harmful to the defendant's case is a sufficient degree of certainty to refuse to allow

the testimony in the case of nondefendant witnesses and to take other remedial steps in the case of a defendant witness).

8. *Jones, supra* note 4.

9. Darden v. Wainwright, 477 U.S. 168, *reh'g denied,* 478 U.S. 1036 (1986) (defendant not denied effective assistance of counsel when lawyer failed to call mitigation witnesses at a sentencing hearing in a capital case, because their testimony would open the door for damaging rebuttal evidence; People v. Miranda, 44 Cal. 3d 57, 744 P.2d 1127 (1987) (en banc), *cert. denied,* 486 U.S. 1038, *reh'g denied,* 487 U.S. 1246 (1988); State v. Davis, 199 Conn. 88, 506 A.2d 86 (1986); *Schultheis, supra* note 5, at 14; *In re* King, 133 Vt. 345, 336 A.2d 195 (1975).

10. *See also* Strickland v. Washington, 466 U.S. 688 (1984); United States v. Wolff, 727 F.2d 656 (7th Cir. 1984) (defense counsel's failure to call a witness who would have aided in the client's defense as a result of negligence and lack of due diligence amounted to ineffective assistance of counsel).

11. EC 7-8; Autry v. McKaskle, 727 F.2d 358, 362 (5th Cir. 1984) (where a defendant knowingly makes a choice not to have mitigating witnesses testify at a sentencing hearing, he cannot later claim ineffective assistance of counsel because his lawyer was simply acceding to his own informed wishes).

12. Faretta v. California, 422 U.S. 806, 819 (1975).

13. State v. Thompson, 625 S.W.2d 115 (Mo. 1981), *cert. denied,* 459 U.S. 1114 (1983) (relying on EC 7-7).

14. *See also Darden, supra* note 9; People v. Deere, 41 Cal. 3d 353, 710 P.2d 925 (1985) (en banc), *cert. denied,* 112 S. Ct. 954 (1992) (not calling mitigating witnesses was ineffective assistance of counsel despite the fact that counsel was acceding to the wishes of his client); People v. Bloom, 48 Cal. 3d 1194, 774 P.2d 688 (1989), *cert. denied,* 110 S. Ct. 1503 (1990).

15. *Strickland, supra* note 10; *Wolff, supra* note 10.

Bibliography

Standards and Opinions

ABA Committee on Ethics and Professional Responsibility, Formal Opinion 87-353 (1987).

ABA MODEL CODE OF PROFESSIONAL RESPONSIBILITY, DR 2-110(B); 2-110(C); 7-101(B)(1); 7-102(A)(4); 7-102(A)(7); 7-102(B); EC 5-12; 7-3; 7-7; 7-8; 9-2 (1980).

ABA MODEL RULES OF PROFESSIONAL CONDUCT, Rules, 1.1; 1.2(a); 1.2(d); 1.2(e), cmt. 1; 1.3; cmt. 1; 1.4; 1.16(a); 1.16(b)(1); cmt. 3; 3.3(a)(2)(4); 3.3(c); cmt. 9 (1983).

ABA STANDARDS FOR CRIMINAL JUSTICE DEFENSE FUNCTION 4-5.2(a)(b)(c); 4-3.7(b); 4-7.5(a); 4-7.7 (3d ed. 1993).

United States Supreme Court Cases

Darden v. Wainwright, 477 U.S. 168, *reh'g denied,* 478 U.S. 1036 (1986).
Estelle v. Williams, 425 U.S. 501 (1976).

Faretta v. California, 422 U.S. 806 (1975).
Harris v. New York, 401 U.S. 222 (1971).
Henry v. Mississippi, 379 U.S. 433 (1965).
Jones v. Barnes, 463 U.S. 745 (1983).
Nix v. Whiteside, 475 U.S. 156 (1986).
Strickland v. Washington, 466 U.S. 688 (1984).
Wainwright v. Sykes, 433 U.S. 72 (1977).

State Court and Circuit Court of Appeals Cases

Autry v. McKaskle, 727 F.2d 358 (5th Cir. 1984).
In re King, 133 Vt. 345, 336 A.2d 195 (1975).
People v. Bloom, 48 Cal. 3d 1194, 774 P.2d 688 (1989), *cert. denied*, 110 S. Ct. 1503 (1990).
People v. Deere, 41 Cal. 3d 353, 710 P.2d 925 (1985) (en banc), *cert. denied*, 112 S. Ct. 954 (1992).
People v. Flores, 128 Ill. 2d 66, 538 N.E.2d 481 (1989).
People v. Guzman, 45 Cal. 3d 915, 755 P.2d 917 (1988).
People v. Lowery, 52 Ill. App. 3d 44, 366 N.E.2d 155 (1977).
People v. Miranda, 44 Cal. 3d 57, 744 P.2d 1127 (1987) (en banc), *cert. denied*, 486 U.S. 1038, *reh'g denied*, 487 U.S. 1246 (1988).
People v. Schultheis, 638 P.2d 8 (Colo. 1981) (en banc).
State v. Davis, 199 Conn. 88, 506 A.2d 86 (1986).
State v. Hightower, 214 N.J. Super. 43, 518 A.2d 482 (1986).
State v. Meeker, 143 Ariz. 256, 693 P.2d 911 (1984).
State v. Thompson, 625 S.W.2d 115 (Mo. 1981), *cert. denied*, 459 U.S. 1114 (1983).
United States v. Long, 857 F.2d 436 (8th Cir. 1988).
United States v. Wolff, 727 F.2d 656 (7th Cir. 1984).
Wilcox v. Johnson, 555 F.2d 115 (3d Cir. 1977).

CHAPTER ◫ 7

Communicating Plea Offers to the Client

Keith N. Bystrom

Is defense counsel ethically required to communicate every plea bargain offered to a client even if counsel feels that the offer is unacceptable?

Simply stated, defense counsel must communicate to a client every plea bargain offer received from the prosecutor. The decision whether to plead guilty is for the accused defendant, not defense counsel. Defense counsel is not only required ethically, but also constitutionally to discuss all plea bargain offers as part of providing effective assistance of counsel.

Trial Counsel's Ethical Duty to Communicate a Plea Bargain Offer

Whether the ABA Model Rules of Professional Conduct (hereinafter Model Rules) or the ABA Model Code of Professional Responsibility (hereinafter Model Code) has been adopted, the ethical duty placed upon criminal defense trial counsel is to communicate to the client every plea bargain offered by the prosecutor.

Model Rule 1.2(a) clearly states this duty to communicate, stating:

> A lawyer shall abide by a client's decision whether to accept an offer of settlement of a matter. In a criminal case, the lawyer shall abide by the client's decision, after consultation with the lawyer, as to a plea to be entered, whether to waive jury trial and whether the client will testify.

Model Rule 1.4 explicitly places upon trial counsel this ethical duty to communicate by stating:

> (a) A lawyer should keep a client reasonably informed about the status of the matter and promptly comply with reasonable requests for information.
> (b) A lawyer shall explain a matter to the extent reasonably necessary to permit the client to make informed decisions regarding the representation.

The commentary to Model Rule 1.4 further explains this communication responsibility in the context of negotiating on behalf of a client when it states:

> For example, a lawyer negotiating on behalf of a client should provide the client with facts relevant to the matter, inform the client of communications from another party and take other reasonable steps that permit the client to make a decision regarding a serious offer from another party. The lawyer who receives from opposing counsel an offer of settlement in a civil controversy or a proffered plea bargain in a criminal case should promptly inform the client of its substance unless prior discussions with the client have left it clear that the proposal will be unacceptable.

The ethical duty to communicate is not as explicitly established under the Model Code. *See* Charles W. Wolfram, *Modern Legal Ethics*, p. 164–66 (West 1986). Nevertheless, adequate communication has been recognized as an essential building block of the client-lawyer relationship. *See generally* Geoffrey C. Hazard, Jr., and W. William Hodes, *The Law of Lawyering: A Handbook on the Model Rules of Professional Conduct*, 2d ed. p. 82 (1990). The Model Code aspirationally provides in Ethical Consideration 7-7:

> A defense lawyer in a criminal case has the duty to advise his client fully on whether a particular plea to a charge appears to be desirable and as to the prospect of success on appeal, but it is for the client to decide what plea should be entered and whether an appeal should be taken.

In addition, Ethical Consideration 7-8 places the responsibility on the lawyer to communicate meaningfully with a client when it states "a lawyer should assert his best efforts to assure that the decisions of his client are made only after the client has been informed of relevant considerations."

The ABA Standards for Criminal Justice have been adopted by many courts, including the United States Supreme Court in *Strickland v. Washington*, 466 U.S. 668, 104 S. Ct. 2052, 80 L. Ed.2d 674 (1984), as guidelines for the ethical responsibilities of participants in the criminal justice system. ABA Standard 14-3.2 Relating to Pleas of Guilty (2d ed. 1980 and Supp. 1986) describes the role defense counsel should play when conducting plea negotiations on behalf of a client as follows:

(a) Defense counsel should conclude a plea agreement only with the consent of the defendant, and should ensure that the decision whether to enter a plea of guilty or nolo contendere is ultimately made by the defendant.

(b) To aid the defendant in reaching a decision, defense counsel, after appropriate investigation, should advise the defendant of the alternatives available and of the considerations deemed important by defense counsel or the defendant in reaching a decision.

Also, ABA Standard 4-6.2 Relating to the Defense Function (3d ed. 1993)[1] concerning plea discussions provides:

(a) Defense counsel should keep the accused advised of developments arising out of plea discussions conducted with the prosecutor.

(b) Defense counsel should promptly communicate and explain to the accused all significant plea proposals made by the prosecution.

The commentary to ABA Standard 4-6.2 further elaborates:

Because plea discussions are usually held without the accused being present, the lawyer has the duty to communicate fully to the client the substance of the discussions. As discussed elsewhere in these Standards, the client should be given sufficient information to participate intelligently in the decision whether to accept or reject a plea proposal. It is important that the accused be informed both of the existence and the content of proposals made by the prosecutor; the accused, not the lawyer, has the right to decide whether to accept or reject a prosecution proposal, even when the proposal is one that the lawyer would not approve. If the accused's choice on the question of a guilty plea is to be an informed one, the accused must act with full awareness of the alternatives, including any that arise from proposals made by the prosecutor. Ordinarily, the information to be provided by counsel is that appropriate for a client who is a comprehending and responsible adult.

ABA Standard 4-3.8 Relating to the Defense Function (3d ed. 1993) provides that defense counsel has a duty to keep the client informed as follows:

> (a) Defense counsel should keep the client informed of the developments in the case and the progress of preparing the defense and should promptly comply with reasonable requests for information.
>
> (b) Defense counsel should explain developments in the case to the extent reasonably necessary to permit the client to make informed decisions regarding the representation.

The ABA Standing Committee on Ethics and Professional Responsibility has determined "that it is the duty of the lawyer to inform his client of every settlement offer made by the opposing party," *see* ABA Committee on Ethics and Professional Responsibility, Formal Opinion 326 (August 9, 1970). This opinion has been specifically determined to require a criminal defense lawyer to transmit a plea bargain offer to the client, *see* ABA Committee on Ethics and Professional Responsibility, Informal Opinion 1373 (December 2, 1976).

Another recent authority to discuss a lawyer's duty to inform and consult with a client is the Proposed Restatement of the Law, *The Law Governing Lawyers* (Tent. Draft No. 5, 1992), being considered by the American Law Institute. Section 31 of the proposed draft states:

> (1) A lawyer must keep a client reasonably informed about the status of a matter and must consult with a client to a reasonable extent concerning decisions to be made by the lawyer under §§ 32–34.
>
> (3) A lawyer must notify a client of decisions to be made by a client under §§ 32–34, such as whether to accept a settlement offer, and must explain a matter to the extent reasonably necessary to permit the client to make informed decisions regarding the representation.

Section 33 of the ALI Proposed Restatement describes the authority specifically reserved to a client. It states:

> As between client and lawyer, decisions such as the following are allocated to the client within the meaning of § 32(3) and may not be irrevocably delegated to the lawyer: whether and on what terms to settle a claim; how to plead in a criminal prosecution; whether to chose to waive jury trial in a criminal prosecution; whether to testify in a criminal prosecution; and whether to appeal in a civil proceeding or criminal prosecution. A client may from

time to time authorize a lawyer to make those decisions for the client, except to the extent that other law (such as criminal procedure rules governing pleas, jury trial, waiver, and defendant testimony) requires the client's personal participation or approval.

In short, leading authorities and ethical standards uniformly agree that trial counsel in a criminal case is ethically mandated to tell the client about all plea bargain offers received from the prosecutor.

Trial Counsel's Constitutional Duty to Communicate a Plea Bargain Offer

In a criminal case, the ethical duty placed on trial counsel to communicate with a client rises to the level of a fundamental constitutional right guaranteed all criminal defendants. This constitutional right emanates from the standards determined by the United States Supreme Court in *Strickland v. Washington*, 466 U.S. 668, 104 S. Ct. 2052, 80 L. Ed.2d 674 (1984). The *Strickland* Court established a two-pronged test for courts to apply to determine whether an accused received ineffective assistance of counsel under the Sixth Amendment to the U.S. Constitution. In *Strickland*, the Court acknowledged that a basic duty of all criminal defense lawyers is "to consult with the defendant on important decisions and to keep the defendant informed of important developments in the course of the prosecution." In *Hill v. Lockhart*, 474 U.S. 52, 106 S. Ct. 366, 88 L. Ed.2d 203 (1985), the *Strickland* standard was made applicable to situations that resulted in a plea of guilty.

The accused defendant has a constitutional right to make certain fundamental decisions regarding the case. At a minimum, those decisions are whether to plead guilty, to waive a jury trial, to testify in his or her own behalf, or to take an appeal. *Jones v. Barnes*, 463 U.S. 745, 103 S. Ct. 3308, 77 L. Ed.2d 987 (1983). A criminal defense lawyer does not have the power to enter a plea of guilty without the defendant's consent and thereby waive the client's constitutional right to plead not guilty and have a trial where witnesses against him can be confronted and cross-examined. *Brookhart v. Janis*, 384 U.S. 1, 86 S. Ct. 1245, 16 L. Ed.2d 314, (1966).[2] Although there may be a debate among leading commentators over exactly how the decision-making authority between a lawyer and a client should be divided and if the proper line should be drawn between "strategy and tactics," "objectives and means," or "substantive and procedural," there is no dispute that the decision to plead guilty is for the client, not the lawyer.[3]

Judicial Scrutiny of Trial Counsel's Performance

Ever since plea bargaining was recognized by the United States Supreme Court as "an essential component of the administration of justice," *Santobello v. New York*, 404 U.S. 257, 260, 92 S. Ct. 495, 498, 30 L. Ed.2d 427 (1971), trial counsel's performance during plea negotiations has been subject to increased scrutiny by the judiciary. Decisions have arisen in three different contexts: disciplinary proceedings, malpractice actions, and post-conviction claims of ineffective assistance of counsel.

Disciplinary Proceedings

Lawyers have been disciplined for the failure to communicate and consult with their clients concerning an offer to settle the client's case. The vast majority of reported opinions involve the unauthorized settlement of civil cases. *See generally* Debra T. Landis, Annotation, 92 A.L.R. 3d 288, *Conduct of Lawyer in Connection with Settlement of Client's Case as Ground for Disciplinary Action* (1979). However, the same ethical rules are violated by trial counsel when a settlement offer in a criminal case is not communicated to the client and defense lawyers have been disciplined for failure to communicate a plea bargain offer to a client. *See generally* Debra T. Landis, Annotation, 69 A.L.R. 4th 410, *Negligence, Inattention or Professional Incompetence of Attorney in Handling Client's Affairs in Criminal Matters as Ground for Disciplinary Action—Modern Cases* (1989).

For example, in *Florida Bar v. Murray*, 489 So. 2d 30, 30 (Fla.1986), the lawyer was disbarred when he "failed to follow through on a plea offer made by the state." Due to trial counsel's failure to communicate the offer, the client lost an opportunity to be placed on probation and was sentenced as an habitual offender. The court determined that trial counsel's conduct violated his duty to pursue or seek the lawful objectives of his client under Disciplinary Rule (DR) 7-101(A)(1). In two companion cases including the same court-appointed counsel, *In Re Stanton*, 470 A.2d 272 (D.C. App. 1983), and 470 A.2d 281, (D.C. App. 1983), *cert. denied*, 466 U.S. 972 (1984), the court determined that trial counsel neglected a legal matter entrusted to him by substituting his judgment over that of his client as to whether to enter a plea of guilty—an area "traditionally reserved solely to the client." Such action violated not only DR 7-101(A)(1) by not pursuing the client's legal objective, but also was neglect under DR 6-101(A)(3). A similar result was reached in *Matter of Rosen*, 470 A.2d 292 (D.C. App. 1983), where trial counsel was suspended after he persisted in forcing a decision to plead his court-appointed client guilty without even a discussion with the client and against the client's wishes.

A finding by the appellate court that trial counsel committed ineffective assistance may lead to subsequent disciplinary proceedings. Richard Klein, *Legal Malpractice, Professional Discipline and Representation of the Indigent Defendant*, 61 Temple L. Rev. 1171, 1184 (1988). In fact, California requires that if a reversal of a judgment is based on misconduct, incompetent representation, or willful misrepresentation by counsel, the court shall refer the matter to the State Bar for further investigation concerning the appropriateness of initiating disciplinary action.[4] In *McAleney v. United States*, 539 F.2d 282 (1st Cir. 1976), trial counsel's error in not accurately communicating a proposed offer to the client caused the appellate court to question trial counsel's continued fitness to represent clients in federal courts.

Legal Malpractice Actions
The failure of trial counsel to communicate a plea bargain offer to the client may lead to a malpractice action against that lawyer.[5] To establish a cause of action for legal malpractice, most jurisdictions require the same elements of proof whether the issue arises from criminal or civil representation.

In *Krahn v. Kinney*, 538 N.E.2d 1058 (Ohio 1989), the court determined that these elements included (1) a lawyer-client relationship giving rise to a duty; (2) a breach of that duty; and (3) damages proximately caused by the breach. *Krahn* explicitly rejected the lawyer's argument that an accused defendant must first obtain a reversal of her conviction on grounds of ineffective assistance of counsel before bringing a malpractice action. Because the claim of ineffective assistance of counsel is based on constitutional guarantees and seeks the reversal of a criminal conviction, and a legal malpractice action is a common law tort action seeking civil monetary damages, the issues are not the same. The proof of one does not necessarily establish the other. Other courts disagree and have determined that issues decided in a post-conviction claim of ineffective assistance may be precluded from being raised again in a malpractice claim.[6]

In *Krahn*, the court reversed a summary judgment and ordered a trial on the issue of whether malpractice was committed when an accused lost the opportunity to plead to a minor misdemeanor due to trial counsel's failure to communicate the original plea bargain offer. Ms. Krahn's claim of damages included severe emotional distress, damage to her good name and reputation, and suffering the stigma of having a criminal conviction including moral turpitude. These damages could have been avoided if her original lawyer had provided her the opportunity to accept the original offer to dismiss the charges in return for testifying against a codefendant also represented by the same lawyer.

Post-Conviction Claims of Ineffective Assistance of Counsel

This issue has surfaced most frequently in the context of post-conviction petitions seeking a determination that trial counsel provided ineffective assistance of counsel by failing to communicate a plea bargain offer. With unanimity, courts that have considered this issue agree that an accused defendant "has a right to be informed about plea bargain offers as part of his participation in the decision-making process surrounding his defense." *Ex parte Wilson,* 724 S.W.2d 72, 74 (Tex. Ct. App. 1987).

A leading case is *Lyles v. State,* 382 N.E.2d 991 (Ind. Ct. App. 1978), where the court determined that the defendant was denied effective assistance of counsel by his lawyer's failure to communicate the state's plea bargain offer to him. During a conference just prior to the commencement of trial, the prosecutor offered Lyles a plea bargain whereby a robbery charge would be reduced to theft along with a recommendation of one to five years in prison. Lyles's lawyer left the judge's chambers to discuss the plea bargain offer with his client. When he returned, counsel informed the prosecutor and the judge that his client "would not do it." Trial was immediately commenced and Lyles was convicted of robbery and sentenced to ten years. From the opinion, it appears that defense counsel told Lyles the plea bargain had fallen through and never informed him of the offer made in chambers. The court found that a criminal defendant in Lyles's situation may not intelligently or voluntarily elect whether to stand trial or plead guilty "without consultation" and certainly not without communication of the prosecutor's offer. The court emphasized that the decision whether or not to plead guilty was of utmost importance and not merely a matter of trial tactics or strategy when it stated "in matters of such importance, the attorney has no option, he must advise his client of the proposed plea agreement."

In a leading federal case, *United States ex rel. Caruso v. Zelinsky,* 689 F.2d 435 (3d Cir. 1982), *aff'd,* 515 F. Supp. 676 (D.N.J. 1982), the federal court determined that the defendant's petition presented a substantial federal constitutional claim concerning his allegation that his criminal defense lawyer failed to advise him of a plea bargain offer. The court ultimately determined that factual issues were in dispute over whether or not the prosecution made any efforts to negotiate a plea with Mr. Caruso's lawyer and, therefore, an evidentiary hearing would be required. Nevertheless, the court did find that the failure of trial counsel to advise his client of a plea bargain would constitute a gross deviation from accepted professional standards. The court said "if the alleged plea offer was, in fact, made to Caruso's counsel and not communicated to Caruso, petitioner was denied his Sixth and Fourteenth Amendment rights to effective assistance of counsel." 515 F. Supp. at 680. Mr. Caruso received a mandatory life sentence for murder, along with consecutive eight to twelve years on other counts. According to his allegation, the proffered plea he never received would have allowed him to receive less than life imprisonment and a dismissal of all other counts.

Similarly, in *State v. Ludwig*, 369 N.W.2d 722 (Wis. 1985), the prosecutor, on the morning of the first day of Ms. Ludwig's trial, suggested that if she would plead no contest or guilty to two unspecified misdemeanor counts, the pending felony would be dismissed. Ms. Ludwig's lawyer rejected the offer immediately without discussing it with her. Later, during a recess in the afternoon session of trial, her lawyer finally mentioned the offer. Prior to trial, Ms. Ludwig had told her lawyer that she did not want to be convicted of a felony, but would take anything else. The court determined that counsel's immediate rejection of the plea bargain offer without prior consultation with the defendant was in total disregard of the principle that the decision of what plea to enter is uniquely the client's, not the lawyer's. Even though counsel later communicated the plea bargain offer to Ms. Ludwig, his consultation with her failed to clearly inform her that the decision of whether to accept or reject the offer was hers and, thereby, deprived her of any opportunity to accept the offer.

In an earlier case, *United States ex rel. Simon v. Murphy*, 349 F. Supp. 818 (E.D. Pa. 1972), counsel's fee arrangement created a conflict of interest that prevented him from communicating a plea bargain to his client charged with the murder of her husband. Counsel's fee arrangement included that his fee would be paid from the life insurance policy on the life of his client's husband. However, under Pennsylvania law, there would be no insurance proceeds available to the wife if she were determined to be the slayer of her husband and the lawyer fee arrangement was valueless unless his client was acquitted. Therefore, a writ of habeas corpus was granted when a proposed plea bargain—which would have substantially reduced the possible penalty of life imprisonment—was offered, but never communicated to the client due to the conflict of interest created by the contingent fee arrangement.

Procedural Issues Involving Ineffective Assistance of Counsel

Certain procedural requirements apply when a prisoner claims that trial counsel was ineffective for failing to disclose that a plea agreement had been offered by the prosecutor. The prisoner will have the burden of proving (1) an offer for a plea was made by the prosecutor; (2) trial counsel failed to inform the accused of the plea bargain offer; (3) trial counsel had no reasonable basis for failing to inform the accused of the plea bargain offer; and (4) the accused was prejudiced by losing the opportunity to enter into a plea bargain. *See Commonwealth v. Copeland,* 554 A.2d 54 (Pa. Super. 1988), *appeal denied,* 565 A.2d 1165 (Pa. 1989).

Courts have relied on different evidence to determine whether an offer for a plea bargain was actually made by the prosecutor. In some cases, evidence that an offer was made is stipulated by the prosecutor or affidavits and testimony is presented from the prosecutor and defense counsel concerning the alleged plea bargain offer. *Rasmussen v. State,* 658 S.W.2d 867 (Ark. 1983), and *State v. Martin,* 350 S.E.2d 63 (N.C. 1986). In fact, testimony from trial counsel about any discussions with the client about an offer is usually the key to determining the issue. *State v. James,* 739 P.2d 1161 (Wash. App. 1987). Without trial counsel's version, the defendant's allegations will stand uncontroverted. If trial counsel denies that an offer was ever made or does not recall that an offer was made, the court must determine by a preponderance of the evidence the existence of the offer. *People v. Alexander,* 518 N.Y.S.2d 872 (N.Y. Sup. 1987). In such cases, the fact that a prosecutor had written notes of the alleged plea bargain offer has assisted the court in making these findings. *Ex parte Wilson,* 724 S.W.2d 72 (Tex. Cr. App. 1987). Notes in the lawyer's file would be persuasive in determining whether a plea bargain was offered and the substance of trial counsel's resulting communication with the client. *Young v. State,* 470 N.E.2d 70 (Ind. 1984).[7]

To avoid confusion, counsel representing persons charged with crimes should routinely document the client file concerning any proposals received from the prosecutor and the communication and consultation with the client about any plea bargain offers. Many experienced criminal defense lawyers also will confirm the offer or agreement with a letter to the prosecutor. This practice ensures that the government's file reflects the actual terms of the offer in case another prosecutor later handles the case. Likewise, a confirmation letter to the client lessens the potential for any misunderstanding about the advice given to the client.

A threshold question in analyzing the issue of failure to communicate a plea bargain is whether, during discussions with the prosecutor, the criminal defense lawyer receives information or proposals that need to be communicated to the client. In *Harris v. State*, 437 N.E.2d 44 (Ind. 1982), the court found that although there were plea discussions between a deputy prosecutor and the defense lawyer, the casual conversations did not rise to the level of "developments or proposals" that should have been communicated promptly to the defendant. However, in *People v. Ferguson*, 413 N.E.2d 135 (Ill. App. 1980), the court rejected efforts on behalf of the parties to label a prosecutor's statement either an "off-hand remark" or an "offer." According to *Ferguson*, the proper focus is not the label for the communication, but to "analyze its content as one worthy of transmittal to defendant in fulfillment of a constitutional right." *Ferguson* at 138. Relying on the ABA Standards for Criminal Justice, the court noted that even the most casual and informal discussion of a case between the prosecutor and defense lawyer can develop information useful to the defense. The criminal defense lawyer should not be relieved of communication and consultation responsibilities to a client when a discussion with the prosecutor does not meet the technical contractual requirements of an offer. For a defendant to make an informed decision on whether or not to plead guilty, the defendant must have whatever information is available that can assist in predicting the consequences of that plea of guilty. Information learned in an "off-hand remark" or "casual conversation" can be very helpful and should be communicated to the defendant.

The tougher question, then, is not whether trial counsel is required to communicate a plea bargain offer, but whether trial counsel must communicate with a client about the negotiations that are taking place with the prosecutor about the client's case. As stated in *State v. James*, 739 P.2d 1161, 1167, (Wash. App. 1987), the communication "must include not only communicating actual offers, but discussion of tentative plea negotiations and the strengths and weaknesses of defendants' case, so the defendants know what to expect and can make an informed judgment whether or not to plead guilty."

The second issue concerning whether trial counsel failed to inform the client about a plea bargain offer can be an equally difficult matter of proof. In *People v. Alexander*, 518 N.Y.S.2d 872 (N.Y. Sup. 1987), the court determined that the defendant had failed to establish by a preponderance of the evidence that trial counsel did not communicate the offer. Important to the court's decision was the fact that trial counsel had represented the defendant for over two years before trial began and had met with the defendant on numerous occasions prior to trial. With this continuing relationship between the defendant and his trial counsel, the court would not infer that trial counsel did not discuss substantive questions of possible pleas with the accused. In some instances, counsel has stipulated to the fact that an offered plea bargain was not communicated to an accused. *See Hanzelka v. State,* 682 S.W.2d 385 (Tex. App. 3 Dist. 1984). As recommended earlier, trial counsel's client file should reflect that a plea bargain offer was not only communicated to the client but fully discussed.

A third issue is whether or not an accused defendant was prejudiced by losing the opportunity to enter into a plea bargain. In many cases, such as *Lyles* and *Hanzelka,* the disparity between the sentence received and the potential outcome, if the plea bargain had been accepted, is sufficient to show that prejudice did occur. In reviewing a claim that trial counsel failed to convey an offer or misadvised the defendant about an offer "a court should scrutinize closely whether a defendant has established a reasonable probability that, with effective representation, he or she would have accepted the proffered plea bargain." *In re Alvernez,* 830 P.2d 747, 756 (Cal. 1992), and *Alvernez v. Ratelle,* 831 F. Supp. 790 (S.D. Cal. 1993).[8]

In fact, petitions for habeas corpus have been denied without prejudice when the prisoner failed to allege that the plea would have been accepted if it had been communicated. *Rasmussen v. State,* 658 S.W.2d 867 (Ark. 1983), and *Elmore v. State,* 684 S.W.2d 263 (Ark. 1985). In *Rasmussen* the accused later amended her petition and the court ordered an evidentiary hearing "to determine the complete circumstances surrounding the offer." *Rasmussen v. State,* 663 S.W.2d 735 (Ark. 1984).

In *Alvernez,* the court encouraged parties to memorialize in some fashion the fact that an offer was made, communicated to the client, the advise provided, and the client's response. The court, recognizing that there will be instances where the parties do not want the trial court to know about failed plea discussions, did not suggest that the memorialization should always occur on the record. *Alvernez, supra* 756 n.7. The court's suggestion would be satisfied by a memorandum to the client's file or a letter of understanding to the prosecutor.

Prejudice is required to be proven when determining if a defendant received ineffective assistance of counsel. However, whether prejudice may occur is not an element of trial counsel's ethical duty to communicate with his client. A decision should not be made whether to inform a client about an offer based on an evaluation of possible prejudice if no discussion occurs and the client never discovers the lost opportunity to plead. Rather, trial counsel must always advise the client about any proposed offer.

Is There Any Reasonable Basis That Would Justify Trial Counsel's Failure to Communicate a Plea Bargain Offer?

What possible justifications could trial counsel put forward to justify a failure to communicate a plea bargain offer to a client?

The official comment to Model Rule 1.4 seems to indicate the ethical duty of communication involves only "a serious offer from another party." That comment also contemplates that communication should take place even when a client has delegated authority to a lawyer concerning possible settlement parameters. Remember, it is the client's decision whether or not to accept a plea bargain offer. It is trial counsel's duty to provide the client with information that is important and necessary to allow the client's meaningful participation in the decision on whether to accept a plea bargain. ABA Standard 4-6.2 (3d ed. 1993) places the duty on defense counsel to communicate "all significant plea proposals." Certainly, an obvious joke, such as offering a life sentence in exchange for a plea to a misdemeanor offense, would not reach the level of significance that requires communication to the client. On the other hand, even though defense counsel feels strongly that a proposed offer is unacceptable, that offer still should be communicated to the client for consultation, discussion, and decision.

This is not to say that plea negotiations need to be stopped each and every time a concession is made and, therefore, the offer has technically changed. Trial counsel should be properly prepared for plea discussions with the prosector by obtaining authority from the client and having knowledge of the client's interest concerning the potential range of available plea agreements. Counsel may be justified in not explaining each concession made by a prosecutor during plea negotiations, but certainly no justification can reasonably be made for not communicating the result of each negotiating session. Even when prior discussions with the client indicate a proposal is unacceptable, the client should be informed that the prosecutor placed the offer on the table. After further discussion with trial counsel, offers that seemed unacceptable earlier may become more agreeable to the client.

In some cases, trial counsel's strong belief in the case led counsel to conclude he was reasonably justified in not communicating a plea bargain offer. In *Lloyd v. State*, 373 S.E.2d 1, 2 (Ga. 1988), the court rejected trial counsel's explanation for failing to communicate a plea bargain offer due to "his strong belief that she would be acquitted because of a persuasive battered women's syndrome defense." Citing ABA Standard, The Defense Function, 4-6.2(a) and its commentary that requires "the accused, not the lawyer, has the right to pass on prosecution proposals, even when a proposal is one which the lawyer would not approve," the court found that trial counsel committed professional error by not communicating a plea bargain offer.

Similarly, in *People v. Whitfield*, 239 N.E.2d 850 (Ill. 1968), and *Ex parte Wilson*, 724 S.W.2d 72, 73 (Tex. Cr. App. 1987), the court rejected trial counsel's justification that "he could win the case." So also, in *People v. Williams*, 429 N.W.2nd 649, 651, (Mich. App. 1988), *remanded*, 434 N.W.2d 411 (Mich. 1989), *cert. denied*, 493 U.S. 956 (1989), trial counsel's justification that he "did not relay the offer to defendant because he believed that defendant stood a good chance of acquittal" was rejected. Trial counsel has the obligation to fairly and objectively evaluate each offer with the client despite counsel's perceived strength of the defense and possible favorable outcome. Trial counsel should not overstate the possibility of an acquittal or understate the possibility of a guilty verdict. In discussing possible alternatives, it would be improper for trial counsel to dramatically understate the quality of the evidence to be presented by the prosecutor for the purpose of persuading the client to reject a plea bargain offer. *United States v. Rodriquez*, 929 F.2d 747 (1st Cir. 1991).[9]

Occasionally, trial counsel will explain to the court that there was just not enough time to communicate a plea bargain offer. With the high volume of legal business in public defender offices, this excuse at first glance might seem reasonable. However, imminent trial dates do not provide a reasonable basis that would justify a failure by trial counsel to communicate a plea bargain offer. As all litigators know, many cases settle on the courthouse steps when trial is imminent and even at different times during trial. Knowing this, trial counsel should talk with her client about the possibility of receiving a last-minute plea bargain offer and be prepared to discuss it while facing a trial deadline. Even when failure to communicate a plea bargain offer occurred "a few moments before the trial," *Curl v. State*, 400 N.E.2d 775, 777 (Ind. 1980); "on the day of trial, before it commenced," *Lyles v. State*, 382 N.E.2d 991, 993 (Ind. Ct. App. 1978); "on the second day of trial," *People v. Williams*, 429 N.W.2d 649, 653 (Mich. App. 1988), *remanded*, 434 N.W.2d 411 (Mich. 1989), *cert. denied*, 493 U.S. 956 (1989); or the "morning of the first day of . . . trial," *Ludwig v. State*, 369 N.W.2d 722, 723 (Wis. 1985), the court has required that trial counsel must still communicate the plea bargain offer. In fact trial counsel has been found ineffective when a deadline on a preindictment proposal of immunity was allowed to pass, subjecting the client to the initiation of adversary criminal proceedings. *United States v. Bowers*, 517 F. Supp 666 (W.D. Pa. 1981). If problems occur with time deadlines, trial counsel should request from the court or prosecutor additional time to consult with the client rather than to fail to communicate a plea bargain offer.

High caseload demands of public defenders and court-appointed lawyers have not provided an excuse for inadequate representation. See Richard Klein, *Legal Malpractice, Professional Discipline and Representation of the Indigent Defendant*, 61 Temple L. Rev. 1171, 1185–86, n. 86 (1988). In a similar vein, a claim that a lawyer was suffering from "burned-out syndrome" because of the excessive amount of work is not a justification for neglecting clients. *In Re Loew*, 642 P.2d 1171 (Or. 1982).

On a few occasions, trial counsel has attempted to justify a failure to communicate a plea bargain offer to a client by explaining that the offer had been discussed with a relative. Obviously, the lawyer's obligation does not stop with consulting a relative. Trial counsel must discuss it with the client. See *People v. Whitfield*, 239 N.E.2d 850 (Ill. 1968), where defendant's mother but not the defendant was consulted, and the court determined that due process required a new trial.

The Seventh Circuit Court of Appeals in *Johnson v. Duckworth*, 793 F.2d 898 (7th Cir. 1986), *cert. denied*, 479 U.S. 937 (1986), has found that a criminal defense lawyer acted reasonably by consulting both his client, a 17-year-old juvenile with an unstable mental state, and his client's parents about a possible plea bargain offer. After this consultation and based on the unique circumstances of representing a confused juvenile client with indications of mental instability, the court found trial counsel acted reasonably when he rejected the plea bargain offer based on the father's disapproval of the offer as well as trial counsel's own belief that the offer was not a good one. Trial counsel facing this situation must be aware of Model Rule 1.14 concerning representing a client under a disability.

Another possible justification for failing to communicate a plea bargain offer has obtained mixed results from the courts; that is, considering the conditional nature of some plea bargain offers, whether trial counsel was justified in not disclosing to the client a proposed offer when one of the conditions had not occurred. In *State v. Simmons*, 309 S.E.2d 493 (N.C. App. 1983), trial counsel believed that an offer to his client by the prosecutor was conditioned upon a codefendant's acceptance of a similar offer. When the codefendant did not accept the offer, trial counsel did not communicate any offer to his client. The court ordered a new trial notwithstanding trial counsel's apparently sincere belief that the offer was conditional. In another case, *Williams v. Arn*, 654 F. Supp. 226 (N.D. Ohio 1986), *appeal dismissed*, 856 F.2d 197 (6th Cir. 1988), *cert. denied*, 488 U.S. 1044 (1989), the court determined that a proposed plea agreement was conditional since the assistant prosecuting lawyer needed to obtain the approval of another prosecutor assigned to the case. Trial counsel did not communicate the proposal to his client, and the offer was withdrawn prior to the commencement of trial. The court declined to order a new trial, placing particular emphasis on the conditional nature of the plea proposal that was under negotiation. In a similar situation, it was determined by the court that discussions between trial counsel and a prosecutor who did not have authority to offer a binding plea bargain were not required to be communicated to the client. *Harris v. State*, 437 N.E.2d 44 (Ind. 1982).

The mere fact that a proposed offer is conditional on another event occurring or might not be officially approved by a prosecutor with authority should not excuse trial counsel's failure to communicate the contents of the conditional proposal. At best, this justification might reasonably lead a court to conclude that trial counsel has met the constitutional duty to the client and, therefore, did not perform ineffective assistance of counsel. However, it should not lead to the same conclusion that trial counsel has met the ethical duty to communicate.

Other Communication Issues in Plea Bargaining

The question that opens this chapter is specifically focused on trial counsel communicating plea bargain offers to a client. There are other related ethical issues involving trial counsel's duty to communicate with the client in the plea bargaining context.[10]

Obviously, it is important to communicate a plea bargain offer, but it is even more critical to consult adequately and advise your client whether or not to accept the offered plea agreement. ABA Standards Relating to The Defense Function 4-5.1 (a & b) (3d ed. 1993). As Anthony Amsterdam succinctly puts it:

> The decision whether to plead guilty or to contest a criminal charge is ordinarily the most important single decision in any criminal case. This decision must ultimately be left to the client's wishes. Counsel cannot plead guilty, or not guilty, against the client's will. (Citation omitted). But counsel may and must give the client the benefit of counsel's professional advice on this crucial decision; and often counsel can protect the client from disaster only by using a considerable amount of persuasion to convince the client that a plea which the client instinctively disfavors is, in fact, in his or her best interest. Anthony G. Amsterdam, Reporter, *Trial Manual 5 for the Defense of Criminal Cases*, Vol. 1, p. 339, ALI-ABA Comm. on Continuing Professional Education (1988).

For an accused to make an informed decision, trial counsel must communicate with the client and make that client as fully aware as possible of the alternatives available and the consequences of choosing a particular alternative. Courts have vacated convictions where a defendant has decided to go to trial based on the inadequate or poor advice of trial counsel. See *Commonwealth v. Napper*, 385 A.2d 521 (Pa. Super. 1978), and *Turner v. State of Tennessee*, 664 F. Supp. 1113 (M.D. Tenn. 19870, *aff'd*, 858 F.2d 1201 (6th Cir. 1988), *rev'd on other grounds*, 492 U.S. 902, (1989). Communicating the reasonable risks of going to trial as well as significant developments in the law as they affect the client's case is the lawyer's responsibility. *Lewandowski v. Makel*, 754 F. Supp. 1142 (W.D. Mich. 1990), *aff'd*, 949 F.2d 884 (6th Cir. 1991). In *Williams v. State*, 605 A.2d 103 (Md. 1992), the court determined that trial counsel provided deficient representation, even though he had disclosed a potential plea offer to his client, when he failed to advise his client of a potential mandatory sentence that attached to the offered plea. In another circumstance a conviction was not vacated, but the court allowed an accused an opportunity to accept a plea to a reduced charge based on his trial counsel's mistaken advice concerning the consequences of the plea. *State v. Kraus*, 397 N.W.2d 671 (Iowa 1986). The court reasoned that such a remedy must be available to restore to the accused the lost opportunity under the formally reached plea bargain.

In communicating a plea bargain offer, counsel has the responsibility to communicate the offer accurately. In *Tucker v. Holland*, 327 S.E.2d 388 (W.Va. 1985), the court found that the defendant was misled by his lawyer into believing the prosecution had consented to a plea of no contest when, in fact, the prosecution had only agreed to permit a plea of guilty. The court found that "in one reprehensible maneuver, the petitioner's lawyer managed to violate his duties to the court, the prosecution and his client." *Tucker* at 395. In another case, *McAleney v. United States*, 539 F.2d 282 (1st Cir. 1976), trial counsel told his client that the prosecutor would recommend a three-year sentence when, in fact, the plea offered by the government did not include such a recommendation. This error in not communicating a proposed offer accurately and completely caused the appellate court to question the trial counsel's continued fitness to represent clients in the federal courts.

In another duty to communicate situation, the court has held that trial counsel has an additional obligation to communicate to the prosecutor the client's acceptance of a plea bargain offer. In *Flores v. State*, 784 S.W.2d 579 (Tex. App.-Ft. Worth 1980), trial counsel's failure to communicate the acceptance of a plea agreement prior to the expiration of the offer fell below an objective standard of reasonableness and required a new trial.[11]

Conclusion

From the foregoing analysis, it is apparent that defense counsel is not only ethically but constitutionally required to communicate all plea bargain offers to a client even if counsel believes that the offers are unacceptable or has another excuse for noncommunication. Defense counsel should comply with this prevailing norm of criminal defense practice that has been recognized by the courts. In addition, good practice requires that information about the terms of a plea bargain offer and the advice given to the client should be completely documented in the client file whenever a plea bargain offer is received.

Notes

1. The standard quoted is from the recently published third edition of the Standards Relating to the Defense Function. More emphasis has now been placed on defense counsel's role in communicating with the accused about plea proposals from the prosecutor. The second edition of Standard 4-6.2 stated "(a) In conducting discussions with the prosecutor the lawyer should keep the accused advised of developments at all times and all proposals made by the prosecutor should be communicated promptly to the accused."

2. *See also* ABA Standards Relating to the Defense Function (3d ed. 1993) 4-5.2(a) and Judith L. Maute, *Allocation of Decisionmaking Authority Under the Model Rules of Professional Conduct*, 17 U.C. Davis L. Rev. 1049, 1095–1105 (1984). The recent amendments to ABA Standard 4-5.2(a) explicitly state that the decision of "whether to accept a plea agreement" is to be made by the accused after full consultation with counsel.

3. Compare the client-centered approach favored by Monroe H. Freedman, Understanding Lawyers' Ethics, p. 43–64 (1990), and David A. Binder, Paul Bergman and Susan C. Price, Lawyers as Counselors: A Client-Centered Approach, p. 266–71 (West 1991), with the ABA Model Rule 1.2(a) requiring the lawyer to "abide by a client's decisions concerning the objectives of representation" and "consult with the client as to the means by which they are pursued," and ABA Standard 4-5.2(b) (3rd Ed. 1993) which states "(b) Strategic and tactical decisions should be made by defense counsel after consultation with the client where feasible and appropriate. Such decisions include what witnesses to call, whether and how to conduct cross-examination, what jurors to accept or strike, what trial motions should be made, and what evidence should be introduced."

4. *See* Cal. Bus. & Prof. Code § 6086.7 (West 1982); People v. Shelley, 202 Cal. Rptr. 874, 881 n.1 (Cal. App. 2d Dist. 1984); and Florida Bar v. Morales, 366 So. 2d 431 (Fla.1978).

5. *See generally* Richard Klein, *Legal Malpractice, Professional Discipline, and Representation of the Indigent Defendant*, 61 TEMPLE L. REV.1171 (1988); Gregory G. Sarno, Annotation, *Legal Malpractice in Defense of Criminal Prosecution*, 4 A.L.R. 5th 273 (1992).

6. *See generally* Gregory G. Sarno, Annotation, *Legal Malpractice in Defense of Criminal Prosecution*, 4 A.L.R. 5th 273 (1992). *See, e.g.*, Wilson v. Britz and Zemmelman, (No. L- 91- 031) (Ohio App. 6th Dist., January 10, 1992), (not published) 1992 WL 2543, where the prisoner was precluded from relitigating in a state malpractice claim the issue of whether the plea bargain proposal was communicated to him by his lawyer since the identical issue had been determined against the prisoner in a federal post-conviction action.

7. If a dispute arises, counsel's frequent contact with the client is likely to indicate that trial counsel was communicating properly. In Barentine v. U.S., 728 F. Supp. 1241 (W.D. N.C. 1990), *aff'd*, 908 F.2d 968 (4th Cir. 1990), the fact that there were more than fifty conversations concerning a potential plea agreement convinced the court that the five-year plea offer had been presented to the defendant and he rejected it.

8. *See also* People v. Polland, 588 Cal. Rptr. 588 (Cal. App. 4th Dist. 1991), *review granted*, 818 P.2d 61 (Cal. 1991), *transferred to court of appeals*, 834 P.2d 695 (Cal. 1992) in light of Alvernez, *supra*, opinion on transfer is not published.

9. *See* ABA STANDARD 4-5.1(a & b) (3d ed. 1993), requiring defense counsel to advise the accused candidly about all aspects of case and give honest assessment of probable outcome without understating or overstating the risks, hazards, and prospects of the case.

10. *See generally* Gregory G. Sarno, Annotation, *Adequacy of Defense Counsel's Representation of Criminal Client Regarding Plea Bargaining*, 8 A.L.R. 4th 660 (1981); Gregory G. Sarno, Annotation, *Adequacy of Defense Counsel's Representation of Criminal Client Regarding Guilty Pleas*, 10 A.L.R. 4th 8 (1981); People v. Brown, 223 Cal. Rptr. 66 (Cal. App. 3d Dist. 1986); JAMES E. BOND, PLEA BARGAINING AND GUILTY PLEAS, Chapter 4 "Role and Responsibility of Defense Counsel in the Guilty Plea Process," pp. 4-1 to 4-58 (2d ed 1983).

11. *See also* United States v. Rodriquez, 929 F.2d 747 (1st Cir. 1991), where an evidentiary hearing was ordered to determine if trial counsel communicated the counteroffer to the prosecutor, and Randle v. State, 847 S.W.2d 576 (Tx. Cr. App. 1993), where a new conviction was vacated when counsel failed to communicate an accepted offer to the prosecutor in a timely manner before the offer expired.

Bibliography

Articles, Reports, and Standards

ABA Center for Professional Responsibility, *Annotated Model Rules of Professional Conduct*, 2d ed., Rules 1.2 and 1.4 (1992).

ABA Committee on Ethics and Professional Responsibility, Formal Opinion 326 (August 9, 1970).

ABA Committee on Ethics and Professional Responsibility, Informal Opinion 1373 (December 2, 1976).

ABA MODEL CODE OF PROFESSIONAL RESPONSIBILITY, EC 7-7, EC 7-8, DR 7-101(A)(1), DR 6-101(A)(3).

ABA MODEL RULES OF PROFESSIONAL CONDUCT, Rules 1.2(a), 1.4.

ABA STANDARDS FOR CRIMINAL JUSTICE, Relating to The Defense Function (3d ed. 1993), Standards 4-3.8(a & b), 4-5.1(a & b), 4-5.2(a & b), 4-6.2(a & b) and Relating to Pleas of Guilty (2d ed 1980 and Supp. 1986), Standard 14-3.2.

ALI-ABA Committee on Continuing Professional Education, *A Practical Guide to Achieving Excellence in the Practice of Law: Standards, Methods, and Self-Evaluation*, Standards 2.2(b), 3.1(d), 3.2(a) (1992).

American Law Institute, Restatement of the Law, *The Law Governing Lawyers* (Tent. Draft No. 5) Ch. 2 ("The Client-Lawyer Relationship" § 31 and 33) (1992).

Anthony G. Amsterdam, *Trial 5 Manual for the Defense of Criminal Cases*, (1988).

David A. Binder, Paul Bergman and Susan C. Price, *Lawyers as Counselors: A Client Centered Approach*, (West 1991).

James E. Bond, *Plea Bargaining and Guilty Pleas*, (Clark Boardman 1983).

John M. Burkhoff, *Criminal Defense Ethics: Law and Liability*, (Clark Boardman, 1988).

Monroe H. Freedman, *Understanding Lawyers' Ethics*, (Matthew Bender 1990).

Geoffrey C. Hazard, Jr. and William W. Hodes, *The Law of Lawyering: A Handbook on the Model Rules of Professional Conduct* (Prentice-Hall Law and Business 1990).

Richard Klein, *Legal Malpractice, Professional Discipline, and Representation of the Indigent Defendant*, 61 Temple L. Rev. 1171 (1988).

Judith L. Maute, *Allocation of Decisionmaking Authority Under the Model Rules of Professional Conduct*, 17 U.C. Davis L. Rev. 1049, 1095–1105 (1984).

Charles W. Wolfram, *Modern Legal Ethics*, (West 1986).

Lawyers Manual on Professional Conduct ABA/BNA § 31:301 (Scope of the Relationship) and § 31:501 (Communication).

Cases

Brookhart v. Janis, 384 U.S. 1, 86 S. Ct. 1245, 16 L. Ed.2d 314 (1966).

Commonwealth v. Copeland, 554 A.2d 54 (Pa. Super. 1988), *appeal denied*, 565 A.2d 1165 (Pa. 1989).

Florida Bar v. Murray, 489 So.2d 30 (Fla. 1986).

Hill v. Lockhart, 474 U.S. 52, 106 S. Ct. 366, 88 L. Ed.2d 203 (1985).

Jones v. Barnes, 463 U.S. 745, 103 S. Ct. 3308, 77 L. Ed.2d 987 (1983).

Krahn v. Kinney, 538 N.E.2d 1058 (Ohio 1989).

Lyles v. State, 382 N.E.2d 991 (Ind. Ct. App. 1978).

People v. Alexander, 518 N.Y.S.2d 872 (N.Y. Sup. 1987).

People v. Williams, 429 N.W.2d 649 (Mich. App. 1988).

State v. James, 739 P.2d 1161 (Wash. App. 1987).

State v. Ludwig, 369 N.W.2d 722 (Wis. 1985).

Strickland v. Washington, 466 U.S. 668, 104 S. Ct. 2052, 80 L. Ed.2d 674 (1984).

United States ex. rel. Caruso v. Zelinsky, 689 F.2d 435 (3d Cir 1981), *aff'd*, 515 F. Supp. 676 (D.N.J. 1982).

Williams v. Arn, 654 F. Supp. 226 (N.D. Ohio 1986), *appeal dismissed*, 856 F.2d 197 (6th Cir. 1988), *cert. denied*, 488 U.S. 1044 (1989).

Ex parte Wilson, 724, S.W.2d (Tex. Cr. App. 1987).

Annotations

Debra T. Landis, Annotation, *Negligence, Inattention, or Professional Incompetence of Attorney in Handling Client's Affairs in Criminal Matters as Ground for Disciplinary Action—Modern Cases*, 69 A.L.R. 4th 410 (1989).

Debra T. Landis, Annotation, *Conduct of Attorney in Connection with Settlement of Client's Case as Ground for Disciplinary Action*, 92 A.L.R. 3d 288 (1979).

Gregory G. Sarno, Annotation, *Legal Malpractice in Defense of Criminal Prosecution*, 4 A.L.R. 5th 273 (1992).

Gregory G. Sarno, Annotation, *Adequacy of Defense Counsel's Representation of Criminal Client Regarding Plea Bargaining*, 8 A.L.R. 4th 660 (1981).

Gregory G. Sarno, Annotation, *Adequacy of Defense Counsel's Representation of Criminal Client Regarding Guilty Pleas*, 10 A.L.R. 4th 8 (1981).

CHAPTER 📖 8

Who Decides: Decision Making in Juvenile Delinquency Proceedings

Wallace J. Mlyniec

When, if ever, is it appropriate in a juvenile delinquency proceeding for a lawyer to ignore a judgment or decision made by a child client and substitute her own judgment or that of the child's parent?

Although twenty-seven years have passed since the Supreme Court decided the case of *In re Gault*, 387 U.S. 1 (1967), controversy concerning a child's right to counsel in juvenile delinquency cases still exists. While the Court explicitly held in *Gault* that children are entitled to the assistance of counsel whenever they are charged in a juvenile court with committing criminal acts, it did not define the precise role that the defense lawyer should play, nor did it consider the other issues that emanate from an entitlement to that right.

Prior to the *Gault* decision, defense counsel rarely appeared in juvenile court. From its establishment in 1899 in Illinois until the due process revolution of the late 1960s and 1970s, juvenile court operated in an informal manner. Cases were presented to the court by police officers and probation officers rather than by government lawyers. Witnesses were seldom compelled and common law evidentiary rules were inapplicable.

The philosophy of the court was rooted in the principles of *paren patriae* and rehabilitation of the child rather than in the principles of free will and punishment. Judges saw themselves not so much as enforcers of societal retribution and imposers of legislatively prescribed punishments, but rather as participants in the great social experiments, begun in the late nineteenth century, which posited that wayward children, no matter what their transgressions, were essentially good and ultimately rehabilitable if placed in appropriate surroundings and given appropriate care. The officials of this court possessed virtually unchecked power and were compared by Roscoe Pound to the denizens of the English Star Chamber. Because court procedures were informal and considered to be nonadversarial, there was no need for prosecutors or defense lawyers, who were seen as disruptive and overly concerned with legal niceties rather than with the rehabilitation of children. In such a court, hidden from view and devoid of democratic principles, abuses were bound to, and did, occur.

The growing number of abuses in juvenile courts was finally checked by the due process revolution. In 1966, in *Kent v. United States,* 383 U.S. 541 (1966), and then more clearly and with greater scope in 1967 in *In re Gault,* the Supreme Court began the redefinition of the juvenile court.[1] In doing so, the Court created a conflict with the juvenile court's traditional processes and philosophy that continues until today.

In re Gault brought the due process clause and the liberties embodied in the Bill of Rights into the juvenile court. The rights to notice of charges, to counsel at the adjudication hearing, to the confrontation and cross-examination of witnesses, and the privilege against self-incrimination all were accorded to children by virtue of the *Gault* decision. Soon, every state began to revise its juvenile court code. Within a very short time, state legislatures accorded many additional rights associated with adult criminal procedures to children facing delinquency charges.[2]

It was the right to counsel, however, that produced the greatest impact. While the Supreme Court made clear that "the guiding hand of counsel [is necessary] at every step in the proceedings against [a child]," 387 U.S. at 36, it did not clarify the role that counsel was to play when participating in juvenile court delinquency proceedings. In the absence of a clear statement, commentators have attempted to accommodate the traditional *parens patriae* philosophy of the juvenile court with the developing adversary nature of the proceedings.[3] Since the *Gault* decision, three models concerning the role of counsel have emerged. *See generally,* IJA/ABA *Juvenile Justice Standards, Standards Related To Counsel For Private Parties* (hereinafter IJA/ABA).

The first model assumes that the role of counsel contemplated by *Gault* is that of an advocate and is no different than that contemplated by the Supreme Court in *Gideon v. Wainwright,* 372 U.S. 335 (1963). Some lawyers have abandoned the traditional advocate model and have replaced it with a guardianship theory of representation. In adopting this second model of representation, a lawyer is concerned with developing a program designed to achieve the best interest of the child irrespective of the child client's stated preference.[4] A third model urges an *amicus curiae* function. In serving as an *amicus*, counsel explains the court process to the child and acts as a intermediary among the participants.[5]

In serving as counsel under the advocacy model, a lawyer assumes that delinquency proceedings are adversarial and develops a traditional lawyer-client relationship, where the client rather than the lawyer directs the course of the litigation and makes the significant decisions concerning the case. In contrast, lawyers operating in accordance with the *guardian ad litem* or *amicus curiae* models, place a greater emphasis on the duty of the lawyer to make significant decisions for the child during the pendency of the case. Indeed, the *guardian ad litem* model permits a lawyer, in some circumstances, to usurp the traditional prerogatives of the client and interpose her own decisions against the wishes of the child.

Attacks on the Advocacy Model

Although a large number of defense lawyers have adopted the advocacy model in delinquency cases, the controversy over the role of the lawyer continues. Commentators continue to question the model. Authors as influential as Bruce Hafen[6] and the trio of Goldstein, Freud, and Solnit[7] have maintained that the Supreme Court did not intend to establish in *Gault* a traditional lawyer-client relationship in delinquency cases or that the model is harmful to children. Moreover, they believe that those who choose to adopt the advocacy model ignore both the importance of parents and other adults in the lives and decision-making processes of children, and disregard the legal rights and duties possessed by parents with respect to their children.

The change in personnel and philosophy of the Supreme Court during the last twenty years has further complicated the issue. While *Gault* and the cases that followed it seemed to suggest that the Supreme Court intended to "criminalize" the delinquency proceedings by granting to children procedural rights that are available to adult defendants, that process came to a halt in the case of *Schall v. Martin*, 467 U.S. 253 (1984). *Schall* did not involve the right to counsel, but the opinion has some impact on the advocacy model of representation.[8] Chief Justice Rehnquist's opinion concerning pretrial detention was premised, in part, on the theory that children were always in "some form of custody." *Id.* at 265. The resurrection of the old notion that children possess only limited autonomy when appearing in the juvenile court can be used by opponents of the advocacy model to support the argument that the Supreme Court has never viewed children as legally competent persons. If a child is not considered autonomous and legally competent, other people, usually parents but also other adults acting in the child's interest, may make decisions for the child client even in delinquency cases.

American society has generally accepted the notion that young children do not have the ability to make their own decisions or to care for themselves. As a cultural custom, society has assigned the primary responsibility for the care of children to their parents. The law has recognized these cultural mores as well. For example, children live under certain legal disabilities. Prior to the age of majority, children are not generally permitted to make decisions regarding their own lives. Children may not marry, drive automobiles, use alcohol or tobacco, control pornography, indulge in sexual activity, consent to medical treatment, enter into contracts, work, choose their place of residence, or indulge in other activities normally accorded to adults without legislative or parental permission. Further, unlike adults, they are required to attend school, obey their parents, and maintain curfews.

In the context of civil litigation, children are not permitted to initiate or to defend lawsuits in their own names. Historically, children sued through their next friend and were defended by a *guardian ad litem*. During the course of a lawsuit, the children do not make decisions affecting the case. The legal representative retains a lawyer, binds them with respect to procedural steps in the litigation, makes arrangements that facilitate the disposition of the case, and may, with the approval of the court, make settlements and waive substantial rights. Horowitz and Davidson, *Legal Rights of Children*, §3.03, (1984). If *Gault* intended to create a traditional lawyer-client relationship between the child and the defense lawyer, it was a major break with the law regarding the legal status of children. In no other legal arena has a child been accorded the autonomy to control the litigation of his or her own case.

Medical and psychological theories concerning child development also seem to undercut the advocacy model.[9] The ability of young children to make decisions and plan for their future is, of course, different from that of adolescents. The law has recognized this difference as well. The age of majority at which children are permitted to make decisions varies from right to right. Legislators have assumed that the exercise of some rights, such as voting, requires greater maturity than others, such as driving, and have accorded the right at a later age. Even constitutional rights such as the right to consent to an abortion are determined by a court on a case-by-case basis in accordance with the "mature minor" doctrine. Some nonconstitutional rights, such as the right to live independently or to obtain medical treatment, are determined in a similar manner. While the standard for maturity purports to be legal in nature, it takes into consideration those factors normally recognized by experts in the field of child development.[10] Thus, even in these situations, the right to make decisions is much more circumscribed than the right to make decisions under the advocacy model of the lawyer-client relationship.

Notwithstanding these legal and developmental objections to the advocacy model, it is safe to say that the major standards-setting groups in America, e.g., the American Bar Association[11] and the National Advocacy Committee on Juvenile Justice,[12] and a large number of defense lawyers subscribe to this role definition. Further, the various codes of professional responsibility appear to permit it.

To determine whether the advocacy model withstands attacks made upon it, one must consider the child client in relation to the state, to his or her lawyer, and to his or her parent. When considering the child in relation to the lawyer, the answer may vary if the child is mentally incompetent rather than competent. When considering the child in relation to his parents, one must understand the differences that may arise in the relationship if the lawyer has been retained by the parent or if the lawyer has been appointed by the state. Finally, one must consider not only Supreme Court decisions from *Kent* to *Schall*, but also the law related to the representation of legally incompetent persons and medical theories about development and maturity of children.

The Child in Relation to the State

In the pre-*Gault* juvenile court, the state through its judges and its probation officers made decisions for children. Because children were incompetent as a matter of law, and because the court was created as a social agency controlled by the concepts of *parens patriae* and rehabilitation, making decisions for children seemed natural and was the common practice of the court. Moreover, the informality of the system eliminated the number of decisions that children had to make. Waivers of legal rights were unnecessary because there were none to waive. Furthermore, since the state presumed the inability of parents to exercise control of their children when it acquired jurisdiction over children, it again seemed natural for state officials to assume the power that the parents possessed to make legal decisions for children.

Gault dramatically altered the power of the state with respect to children appearing before the juvenile court in delinquency cases.

While juvenile court judges retained the power after *Gault* to impose rehabilitative or punitive sanctions for the commission of a crime, the Supreme Court withdrew from judges and probation officers all power to make personal litigation decisions for children during the course of the proceedings prior to an adjudication of guilt.[13] Judges could no longer dispense with formal notice of charges. Neither judges nor police officers were permitted to question the child in a manner normally reserved for parents. Neither judges nor probation officers were permitted to acknowledge guilt on behalf of children, nor to waive any of the constitutional rights that *Gault* and later cases accorded to children. While the *Gault* court did not specifically delineate the responsibilities of lawyers representing child clients in these situations, it made clear that the control of a child's rights and litigation decisions are not the province of the state. *Gault*, 387 U.S. at 36. While *Shall v. Martin* may have restricted the autonomy of the child client by noting that he or she is always in some form of custody, it did not alter the pronouncement in *Gault* that there was no identity of interest between the state and the children brought before the court. *Schall* permitted juvenile court judges to rule on procedural issues and assert authority over the child in a manner greater than the way a court could assert its authority over adults accused of crimes.[14] It did not, however, eliminate the requirement of due process of law, nor did it suggest a retreat from the basic principle that judges were adjudicators in a contest between the state acting primarily in its interest and the child acting primarily in his or her interest. Protestations by judges or probation officers that a course of conduct is contrary to a child's best interest cannot override a decision made by a child client and counsel to pursue that course of conduct. While lawyers may feel uncomfortable pursuing such a course in the face of official disapproval, counsel must be steadfast and sure in the knowledge that the law requires no less.

The Child in Relation to the Lawyer

When one looks for guidance to implement the advocacy model of child representation, one must look to the Model Rules of Professional Conduct (hereinafter MR) or the Code of Professional Responsibility (hereinafter CPR), which describe the relationship between the lawyer and the adult client. MR 1.2 (a) states that

> a lawyer should abide by a client's decisions concerning the objectives of representation, . . . and shall consult with a client as to the means by which they are to be pursued. A lawyer should abide by a client's decision whether to accept an offer of settlement of a

matter. In a criminal case, the lawyer shall abide by the client's decision after consultation with the lawyer as to a plea to be entered, whether to waive a jury trial, and whether the client will testify.

Comments to this ethical rule and to MR 1.3 concerning a lawyer's diligence indicate that the duty of a lawyer, both to the client and to the legal system, is to represent the client zealously within the bounds of the law. A lawyer has a duty to pursue matters on behalf of a client with commitment and dedication. Finally, the client has the ultimate authority to determine the purposes to be served by legal representation within the limits imposed by the law and the lawyer's professional obligations.

The admonitions of the CPR Disciplinary Rules (hereinafter DR) are no different. DR 7-101 states that "a lawyer shall not intentionally fail to seek the lawful objectives of his client through reasonably available means permitted by law." The Ethical Considerations (hereinafter EC) expand upon the disciplinary rules. EC 7-1 states that the duty of a lawyer both to his client and to the legal system is to represent the client zealously. EC 7-7 cautions that the authority to make decisions is exclusively that of the client and, if made within the framework of the law, such decisions are binding on the lawyer. While "a defense lawyer in a criminal case has the duty to advise a client fully on whether a particular plea or charge appears to be desirable and as to the prospect of success on appeal, . . . it is for the client to decide what plea should be entered and whether an appeal should be taken." *Id.* These rules and ethical considerations make clear beyond any doubt that a lawyer owes to an adult client loyalty, diligence, zealous representation, and respect for the client's decisions in matters pertaining to the case. The lawyer is merely the agent, albeit a skilled one, for a person engaging in the legal process. Once the lawyer undertakes representation of an adult client, the duties are clear.

If the lawyer assumes that *Gault* eliminated legal incompetency because of age in the context of juvenile delinquency proceedings, fulfilling the advocacy model of representation is not difficult. The child must be represented zealously at each stage of the proceeding. He or she must be advised of potential decisions and the ramifications resulting from those decisions. Once the child client has been so informed, he or she makes the decision. It does not matter whether the lawyer endorses the choice or not. While the lawyer is entitled, by virtue of various ethical rules and the norms of good practice, to render advice concerning her reluctance to pursue tactics or goals chosen by the child client, the lawyer must pursue the goals and tactics once the decision is made. If the lawyer cannot do so, she must seek to withdraw rather than substitute judgment.

While it remains arguable that *Gault* did not eliminate legal incompetency based on age in juvenile delinquency proceedings, lawyers who reject the adversary model do not possess the right to substitute their own judgment for that of the child client. Ethical codes generally prohibit lawyers from making substantive decisions for clients in the absence of a clear *guardian ad litem* relationship.

MR 1.14 recognizes that not all clients will be comprehending and responsible. Moreover, the comment to this rule recognizes that from time to time lawyers will have clients who are children. When they do, MR 1.14 guides the lawyers action. The rule states that

> when a client's ability to make adequately considered decisions in connection with representation is impaired . . . because of minority . . . the lawyer shall as far as reasonably possible maintain a normal client relationship with the client. A lawyer may seek an appointment of a *guardian ad litem* or take other protective action with respect to a client only when the lawyer reasonably believes that the client can not adequately act in the client's own interest.

The comments to the rule do not resolve whether *Gault* eliminated age as a factor in legal incompetence. While the comments recognize that incapacitated persons may not have the power to make legally binding decisions, they also recognize that clients lacking legal competence often have the ability to understand, deliberate upon, and reach conclusions about a matter affecting their own well-being. Further, the comments state that lawyers should seek the appointment of a *guardian ad litem* when it is necessary to serve the client's best interest. When to seek such appointments is left to the professional judgment of the lawyer. Neither MR 1.14 nor the comments suggest that the lawyer possesses the authority to substitute her own judgment for the child client.

The Code of Professional Responsibility resolves this issue in a similar fashion. EC 7-11 suggests that the responsibilities of a lawyer may vary according to the intelligence, experience, mental condition, or age of a client. EC 7-12 indicates that when clients under legal disabilities have no legal representative, the lawyer may be compelled to make decisions on behalf of the client. On the other hand, when the client is capable of understanding the matter in question or of contributing to the advancement of his interest the lawyer must obtain all possible aid from the client. The Ethical Considerations caution, however, that a lawyer may not perform any act or make any decision that the law requires the client to perform.

The CPR was developed shortly after the *Gault* decision. The drafters did not have much experience with the newly regulated juvenile court when promulgating the code. The Model Rules, which are newer than the CPR, seem to recognize a greater range of authority for incompetent clients than does the code. By the time the Model Rules were written, the drafters had the benefit of twenty years of experience with the due process model. Nonetheless, both recognize that clients who are legally incompetent by virtue of age may possess the ability to assist a lawyer and to make decisions in their own right.

The drafters of the Model Rules also had the benefit of the Juvenile Justice Standards drafted under the auspices of the Institute of Judicial Administration and the American Bar Association. In its *Standards Relating to Counsel for Private Parties,* the IJA/ABA drafters recognized that adult clients are not necessarily required to possess wisdom when weighing the immediate and remote benefits associated with available options. Ordinarily, it is sufficient that adult clients understand the nature and purposes of the proceedings and the general consequences of actions when formulating their desires concerning the legal proceedings. IJA/ABA at 8. The drafters recognized that most adolescents confront decision making comparably and that more should not be required of them. *Id.* The drafters suggest that because of the client's youth and inexperience, lawyers must make special efforts to explain the nature and potential results of an action to a child client. Nonetheless, the need to make special efforts do not justify a lawyer's abandoning the advocacy role in the juvenile court. While the drafters recognized that occasions for abandoning that role may occur in rare instances, the opportunities to do so may not properly be extended through manipulation of the general standard for competence. *Id.*

Thus, the ethical rules seem to suggest that a lawyer must remain an advocate for the choices of even a legally incompetent client unless he is also appointed as a *guardian ad litem*. In circumstances where the lawyer believes that the child is legally incompetent by virtue of age and special efforts do not enable the child client to make a decision, the lawyer is required to petition the court for the appointment of a *guardian ad litem.*

The CPR, the Model Rules, and the IJA/ABA Standards all suggest that while lawyers may make some minor decisions in the course of representing incompetent people, they are not permitted to make those decisions that ordinarily the client is expected to make. If the client is incapable of making a significant decision normally entrusted to the client, a *guardian ad litem* must be appointed. Lawyers who believe that *Gault* left intact legal incompetence based on age and who make decisions themselves rather than seek guidance from the child client or seek the appointment of a *guardian ad litem*, appear to be violating the ethical rules of the profession unless the lawyer's appointment includes the authority to act as a *guardian ad litem*. On the other hand, lawyers who believe that *Gault* eliminated the doctrine of legal incapacity based on age in delinquency cases find authority within the codes and from the commentators to continue representing the child as if he or she were an adult. In those instances where such representation is impossible because the child's maturity level is such that the client cannot make reasonable decisions after considering the available options, the lawyer must request the appointment of a *guardian ad litem*.

The Child in Relation to the Parent

Common sense, if not the law, suggests that parents have a role to play in juvenile delinquency cases. *Gault* seems to recognize this. Throughout the opinion, the Supreme Court referred to the requirement of then existing state statutes and model acts that both parents and children be notified of the right to counsel. In fact, the Supreme Court in *Gault* required that children *and* parents be notified of the right to counsel.[15] When children have been declared incompetent by the court, parents are presumed to be the child's guardian for all legal proceedings. Further, when a lawyer becomes concerned that the child may not be competent to understand the proceedings, MR 1.14, EC 7-12, and the IJA/ABA Standards all require that the lawyer seek the appointment of a *guardian ad litem* who will in most cases be a parent. Even in the absence of an incompetency determination, parents have a major role to play in their child's decision making. Lawyers must be sensitive to the concerns of parents. That sensitivity, however, must not be subordinated to the lawyer's loyalty to the client.

When lawyers follow the advocacy model of the lawyer-client relationship and presume that the child is competent to give guidance during the course of the juvenile delinquency proceeding, conflict with parents may arise. As a practical matter, most parents can be expected to be concerned about their child's legal rights and social needs. Since most parents make major decisions in their child's life, they may be surprised and resentful at the lawyer's attempts to exclude them from the lawyer-client relationship. They may also seek to exercise client control over the lawyer's actions. Moreover, lawyers who are retained by parents may find that this situation is exacerbated by the parents' financial commitment. Finally, some states have enacted statutes establishing parental liability for a child's willful and malicious acts or for restitution for damages resulting from the commission of a crime. When parents have a real financial interest in the outcome of their child's case, they may assume that the lawyer must either represent them as well as the child, or in representing the child, be sensitive to their financial exposure.

Lawyers following the advocacy model have both good reason and ethical justification for excluding parents from the decision-making process. Few states have created a parent/child privilege.[16] In most states, parents may be subpoenaed and forced to testify against a child who has divulged damaging information to them. Lawyers must explain to parents that ill will is not the reason that they are being excluded from conversations between the lawyer and the child concerning alleged criminal acts. There is a very real danger, especially if the crimes charged are serious, that the prosecuting authority will use the power of the subpoena to compel a parent to testify against his or her child. Additionally, children are often more fearful of parental authority than judicial authority or are too embarrassed to provide an accurate account of the events in the presence of their parents. A lawyer seeking complete information concerning the events that precipitated an arrest will often obtain more and more accurate information if the parents are not included in the conversation.

Several ethical rules protect a lawyer who seeks to minimize parental involvement. MR 1. 6 concerning confidentiality of information as well as DR 4-101 and the ethical considerations concerning Canon Four of the CPR require that the lawyer preserve a client's confidences.

The rules also protect counsel when parents compensate the lawyer for the child client's representation. Such compensation does not diminish the lawyer's obligations to the client. MR 1. 8 states that a client must consent to an arrangement whereby a lawyer receives compensation from a third party. Even when the parent-child relationship make such consent impractical, MR 1. 8 dictates that there be no interference with the lawyer's independence or professional judgment or with the lawyer client-relationship. It also provides that information relating to representation of the client must remain protected. The CPR is no different. DR 5-107 forbids the acceptance of compensation for legal services from someone other than the client without the client's consent. EC 5-1 cautions the lawyer not to dilute her loyalty to the client based on the desires of third persons. Finally, EC 5-21 specifically advises the lawyer to disregard the desires of others that might impair free judgment and cautions the lawyer to be aware of even subtle influences.

Parents in states where financial exposure is possible and who seek to avoid such liability may have interests that are in substantial conflict with the interests of the child client. MR 1.7 forbids a lawyer from representing two people who take adverse positions in the same actions. DR 5-105 contains similar provisions. If a lawyer is appointed by the court, clearly his duty is to the client. There is no professional relationship created with the parents when representation of the child is undertaken by virtue of the court appointment. The lawyer is prohibited from considering the interests of the parents who face statutory liability for their children's acts under parental liability statutes. The same is true in cases where the parent retains the lawyer for the child. The lawyer does not represent the parent. If the parent seeks to engage the lawyer in a lawyer-client relationship for him or herself as well as for the child in states where parental liability statutes may create a conflict, the ethical codes preclude the lawyer from accepting such employment since the interest of the parent and the child will be adverse.

Conclusion

There is no question that the cases from *Gault* to *Schall*, when read in the context of the common law rights and duties of parents and the scientific literature regarding child development, have created uncertainty concerning the role of the lawyer in juvenile delinquency proceedings. Although the juvenile court is "fundamentally different," *Schall v. Martin*, 467 U.S. at 263, than the adult criminal court, the differences are not so pronounced that the child client is without the autonomy to make decisions regarding the course of his or her representation. Support for such power can be found in the cases, as well as in the ethical codes and the standards established for the practice of law in these courts. While parents may reserve some rights to control the decision making, clearly neither the lawyer nor state officials may substitute their will for that of the child. The extent of the parents' authority remains to be clarified. Even if parents retain some authority, it must be restricted when the potential for financial or other conflict exists between the child and the parent.

Notes

1. The cases redefining the court are: Kent v. United States, 383 U.S. 541 (1966) (applying constitutional principles to the District of Columbia procedures for waiving juvenile court jurisdiction); In re Gault, 387 U.S. 1 (1967) (applying the due process clause to state juvenile delinquency proceeding); *In re* Winship, 397 U.S. 358 (1970); (requiring proof beyond a reasonable doubt in

juvenile delinquency cases); McKeiver v. Pennsylvania, 403 U.S. 528 (1971); (refusing to require jury trials or public trials in juvenile delinquency cases); Breed v. Jones, 421 U.S. 519 (1975) (applying the double jeopardy clause to juvenile delinquency proceedings); Fare v. Michael C., 442 U.S. 707 (1979) (applying *Miranda* principles to confessions in juvenile delinquency proceedings); Schall v. Martin, 467 U.S. 253 (1984) (permitting preventive detention in the juvenile court).

2. Child welfare cases have also been redefined as a result of Supreme Court cases. *See, e.g.,* Stanley v. Illinois, 405 U.S. 645 (1972) (requiring notice to fathers in neglect cases); Lehr v. Robertson, 463 U.S. 248 (1983) (establishing the rights of noncustodial fathers); Lassiter v. Department of Social Services, 452 U.S. 18 (1981) (establishing the right to counsel in some termination of parental rights cases).

3. *See* Bibliography, *infra.*

4. This model is most often used and often required in child welfare cases.

5. It is difficult to understand how this model can be justified in delinquency cases. While it may work properly in contested divorce cases, neither *Gault* nor the state statutes granting the right to counsel could possibly contemplate such a passive role. The Model Rules and Code of Professional Responsibility probably do not permit it.

6. Bruce R. Hafen, Book Review, 100 HARV. L. REV. 435 (1986) reviewing ROBERT H. MNOOKIN, ET AL., EXPLORING TEST CASES IN CHILD ADVOCACY IN THE INTEREST OF CHILDREN: ADVOCACY, LAW REFORM, AND PUBLIC POLICY.

7. J. GOLDSTEIN, A. FREUD, AND A. SOLNIT, BEFORE THE BEST INTEREST OF THE CHILD (1980).

8. *Schall* concerned a New York statute permitting preventive detention in delinquency cases.

9. The literature about child development is voluminous. For a discussion of child development as it applies to legal advocacy, *see, e.g.,* JACK C. WESTMAN, WHO SPEAKS FOR THE CHILDREN, chap. 3 (1991).

10. The "mature minor" doctrine has been most often discussed in cases involving a child's right to an abortion.

11. INSTITUTE OF JUDICIAL ADMINISTRATION AND AMERICAN BAR ASSOCIATION, JUVENILE JUSTICE STANDARDS, STANDARDS RELATING TO COUNSEL FOR PRIVATE PARTIES (1980).

12. STANDARDS FOR THE ADMINISTRATION OF JUVENILE JUSTICE, REPORT OF THE NATIONAL ADVISORY COMMITTEE FOR JUVENILE JUSTICE AND DELINQUENCY PREVENTION (1980).

13. The *Gault* opinion specifically left unresolved issues surrounding the dispositional phase of delinquency proceedings.

14. The *Schall* court faced the issue of preventive detention for children before it faced the issue in the case of an adult defendant. At the time *Schall* was decided, lower courts had assumed that adults could not generally be preventively detained.

15. *In re* Gault, 387 U.S. at 41. The *Gault* court assumed an identity of interest between Mrs. Gault and her son. As a matter of fact, such an identity of

fact existed. Thus, the *Gault* opinion offers no guidance with respect to the right to counsel when parent and child disagree about specific decisions. Assuming the right belongs to each, each might be entitled to separate counsel.

16. Annotation, *Testimonial Privilege for Confidential Communications Between Relatives Other Than Husband and Wife*, 6 A.L.R. 4th 544 (1993).

Bibliography

Kerin S. Bishchoff, *The Voice of a Child: Independent Legal Representation of Children in Private Custody Disputes when Sexual Abuse is Alleged*, 138 U. PA. L. Rev. 1383 (May 1990).

Donald Bross, "An Introduction to Child Representation," in *Foundations of Child Advocacy* (D. Bross & L. Michaels, eds) (1987).

Howard A. Davidson, *Symposium Issue on Children and the Law: The Child's Right to be Heard and Represented in Judicial Proceedings*, 18 Pepp. L. Rev. 255 (Jan. 1991).

Jinanne S. J. Elder, *The Role of Counsel for Children: A Proposal for Addressing a Troubling Question*, 35 B.B.J. 6 (Feb. 1991).

Barry C. Feld, *The Right to Counsel in Juvenile Court: An Empirical Study of When Lawyers Appear and the Difference They Make*, 79 J. Crim. L. & Criminology (Win. 1989).

Marsha Garrison, *Child Welfare Decisionmaking: In Search of the Least Drastic Alternative*, 75 Geo. L. J. 1745 (Aug. 1987).

Martin Guggenheim, *The Right to Be Represented But Not Heard: Reflections on Legal Representation for Children*, 59 N.Y.U. L. Rev. 76 (Apr. 1984).

Bruce C. Hafen, Book Review, 100 Harv. L. Rev. 435 (Dec. 1986)(of Robert H. Mnookin, *Exploring Test Cases in Child Advocacy in the Interest of Children: Advocacy, Law Reform, and Public Policy* (1985)).

Mark Hardin, *Guardians ad Litem for Child Victims in Criminal Proceedings*, 25 J. Fam. L. 687 (1986-1987).

Juvenile Law—What Ever Happened in In re Gault [87 S. Ct. 1428] and Fundamental Fairness in Juvenile Delinquency Proceedings?—Schall v. Martin [104 S.Ct. 2403], 22 Wake Forest L. Rev. 347 (1987).

Robyn-Marie Lyon, *Speaking for a Child: The Role of Independent Counsel for Minors*, 75 Cal. L. Rev. 681 (Mar. 1987).

Patricia M. Wald, *The Kindness of Strangers*, 97 Yale L. J. 1477 (June 1988) (Book review of J. Goldstein, A. Freud, J. Solnit & M. Goldstein, *In the Best Interests of the Child*).

Jack C. Westman, *Who Speaks for the Children*, chap. 3 (1991).

CHAPTER 📖 9

Who Decides: The Role of Parent or Guardian in Juvenile Delinquency Representation

Janet R. Fink

What is the role, if any, of the parent or guardian of an accused juvenile delinquent in making decisions during the course of legal representation of the juvenile? Is this role affected in any way by the fact that the parent or guardian has retained counsel for an accused juvenile delinquent or is obligated by law or court order to pay for the cost of assigned counsel or public defender services for the juvenile? What, if any, impact do laws or precedents requiring parental involvement in waivers of their child's rights, parental contributions to the costs of placements or other dispositions, or parental participation in counseling or other juvenile dispositional programs have upon counsel's representation of an accused juvenile?

Facing trial in an adult or juvenile court for acts of juvenile delinquency may be a bewildering, even terrifying, experience for a child, an ordeal for which the child is deeply in need of parental support and assistance. The parent thus has an important role to play during the course of a juvenile delinquency proceeding. However, constitutional due process strictures, ethical mandates, and juvenile justice standards all underscore the fact that it is the child, not the parent, who is the client and decision maker. It is the juvenile, not the parent or guardian, who faces a potential loss of liberty at the pretrial detention and dispositional stages of the proceeding. It is the juvenile, therefore, who possesses a fundamental due process right to legal representation, pursuant to the decision of the United State Supreme Court in *In re Gault*, 387 U.S. 1, 36 (1967):

There is no material difference in this respect between adult and juvenile proceedings of the sort here involved. . . . A proceeding where the issue is whether the child will be found "delinquent" and subjected to the loss of his liberty for years is comparable in seriousness to a felony prosecution. The juvenile needs the assistance of counsel to cope with problems of law, to make skilled inquiry into the facts, to insist upon regularity of the proceedings, and to ascertain whether he has a defense and to prepare and submit it. The child requires "the guiding hand of counsel at every step in the proceedings against him."

As both a constitutional and ethical matter, counsel's independence must be a sine qua non of that representation.

Rule 1.14(a) of the American Bar Association's Model Rules of Professional Conduct requires counsel to "maintain a normal client-lawyer relationship" as far as "reasonably possible," regardless of a client's minority. Noting in the Commentary that "a client lacking legal competence often has the ability to understand, deliberate upon, and reach conclusions about matters affecting the client's own well-being," the Model Rules accord the client authority to make key decisions during the course of representation. Under Rule 1.14(b), a lawyer is authorized to seek appointment of a *guardian ad litem* as a substitute decision maker "only when the lawyer reasonably believes that the client cannot adequately act in the client's own interest"—a rare eventuality in the context of juvenile delinquency proceedings, the overwhelming majority of which involve adolescents, rather than young children.

Likewise, assuming the general case where the juvenile is capable of "considered judgment," the Model Code of Professional Responsibility provides that a juvenile client's wishes govern fundamental issues of trial strategy and of the exercise of legal rights. The authority to make key decisions resides exclusively with the client and, if made within the framework of the law, such decisions are binding upon the lawyer. [Ethical Considerations §§ 7-3, 7-7.] While recognizing that the responsibilities of a lawyer vary according to the age or other disability of the client, the Model Code [EC 7-12] provides that, regardless of disability, "[i]f the client is capable of understanding . . . or contributing to the advancement of his interests, . . . the lawyer should obtain from him all possible aid." Where a legally incompetent client is acting through a *guardian ad litem* or other representative, the lawyer must look to the representative for decisions normally made by the client, but where no such representative has been appointed, the lawyer "should consider all circumstances then prevailing and act with care to safeguard and advance the interests of his client." [Ethical Considerations §§ 7-11, 7-12.]

In construing these mandates in the juvenile court context, the American Bar Association has declared that a lawyer for a juvenile owes "a primary duty of loyalty to the client, the observance of which is tempered by the lawyer's right to use professional judgment. . . ." The lawyer's duty to seek exoneration of the client through all lawful means was held not to differ in a juvenile delinquency matter from the obligation in representing adults accused of crimes. ABA Committee on Ethics and Professional Responsibility, Informal Op. 1160 (1971).

Standards that have been developed regarding juvenile delinquency cases echo the theme of zealous representation in which the parameters are determined by the juvenile clients themselves to the extent possible. The Juvenile Justice Standards, developed by a joint project of the Institute for Judicial Administration and the American Bar Association and approved by the ABA in 1979, provide that "[h]owever engaged, the lawyer's principal duty is the representation of the client's legitimate interests." The Standards go on to observe:

> Counsel for the respondent in a delinquency or in need of supervision proceeding should ordinarily be bound by the client's definition of his or her interests with respect to admission or denial of the facts or conditions alleged. It is appropriate and desirable for counsel to advise the client concerning the probable success and consequences of adopting any posture with respect to those proceedings.[1]

In those cases where juveniles are not competent to make decisions and where a separate *guardian ad litem* has been appointed, primary decision-making authority rests with the guardian and the juvenile. In any case where a separate guardian has not been appointed, the lawyer must "inquire thoroughly into all circumstances" and opt for the least restrictive alternative for the juvenile or (generally only in child protective proceedings) remain neutral.[2]

The standards established in 1976 by the Task Force on Juvenile Delinquency of the National Advisory Committee on Criminal Justice Standards and Goals similarly stress the primacy and self-determination of the child client. While requiring counsel to advise clients on the consequences of case-related decisions, the "ultimate responsibility for making any decision that determines the client's interests within the bounds of the law remains with the client"; counsel has a duty to "represent zealously a client's legitimate interests under the law."[3] The Standards require the lawyer to request appointment of a separate *guardian ad litem* only if the client is incompetent to understand the ramifications or to make decisions on the case.

Because the child, not the parent or guardian, is the client, it is the child who "has the ultimate authority to make certain fundamental decisions regarding the case, as to whether to plead guilty, waive a jury, testify in his or her own behalf, or take an appeal." *Jones v. Barnes*, 403 U.S. 745, 751 (1983). In the unique context of juvenile delinquency cases, the IJA/ABA Juvenile Justice Standards also afford juveniles authority to make decisions regarding trial in juvenile or adult court, case diversion plans, or particular dispositions. Strategic decisions, such as whether to call particular witnesses, submit motions, or select particular jurors, are deemed appropriate for the lawyer to make after consultation with the client.[4] Prerogatives, such as whether to waive the right to counsel, to plead guilty, to consent to searches of personal property in the child's private areas, or to waive *Miranda* rights, are deemed personal to the child and may not be waived by a parent or other individual.[5] This is particularly true where an adversity of interests may be said to exist between parent and child.[6]

Counsel's independence, loyalty to the juvenile client, and deference to the client's decision-making authority must characterize the representation, regardless of whether the child's parent or guardian has retained the lawyer or is contributing to the legal costs. The Model Code of Professional Responsibility, in Disciplinary Rule § 5-107(B), mandates that counsel must be free of third-party influences, regardless of who pays the fee:

> A lawyer shall not permit a person who recommends, employs or pays him to render legal services for another to direct or regulate his professional judgment in rendering legal services.

Ethical Consideration § 5-1 elaborates further:

> The professional judgment of a lawyer should be exercised, within the bounds of the law, solely for the benefit of his client and free of compromising influences and loyalties. Neither his personal interests, the interests of other clients, nor the desires of third persons should be permitted to dilute his loyalty to his client.

In the same vein, Ethical Consideration § 5-21 provides:

> The obligation of a lawyer to exercise professional judgment solely on behalf of his client requires that he disregard the desires of others that might impair his free judgment.

Standards established by the Hawaii State Law Enforcement and Juvenile Delinquency Planning Agency in 1977 explicitly translate this need for independence into the juvenile delinquency context:

§ 4.1(3). Whenever a juvenile denies an allegation in a law violation case, defense counsel may use any method permissible in a criminal prosecution.

* * *

(b). Counsel's actions shall be unaffected by the wishes of the juvenile's parents or guardian if those differ from the wishes of the juvenile.[7]

To insure the independence of the juvenile's counsel, the IJA/ABA Juvenile Justice Standards caution against requiring parental reimbursement for the costs of court-appointed counsel, regardless of the parents' financial circumstances.[8] Nonetheless, many jurisdictions impose a parental means test before counsel is appointed for a child and courts have found parents financially responsible for assuming the costs of their children's representation. *See, e.g., Matter of Cheri H.,* 121 Misc. 2d 973, 469 N.Y.S.2d 551 (Fam. Ct., Bronx Co. 1983).

Conflicts arising between parent and child are not hypothetical. A parent may retain counsel and instruct counsel not to seek immediate bail or pretrial release to "teach the child a lesson" or because the parent faces eviction from public or other housing if a troublesome child is not placed out of the home. A parent may prefer to have the child placed, rather than be ordered to participate in family counseling or other dispositional plan preferred by the child. A parent may have been involved in other proceedings where an adversity of interests may have existed with the child, e.g., child abuse or neglect or status offense ("in need of supervision") cases. State laws imposing financial liability upon parents for the wrongful acts of their children, as well as restitution laws, inevitably affect parents' perceptions of desired case outcomes. As the Commentary to the IJA/ABA Standards notes: "Parents often resent their children for the trouble, embarrassment and expense brought upon the family by court involvement."[9]

Each of the sets of standards promulgated regarding juvenile delinquency cases provide guidance as to the resolution of such conflicts. Clearly, a lawyer who has represented a child's parent in a proceeding where an identity of interest with the juvenile may not have existed, should not undertake representation of the child in a delinquency matter. The Standards for Administration of Juvenile Justice, issued in 1980 by the National Advisory Committee on Juvenile Justice and Delinquency Prevention, require separate, independent counsel to be appointed in cases where the lawyer had represented the parents in a child protective, custody, or supervision matter; in cases where the parent's contentions might prejudice the juvenile's interests; and "whenever the juvenile's lawyer would have to accommodate the juvenile's interests to those of some third person or institution. . . ." Standard § 3.132 (Commentary). The Juvenile Delinquency Standards of the National Advisory Committee on Criminal Justice Standards and Goals, *supra*, require separate counsel to be appointed for the parent in cases where the parent might be required to participate in a particular dispositional plan. Standard § 16-6. The IJA/ABA Juvenile Justice Standards impose a duty upon the court to assure the independence of counsel:

> If the parent has retained counsel for the juvenile and it appears to the court that the parent's interest in the case conflicts with the juvenile's interest, the court should caution both the parent and counsel as to counsel's duty of loyalty to the juvenile's interests. If the parent's dominant language is not English, the court's caution should be communicated in a language understood by the parent.[10]

Parents and legal guardians play a vital, supportive role for juveniles facing juvenile delinquency proceedings. Children often benefit from the assistance of parents and legal guardians in making the significant decisions affecting the outcomes of their cases and in facing the attendant trauma. In light of the immaturity and lack of sophistication of youth, many jurisdictions, in fact, require parental presence at interrogations and court appearances involving their children, require parents to be notified of their children's rights, and involve the parents in plea allocutions and dispositions. *See, e.g.,* N.Y. Fam. Ct. Act §§ 305.2(7), 320.3, 341.2; *Matter of Kim F.,* 109 A.D.2d 706, 487 N.Y.S.2d 31 (1st Dept. 1985) (plea vacated because of insufficient efforts to procure presence of parent). Barring cases where there is an adversity of interests between parents and children, juvenile delinquency standards also require lawyers to counsel and consult with parents so that they are able to advise their children appropriately.[11]

While involving the parents to the extent possible, counsel must, nonetheless, confer with the juvenile alone. Not only is this essential to establish the child's total trust, but it is advisable in light of the lack of parent-child privilege protecting such communications in many jurisdictions.[12] Significantly, it is arguable, but by no means guaranteed, that communications between a lawyer and child client in the presence of the child's parent would be protected by the lawyer-client privilege. At the same time, if the lawyer confers with the parent alone, the lawyer must advise the parent that it may not always be possible to preserve the parents' secrets. The lawyer should remind the parent that the child, rather than the parent, is the client, regardless of who is paying the fee. Disclosure of the parent's communications "may become necessary to full and effective representation of the client," although to the extent possible, consent of the parent should be obtained prior to disclosure or usage of the parent's statements.[13]

In *Parham v. J.R.*, 442 U.S. 584 (1979), the United States Supreme Court held:

> The law's concept of the family rests on a presumption that parents possess what a child lacks in maturity, experience, and capacity for judgment required for making life's difficult decisions. More importantly, historically it has recognized that natural bonds of affection lead parents to act in the best interests of their children. 442 U.S. at 603 [citing 1 Blackstone, *Commentaries* 447; 2 Kent, *Commentaries on American Law* 190].

Many would question whether this presumption is accurate in the context of parental advice to, or actions on behalf of, their children, particularly in the context of court proceedings. Indeed, studies of children's waiver of their *Miranda* rights in interrogations have demonstrated, respectively, that 80 percent of the parents gave no advice whatsoever to their children to assist them in the preinterrogation process and that "no significant differences [existed] between the legal understanding of parents and their children."[14] Further, an attitudinal study revealed that 75 percent of the parents did not believe that children should possess a right to silence comparable to their own.[15]

Conclusion

Although no one would doubt the appropriateness of involving the parent during the course of representing a juvenile accused of delinquency to the degree that a conflict is not presented, the importance of independent counsel for children can not be over-emphasized. Counsel must never lose sight of the fact that it is the child who is the client; it is the child whose prerogatives bind the lawyer, regardless of who has retained the lawyer or contributed to the fee. In any conflict between parent and child, it is the child to whom the lawyer's loyalty is due.

Notes

1. INSTITUTE FOR JUDICIAL ADMINISTRATION/AMERICAN BAR ASSOCIATION JUVENILE JUSTICE STANDARDS PROJECT ("IJA/ABA JUVENILE JUSTICE STANDARDS"), STANDARDS RELATING TO COUNSEL FOR PRIVATE PARTIES, § 3-1 (approved draft

1979). *See generally* Costello, *Ethical Issues in Representing Juvenile Clients: A Review of the IJA-ABA Standards on Representing Private Parties*, 10 N.M. L. Rev. 255 (1980).

2. *Id.* at § 3.1(c).

3. National Advisory Committee on Criminal Justice Standards and Goals, Report of the Task Force on Juvenile Delinquency, Standards §§ 16.2, 16.3 (1976).

4. IJA/ABA Juvenile Justice Standards, Standards Relating to Counsel for Private Parties, § 5.2.

5. *See, e.g.*, Matter of Cheri H., 121 Misc. 2d 973, 469 N.Y.S.2d 551 (Fam. Ct., Bronx Co. 1983) (waiver of counsel); Matter of Scott K., 24 Cal. 3d 395, 595 P.2d 105, 155 Cal. Rptr. 671 (1979), *cert. denied*, 444 U.S. 973 (1973) (consent to search locked toolbox); State v. Peterson, 525 S.W.2d 599, 608-9 (Mo. App. 1975) (consent to search child's room); People v. Flowers, 23 Mich. App. 523, 527, 179 N.W.2d 56, 58 (1970) (consent to search); Matter of Schaefer, 97 Misc. 2d 487, 411 N.Y.S.2d 977 (Fam. Ct., N.Y. Co. 1978) (waiver of *Miranda* rights); Smith v. State, 484 So. 2d 560, 561 (Ala. Crim. App. 1986) (waiver of *Miranda* rights); *In re* S.W.T., 277 N.W.2d 507, 512–13 (Minn. 1979) (waiver of *Miranda* rights). *But see* United States v. Stone, 401 F.2d 32, 34 (7th Cir. 1968) (allow parental waiver of right to search); Maxwell v. Stephens, 348 F.2d 325, 336–38 (8th Cir. 1965), *cert. denied*, 382 U.S. 944 (1965) (allow parental waiver of right to search). *See generally* Randy Hertz, Martin Guggenheim & Anthony Amsterdam, Juvenile Court Trial Manual, §§ 2-03, 23.18(b) (ALI-ABA 1991).

6. *See, e.g.*, Matter of Michelet P. v. Gold, 70 A.D.2d 68, 419 N.Y.S.2d 704 (2d Dept. 1979) (admission inadmissible as involuntary where victim's son acted as adult to whom police gave notification regarding interrogation of juvenile); In re P.L.V., 490 P.2d 685 (Sup. Ct., Colo. 1971) (parents who suspected child of burglarizing their home could not waive child's *Miranda* rights). *But see* People v. Hayhurst, 571 P.2d 721 (Sup. Ct., Colo. 1977) (while father upset with son, relationship was not so adversarial as to disqualify him from consenting to warrantless search of son's van).

7. Hawaii State Law Enforcement and Juvenile Delinquency Planning Agency, *Hawaii Criminal Justice Standards and Goals: Juvenile Justice,* cited in Healy, *Legal Ethics in Juvenile Matters,* 16 Haw. Bar J. 75, 77 (Summer, 1981).

8. IJA/ABA Juvenile Justice Standards, Standards Relating to Pretrial Court Proceedings, § 5.3A.

9. IJA/ABA Juvenile Justice Standards, Standards Relating to Pretrial Court Proceedings, § 5.3 (Commentary). *See generally* Flicker, Providing Counsel for Accused Juveniles (ABA 1983); Hertz, Guggenheim & Amsterdam, Juvenile Court Trial Manual § 4-04 (ALI-ABA 1991); Robyn-Marie Lyon, *Speaking for a Child: The Role of Independent Counsel for Minors,* 75 Cal. L. Rev. 681, 686 (1987); National Advisory Committee on Criminal Justice Standards and Goals, Report of the Task Force on Juvenile Delinquency, Standard § 16.6 (Commentary) (1976).

10. IJA/ABA J$_{UVENILE}$ J$_{USTICE}$ S$_{TANDARDS}$, S$_{TANDARDS}$ R$_{ELATING}$ $_{TO}$ P$_{RETRIAL}$ C$_{OURT}$ P$_{ROCEEDINGS}$, § 5-3(C). *See also* H$_{ERTZ}$, G$_{UGGENHEIM}$ & A$_{MSTERDAM}$, J$_{UVE-}$ $_{NILE}$ C$_{OURT}$ T$_{RIAL}$ M$_{ANUAL}$, § 4.04 (ALI-ABA 1991). Court intervention was also deemed the appropriate approach in a tort case where a conflict arose as to whether a particular course of action sought by the parent was considered by retained counsel to contravene the interests of the child client. The lawyer was counseled to bring the matter to the court's attention so that the court could determine, *inter alia*, whether withdrawal by the lawyer would be necessary. Association of the Bar of the City of New York, Ethics Opinion 82-18, N. Y. L.J., Oct. 18, 1983, p.5, col. 1.

11. IJA/ABA J$_{UVENILE}$ J$_{USTICE}$ S$_{TANDARDS}$, S$_{TANDARDS}$ R$_{ELATING}$ $_{TO}$ C$_{OUNSEL}$ $_{FOR}$ P$_{RIVATE}$ P$_{ARTIES}$, § 7.5; S$_{TANDARDS}$ R$_{ELATING}$ $_{TO}$ A$_{DJUDICATION}$, § 3.7; S$_{TAN-}$ $_{DARDS}$ R$_{ELATING}$ $_{TO}$ P$_{RETRIAL}$ C$_{OURT}$ P$_{ROCEEDINGS}$, §§ 6.2, 6.5; N$_{ATIONAL}$ A$_{DVISORY}$ C$_{OMMITTEE}$ $_{FOR}$ J$_{UVENILE}$ J$_{USTICE}$ $_{AND}$ D$_{ELINQUENCY}$ P$_{REVENTION}$, S$_{TANDARDS}$ $_{FOR}$ A$_{DMINISTRATION}$ $_{OF}$ J$_{UVENILE}$ J$_{USTICE}$, § 3.169 (1980).

12. *See, e.g.,* Matter of Mark G., 65 A.D.2d 917, 410 N.Y.S.2d 464,465 (4th Dept. 1978) (child's admission to parent admitted where "not made in confidence and for the purpose of obtaining support, advice or guidance"). *See generally* H$_{ERTZ}$, G$_{UGGENHEIM}$ & A$_{MSTERDAM}$, J$_{UVENILE}$ C$_{OURT}$ T$_{RIAL}$ M$_{ANUAL}$, § 5.03(a) (ALI-ABA 1991).

13. IJA/ABA J$_{UVENILE}$ J$_{USTICE}$ S$_{TANDARDS}$, S$_{TANDARDS}$ R$_{ELATING}$ $_{TO}$ C$_{OUNSEL}$ $_{FOR}$ P$_{RIVATE}$ P$_{ARTIES}$, § 3.3(C).

14. G$_{RISSO}$, J$_{UVENILE'S}$ W$_{AIVER}$ $_{OF}$ R$_{IGHTS}$: L$_{EGAL}$ $_{AND}$ P$_{SYCHOLOGICAL}$ C$_{OMPE-}$ $_{TENCE}$ 190, 193 (Plenum 1981); Lawrence, *The Role of Legal Counsel in Juveniles' Understanding of Their Rights,* J$_{UV}$. & F$_{AM}$. C$_{T}$. J. 49, 54 (Winter 1983–84).

15. Grisso & Ring, *Parents' Attitudes Towards Juveniles' Rights in Interrogation,* 6 C$_{RIM}$. J$_{UST}$. & B$_{EH}$. 221–26 (1979).

Bibliography

Articles, Reports, and Standards

ABA M$_{ODEL}$ R$_{ULES}$ $_{OF}$ P$_{ROFESSIONAL}$ C$_{ONDUCT}$, 1.14(a), (b).

ABA M$_{ODEL}$ C$_{ODE}$ $_{OF}$ P$_{ROFESSIONAL}$ R$_{ESPONSIBILITY}$ EC 5-1, 5-21, 7-3, 7-7, 7-11, 7-12.

ABA M$_{ODEL}$ C$_{ODE}$ $_{OF}$ P$_{ROFESSIONAL}$ R$_{ESPONSIBILITY}$ DR 5-107(B)

ABA Committee on Ethics and Professional Responsibility, Informal Op. 1160 (1971)

Association of the Bar of the City of New York, Ethics Opinion 82-18, N.Y. L. J., Oct. 18, 1983, p.5, col. 1.

Costello, *Ethical Issues in Representing Juvenile Clients: A Review of the IJA-ABA Standards on Representing Private Parties,* 10 N.M. L. Rev. 255 (1980).

Flicker, *Providing Counsel for Accused Juveniles* (ABA 1983).

Grisso, *Juvenile's Waiver of Rights: Legal and Psychological Competence* 190, 193 (Plenum 1981).

Grisso & Ring, *Parents' Attitudes Towards Juveniles' Rights in Interrogation*, 6 Crim. Just. & Beh. 221–26 (1979).

Randy Hertz, Martin Guggenheim & Anthony Amsterdam, *Juvenile Court Trial Manual*, §§ 2.03, 4-04, 5.03(a), 23.18(b) (ALI-ABA 1991).

Hawaii State Law Enforcement and Juvenile Delinquency Planning Agency, Hawaii Criminal Justice Standards and Goals: *Juvenile Justice*, ch. 4 [Counsel] at 85(1977) [cited in Healy, *Legal Ethics in Juvenile Matters*, 16 Haw. Bar J. 75, 77 (Summer, 1981)].

IJA/ABA Juvenile Justice Standards Project, *Standards Relating to Counsel for Private Parties*, §§ 3.1, 3.3(C), 5.2, 7.5.

IJA/ABA Juvenile Justice Standards Project, *Standards Relating to Adjudication*, § 3.7

IJA/ABA Juvenile Justice Standards Project, *Standards Relating to Pretrial Court Proceedings*, §§ 5.3(A),5.3(C), 6.2, 6.5.

National Advisory Committee on Criminal Justice Standards and Goals, *Juvenile Delinquency Standards*, Standard §§ 16.2, 16.3, 16.6 (1976).

National Advisory Committee on Juvenile Justice and Delinquency Prevention, *Standards for Administration of Juvenile Justice*, Standard §§ 3.132, 3.169 (1980).

Lawrence, *The Role of Legal Counsel in Juvenile's Understanding of Their Rights*, Juv. and Fam. Ct. J. 49, 54 (Winter 1983–84).

Robyn-Marie Lyon, *Speaking for a Child: The Role of Independent Counsel for Minors*, 75 Cal. L. Rev. 681, 686 (1987).

Cases and Statutes

In re Gault, 387 U.S. 1, 36 (1967).

Jones v. Barnes, 403 U.S. 745, 751 (1983).

Matter of Cheri H., 121 Misc. 2d 973, 469 N.Y.S.2d 551 (Fam. Ct., Bronx. Co. 1983).

Matter of Kim F., 109 A.D.2d 706, 487 N.Y.S.2d 31 (1st Dept. 1985).

Matter of Mark G., 65 A.D.2d 917, 410 N.Y.S.2d 464,465 (4th Dept. 1978).

Matter of Michelet P. v. Gold, 70 A.D.2d 68, 419 N.Y.S.2d 704 (2d Dept. 1979).

Matter of Schaefer, 97 Misc. 2d 487, 411 N.Y.S.2d 977 (Fam. Ct., N.Y. Co. 1978).

Matter of Scott K., 24 Cal. 3d 395, 595 P.2d 105, 155 Cal. Rptr. 671 (1979), *cert. denied*, 444 U.S. 973 (1973).

Maxwell v. Stephens, 348 F.2d 325, 336–38 (8th Cir. 1965), *cert. denied*, 382 U.S. 944 (1965).

Parham v. J.R., 442 U.S. 584 (1979).

People v. Flowers, 23 Mich. App. 523, 527, 179 N.W.2d 56, 58 (1970).

People v. Hayhurst, 571 P.2d 721 (Sup. Ct., Colo. 1977).

In re P.L.V., 490 P.2d 685 (Sup. Ct., Colo. 1971).

Smith v. State, 484 So. 2d 560, 561 (Ala. Crim. App. 1986).

State v. Peterson, 525 S.W.2d 599, 608–9 (Mo. App. 1975).

In re S.W.T., 277 N.W.2d 507, 512–13 (Minn. 1979).

United States v. Stone, 401 F.2d 32, 34 (7th Cir. 1968).

N.Y. Fam. Ct. Act §§ 305.2(7), 320.3, 341.2.

PART II

Confidentiality and Defense Counsel's Duty to Disclose

For most lawyers, especially those who defend a person accused of a crime, trust between lawyer and client is the cornerstone of a meaningful lawyer-client relationship. Most commentators and practicing lawyers also agree that this relationship as well as counsel's ability to provide effective representation depend on the lawyer's assurances to the client that counsel will not betray the client's confidences. Counsel's obligation to safeguard the confidences and secrets of a client is enshrined in both the Model Code and Model Rules and intertwined with state and federal constitutional protections. Coupled with the duty to provide zealous representation, counsel's duty to preserve a client's confidential communications assures a client that defense counsel will work to advance the client's best interests.

The difficult ethical dilemmas addressed in Part II of this book arise when the criminal defense lawyer is called upon to balance client loyalty and this deeply felt and long-standing obligation to preserve a client's confidences with the lawyer's duties as an officer of the legal system. Thus, the next six chapters examine the extent to which defense counsel's "overarching duty to advocate the defendant's cause"[1] is tempered by counsel's duty to be candid with the court and to avoid assisting a criminal or fraudulent act of the client. As in Part I, the authors in Part II suggest different approaches to the ethical dilemmas presented by this clash of responsibilities. Above all, these six chapters vividly capture the difficult and delicate balancing act that defense counsel faces when struggling with one of these dilemmas.

It is fitting, then, that Chapter 10 by Monroe Freedman leads off the discussion of the complexity of defense counsel's struggle to preserve client confidentiality without violating counsel's duty to the court. For as Terence MacCarthy and Carol Brook note, it was Freedman's oft-cited article "The Three Hardest Questions"[2] that focused attention on the trilemma facing criminal defense lawyers. Freedman's chapter outlines defense counsel's conflicting responsibilities when confronting the problem of a client's intended perjury and reminds lawyers that before attempting to resolve this trilemma the lawyer must "know" with a sufficient degree of certitude that the client will, in fact, commit perjury. Freedman insists that defense counsel who jumps the gun and accuses a client of perjury without a firm factual basis fails to function as the client's champion and advocate as required by ethical and constitutional mandates.

In Chapter 11, MacCarthy and Brook share Freedman's concern that criminal defense lawyers not unduly compromise the constitutional rights of their clients. Nevertheless, as they point out, courts and ethics committees seem increasingly sympathetic to a view—at odds with that championed by Freedman—that a lawyer's obligation to the court outweighs counsel's duty to maintain a client's confidences. And yet, as MacCarthy and Brook sketch out in considerable detail, despite *Nix v. Whiteside*, 475 U.S 157 (1986) and an abundance of legal writing, the criminal defense lawyer facing a perjury problem still lacks a definitive answer to this troublesome problem. MacCarthy and Brook readily admit they offer no definitive answer. Chapter 11 does provide, however, considerable assistance to the lawyer struggling with the elusive perjury question.

In Chapter 12, Richard Wilson looks at another dimension of this same clash of ethical obligations. Wilson explores the conflicted position of a public defender who learns as a result of confidential communications that a client has committed fraud to obtain court-appointed counsel. In Wilson's view, counsel cannot "be loyal to the one duty without being disloyal to the other." Counsel faced with the choice of upholding one duty at the expense of another must look to the specific language of the ethical provision in that jurisdiction as well as other relevant authority before taking the drastic step of revealing a client's fraud. Nonetheless, lawyers in certain jurisdictions—Oregon, Ohio, and other states whose version of DR 7-102(B) does not include the phrase "except when the information is protected as a privileged communication"—may be compelled to reveal client fraud despite the harm such a disclosure may cause to the client. Similarly, lawyers in many Model Rules states will find that the duty of candor to the tribunal appears to trump the duty to protect the client's confidential communications.

Like Wilson, Marilyn Bednarski, William Talley, and Eva Nilsen all begin by stressing the importance of defense counsel's duty to be a loyal, zealous advocate. Client loyalty includes "the responsibility of furthering the defendant's interest to the fullest extent that the law and the applicable standards of professional conduct permit."[3] Yet, in limited situations, counsel's duty of loyalty to the client is superseded by a lawyer's obligation to the judicial system. The rub, of course, is that unless ethical standards clearly command or proscribe certain conduct, a defense lawyer will be particularly reluctant to take action that will be detrimental to a client.

Bednarski, Talley, and Nilsen, therefore, analyze reoccurring situations where defense lawyers must decide whether to disclose information that, if revealed, will be adverse to or harm their client. Not surprisingly, each advises defense lawyers to try to find ways of extricating themselves from their ethical dilemmas without having to betray their clients. Each author acknowledges that these dilemmas force defense counsel to walk an ethical tightrope and to do so without making any misrepresentations to the court. In the end, however, each recognizes, albeit somewhat begrudgingly, especially in Talley's case, that defense counsel may be ethically bound to disclose adverse legal authority, reveal a client's fraud, or disclose a client's true identity. Nevertheless, they remind defense lawyers that the defendant's constitutional rights may override a lawyer's ethical obligations. They urge defenders, therefore, to even consider risking ethical sanctions in certain instances rather than take action that would compromise their clients' rights and best interests.

Notes

1. Strickland v. Washington, 466 U.S. 668, 688 (1984).
2. Monroe H. Freedman, *Professional Responsibility of the Criminal Defense Lawyer: The Three Hardest Questions*, 64 MICH. L. REV. 1469 (1966).
3. ABA STANDARDS FOR CRIMINAL JUSTICE, Standard 4-1.2 (3d ed. 1993).

CHAPTER 📖 10

But Only If You "Know"

Monroe H. Freedman

When does a criminal defense lawyer know that a defendant or defense witness intends to commit or has committed perjury?

For over a quarter of a century, the bar has been trying to resolve the perjury trilemma.[1] The phrase refers to three ethical obligations imposed upon the criminal defense lawyer.

First, to provide effective assistance of counsel, the lawyer is required to seek out all relevant facts.[2] In the words of Edward Bennett Williams, "Any lawyer surprised by facts at trial has failed in the preparation. It's that simple."[3] Accordingly, Williams added, "I demand complete candor and honesty from the client—no holding back."[4]

Second, to assure that clients will not hold back essential facts from their lawyers, and to protect the clients' Fifth and Sixth Amendment rights, the lawyer has a professional responsibility of confidentiality.[5] Trust between lawyer and client is the "cornerstone of the adversary system and effective assistance of counsel,"[6] and fidelity to that trust is "the glory of our profession."[7]

Third, the lawyer is required to be candid with the court, even to the point of betraying the client's confidences by revealing client perjury.[8]

A moment's reflection makes it clear that a lawyer cannot do all three of those things—know everything, keep it in confidence, and reveal it to the court without the client's informed and voluntary consent. To resolve the trilemma, one of the three duties must give way.

The traditional view is that full information and confidentiality are the overriding obligations, both ethically and constitutionally.[9] Thus,

135

the lawyer should know the truth but, despite that knowledge, should not betray the client's confidences and secrets by conveying to the judge and/or the jury that the client intends to commit perjury or that the client has done so. This means that the lawyer may not inform the judge obliquely of "ethical problems," require the client to testify in narrative fashion, or fail to argue the client's testimony to the jury for other than tactical reasons.

Thus, consistent with the lawyer's constitutional and ethical responsibilities, the proper way for the lawyer to deal with foreknowledge of client perjury is as follows.[10] The lawyer may act on the assumption that the client intends to commit perjury only if the lawyer believes this to be so beyond a reasonable doubt. The lawyer must make good faith, ongoing efforts to dissuade the client from committing perjury. The lawyer may seek leave to withdraw, but only if this can be accomplished without either directly or indirectly revealing the client's confidences or secrets or otherwise prejudicing the client's rights. If the lawyer is unable to dissuade the client or to withdraw without prejudicing the client, the lawyer may not assist the client to improve upon the perjury, but must maintain the client's confidences and secrets, examine the client in the ordinary way, and, to the extent tactically desirable, argue the client's testimony to the jury as evidence in the case.[11]

The Model Code of Professional Responsibility, as construed by the ABA Standing Committee on Ethics and Professional Responsibility, is consistent with this position.[12] The committee has held that, under the Model Code, the lawyer is forbidden to reveal knowledge of client perjury gained after the fact, and that the lawyer has discretion to withhold foreknowledge of perjury.[13]

This is consistent with the committee's earlier holding in Formal Opinion 341. There the committee observed that "the conflicting duties to reveal fraud and to preserve confidences have existed side-by-side for some time." Relying upon "tradition . . . backed by substantial policy considerations," Opinion 341 held that confidentiality should prevail. The committee noted that "it is clear that there has long been an accommodation in favor of preserving confidences either through practice or interpretation."[14]

In MR 3.3 of the Model Rules of Professional Conduct, however, the ABA appears to have reversed this long-standing tradition. The lawyer appears to be required to reveal client perjury either before[15] or after the fact.[16] But this appearance is deceptive for a number of reasons.[17] Chief among these is the opening phrase of MR 3.3(a): "A lawyer shall not *knowingly* . . . ."[18] That is, you are required to violate confidentiality by revealing client perjury, but only if you "know" that the client intends to or has committed perjury.

Since 1975, it has been recognized that the knowing standard has been used disingenuously in ethics rules and opinions to permit the bar to have it both ways—both to publish strict rules on difficult ethical issues and to allow those rules to be ignored in practice.[19] It is fair to infer, therefore, that the drafters of the Model Rules were well aware of what they were doing in using the knowing standard in MR 3.3. This inference has been confirmed by the subsequent history of official and unofficial interpretations of the rule (discussed below).

The apparent obligation to disclose client perjury was taken at face value in *Nix v. Whiteside*,[20] where Chief Justice Warren Burger said in dictum that MR 3.3 imposes a duty upon the lawyer to disclose client perjury "even if disclosure compromises client confidences."[21] Within weeks of the decision in *Nix*, the American Bar Association, with the American Law Institute, produced a videotape on which several experts on the ethics of criminal defense lawyers commented on the case and on MR 3.3. The ABA/ALI commentators make it clear that the trial lawyer's conduct approved by the majority in *Nix* represented a radical departure from traditional, standard practice.

Defense counsel in *Nix* is described as having gone "bonkers" in concluding that his client was going to commit perjury and in his "brutal" reaction. Further, the notion that a criminal defense lawyer might be required to divulge his client's perjury is characterized as "startling," "unworkable," and out-of-touch with the dynamics of the lawyer-client relationship. With regard to the "knowing" standard, one commentator on the ABA/ALI videotape says that a lawyer has an obligation to reveal client perjury only if the lawyer has "absolutely no doubt whatsoever" that the client will commit a "serious" fraud on the court. (The perjury in *Nix* is defined as falling short of "serious" fraud.)[22]

Also, soon after *Nix*, the deputy attorney general who won the case was quoted in the *ABA Journal* as saying that if the lawyer does not "know for sure" that a witness's evidence is false, the lawyer should put the evidence on.[23] In the same article a former prosecutor said that a client may stick to a story that "you know in your heart of hearts is false." As long as the client "never admits that it is false," however, most lawyers "suspend judgment and do the best they can." He added that any different standard of "knowing" would be "at war with the duty to represent the client zealously."[24] Similarly, ABA Formal Opinion 87-353 insists that it is only the "unusual case" where the lawyer does "know." The Opinion requires that knowing be established by the client's "clearly stated intention" that he will commit perjury at trial—and this surely will be the "unusual case."

Courts, too, have insisted upon stringent standards of "knowing" before lawyers have an obligation to reveal client perjury. The majority in *Nix* posits that the case involved "an intent to commit perjury, communicated to counsel,"[25] and says that its decision relates to the case of a client's "announced plans" to commit the crime.[26] Justice Blackmun notes that "[e]xcept in the rarest of cases, lawyers who adopt 'the role of the judge or jury to determine the facts,' pose a danger of depriving their clients of the zealous and loyal advocacy required by the Sixth Amendment."[27]

Justice Stevens elaborates on this theme:[28]

> Justice Holmes taught us that a word is but the skin of a living thought. A "fact" may also have a life of its own. From the perspective of an appellate judge, after a case has been tried and the evidence has been sifted by another judge, a particular fact may be as clear and certain as a piece of crystal or a small diamond. A trial lawyer, however, must often deal with mixtures of sand and clay. Even a pebble that seems clear enough at first glance may take on a different hue in a handful of gravel.
>
> * * *
>
> . . . [B]eneath the surface of this case there are areas of uncertainty that cannot be resolved today. A lawyer's certainty that a change in his client's recollection is a harbinger of intended perjury—as well as judicial review of such apparent certainty—should be tempered by the realization that, after reflection, the most honest witness may recall (or sincerely believe he recalls) details that he previously overlooked.

A common phrase in the literature of "knowing" has been taken from *United States ex rel. Wilcox v. Johnson:* the lawyer is forbidden to act on the belief that the client is committing perjury unless she has a "firm factual basis" for that conclusion.[29] In explaining what constitutes a firm factual basis, the courts generally have set an extremely high standard. The Eighth Circuit has insisted upon a direct admission of perjury by the client to establish a firm factual basis.[30] The court held that a lawyer must use "extreme caution" before deciding that a client intends to commit perjury,[31] and that nothing but "a clear expression of intent" will justify the lawyer's disclosure to the judge.[32] The Eighth Circuit has added, quoting Justice Blackmun, that it will be only "the rarest of cases" in which this factual requirement is met.[33]

Similarly, the Second Circuit has interpreted a firm factual basis to require a "clearly established" or "actual knowledge" standard based upon an admission by the client.[34] In doing so, the court approved a definition providing that information is "clearly established" only when the client "acknowledges" the perjury to the lawyer.[35] The court observed that under any standard less than actual knowledge, courts would be "inundated" with lawyers' reports of perjury.[36]

At another point in its opinion, the Second Circuit went further, indicating that an admission alone will not be sufficient to justify disclosure by a lawyer. After explaining that knowledge by the lawyer means "actual knowledge," the court went on to say that the lawyer should disclose "only that information which [1] the attorney reasonably knows to be a fact and which, [2] when combined with other facts in his knowledge, would [3] clearly establish the existence of a fraud on the tribunal."[37] Thus, the client's admission does not suffice unless it is corroborated by "other facts" that "clearly establish" the perjury.

The standard of "beyond a reasonable doubt" has also been adopted by courts[38] and commentators.[39] Some have gone further, using such phrases as "at least beyond a reasonable doubt,"[40] an "undeniable conclusion,"[41] and "absolutely no doubt."[42] In the words of one court, it is "crucial" that the lawyer "know for sure" that "actual perjury" is involved before acting contrary to the client's interests.[43]

Before revealing her knowledge of client perjury or otherwise acting against the client's interests, there is a further requirement. Not only must the lawyer meet the appropriate standard of knowing, but "the lawyer must also have attempted to dissuade the client from committing the perjury."[44] If a lawyer intimates knowledge of perjury to the court "without first communicating his suspicions to his clients and trying to dissuade them from false testimony, he violate[s] his duty of loyalty to his client."[45]

Finally, when the defense lawyer makes the decision that she does not "know" that the client is committing perjury, the standard of review is likely to be that established by *Strickland v. Washington.*[46] That is, the court must "indulge a strong presumption" that counsel's conduct falls within the "wide range of reasonable professional assistance."[47] As expressed by one court, defense counsel has "great discretion" in deciding whether the client's testimony is truthful.[48]

For example, in *Strickland* itself, the defense lawyer employed tactics deliberately designed to cover up the client's false statements to the court that he had no significant criminal record and that he had committed the crime under emotional stress. The lawyer then argued to the court what he must have known to be false statements made by the client. Nevertheless, the Supreme Court held that the lawyer's conduct fell within the "wide range of reasonable professional assistance," and no member of the Court suggested that the lawyer had acted improperly in using these tactics.

Another example of the wide range of discretion that is accorded to the lawyer with regard to "knowing" is *New Jersey v. Portash*.[49] Portash had been granted use immunity for grand jury testimony. When he was subsequently prosecuted, the trial court ruled that if he presented an alibi that was inconsistent with his self-incriminatory grand jury testimony, the prosecution would be able to use the grand jury testimony to impeach him. The Supreme Court assumed that Portash's grand jury testimony was truthful and that the alibi was therefore perjurious.[50] Nevertheless, the Court reversed, holding that Portash had a constitutional right to present his alibi without being impeached with his inconsistent grand jury testimony. There was no suggestion that Portash's lawyer had acted improperly in offering what was assumed to have been a perjurious alibi.

In almost all of the cases discussing client perjury, the issue has been raised by a defense lawyer (rather than by a client or a judge) who has concluded that the client is committing perjury. In *State v. Skjonsby*,[51] however, the client raised the issue, complaining that the lawyer rendered ineffective assistance of counsel by failing to recognize that the client's self-defense testimony was perjurious and ineffectual.[52]

In rejecting that claim, the court followed a line of analysis paralleling that suggested here. "[O]ur scrutiny of counsel's performance must be highly deferential," the court said, "and must be evaluated from counsel's perspective at the time."[53] Continuing to quote from *Strickland*, the court added that "every effort [must] be made to eliminate the distorting effects of hindsight" and to recognize "the difficulties inherent in making the evaluation."[54] The court concluded that it "must indulge a strong presumption that counsel's conduct falls within the wide range of reasonable professional assistance."[55]

The court in *Skjonsby* also noted that "[l]awyers are not to perform the functions of judges or jurors,"[56] adding:[57]

> To compel attorneys to monitor their clients' behavior, to pursue vigorously any suspicions that might occur to them about possible wrongdoing by the clients, and to develop evidence against the people they represent, would undermine the fundamental character of the attorney-client relationship and bastardize the role of defense counsel. Imposing such obligations on attorneys also would create pressure on clients to conceal information from their

lawyers and to try to make the tactical judgments about the use of evidence that only attorneys are fully equipped to make.

Thus, because of the "knowing" requirement, the apparent requirement of Model Rule 3.3 to reveal client perjury is virtually inoperative, and lawyers can in effect follow the traditional position described in the beginning of this chapter.

Unfortunately, however, there is a small but important number of cases in which defense lawyers do decide that the client is committing perjury and have revealed that conclusion to the court. And, disproportionately, these cases have involved minority-group clients represented by public defenders or court-appointed lawyers.[58] That is, as found by Prof. Jay Silver of St. Thomas Law School, there is "a race- and class-based double standard" in effect when lawyers decide to turn on their clients.[59]

It is important, therefore, that public defenders and court-appointed lawyers begin to apply the same standard of "knowing" that is used by lawyers for fee-paying clients. Until they do, the Fifth and Sixth Amendments will continue to mean less for the indigent accused than for the criminal defendant who is able to pay a lawyer's fee.

Conclusion

In MR 3.3 of the Model Rules of Professional Conduct, the American Bar Association appears to require criminal defense lawyers to reveal client perjury to the court. This position is inconsistent with the traditions of the profession, with the beliefs and practice of most criminal defense lawyers, and with the Fifth and Sixth Amendments to the Constitution.

The apparent requirement of disclosure in MR 3.3 is undercut, however, by the requirement in the rule that the lawyer maintain confidentiality unless she "knows" that the client is committing perjury. The ABA itself, as well as courts and commentators, have interpreted the "knowing" standard to require an extremely high degree of certitude. The authorities use phrases such as "actual knowledge," "a firm factual basis," "beyond a reasonable doubt," "know for sure," and "absolutely no doubt."

Also, most courts require that the lawyer's knowledge come from a direct admission by the client, and some insist that the admission be corroborated by independent investigation by the lawyer. Another condition on disclosure is that the lawyer must first make good faith efforts to dissuade the client from the perjury.

Even if there are strong indications that the client's testimony is false, if the lawyer concludes that she does not "know" that the client is committing perjury, the court must indulge a strong presumption that the lawyer's decision is within the wide range of reasonable discretion afforded to trial counsel.

It will only be the rarest of cases, therefore, in which a lawyer need feel compelled to act as her client's judge or jury, much less as her client's prosecutor. Contrary to the apparent requirement of MR 3.3, and consistent with her constitutional and ethical role, the defense lawyer remains her client's "champion against a hostile world."[60]

Notes

1. *See* Monroe H. Freedman, *Professional Responsibility of the Criminal Defense Lawyer: The Three Hardest Questions*, 64 MICH. L. REV. 1469 (1966); Norman Lefstein, *Client Perjury in Criminal Cases: Still in Search of an Answer*, 1 GEO. J. LEGAL ETHICS 521 (1988).

2. "Facts form the basis of effective representation." ABA STANDARDS FOR CRIMINAL JUSTICE, Comment to 4-4.1 (3d ed., 1993). *See also* ABA MODEL CODE OF PROFESSIONAL RESPONSIBILITY EC 4-1 (1980).

3. Schwab, "Interview with Edward Bennett Williams," in ABA, THE LITIGATION MANUAL: A PRIMER FOR TRIAL LAWYERS 1178, 1180 (J.G. Koeltl, ed., 1989).

4. *Id.* at 1182. In the same *Primer for Trial Lawyers,* Irving Younger wrote: "Nothing should come as a surprise. . . . Everything must be anticipated. . . . If a lawyer doesn't . . . know what the case is all about, he shouldn't be trying it." Younger, "Cicero on Cross-Examination," in *id.* at 532, 533, 535.

5. Upjohn Co. v. United States, 449 U.S. 383 (1981), quoting ABA MODEL CODE OF PROFESSIONAL RESPONSIBILITY EC 4-1 and Hunt v. Blackburn, 128 U.S. 464, 470 (1888); Fisher v. United States, 425 U.S. 391, 403 (1976). For analysis showing that Nix v. Whiteside, 475 U.S. 157 (1986), did not foreclose all challenges under the Sixth Amendment, and that it did not involve the Fifth Amendment, *see* MONROE H. FREEDMAN, UNDERSTANDING LAWYERS' ETHICS 132–39 (1990).

6. Linton v. Perrini, 656 F.2d 207, 212 (6th Cir. 1981), quoted with approval, Morris v. Slappy, 461 U.S. 1, 21 n.4 (1983) (Brennan, J., concurring).

7. United States v. Costen, 38 Fed. 24 (1889) (upholding the disbarment of a lawyer for violating his client's confidences).

8. ABA MODEL RULES OF PROFESSIONAL CONDUCT 3.3.

9. See MONROE H. FREEDMAN, UNDERSTANDING LAWYERS' ETHICS Chs. 5 and 6 (1990); Monroe H. Freedman, *Client Confidences and Client Perjury: Some Unanswered Questions*, 136 PA. L. REV. 1939 (1988).

10. This position has been adopted in Opin. 92-2 of the National Association of Criminal Defense Lawyers.

11. An overwhelming proportion of trial lawyers agree with this position. *See, e.g.,* Steven A. Friedman, *Professional Responsibility in D.C.: A Survey,* 1972 Res Ipsa Loquitur 60. Similar results were reported at the Sixth Annual Judicial Conference of the District of Columbia, held in June, 1981. The conclusion is

also confirmed by extensive discussions I have had at innumerable profes-sional meetings around the country over the course of more than twenty-five years. *See also* National Association of Criminal Defense Lawyers, Opin. 92-2.

Law professors, however, generally disagree with this position. Signifi-cantly, law professors have made a career choice that removes them from service to clients. The former dean of the Yale Law School has found law professors to be increasingly "less professionally oriented." Harry H. Wellington, *Challenges to Legal Education: The "Two Cultures" Phenomenon,* 37 J. LEGAL EDUC. 327 (1987). Also, a distinguished federal appellate judge has expressed concern that law professors are "indifferent to or hopelessly naive about the problems of prac-tice." Harry T. Edwards, *The Role of Legal Education in Shaping the Profession,* 38 J. LEGAL EDUC. 285 (1988).

12. ABA Inf. Opin. 1314 (1975) had held otherwise, but was overruled in ABA Formal Opin. 87-353 (1987), which held (emphasis in the original):

> [N]one of these prohibitions [of the Model Code] *requires* disclosure to the tribunal of any information otherwise protected by DR 4-101. Although 4-101(C)(3) permits a lawyer to reveal a client's stated intention to commit perjury, this exception to the lawyer's duty to preserve the client's con-fidences and secrets is only discretionary on the part of the lawyer.

13. *Id.* Also, interpreting both the Model Code and the Model Rules, the committee has expressly rejected both the narrative solution and selective or intentional ignorance on the part of the lawyer. *Id.* For analysis of these and other proposed solutions to the perjury trilemma, *see* MONROE H. FREEDMAN, UNDERSTANDING LAWYERS' ETHICS 109–41 (1990).

14. The committee's phrase "through practice" is a recognition that the practicing bar has made the accommodation in favor of confidentiality regard-less of what the ethical rules might have appeared to require.

15. MODEL RULE 3.3(a)(2) and (4).

16. MODEL RULE 3.3(a)(4).

17. These are discussed in MONROE H. FREEDMAN, UNDERSTANDING LAWYERS' ETHICS 129–41 (1990).

18. Emphasis added.

19. MONROE H. FREEDMAN, LAWYERS' ETHICS IN AN ADVERSARY SYSTEM, Ch. 5, "What Does a Lawyer Really 'Know': The Epistemology of Legal Ethics" (1975). This chapter has been updated in MONROE H. FREEDMAN, UNDERSTANDING LAWYERS' ETHICS, App. B (1990).

20. Nix v. Whiteside, 475 U.S. 157 (1986). *Nix* is analyzed in MONROE H. FREEDMAN, UNDERSTANDING LAWYERS' ETHICS 132–41 (1990) and in Monroe H. Freedman, *Client Confidences and Client Perjury: Some Unanswered Questions,* 136 PA. L. REV. 1939 (1988).

21. *Nix* at 168. The Chief Justice's conclusions, analysis, and use of au-thorities in *Nix* have been severely criticized. Dean Norman Lefstein has ob-served that the majority opinion "contains a shocking misstatement of the law pertaining to client perjury." Norman Lefstein, *Reflections on the Client Perjury Dilemma and* Nix v. Whiteside, CRIM. JUST. 27, 28 (Summer, 1986). Another critic

of the Chief Justice's inaccuracies is Brent Appel, the Iowa deputy attorney general who argued and won *Nix v. Whiteside*. Brent R. Appel, Nix v. Whiteside: *The Role of Apples, Oranges, and the Great Houdini in Constitutional Adjudication*, 23 Crim. L. Bull. 5 (1987).

22. To help ensure that the lawyer will not "know" the truth within the meaning of these standards, the ABA/ALI videotape has Prof. Geoffrey C. Hazard, Jr., the former reporter for the Model Rules, advise how lawyers can avoid having to reveal client perjury while still knowing everything about the case. The lawyer, Prof. Hazard explains, can ask the client *what the prosecution is likely to say* about his involvement in the crime. (A similar formula is to ask the client what lies his worst enemy might tell to get him convicted.) Thus, the lawyer can learn the truth without making the client commit himself to a particular version of the facts.

23. A.B.A.J. 84, 88 (May 1, 1986).

24. *Id.*

25. *Nix* at 163. This is another example of Chief Justice Burger's questionable way of dealing with the facts of the case, but his statement of fact necessarily constitutes a factual premise of the majority opinion.

26. *Id.* at 167.

27. *Id.* at 189, *citing* United States *ex rel.* Wilcox v. Johnson, 555 F.2d 115, 122 (3d Cir. 1977).

28. *Id.* at 190.

29. 555 F.2d at 122.

30. United States v. Long, 857 F.2d 436, 445 (8th Cir. 1988).

31. *Id.* at 447.

32. *Id.* at 445.

33. *Id.* at 447.

34. Doe v. Federal Grievance Committee, 847 F.2d 57 (2d Cir. 1988).

35. *Id.* at 62.

36. *Id.* at 63.

37. *Id.*

38. *See, e.g.*, United States v. Del Carpio-Cotrina, 733 F. Supp. 95 (1990); Shockley v. State, 565 A.2d 1373 (Del. 1989).

39. *See, e.g.*, Edward L. Kimball, *When Does a Lawyer 'Know' Her Client Will Commit Perjury?* 2 Geo. J. Legal Ethics 579, 581 (1988).

40. Wayne D. Brasil, *Unanticipated Client Perjury and the Collision of Rules of Ethics, Evidence and Constitutional Law*, 44 Mo. L. Rev. 601, 608–9 (1979).

41. *Id.* at 614.

42. Norman Lefstein, *Client Perjury in Criminal Cases: Still in Search of an Answer*, 1 Geo. J. Legal Ethics 521, 528 (1988).

43. Commonwealth v. Wolfe, 301 Pa. Super. 187, 447 A.2d 305, 310 n.7 (1982).

44. United States v. Long, 857 F.2d 436, 446 n.6 (8th Cir. 1988), *citing* Nix v. Whiteside, 475 U.S. at 169, 106 S. Ct. at 996.

45. State v. James, 739 P.2d 1161, 1169 (Wash. App. 1987).

46. 466 U.S. 668, 691 (1984).

47. Nix v. Whiteside, 475 U.S. at 166, quoting Strickland v. Washington, 466 U.S. at 689, 690.

48. People v. Bartee, 566 N.E.2d 855, 857 (Ill. App. 1991). In view of this broad range of discretion granted to defense counsel, it does not appear to be material that the court in *Bartee* rejects the "beyond a reasonable doubt" standard.

49. 440 U.S. 450 (1979).

50. *Id.* at 452-453.

51. 417 N.W.2d 818 (N.D. 1987).

52. A similar case is Commonwealth v. McNeil, 506 Pa. 607, 487 A.2d 802 (1985).

53. *Skjonsby* at 828.

54. *Id.*

55. *Id.*

56. *Id.* at 827, quoting Wayne D. Brasil, *Unanticipated Client Perjury and the Collision of Rules of Ethics, Evidence, and Constitutional Law*, 44 Mo. L. Rev. 601, 614 (1979).

57. *Id.*

58. A rare exception is State v. Fleck, 744 P.2d 628 (Ct. App., Wash. 1987). Retained counsel in that case became angry when he learned that his client was boasting at the jail that he was guilty but that he was successfully conning his "Christian attorney." The lawyer then had the client take a lie detector test; the client failed the test and tacitly admitted its accuracy.

59. Jay Silver, *Truth, Justice, and the American Way: The Case Against the Client Perjury Rules* (unpublished manuscript).

60. See ABA Defense Function Standards, Introduction (Approved Draft, 1971).

Bibliography

Articles, Reports, and Standards

ABA Committee on Ethics and Professional Responsibility, Formal Opinion 87-353 (1987).

ABA Committee on Ethics and Professional Responsibility, Informal Opinion 1314 (1975).

ABA Defense Function Standards, Introduction (Approved Draft, 1971).

ABA Model Code Of Professional Responsibility, EC 4-1 (1980).

ABA Model Rules Of Professional Conduct, Rules, 3.3; 3.3(a)(2); 3.3(a)(4).

ABA Standards For Criminal Justice, 4-4.1 and Cmt. (3d ed., 1993).

Brent R. Appel, Nix v. Whiteside: *The Role of Apples, Oranges, and the Great Houdini in Constitutional Adjudication*, 23 Crim. L. Bull. 5 (1987).

Wayne D. Brasil, *Unanticipated Client Perjury and the Collision of Rules of Ethics, Evidence and Constitutional Law*, 44 Mo. L. Rev. 601 (1979).

Harry T. Edwards, *The Role of Legal Education in Shaping the Profession*, 38 J. Legal Educ. 285 (1988).

Monroe H. Freedman, *Client Confidences and Client Perjury: Some Unanswered Questions*, 136 U. Pa. L. Rev. 1939 (1988).

Monroe H. Freedman, *Lawyers' Ethics In An Advesary System*, (1975).

Monroe H. Freedman, *Professional Responsibility of the Criminal Defense Lawyer: The Three Hardest Questions*, 64 Mich. L. Rev. 1469 (1966).

Monroe H. Freedman, *Understanding Lawyers' Ethics*, (1990).

Steven A. Friedman, *Professional Responsibility in D.C.: A Survey*, 1972 Res Ipsa Loquitur 60.

Edward L. Kimball, *When Does a Lawyer "Know" Her Client Will Commit Perjury?* 2 Geo. J. Legal Ethics 579 (1988).

Norman Lefstein, *Client Perjury in Criminal Cases: Still in Search of an Answer*, 1 Geo. J. Legal Ethics 521 (1988).

Norman Lefstein, *Reflections on the Client Perjury Dilemma and* Nix v. Whiteside, Crim. Just. 26, 28 (Summer, 1986).

National Association of Criminal Defense Lawyers, Opinion 92-2 (1992).

Schwab, "Interview with Edward Bennett Williams," in ABA, *The Litigation Manual: A Primer for Trial Lawyers*, 1178 (J.G. Koeltl, ed., 1989).

Jay Silver, Truth, Justice, and the American Way: The Case Against the Client Perjury Rules, (unpublished manuscript).

David O. Stewart, *Drawing the Line at Lying*, ABA Journal 84, 88 (May 1, 1986).

Harry H. Wellington, *Challenges to Legal Education: The "Two Cultures" Phenomenon*, 37 J. Legal Educ. 327 (1987).

Irving Younger, "Cicero on Cross-Examination," *The Litigation Manual: A Primer for Trial Lawyers*, 1178 (J.G. Koeltl, ed., 1989).

Cases

Commonwealth v. McNeil, 506 Pa. 607, 487 A.2d 802 (1985).

Commonwealth v. Wolfe, 301 Pa. Super. 187, 447 A.2d 305 (1982).

Doe v. Federal Grievance Committee, 847 F.2d 57 (2d Cir. 1988).

Fisher v. United States, 425 U.S. 391 (1976).

Hunt v. Blackburn, 128 U.S. 464 (1888).

Linton v. Perrini, 656 F.2d 207 (6th Cir. 1981).

Morris v. Slappy, 461 U.S. 1 (1983).

New Jersey v. Portash, 440 U.S. 450 (1979).

Nix v. Whiteside, 475 U.S. 157 (1986).

People v. Bartee, 566 N.E.2d 855 (Ill. App. 1991).

Shockley v. State, 565 A.2d 1373 (Del. 1989).

State v. Fleck, 744 P.2d 628 (Wash. App. 1987).

State v. James, 739 P.2d 1161 (Wash. App. 1987).

State v. Skjonsby, 417 N.W.2d 818 (N.D. 1987).

Strickland v. Washington, 466 U.S. 668 (1984).

United States v. Costen, 38 Fed. 24 (1889).

United States v. Del Carpio-Cotrina, 733 F. Supp. 95 (1990).

United States v. Long, 857 F.2d 436 (8th Cir. 1988).

United States ex rel. Wilcox v. Johnson, 555 F.2d 115 (3d Cir. 1977).

Upjohn Co. v. United States, 449 U.S. 383 (1981).

CHAPTER 📖 11

Anticipated Client Perjury: Truth or Dare Comes to Court

Terence F. MacCarthy and Carol A. Brook

What must defense counsel ethically do when she learns that her client intends to testify falsely at trial?

Despite the scores of articles written about client perjury and the problems it creates for criminal defense lawyers, it was Monroe Freedman, the one who started it all[1] (the discussion, not the perjury), who said it best. Client perjury, he said, confronts the lawyer "with what we may call a trilemma—that is, the lawyer is required to know everything, to keep it in confidence, and to reveal it to the court." M. FREEDMAN, LAWYERS' ETHICS IN AN ADVERSARY SYSTEM 28 (1975). This articulation of the problem brings into sharp relief the tension between criminal defense lawyers' constitutional obligations to their clients and their ethical obligations to the courts.

Although the problem of client perjury rarely arises during a defense lawyer's career, once is more than enough. Yet, despite both the importance and the immediacy of the problem, the conflict between relevant ethical rules and constitutional strictures is not destined to be resolved soon. Indeed, the one time the Supreme Court specifically addressed the issue, it left the subject more confused than ever. *See* Nix v. Whiteside, 475 U.S. 157, 165 (1986)(where the Court noted, with admirable understatement: "In some future case . . ., we may need to define with greater precision the weight to be given to recognized canons of ethics, the standards established by the state in statutes or professional codes, and the Sixth Amendment . . . ."). Sadly, words written a decade ago are even more true today: "The sorry fact is that, to date, there is no acceptable answer to this most troubling of questions for the criminal defense attorney." MacCarthy & Mejia, *The Perjurious Client Question: Putting Criminal Defense Lawyers Between a Rock and a Hard Place*, 75 J. CRIM. L. & CRIMINAL. 1197, 1198 (1984).

But criminal defense lawyers do not have the luxury of waiting for some future case when confronted with a client who clearly intends to commit perjury tomorrow, or perhaps even this afternoon. It is our hope, therefore, that this chapter will provide some guidance to the criminal defense lawyers who find themselves in that unhappy position. It should be noted that this problem is unique to the criminal defense lawyer. It is not a civil problem; nor is it a prosecution problem—for only criminal defendants have a constitutionally protected right to testify. Yet, in the main, those who have attempted to resolve this most difficult problem have failed to fully understand the unique circumstances facing a criminal defense lawyer.

Because of this failure, reading the literature on the perjurious defendant reminds one of nothing so much as the White Rabbit scurrying along muttering: "The hurrieder I go, the behinder I get." L. CARROLL, THROUGH THE LOOKING GLASS (Signet 1960). In our case, the more one reads, the more confused one is likely to become. It is at least apparent, however, that the pendulum has swung away from the view that lawyers' obligations to their clients are paramount and toward the view that lawyers' obligations to the court system must take precedence.

Although this is not a surprising shift in light of the continual erosion of criminal defendants' rights over the past two decades,[2] it is nonetheless ironic that rules governing client perjury have become increasingly antidefendant at a time when studies indicate that 93 percent of all participants involved in the criminal justice system of at least one major city believe prosecutors know or have reason to know that law enforcement officers lie under oath at least some of the time. *See* Orfield, *Deterrence, Perjury and the Heater Factor: An Exclusionary Rule in the Chicago Criminal Courts*, 63 UNIV. COLO. L. REV. 75, 109 (1992).[3] A further irony is that "this excursion into defense lawyer ethics stands in sharp contrast to the Court's historic unwillingness to impose ethical rules for prosecutors or other government officials." Gershman, *Attorney Loyalty and Client Perjury—A Postscript to* Nix v. Whiteside, 14 AM. J. CRIM. L. 97, 103 (1987).

The solution currently offered by the ABA Standing Committee on Ethics and Professional Responsibility in its most recent opinion, Formal Opinion No. 87-353 (April 20, 1987), is an example of the shift away from protecting client communications. Formal Opinion 87-353 is based on Rule 3.3 of the ABA Model Rules of Professional Responsibility and the Supreme Court's decision in *Nix v. Whiteside*, 475 U.S. 157

(1986). Although not binding, the opinion is relevant to lawyers who practice in jurisdictions that have adopted ABA Model Rule 3.3. Because thirty-eight states and the District of Columbia have adopted some version of the Model Rules,[4] the ABA view of what a lawyer should do is a useful place to start our discussion.

ABA Opinion 87-353 advises lawyers who are convinced their clients will commit perjury to first attempt to dissuade their clients by "informing the[m] . . . of the consequences of giving false testimony, including the lawyer's duty of disclosure to the tribunal." This admonition assumes that the consequences are clear and that there is such a duty of disclosure in every state. As we will see, neither of these propositions is true.

The opinion further assumes that the lawyers' exhortations were successful and so it allows them to proceed as if everything is as it should be. In the words of the ABA: "Ordinarily, after warning the client of the consequences of the client's perjury, including the lawyer's duty to disclose it to the court, the lawyer can reasonably believe that the client will be persuaded not to testify falsely at trial." Commentary to Formal Opinion No. 87-353, ABA/BNA LAWYERS MANUAL ON PROFESSIONAL CONDUCT 901:106. What this means is that in most cases, once a client says something the lawyer believes would be perjurious and the lawyer properly warns the client about the potential consequences of committing perjury, nothing more need or should happen.

If the lawyers somehow know, however, that their efforts at persuasion have been unsuccessful, they must move to withdraw. If that motion is denied, as all experienced trial lawyers and judges well know it will be, lawyers must "either limit the examination of the client to subjects on which the lawyer believes the client will testify truthfully; or, if there are none, not permit the client to testify [however one is supposed to do this]; or, if this is not feasible, disclose the client's intention to testify falsely to the tribunal." None of these choices are palatable to a criminal defense lawyer and, depending on where you practice, they may be neither ethical nor constitutional.

Take first the motion to withdraw. What does one say in the motion? Is a motion to withdraw even with no reason given always a signal to the judge that perjury is about to be committed? If so, does sending this signal to the judge violate a defendant's constitutional rights? Exactly how much information *must* the lawyer give? How much *may* the lawyer give? How much *should* the lawyer give?

What of the ABA mandate to keep a client off the stand? As Dean Lefstein points out in *Client Perjury in Criminal Cases: Still in Search of an Answer,* 1 Geo. J. Legal Ethics 521, 536-37 (1988), a lawyer's unilateral decision to prevent a client from testifying surely does not comport with the well-established legal principle that it is the client, not the lawyer, who decides whether to take the stand. *See* Jones v. Barnes, 463 U.S. 745, 751 (1983)(*dicta*)("accused has the ultimate authority to make certain fundamental decisions regarding the case, [including] . . . whether to . . . testify. . .."); MODEL RULE 1.2(a); ABA STANDARDS FOR CRIMINAL JUSTICE, The Defense Function § 4-5.2(a) (3d ed. 1993).

Moreover, it is now clear that a defendant has a constitutional right to testify. Rock v. Arkansas, 483 U.S. 44, 53 n.10 (1987)("the right to testify on one's own behalf in defense to a criminal charge is a fundamental constitutional right"). Although there may be "no constitutional right to testify falsely," Nix v. Whiteside, 475 U.S. at 173, that should not translate to no right to testify at all. Even ABA Opinion 87-353 recognizes the possibility that a defendant who intends to commit perjury may be able *and should be allowed* to testify truthfully on some points. How on earth such a direct examination could be successfully executed by the defense lawyer is truly one of life's great mysteries. Nonetheless, there are cases holding that counsel's refusal to put a client on the witness stand because the client intended to commit perjury did not violate the client's right to testify or right to counsel. *See, e.g.,* United States v. Curtis, 742 F.2d 1070 (7th Cir. 1984), *cert. denied,* 475 U.S. 1064 (1986).

What about those jurisdictions that require trial judges to personally inquire of defendants whether they knowingly waive their right to testify? If the defendant says he or she does not knowingly waive the right, what then? At a minimum, a court, not the defendant's lawyer, must resolve the dilemma at an ex parte hearing with the defendant present. But regardless of the outcome, it is too late—the judge has already been told the client intends to commit perjury.

In apparent recognition of these problems, the ABA adopted the following caveat entitled "Constitutional Requirements" as part of its official Comment to Model Rule 3.3:

> The general rule—that an advocate must disclose the existence of perjury with respect to a material fact, even that of a client— applies to defense counsel in criminal cases, as well as in other instances. However, the definition of the lawyer's ethical duty in such a situation may be qualified by constitutional provisions for due process and the right to counsel in criminal cases. In some jurisdictions these provisions have been construed to require that counsel present an accused as a witness if the accused wishes to

testify, even if counsel knows the testimony will be false. The obligation of the advocate under these Rules is subordinate to such a constitutional requirement.

Unfortunately, because this Comment was adopted pre-*Whiteside* its value now lies more in state constitutional claims than in federal.

Only one point in ABA Opinion 87-353 is and has been universally accepted. If you become *absolutely convinced* your client intends to commit perjury, you must try to dissuade your client from doing so. *See* MODEL RULE 3.3; *Nix v. Whiteside*, 475 U.S. at 169. What you may permissibly tell your client is not as clear and will, therefore, be discussed in more detail below.

If you are unsuccessful in dissuading your clients from their perjurious intentions, there is general, although not universal, consensus that you should move to withdraw. *Whiteside* at 170. This procedure, however, has spawned two lines of criticism. One line suggests that motions to withdraw are contrary to the traditional notion that clients are entitled to full and zealous representation, and that the most counsel can do consistent with such representation is attempt to dissuade them from committing perjury. The arguments in support of this position are, first, a motion to withdraw signals the court that perjury may be committed, contrary to the client's interests, and, second, a motion to withdraw violates a client's Fifth Amendment privilege. *See, e.g.*, Lowery v. Cardwell, 575 F.2d 727 (9th Cir. 1978)(*during* defendant's direct testimony, defense counsel's request to withdraw *in bench trial* denied defendant due process of law); FREEDMAN, LAWYER'S ETHICS IN AN ADVERSARY SYSTEM at 33–34; Gershman, *supra* at 104–5.

The gist of the second line of criticism is that withdrawal, even where granted, simply throws the problem onto the next lawyer's lap and does nothing to resolve the issue in a principled way. *See, e.g.*, United States v. Scott, 909 F.2d 488, 492 n.4 (11th Cir. 1990); Lefstein, *supra* at 525–27; Hall, *Handling Client Perjury After* Nix v. Whiteside: *A Criminal Defense Lawyer's View*, 42 MERCER L. REV. 769, 800–801 (1991).

The authors believe, however, that a motion to withdraw, at least when made prior to trial, may be the appropriate action to allow clients to start over, properly warned, with a real understanding of the consequences of their actions. The cases do not bear out the fear that granting a motion to withdraw will inevitably create an endless cycle of "eleventh-hour motions" as posited in opinions such as *Sanborn v. State*, 474 So. 2d 309, 314 (Fla. Dist. Ct. App. 1985) and by commentators such as Lefstein, *supra* at 526–27. What you may say in a motion to withdraw is, naturally, not clear, and will also be discussed below.

If the motion to withdraw is denied, as most would be, darkness descends. Counsel must then decide whether to (1) put the client on the stand in the normal manner as suggested by Opinion 92-2 of the National Association of Criminal Defense Lawyers and Monroe Freedman; (2) put the client on the stand and ask for narrative testimony as suggested by Standard 4-7.7 of the ABA Defense Function Standards for Criminal Justice (now withdrawn but not forgotten) and by cases such as *United States v. Long*, 857 F.2d 436 (8th Cir. 1988); (3) put the client on the stand and only ask questions relating to what the lawyer believes is the client's truthful testimony as suggested in ABA Formal Opinion 87-353; or (4) refuse to put the client on the stand as also suggested by Formal Opinion 87-353 and by cases such as *United States v. Henkel*, 799 F.2d 369 (7th Cir. 1986), *cert. denied*, 479 U.S. 1101 (1987). In addition, the lawyer must decide what, if anything, to tell the judge.

To answer these questions, we must review the history of the ABA ethical rules, the evolution of the case law, and the thoughts of legal commentators, many of whom have expressed an abiding interest in the subject.

Canons of Professional Ethics

The ABA developed its Canons of Professional Ethics in 1908. The canons, like the codes that followed, were ambiguous about the lawyer's role in the system. In 1953, the ABA issued its only opinion dealing with client perjury under the early canons. In Formal Opinion 287, the ABA responded to a question concerning a lawyer's obligation when a client makes a false statement at a sentencing proceeding. The opinion instructed the lawyer to attempt to persuade the client to recant the statement, and failing that, to seek to withdraw.

That is where the similarity between that opinion and Formal Opinion 87-353 ends. The earlier opinion clearly stated that even if the motion to withdraw was denied, the lawyer *could not* disclose the false statement to the court if the lawyer knew, based on client confidences or secrets, that the statement was false. Formal Opinion 87-353 reaches an opposite conclusion.

The Model Code of Professional Responsibility

In 1969, the ABA Canons of Professional Responsibility evolved into the ABA Model Code of Professional Responsibility. Although the Model Code was replaced by the ABA Model Rules of Professional Conduct in 1983, a version of the Model Code is still followed in some states.[5] Thus, practitioners in those jurisdictions must be aware of

Model Code proscriptions. In addition, the Supreme Court in *Nix v. Whiteside* relied in part on the teachings of the Model Code, making them relevant, at the very least, to an understanding of that decision.

The Model Code consists of seven canons, described by the ABA as "axiomatic norms." Each canon is followed by a number of Ethical Considerations (EC), said to be "aspirational in character," and Disciplinary Rules (DR), which are mandatory. *See* ABA MODEL CODE OF PROFESSIONAL RESPONSIBILITY (1979), Preliminary Statement.

Several different provisions are relevant to the client perjury dilemma. Canon 4 states: "A lawyer should preserve the confidences and secrets of a client." One Disciplinary Rule following this canon, DR 4-101(B)(1), prohibits lawyers from revealing client confidences or secrets unless permitted under DR 4-101(C). DR 4-101(C)(2) permits, but does not require, disclosure of client confidences or secrets "when permitted under Disciplinary Rules or required by law or court order." DR 4-101(C)(3) permits, but again does not require, disclosure of client confidences or secrets if they relate to the client's intention "to commit a crime and the information necessary to prevent the crime." Thus, this canon makes the protection of client confidences and secrets paramount.

Tempering this protection of client communications is Canon 7, which states: "A lawyer should represent a client zealously within the bounds of the law." On the other hand, DR 7-101(A)(3) prohibits the lawyer from intentionally prejudicing or damaging a client, except as required under DR 7-102(B). And DR 7-102(B) only *requires* lawyers to reveal to the court a client's *past* fraud upon the court if the client will not do so, and even then only when the information is not privileged. Thus, this rule does not apply to anticipated perjury.

Two Ethical Considerations must be added to the mix. EC 7-5 states in part that a lawyer may not "knowingly assist the client to engage in illegal conduct. . . ." It further prohibits a lawyer from encouraging or aiding a "client to commit criminal acts. . . ." (Query: just what is the difference, if any, between "commit[ting] criminal acts" and "engag[ing] in illegal conduct" or between "knowingly assist[ing]" and "encouraging or aiding"?) EC 7-26 states, in part, that: "The law and Disciplinary Rules prohibit the use of . . . perjured testimony . . . ." It further states: "A lawyer who knowingly participates in introduction of such testimony . . . is subject to discipline."

So under the Model Code you cannot assist in illegal conduct and perjury is illegal. And, under DR 4-101(C)(2) of the Model Code, you may, but need not, reveal client confidences or secrets to prevent an illegal act. Thus, the question becomes: When you learn of your client's intent to commit perjury through client confidences or secrets, to whom do you owe your primary loyalty—your client or the court?[6]

In 1971, in an apparent attempt to answer this question, the ABA promulgated Standard 4-7.7 of The Defense Function Standards (1980 & Supp. 1986). Standard 7.7 applied only in criminal cases and was the first straightforward attempt to grapple with the problem and to provide guidance to criminal defense lawyers. It required lawyers convinced of their clients' perjurious intentions to counsel their clients against committing perjury. If unsuccessful, lawyers were advised to move to withdraw from the case without telling the court the reason for the motion. If the lawyers' withdrawal motions were denied, Standard 7.7 expressly permitted defendants to testify in narrative fashion. The standard also prohibited lawyers from referring to their clients' perjurious testimony in closing argument. Finally, the standard required counsel to somehow and somewhere make a record of the fact that the client took the stand over counsel's objection without revealing that fact to the court.

Although the end result was a clearer stance in favor of protection of client communications, the Supreme Court specifically denounced the narrative approach in *Whiteside*. Following *Whiteside*, the ABA explicitly disavowed the standard in its commentary to Formal Opinion 87-353, although, apparently unnoticed by many, the standard had already been withdrawn by the ABA in 1979. Nonetheless, courts and commentators have continued to tout the standard, perhaps because it still seems to be the best of a bad lot. *See, e.g.*, cases cited in MacCarthy & Mejia, *supra* at 1205 & n.43; Lefstein, *supra* at 523; District of Columbia Rule 3.3.

The Model Rules of Professional Conduct

In 1983 the ABA released its Model Rules of Professional Conduct, which take a stronger position in favor of disclosing intended client perjury. Although Model Rule 1.6 precludes the revelation of "information relating to representation of a client" and exempts certain information from disclosure, those areas of nondisclosure are trumped by Rule 3.3, "Candor Toward the Tribunal."

Rule 3.3 and its accompanying comment, which was also specifically adopted by the ABA (one of the few places where the ABA has adopted both a rule *and* its supporting commentary), forbid a lawyer from knowingly making or "fail[ing] to disclose a material fact to a tribunal when disclosure is necessary to avoid assisting a criminal or fraudulent act by the client." MODEL RULE 3.3(a)(1) & (2). The rule also prohibits a lawyer from "offer[ing] evidence that the lawyer knows to be false." MODEL RULE 3.3(a)(4). It does not delineate how a lawyer is to disclose client perjury, nor does it delineate how a lawyer is to proceed if the motion to withdraw is denied.

Nix v. Whiteside

Now let us look at the opinion in *Whiteside*. Emmanuel Charles Whiteside was charged with the murder of Calvin Love. Prior to trial Whiteside told his lawyer that he had gone to Love's apartment to purchase some marijuana and found Love and his girlfriend in bed. An argument ensued, Love told his girlfriend to get his "piece," then got up and returned to the bed where he started to reach under his pillow and move toward Whiteside. Nix v. Whiteside, 475 U.S. at 160. According to the Supreme Court opinion, Whiteside originally said he never actually saw a gun, but believed Love had one in his hand. Later, Whiteside said he had seen something "metallic" in Love's hand. His explanation for the change as it appears in the majority opinion was that: "If I don't say I saw a gun, I'm dead." *Id.* at 161. (That this scenario meets the standard for "knowing" a client intends to commit perjury is hardly clear, but we leave that to another chapter.)

According to the Supreme Court, Whiteside's lawyer told Whiteside he did not believe he saw something metallic and so could not allow him to testify to it. Whiteside's lawyer told Whiteside if he testified that way he would have to advise the court that Whiteside had committed perjury. His lawyer also told him he would "probably" be allowed to impeach Whiteside's testimony. *Id.*[7]

Whiteside did testify at trial, but he did not testify he ever saw anything in Love's hand. He was convicted of second degree murder.

A series of appeals ensued. Whiteside lost in the state courts on direct appeal and in the federal district court on his habeas petition. But the Eighth Circuit saw things differently and reversed in *Whiteside v. Scurr*, 744 F.2d 1323 (1984). That court concluded that the lawyer's threat to inform the trial judge of Whiteside's intended perjury forced the defendant to choose between his right to testify and his right to effective assistance of counsel, violating both. It also found that Whiteside's lawyer's actions violated due process and threatened to violate the lawyer's ethical obligation to preserve client confidences. The court held that this threatened violation created a conflict of interest that made the lawyer ineffective under the Sixth Amendment, with no finding of prejudice required.

The Supreme Court disagreed. At the outset, it must be kept in mind that the defendant *did* testify in *Whiteside*. Further, *Whiteside* was a habeas case and the four concurring justices joined in the opinion only on the finding of no prejudice under *Strickland v. Washington*, 466 U.S. 668 (1984). Finally, the question in *Whiteside* was not what counsel should have done pursuant to ethical guidelines, but whether what counsel actually did violated any *constitutional* rights of the defendant or caused him any actionable prejudice. *Nix v. Whiteside*, 475 U.S. at 166.

Yet, the constitutional questions appeared to be of little interest to the Court. The Court initially announced that the actions of Whiteside's lawyers, including the threats to withdraw and to reveal the client's perjury, fell "well within accepted standards of professional conduct and the range of reasonable professional conduct acceptable under *Strickland*." *Id*. at 171. Regarding the defendant's constitutional right to testify, the Court said simply that whether or not such a right exists, it does not include a right to testify falsely. *Id*. at 173. As for the perceived conflict between a lawyer's ethical obligations and the client's right to testify, the Court found no conflict where the lawyer was seeking to prevent the client from engaging in future criminal conduct such as perjury. *Id*. at 174.[8]

Although Chief Justice Burger stated in *Whiteside* that under both the ABA Model Code and Model Rules a lawyer is not only authorized, but required, to disclose client perjury, *Whiteside* at 168, this declaration is both inaccurate and beside the point. It is inaccurate because, as discussed above at 12–13, although the Model Code may permit disclosure of intended perjury, it does not *require* a lawyer to do anything until *after* perjury has been committed. Moreover, the *Comment* to Model Rule 3.3 (although not the rule itself) is written as if the requirements of that rule also apply only *after* perjury has been committed. Gershman, *Attorney Loyalty and Client Perjury—A Postscript to* Nix v. Whiteside, 14 AM. J. CRIM. L. 97, 101 n.22 (1987). Finally, because the rule permits lawyers to assume they have convinced their clients not to testify perjuriously, lawyers should make this assumption in the vast majority of cases. Thus, under Rule 3.3, once a client has been admonished, lawyers should ordinarily do nothing until after a defendant testifies.

Regarding the relevance of Chief Justice Burger's assertion, it has been pointed out by numerous commentators, including the deputy attorney general who represented the State of Iowa in *Whiteside*, that the Supreme Court is not the arbitrar of ethics rules. What is ethically required in any particular jurisdiction is a question of local law. Appel, Nix v. Whiteside: *The Role of Apples, Oranges, and the Great Houdini in Constitutional Adjudication*, 23 CRIM. L. BULL. 5, 20 (1987).

Thus, Justice Brennan declared in his concurring opinion:

[T]he Court seems unable to resist the temptation of sharing with the legal community its vision of ethical conduct. But let there be no mistake: the Court's essay regarding what constitutes the correct response to a criminal client's suggestion that he will perjure himself is pure discourse without force of law. * * * Lawyers, judges, bar associations, students, and others should understand that the problem has not now been "decided."

Nix v. Whiteside, 475 U.S. at 177. *Accord* United States v. Del Carpio-Cotrina, 733 F. Supp. 95, 97 (S.D. Fla. 1990)("In determining whether an ethical violation has occurred, the Court should look to the controlling ethical principles of the forum state for guidance").

Unfortunately, although most of what is contained in the majority opinion is sheer speculation, several courts have incorrectly interpreted it as having the force of law. *See generally* Appel, *The Limited Impact of* Nix v. Whiteside *on Attorney-Client Relations,* 136 U. Pa. L. Rev. 1913 (1988) (hereinafter *The Limited Impact of* Nix v. Whiteside). Beware of such cases.

For example, in *United States v. Carbone,* 798 F.2d 21, 28 (1st Cir. 1986), the court cited *Whiteside* for the proposition that the lawyer-client privilege does not cover perjury. That is not what *Whiteside* said—*Whiteside* said states need not *require* that perjury be protected by the privilege; it never said they are precluded from protecting it.

Likewise, in *In re Curl,* 803 F.2d 1004, 1006–7 (9th Cir. 1986), *overruled on other grounds, Partington v. Gedan,* 923 F.2d 686 (9th Cir. 1991) (en banc), the court indicated its belief that *Whiteside* forbids a lawyer from putting a client on the witness stand if the lawyer has reason to know the client is committing perjury. Yet *Whiteside* leaves it to the individual states to decide which approach to condone when a lawyer believes her client will commit perjury. *See,* Appel, *The Limited Impact of* Nix v. Whiteside at 1936.

Where Do We Go from Here?

Many questions remain unanswered. First, what methods of inducement may a lawyer legitimately use to dissuade a client from testifying? There is general agreement that lawyers have a wealth of reasons at their fingertips to attempt to dissuade clients from perjuring themselves. *See, e.g.,* Hall, *supra* at 797–98. The client should be told that perjury is a crime and that if the prosecution believes it occurred, the client may be charged with that crime. In addition, the client should be told that you, the lawyer, may be indicted for subornation of perjury. The client should understand why the perjured testimony will not be believable to the jury (including the fact that you yourself may break out laughing) and how this will hurt the client's case, including its effect on the lawyer's choice of defenses. The client should understand how the prosecution will cross-examine him. The client should be told that the judge may consider perjury to enhance the sentence. *See* United States v. Grayson, 438 U.S. 41 (1978). In federal court, the client should understand that the federal sentencing guidelines *mandate* that the judge increase the client's offense level if the judge thinks the client lied on the stand. *See* Guideline § 3C1.1; United States v. Dunnigan, 113 S. Ct. 1111, 1119 (1993)("Upon a proper determination that the accused has committed perjury at trial, an enhancement of sentence is required by the Sentencing Guidelines"). Finally, the client should understand that the lawyer will move to withdraw if the client persists in a clear intent to commit perjury.

Is it permissible to go further and threaten to reveal your client's perjury and also threaten to testify against them? *Whiteside* says it is within the range of permissible federal *constitutional* behavior and, thus, is not ineffective assistance of counsel under the Fifth or Sixth Amendments. It does not say you must engage in this behavior, nor is there any reason to inform your client of such a possibility unless you believe that would be the only option available to you. The Supreme Court cannot say what is ethically or constitutionally required *or prohibited* in your state. And it is certainly possible that a state's ethics rules may either prohibit disclosure of information leading to the lawyer's belief that the information came in the form of client confidences, or at least not mandate such disclosure.

In Iowa, for example, the Iowa Code of Professional Responsibility for Lawyers in effect at the time of *Whiteside* prohibited lawyers from giving testimony concerning any confidential communications received in their professional capacity. Several commentators have noted that this provision "strongly suggests that threatening testimonial disclosure is . . . prohibited and unethical under Iowa law." *See, e.g.,* Auerbach, *What Are Law Clerks For?—Comments on* Nix v. Whiteside, 5 S. DIEGO L. REV. 979, 987 (1986). Nonetheless, the Supreme Court did not see fit to mention this point, perhaps because the Iowa Supreme Court did not mention it either. State v. Whiteside, 272 N.W.2d 468 (Iowa 1978). *But see* Auerbach, *supra* at 987: "Surely the Court should have considered the implications of . . . [the Iowa rule]."

In *United States v. Long*, 857 F.2d 436 (8th Cir. 1988), however, the Eighth Circuit seemingly approved (but did not require) disclosure of

client perjury. There it said a defendant should be informed of the following possible consequences of giving perjured testimony: "(1) the
lawyer may reveal to the court what he believes to be false; (2) the lawyer may refrain from referring to the false testimony in final argument;
and (3) the defendant may be prosecuted for perjury." *Id.* at 446 n.8.

If unsuccessful in dissuading your client from committing perjury,
what then? Assuming a motion to withdraw is permissible in your jurisdiction, that is your next step. But what should you tell the court in
seeking to withdraw? The point of moving to withdraw is to avoid
being involved in the client's perjury, not to hurt the client. Thus, the
less said, the better. Whether even a bare motion citing irreconcilable
conflict of interest gives away the real reason for the motion largely
depends on when the motion is made. As MacCarthy and Mejia point
out at 215 n.119: "Criminal defense lawyers move to withdraw for a
number of reasons, such as a personality conflict with the defendant,
knowledge by an appointed attorney that a defendant does have, but
did not admit to, sufficient funds to retain counsel, a conflict of interest,
a serious difference of opinion regarding trial strategy, failure of the
defendant to pay the attorney's fees, schedule conflicts, etc."

Motions made during the defense case are more likely to signal the
lawyer's belief that the client intends to commit perjury.[9] *See, e.g.,*
United States v. Henkel, 799 F.2d 369, 370 (7th Cir. 1986) *cert. denied*, 479
U.S. 1101 (1987) ("Coming at the time and manner in which it did, the
motion to withdraw had only one reasonable predicate"); United
States v. Scott, 909 F.2d 488, 492 n.3 (11th Cir. 1990) (district court "assumed" reason for withdrawal motion made during trial was lawyer's
belief her client would commit perjury). In *Henkel*, defense counsel's
actions, clearly signaling a belief that the client intended to commit
perjury, were held to be permissible because "the defendant was entitled only to ethical representation and had no right to commit perjury
or have an attorney . . . assist him in this endeavor. . . ." 799 F.2d at 370.
In *Lowery v. Cardwell*, 575 F.2d 727 (9th Cir. 1978), however, the court
held that in a bench trial, defense counsel's motion to withdraw made
during the defense case with no reason given was impermissible.
"[T]his conduct affirmatively and emphatically called the attention of
the fact finder to the problem counsel was facing." *Id.* at 731.

This rebuke leads us to the third issue: What actions should lawyers take if denied leave to withdraw, knowing their client intends to
commit perjury? The first option is to put the client on the stand as
you would any other witness. The arguments in favor of this course are
that it is clearly the most effective representation of the client and preserves the client's Fifth Amendment privilege. *See* Opinion 92-2 of the

National Association of Criminal Defense Lawyers. The arguments against it are that most ethical rules forbid lawyers from actively presenting known perjurious testimony and the Fifth Amendment does not protect statements of future crimes. *See* Lefstein, *supra* at 524–25. Lefstein warns that lawyers who engage in full representation of clients whom they know will commit perjury may find themselves with no defense. *Id.* at 522–23. Nonetheless, "the effect of the Fifth Amendment on revelation of client confidences relating to perjury," has not yet been decided by the Supreme Court. United States v. Scott, 909 F.2d 488, 492 n.2 (1990), *citing* Freedman, *Client Confidences and Client Perjury: Some Unanswered Questions,* 136 U. PA. L. REV. 1939 (1988).

If the full representation approach is not taken and a motion to withdraw is denied, is a narrative permissible after *Whiteside*? Maybe. It depends upon the ethical rules in your state. A number of jurisdictions have approved the narrative approach in their versions of Model Rule 3.3.[10] Indeed, several courts have ordered defendants to proceed in narrative fashion. *See, e.g.,* United States v. Long, 857 F.2d 436, 446 & n.7 (8th Cir. 1988) (although narrative has been criticized because it indicates to the judge and some jurors that the lawyer does not believe the client and because it requires the lawyer to play a passive role in the client's perjury, these concerns "were largely removed [in *Long*] because the judge had already been notified of the potential perjury and because the judge had instructed the attorney to proceed in this manner").[11]

Under former Standard 7.7, when a narrative is allowed defense counsel should not refer to the perjured narrative testimony in closing argument. Where defense counsel complies with this advice, and the prosecutor seizes upon counsel's silence to argue to the jury that the defendant lied, at least one court has reversed the defendant's conviction. In *State v. Long*, 714 P.2d 465, 467 (Ariz. App. 1986) (a different Long this time), the prosecutor told the jury that defense counsel did not refer to his client's testimony in closing because defense counsel would have "choke[d]" on it. The court said: "We find this effort to make affirmative evidence of guilt out of defense counsel's ethical behavior to be prejudicial error." *Id.* Like the Ninth Circuit in *Lowery v. Cardwell, supra,* the court held that due process is violated where the factfinder is told of defense counsel's belief that the defendant committed perjury.

A judge's order to use a narrative should insulate the lawyer from disciplinary proceedings if the lawyer is found to have passively engaged in client perjury. *Cf.* The Florida Bar v. Rubin, 549 So. 2d 1000 (Fla. 1989). In *Rubin,* counsel moved to withdraw, apparently based on his belief that his client intended to commit perjury. The court denied the motion, but ordered the lawyer to allow the defendant to testify in narrative fashion. The lawyer refused. After a disciplinary hearing, the Florida Supreme Court held that the lawyer's refusal was unjustified because the court's order gave counsel "a good, and most likely a complete, defense" to disciplinary charges. 549 So. 2d at 1003.

If the narrative is unworkable, what about putting on a client just to testify to the truthful parts as Model Rule 3.3 suggests? To us, this is the worst approach of all. What it means is you cannot let your client testify to the one point the jury really wants to hear: Did your client do it. It would be like putting Whiteside on the stand to testify he went to Love's apartment, saw Love and his girlfriend in bed . . . and then left the building. This would be far worse for the client than saying nothing, not to mention that it would be virtually impossible to control once the client takes the stand. And what about cross? How can you possibly prepare your clients for that? Tell them not to answer any questions that they do not like?

This leaves us with the final option: May counsel unilaterally refuse to let a client testify? We think not. (Parenthetically, the defendant in *Whiteside did* testify so that case does not control on this issue.) So what to do? Do you say: "Judge, I believe my client will commit perjury so I will not let my client testify?" In the *Long* case, the Eighth Circuit said of this choice: "The most weighty decision in a case of possible client perjury is made by the lawyer who decides to inform the court, and perhaps incidentally his adversary and the jury, of his client's possible perjury." United States v. Long, 857 F.2d 436, 447 (8th Cir. 1988). Nonetheless, in *Long,* after remanding for a hearing to determine if the defendant was prejudiced by the lawyer's statement (somewhat of a foregone conclusion, no?), the court ruled that the lawyer's statement was proper. Jackson v. United States, 928 F.2d 245, 248 (8th Cir.), *cert. denied,* 112 S. Ct. 98 (1991). Similarly, in *United States v. Litchfield,* 959 F.2d 1514 (10th Cir. 1992), the lawyer expressed concern to the judge about whether the client would tell the truth at trial. The lawyer was concerned *not* because of what the client had told him, but rather because the lawyer had told the client that the only way to defend the case was to have the client testify! The Tenth Circuit held that under Wyoming Rule of Professional Conduct 3.3, it was not unethical for the lawyer to discuss his concerns ex parte with the judge (without the defendant), nor did the lawyer's conduct create any Sixth Amendment claim. Yet, it is unclear why the lawyer thought the judge was the appropriate person from whom to receive absolution, if indeed absolution was even necessary.

Indeed, it is questionable that this conference could occur constitutionally without the defendant's presence. An accused undoubtedly has a fundamental right to be present at every stage of her trial. Illinois

v. Allen, 397 U.S. 337, 338 (1970). The right extends to all proceedings where the accused's presence "has a relation, reasonably substantial, to the fullness of his opportunity to defend against the charge." United States v. Gagnon, 470 U.S. 522, 526 (1985), *quoting* Snyder v. Massachusetts, 291 U.S. 97, 105–6 (1934). Further, due process requires an accused's presence "'to the extent that a fair and just hearing would be thwarted by [the accused's] absence. . . .'" Kentucky v. Stincer, 482 U.S. 730, 745 (1987), *quoting Snyder* at 108. Since *Rock v. Arkansas, supra,* determined that the right to testify is a fundamental constitutional right, it inexorably follows that the accused's presence at a time when the judge will determine whether and how the accused may testify bears more than a "reasonably substantial" relationship to the accused's right to defend against the charge.

In addition, the defendant must be told about the information relied upon by the court in sentencing the defendant. That is because due process prohibits the sentencing of defendants based on materially inaccurate information, *Townsend v. Burke,* 334 U.S. 736 (1948), and such sentencings arguably can only be prevented by disclosure of the information relied upon. *See, e.g.,* United States v. Berzon, 941 F.2d 8, 21 (1st Cir. 1991) ("a defendant may not be placed in a position where, because of his ignorance of the information being used against him, he is effectively denied an opportunity to comment on or otherwise challenge material information considered by the district court").[12]

Several courts and commentators have suggested more acceptable (although far from great) ways to deal with the problem. One commentator suggests an in camera ex parte hearing with a judge other than the presiding judge where the defendant could testify if he so desired. The record of the hearing would be sealed and nothing in it could later be used against the client. Rieger, *Client Perjury: A Proposed Resolution of the Constitutional and Ethical Issues,* 70 MINN. L. REV. 121, 151–53 (1985). Of course, convincing a jurisdiction to accept such a time-consuming procedure (why is it that all fair procedures are time consuming and unfair ones are not?) would not be easy. *See, e.g., People v. Bartee, supra* (court declined to require *Long* hearing before ordering defendant to testify in narrative).

Another commentator, indeed the distinguished former chief justice of the Colorado Supreme Court, suggests creating a board of lawyers to decide ethical issues. Erickson, *The Perjurious Defendant: A Proposed Solution to the Defense Lawyer's Conflicting Ethical Obligations to the Court and to His Client,* 59 DEN. L. J. 75, 88–91 (1981).

And in *Long, supra,* the Eighth Circuit suggested that any prejudice could be sufficiently ameliorated if the trial judge discussed the po-

tential lawyer-client conflict only with the defense lawyer and the defendant, prevented any further disclosure of client confidences, and
clarified that the defendant understood his rights and his lawyer's
ethical obligations. Unfortunately this is no solution at all, since one of
the lawyer's ethical obligations in *Long* was said to be disclosure of
client perjury. Which brings us back full circle.

Where Are We Now?

We began this chapter stating our hope to provide defense lawyers
with "some" guidance. It must now be obvious why we kept our hopes
so modest. If the quality of a civilization is indeed judged by its treatment of those charged with violating its laws,[13] our society has a long,
long way to go. Not until we have traveled much father toward that
goal will there be any clarity in the area of anticipated client perjury.

Notes

The authors gratefully acknowledge the assistance of Lisa Berman,
which she provided while a law student at California Western Law
School.

1. Dean Freedman began the public debate in 1966 when he told the
Criminal Law Institute that criminal defense lawyers should present their clients' perjured testimony in the same way they present any other testimony.
Lecture by Monroe H. Freedman to the Criminal Law Institute (Washington,
D.C. 1966). *See also* articles cited at the end of this chapter. Freedman's position
shocked many and was immediately denounced by former Chief Justice Warren Burger, among others. *See, e.g.,* Warren G. Burger, *Standards of Conduct for
Prosecution and Defense Personnel: A Judge's Viewpoint,* 5 AM. CRIM. L.Q. 11 (1966).
2. *See, e.g.,* Charles J. Ogletree, *The Future of Defense Advocacy,* 136 U. PA.
L. REV. 1903 (1988).
3. In a fascinating study of the Chicago courts, the author found, among
other things, that prosecutors, public defenders, and judges believe that police
officers commit perjury between 20 and 50 percent of the time when testifying
about Fourth Amendment issues Orfield, *supra* at 83.
4. *See* ABA/BNA LAWYERS MANUAL ON PROFESSIONAL CONDUCT, Model
Standards at 01 (2/23/94). Of the remaining states, five—Illinois, New York,
North Carolina, Oregon, and Virginia—have amended their ethics rules since
the 1983 passage of the ABA Model Rules to incorporate some of the substance
of those Rules. *Id.* Another state—California—has revised its rules since 1983,
but has adopted neither the Model Code nor the Model Rules. *Id.*
5. *See, e.g.,* Georgia, New York, Oregon, Tennessee, and Virginia.
6. This question of loyalty is the foundation of all ethical analysis of
lawyer-client relationships. *See, e.g.,* Michael K. McChrystal, *Lawyers and Loy-*

alty, 33 WILLIAM & MARY L. REV. 367 (1992) ("The concept of loyalty is a fulcrum in the persistent struggle to define the nature of lawyering"); Geoffrey C. Hazard, *Triangular Lawyer Relationships: An Exploratory Analysis,* 1 GEO. J. LEGAL ETHICS 15, 21 (1987).

7. As trial lawyers, we have more than a little difficulty envisioning how a direct examination by a defense lawyer could include the lawyer's impeachment of his or her client. Contemplate, if you can, a criminal defense lawyer suddenly interrupting the flow of direct examination of her client with the following: "You are *now* telling this jury you actually saw a metallic object. I want to ask you some questions about what I asked you and what you told me last night in my office. I asked you what, if anything, you saw. You told me you saw nothing. You never told me you saw a metallic object."

8. Compare this finding with the Court's holding in *Strickland* where the defendant told the trial court during his plea proceeding that he had no prior criminal record. Although defense counsel knew that his client had a "rap sheet," counsel argued at his client's capital sentencing hearing that the judge should favorably consider the fact that his client had no prior criminal record. In its opinion upholding Strickland's death sentence, the Supreme Court not only approved counsel's affirmative misstatement to the court, but characterized counsel's actions as "the result of reasonable professional judgment." 466 U.S. at 699. In reaching this decision, the Supreme Court interpreted the Sixth Amendment to require an "overarching duty to advocate the defendant's cause. . . ." *Id.* at 688. The only consistency we can find between *Strickland* and *Whiteside* is that both cases affirmed the convictions and sentences of criminal defendants.

9. This is not always a correct assumption. A lawyer may seek to withdraw mid-trial because of other serious conflicts with a client, such as a case where the client insists upon testifying even though the lawyer is adamantly opposed to the testimony because a prejudicial prior conviction would be disclosed to the jury.

10. *See* Connecticut Bar Ass'n Committee on Professional Ethics, Formal Opinion 42 (3/13/92) (where lawyer is unsuccessful in dissuading client from testifying perjuriously and lawyer's motion to withdraw is denied, client may testify in narrative form without lawyer's assistance); Legal Ethics Committee of the D.C. Bar, Formal Opinion 234 (1993) (where lawyer is unsuccessful in dissuading client from testifying perjuriously and lawyer's motion to withdraw is denied *or would cause "serious harm" to the client,* client may testify in narrative form).

11. *See also* People v. Bartee, 208 Ill. App. 3d 105, 566 N.E.2d 855 (Ill. App. 1991) (where lawyer's mid-trial motion to withdraw is denied, trial court properly ordered defendant to testify in narrative form), *app. denied,* 139 Ill. 2d 598, *cert. denied,* 112 S. Ct. 661 (1991). *See also* Hall, *supra* at 806–8, *citing* Benedict v. Henderson, 721 F. Supp. 1560 (N.D.N.Y. 1989) (narrative approach consistent with New York Code of Professional Responsibility then in effect), *aff'd without op.,* 904 F.2d 34 (2d Cir.), *cert. denied,* 498 U.S. 867 (1990); People v. Guzman, 755

P.2d 917 (Cal. 1988) (neither California Rules of Professional Conduct nor Sixth Amendment violated by use of narrative), *cert. denied*, 488 U.S. 1050 (1989); State v. Fosnight, 679 P.2d 174 (Kan. 1984); *In re* Goodwin, 305 S.E.2d 578 (S.C. 1983); Coleman v. State, 621 P.2d 869 (Alaska 1980).

12. *Cf.* Burns v. United States, 501 U.S. 129 (1991) (Fed. R. Crim. P. 32 requires courts to give notice to defendants of court's intent to depart upward because right to comment on sentencing information under the rule is otherwise rendered meaningless).

13. Irvin v. Dowd, 366 U.S. 717, 729 (1961) (Frankfurter, J., concurring).

Bibliography

Books and Law Review Articles

ABA/BNA LAWYERS MANUAL ON PROFESSIONAL CONDUCT.

Brent R. Appel, Nix v. Whiteside: *The Role of Apples, Oranges, and the Great Houdini in Constitutional Adjudication*, 23 Crim. L. Bull. 5 (1987).

Brent R. Appel, *The Limited Impact of* Nix v. Whiteside *on Attorney-Client Relations*, 136 U. Pa. L. Rev. 1913 (1988).

Carl A. Auerbach, *What Are Law Clerks For?—Comments on* Nix v. Whiteside, 23 S. Diego L. Rev. 979 (1986).

Michael L. Bender, Nix v. Whiteside: *The Perjurious Client Dilemma— What Should Defense Counsel Do?* 15 Colo. Law. 21 (1986).

Warren G. Burger, *Standards of Conduct for Prosecution and Defense Personnel: A Judge's Viewpoint*, 5 Am. Crim. L.Q. 11 (1966).

William H. Erickson, *The Perjurious Defendant: A Proposed Solution to the Defense Lawyer's Conflicting Ethical Obligations to the Court and to His Client*, 59 Den. L.J. 75 (1981).

Monroe H. Freedman, *Client Confidences and Client Perjury: Some Unanswered Questions*, 136 U. Pa. L. Rev. 1913 (1988).

Monroe H. Freedman, *Lawyer's Ethics in an Adversary System* (1975).

Monroe H. Freedman, *Perjury: The Lawyer's Trilemma*, 1 Litigation 26 (1975).

Monroe H. Freedman, *Professional Responsibility of the Criminal Defense Lawyer: The Three Hardest Questions*, 64 Mich. L. Rev. 1469 (1966).

Bennett L. Gershman, *Attorney Loyalty and Client Perjury—A Postscript to* Nix v. Whiteside, 14 Am J. Crim. L. 97 (1987).

Linda H. Gottlieb, *Pinocchio for the Defense*, 14 Fla. St. U. L. Rev. 891 (1987).

Patrick R. Grady, Nix v. Whiteside: *Client Perjury and the Criminal Justice System: The Defendant's Position*, 23 Am. Crim. L. Rev. 1 (1985).

Hall, *Handling Client Perjury After* Nix v. Whiteside: *A Criminal Defense Lawyer's View*, 42 Mercer L. Rev. 769 (1991).

Geoffrey C. Hazard, *Triangular Lawyer Relationships: An Exploratory Analysis*, 1 Geo. J. Legal Ethics 15 (1987).

Norman Lefstein, *Client Perjury in Criminal Cases: Still in Search of an Answer*, 1 Geo. J. Legal Ethics 521 (1988).

Terence F. MacCarthy & Kathy Morris Mejia, T*he Perjurious Client Question: Putting Criminal Defense Lawyers Between a Rock and a Hard Place*, 75 J. Crim. L. & Criminol. 1197 (1984).

McCall, Nix v. Whiteside: *The Lawyer's Role in Response to Perjury*, 13 Hastings Const. L.Q. 443 (1986).

Michael K. McChrystal, *Lawyers and Loyalty*, 33 William & Mary L. Rev. 367 (1992).

John T. Noonan, Jr., *The Purposes of Advocacy and the Limits of Confidentiality*, 64 Mich. L. Rev. 1485 (1966).

Note, *Legal Ethics, Client Perjury and the Privilege Against Self-Incrimination*, 13 Hastings Const. L.Q. 545 (1986).

Charles J. Ogletree, *The Future of Defense Advocacy*, 136 U. Pa. L. Rev. 1903 (1988)

Myron W. Orfield, *Deterrence, Perjury, and the Heater Factor: An Exclusionary Rule in the Chicago Criminal Courts*, 63 Univ. Colo. L. Rev. 75, 109 (1992).

Lee A. Pizzimenti, *The Lawyer's Duty to Warn Clients about Limits on Confidentiality*, 39 Cath. U. L. Rev. 441 (1990).

Carol T. Rieger, *Client Perjury: A Proposed Resolution of the Constitutional and Ethical Issues*, 70 Minn. L. Rev. 121 (1985)

CHAPTER 📖 12

Disclose or Not: The Client Who Falsely Obtains Appointed Counsel

Richard J. Wilson

During a confidential discussion with her client, a public defender learns information about her client that suggests the client may have provided false information to qualify for appointed/assigned counsel. What obligation, if any, does a public defender have to investigate or to reveal information relating to client eligibility or fraud in obtaining court-appointed counsel? Is that obligation affected by the fact that the defender and her office are burdened by high caseloads that limit the number of indigent clients who can be served?

Proposed answers to this ethical dilemma must be explored at the intersection of two fundamentally conflicting obligations of any defense lawyer. The first duty of counsel is to protect the confidential and secret communications from a client. Here, the question assumes confidential communication of new information indicating lack of indigency, which puts the lawyer in the difficult position of judging whether that information is evidence of a crime or fraud, and whether, if it is a crime, the crime is completed or ongoing.

The second duty of counsel is to be candid with the court. That duty flows both from counsel's traditional role as an "officer of the court" and from the additional fiduciary obligations that appointed counsel has to protection of the public fisc. Counsel cannot, it is suggested here, be loyal to one duty without being disloyal to the other. Neither the Model Code nor the Model Rules neatly resolve the issue of the lawyer's competing obligations of confidentiality of client communications and candor to the tribunal.

ABA Model Code of Professional Responsibility

It is assumed, for purposes of discussion here, that actual evidence of false information is provided by the client. The issue of the obligation of the defender to investigate "information" provided by the client that indicates falsity in the application for counsel is explored below. Under the Model Code, DR 4-101 provides that a lawyer must protect the confidences and secrets of a client. Here, the question itself assumes confidentiality, and there is little doubt that the communication also qualifies as a "secret," which is defined as "information gained in the professional relationship . . . the disclosure of which . . . would be likely to be detrimental to the client." MODEL CODE, DR 4-101(A). The rule goes on to describe situations where the lawyer *may* reveal confidences or secrets of a client. That is, when the client consents after full disclosure, when the Disciplinary Rules or law so require, when the court orders disclosure, or when the revelation is necessary to collect a fee or protect against charges of wrongful conduct. MODEL CODE, DR 4-101(C)(1),(2) and (4).

While neither state nor federal law requires the revelation of information of falsity in the application for defense services, federal and state statutes sometimes deal with the consequences of revelation of such information. Nebraska, for example, has a statute which provides:

> Whenever any court finds subsequent to its appointment of the public defender or other counsel to represent a felony defendant that its initial determination of indigency was incorrect, or that during the course of representation by appointed counsel the felony defendant has become no longer indigent, the court may order such felony defendant to reimburse the county for all or part of the reasonable cost of providing such representation. NEB. REV. STAT. § 29-3908 (Supp. 1990). *Cf.,* 18 U.S.C. §§ 3006A(c) and (f) (1992).

It should be noted that this statute does not assess the manner by which the defendant becomes solvent, nor the means by which the court "finds" the information. The ABA Standards for Criminal Justice suggest that a finding of reimbursement should be entered *only* when there has been "fraud in obtaining the determination of eligibility." ABA STANDARDS FOR CRIMINAL JUSTICE, *Providing Defense Services,* Standard 5-7.2(a) (3d ed. 1992).

DR 4-101(C)(3) provides the situation closest to the one posed here. It provides that a lawyer "may reveal . . . [t]he intention of his client to commit a crime and the information necessary to prevent a crime." The question thus arises as to whether the provision of false information at the time of appointment of counsel or the failure to disclose such information later constitutes a crime, and whether the crime is complete or ongoing.

It seems that any crime that the client may have committed is complete at the time of the provision of counsel. Unless the client has executed an affidavit of indigency, no crime of perjury has been committed, particularly if confidentiality is protected in the initial provision of counsel, as is suggested by the ABA Criminal Justice Standards. ABA STANDARDS FOR CRIMINAL JUSTICE, *Providing Defense Services*, Standard 5-7.3 (3d ed. 1992).[1]

Even if the conduct involved in the nondisclosure of information at the time of appointment amounts to perjury, however, the crime has already been committed. The same seems to be true of other potential crimes such as theft of services or obtaining money by false pretenses. This result accords with the well-reasoned Opinion No. 78-2 of the Nebraska State Bar Association, which concluded that the defender may not disclose the new information to the court without client consent and may not seek to withdraw from representation on grounds that the client is not indigent. Revelation of the confidentially disclosed information is inappropriate, the Nebraska Bar Opinion reasoned, because of the latitude in interpretation of the definition of indigency and the need to maintain the integrity of the lawyer-client relationship. The opinion notes the ongoing responsibility of the court to inquire into eligibility. In reaching its conclusion, the bar found support in ABA Formal Opinion 287 and ABA Informal Opinions 1314, 1137, and 1141.

An opposite conclusion is reached by the Oregon Bar Association in its Opinion No. 263 (May 11, 1974). The opinion concludes that the client who tells a public defender that false information was provided to obtain criminal defense services commits the crime of theft of services, and that the crime is ongoing. Under Oregon law the crime of theft of services occurs when one obtains services by "deception," and deception occurs when a person "fails to correct a false impression which he previously created or confirmed...." OR. REV. STAT. § 164.085(1)(b) (1991).

The Oregon Bar Association opinion, however, focuses its ethical analysis primarily on the provisions of DR 7-102(A) of the Model Code, which deal with representation of a client within the bounds of the law. That provision states, in relevant part, that a lawyer shall not:

(3) Conceal or knowingly fail to disclose that which he is required by law to reveal.
(4) Knowingly use perjured testimony or false evidence.

(5) Knowingly make a false statement of law or fact.

(6) Participate in the creation or preservation of evidence when he knows or it is obvious that the evidence is false.

(7) Counsel or assist his client in conduct that the lawyer knows to be illegal or fraudulent.

(8) Knowingly engage in other illegal conduct or conduct contrary to a Disciplinary Rule.

The opinion also utilizes DR 7-102(B), which, in Oregon, provides that:

(B) A lawyer who receives information clearly establishing that: (1) His client has, in the course of representation, perpetrated a fraud upon a person or tribunal shall promptly call upon his client to rectify the same, and if his client refuses or is unable to do so, he shall reveal the fraud to the affected person or tribunal.

The latter provision seems to make clear the lawyer's responsibilities in Oregon.[2] There is little doubt that, whether the false information revealed by the client is "evidence" under DR 7-102(A), it is a "fraud upon a . . . tribunal" under DR 7-102(B).

The lawyer, therefore, should call on the client to reveal the false information to the court, according to the Oregon Bar's analysis, and if the client refuses, the lawyer should reveal the information to the tribunal. The first part of this analysis seems appropriate in most other states as well, since it is almost always appropriate to advise the client to reveal unlawful conduct to the tribunal, even when there are issues of confidentiality. However, revelation here seems to fly directly in the face of the amended provisions of DR 7-102(B)(1) of the ABA Model Code.

In fact, there is a significant omission in the Oregon version of DR 7-102. The language of the ABA Model Code is exactly the same as that of the Oregon Code, but the following clause is added at the end of the section:

(B) A lawyer who receives information clearly establishing that: (1) His client has, in the course of representation, perpetrated a fraud upon a person or tribunal shall promptly call upon his client to rectify the same, and if his client refuses or is unable to do so, he shall reveal the fraud to the affected person or tribunal, *except when the information is protected as a privileged communication.*

Thus, under the language of the Model Code (and of the Nebraska ethics code, cited in Opinion 78-2 above), the lawyer would be required to value the lawyer-client privilege over the duty to reveal the client's fraud in this circumstance.[3]

Two other state bars provide some guidance to the solution of this problem, drawing on the equivalents of Model Code provisions in their states. In Michigan, the ethics committee has provided a series of opinions on this precise issue and concludes, as did the Oregon Bar, that the lawyer must "cause the client to disclose the true facts concerning the defendant's financial ability to the court, and abide by the court's redetermination of the client's indigency, before withdrawing from the case or making any other employment arrangement with the client." Michigan Syllabus CI-785 (June 23, 1982); *see also,* Michigan Syllabus CI-324 (June 30, 1977); Michigan Opinion 127 (Oct. 1949). Unfortunately, the later informal opinions uniformly draw from the 1949 formal opinion, which seems guided by ethical norms that had not yet grappled with the difficult issues of balance of candor to the tribunal and protection of client confidences.

Finally, the Illinois Bar, using the same ethical rules, provides something of a middle ground. It concludes that the defender should not report or reveal any information concerning the specific assets that have been concealed by the client, but if the client refuses to voluntarily correct the omission, the defender should file a motion for leave to withdraw from the case on the stated general grounds that the client does not qualify for public defender services. Illinois Opinion No. 533 (Feb. 13, 1976).

Taken together with the provisions of the Model Code, these state ethics opinions suggest that, in states where the Model Code's language in DR 7-102(B) has been adopted, the privilege prevails over the obligation to reveal, except that the lawyer is left with the exercise of discretion in keeping the information confidential.[4] Prof. John Burkoff calls this an instance where "professional ethics defer to personal ethics. A lawyer cannot avoid responsibility for a revelation . . .; rather, the lawyer must personally decide in such a situation precisely what he or she thinks is the morally correct and appropriate thing to do—and then do it." John M. Burkoff, *Criminal Defense Ethics: Law and Liability,* § 6.5(f) (1992).

Both the Michigan and Nebraska opinions suggest a different but related ethical issue that can arise: the potential for conflict of interest created when the defender is part-time and is also permitted to engage in private practice. If the lawyer also provides private criminal defense representation, then the lawyer has a clear financial incentive to transfer the nonpaying client onto the docket of paying customers. This conflict is real, not potential, and may put the defender in the position of promoting a redetermination of indigency in order to garner a fee that is higher than the amount paid by the government for defense of an indigent client. It is for just these reasons that the ABA Criminal Justice Standards strongly suggest that part-time defenders not provide private defense representation in the same jurisdiction where they serve as a public defender. ABA STANDARDS FOR CRIMINAL JUSTICE, *Providing Defense Services*, Standard 5-4.2, Commentary at 59 (3d ed. 1992).

Two cases provide some helpful insights into the circumstances presented by the problem. Both deal with legal issues, not ethical problems, in the redetermination of indigency, but each sheds some light on the resolution of such ethical dilemmas. First, in *State v. Keswick*, 680 P.2d 182 (Ariz. Ct. App. 1984), the facts indicate that the public defender, in the course of representation of appellant Keswick, concluded that he "had serious doubts as to whether appellant was indigent." *Id.* at 183. Keswick had apparently owned a parcel of land valued at approximately $225,000 at the time of appointment of counsel, but had transferred title to the land to his sister and argued that he had no control over the property. The defender followed the procedure suggested by the Illinois ethics opinion above, filing a "motion for determination of counsel which, in substance, was a motion for reconsideration of the determination of indigency. . . ." *Id.* at 183–84. After revelation of the defendant's property interest, the defender was permitted to withdraw and Keswick retained counsel.[5] The remainder of the opinion dealt with the issue of the appropriate calculation of lawyer's fees to reimburse the county for the hours expended in representation.

Another informative decision is *United States v. Jimenez*, 600 F.2d 1172 (5th Cir. 1979). In that case, the prosecution filed a motion after conviction asking the court to reconsider the order appointing counsel, arguing that Jimenez had not been indigent when he applied for counsel and that appointment of counsel had been in error. The trial court agreed but concluded that since the trial Jimenez had become indigent and could not afford to pay any future lawyer's fees. Nonetheless, the court ordered that Jimenez reimburse the government for the costs of counsel as a condition of probation. The court of appeals overturned the latter order, finding that the condition of probation was unconstitutional under the decision in *Fuller v. Oregon*, 417 U.S. 40 (1974). That case upheld a state statute permitting recovery of lawyer's fees but specifically excepted those who have no current ability to pay.

ABA Model Rules of Professional Conduct

The Model Code, because of its longevity, has a rich basis of opinions and cases that interpret its provisions. The ABA Model Rules, on the other hand, are relatively recent and have little interpretive material to provide guidance to the practitioner. Moreover, the newer rules were adopted in part because of a public perception that lawyers were not as candid and honest in their dealings with the public as they could be. Therefore, although the Model Rules draw from the experience of the Model Code, their solutions to the dilemmas alluded to in this problem leave the public defender with no clear sense of a solution.

The first major difference in the Model Rules is the scope of coverage of confidential communications, particularly at the outset of the relationship. The Model Rules provide, in relevant part, that a lawyer's duty of confidentiality extends to all information "relating to representation of a client" unless the client knowingly consents to the revelation. MODEL RULE 1.6(a). It seems clear that information about eligibility, given in confidence during the course of representation, "relates to" representation and is covered by the Model Rules.

The only relevant exception provided for revelation of confidences states that the lawyer *may* reveal information, to the extent the lawyer reasonably believes necessary, "to prevent the client from committing a criminal act" that the lawyer believes is likely to result in "imminent death or substantial bodily harm." MODEL RULE 1.6 (b)(1). This provision is similar to that found in the Model Code in DR 4-101(C)(3), with some slight changes.

Under the Model Rules, the revelation of intent to commit a future criminal act is limited in a way that the Model Code was not. The withholding of financial information to obtain appointed counsel, which may or may not constitute a completed or ongoing crime, is surely not sufficient to qualify for optional revelation as permitted under the above rule, which limits revelation only of those future crimes likely to result in death or great bodily harm.

In 1991, the ABA House of Delegates rejected an Ethics Committee recommendation that it modify the language of Model Rule 1.6 to create an exception to the general rule of confidentiality "to rectify the consequences of a client's criminal or fraudulent act in the furtherance of which the lawyer's services had been used." (*See Selected Statutes, Rules and Standards on the Legal Profession* 21 (1992 ed.)). This amendment seemingly was offered to correct a perceived defect in the Model Rules concerning the potential complicity of the lawyer in the ongoing criminal or fraudulent conduct of the client. Under the Model Rules, then, even fraudulent withholding of information by the client from the public defender falls within the protection of the rule of confidentiality and a reasonable reading of Model Rule 1.6 leads to the conclusion that not only is the lawyer not required to reveal the false information, but is not permitted to do so. However, defenders should be aware that certain states have adopted the exception to Model Rule 1.6(b) (*See, e.g.,* Oklahoma Model Rule 1.6(b)(2)). In states where the exception has been adopted, defenders arguably would be permitted to disclose a client's fraud used to obtain legal services.

The unambiguous Model Rule 1.6 is, unfortunately, muddied by another section of the Model Rules. Model Rule 3.3(a)(2) states that a lawyer shall not knowingly "fail to disclose a material fact to a tribunal when disclosure is necessary to avoid assisting a criminal or fraudulent act by the client." Subsection (a)(4) prohibits the lawyer from knowingly offering "evidence which the lawyer knows to be false." Subsection (b) of Model Rule 3.3 states explicitly that the duty to disclose under paragraph (a) applies *"even if compliance requires disclosure of information otherwise protected by rule 1.6,"* but only until "the conclusion of the proceeding." Subsection (d) requires that a lawyer involved in an ex parte proceeding disclose all material facts known to the lawyer.[6] Model Rule 3.3, then, reaches exactly the opposite conclusion to that suggested by Model Code DR 7-102(B)(1), which concludes that the duty of disclosure does *not* apply to information protected by the privilege, whenever it may be revealed.

The explicit requirement of disclosure in Model Rule 3.3 would seem to prevail over the general rule of confidentiality found in Model Rule 1.6. However, a number of perplexing problems regarding revelation persist. First, subsection (a)(4) prohibits the lawyer only from "offering" known false evidence. When a lawyer confidentially obtains information indicating a previous falsity by the client in obtaining counsel, there is no context in which the lawyer is likely to "offer" such evidence. Second, subsection (a)(2) requires disclosure of "material facts" to the tribunal when disclosure is necessary to avoid assisting "criminal or fraudulent acts" by the client. Does this refer to future criminal activity only, as is suggested by Model Rule 1.6, or does it also refer to completed crimes? Is fraud in an application for appointment of counsel "material" to the proof of criminal charges against the client, when evidence is immaterial if it is "offered to prove a proposition which is not a matter in issue," and what is "in issue" is what is "within the range of the litigated controversy as determined mainly by the pleadings"? Edward J. Cleary, et al., *McCormick on Evidence* (3d ed. 1984). If the application is unsworn, is there any crime at all?

Third, the commentary to Model Rule 1.6 seems at odds with the black letter. In the section "False Evidence," the commentary states, in paragraph [6], *"Except in the defense of a criminal accused,* the rule generally recognized is that, if necessary to rectify the situation, an advocate must disclose the existence of the client's deception to the court or to the other party." This major exception is nowhere to be found in the text of the Model Rule. Moreover, the remainder of the commentary deals with the much more complex ethical issue of perjury by a criminal defendant. See commentary to Model Rule 3.3, paragraphs [7] to [12]. As noted in the discussion of the Model Code above, the crime of perjury, if it has been committed in this factual context, seems to have been completed at the time of the signing of an initial affidavit of indigency, assuming the client knowingly withheld the false information at that time. Finally, the rejected amendment to Model Rule 1.6, proposed by the ABA Ethics Committee in 1991 and set forth above, seems to suggest both the committee's concern that the rules were not specific enough in their requirements of disclosure and that the provisions of Model Rule 3.3 could not be interpreted in such a manner as to overcome this potential defect.

The commentary to Model Rule 1.6 refers frequently to parallel language in Model Rule 1.2, which states, in subsection (d), that a lawyer "shall not counsel a client to engage, or assist a client, in conduct that the lawyer knows is criminal or fraudulent, but the lawyer may discuss the legal consequences of any proposed course of conduct with a client and may counsel or assist a client to make a good faith effort to determine the validity, scope, meaning or application of the law." Section 1.2 deals with the options a lawyer has when counseling her client about criminal or fraudulent conduct while Model Rule 1.6 deals with the lawyer's obligations to the tribunal.

The commentary to Model Rule 1.2 offers some specific guidance to the problem alluded to above in discussion of the Model Code provisions—the issue of counsel's potential complicity in an ongoing crime by the client once the false information is revealed in a confidential communication. The commentary states:

> When the client's course of action has already begun and is continuing, the lawyer's responsibility is especially delicate. The lawyer is not permitted to reveal the client's wrongdoing, except where permitted by Rule 1.6 [the confidentiality provision]. However, the lawyer is required to avoid furthering the purpose, for example, by suggesting how it might be concealed. A lawyer may not continue assisting a client in conduct that the lawyer originally supposes is legally proper but then discovers is criminal or fraudulent. Withdrawal from the representation, therefore, may be required. MODEL RULE 1.2, Comment, paragraph 7.

This is the only place in the Model Rules where a course of action for the lawyer, in the context of the instant problem, is suggested.

The totality of the new Model Rules provisions suggest a course of action similar to that arrived at under the Model Code in dealing with the client who confidentially reveals that false information was provided to qualify for appointed counsel. The lawyer should discuss the issue fully and urge the client to take steps to remedy the situation by revealing the information to the tribunal. However, the Model Rules seem to suggest a different course of action for the lawyer when the client refuses to reveal the false information. Unlike the Model Code solution, which permits but does not mandate the lawyer to reveal the existence of a fraud, the Model Rules seem to suggest an affirmative obligation to reveal the information in question, so long as the new information is acquired in the course of the proceeding for which counsel has been appointed.[7] Commentary to the Model Rules suggests that withdrawal of counsel may be necessary, without guidance as to how revelation of the fraud is to occur.

Other Sources

The ABA Standards for Criminal Justice explicitly deal with the issue of fraud in obtaining counsel. Standard 5-7.2(a) states as follows:

> Reimbursement of counsel or the organization or the governmental unit providing counsel should not be required, *except on the ground of fraud in obtaining the determination of eligibility.* ABA STANDARDS FOR CRIMINAL JUSTICE, *Providing Defense Services*, Standard 5-7.2(a) (3d ed. 1992) (emphasis added).

This standard, of course, deals more specifically with the question of the propriety of reimbursement in general and not with the ethical issue of counsel's duty to reveal the fraud when it is revealed in a confidential conversation with the client. The commentary to the standard, however, more specifically addresses that issue. Citing to Model Rule 3.3(a)(2), the commentary states that defendants who misrepresent financial eligibility "should not be permitted to benefit from their deceit, and the defendant's lawyer has an ethical duty to reveal the misrepresentation to the court." ABA STANDARDS FOR CRIMINAL JUSTICE, *Providing Defense Services*, Standard 5-7.2, Commentary at 95 (3d ed. 1992). No authority is cited in support of this obligation, however, and the rule itself deals only with reimbursement, not ethical obligations.

In 1986, the U.S. Department of Justice conducted a national study of eligibility screening and the use of recoupment of lawyer's fees from "partially indigent" defendants. That study did not provide any specific recommendations on the question presented in this problem, but the text of the report provides a summary of some of the issues discussed above. The report states:

> An obvious problem occurs when appointed counsel believes that the defendant committed perjury in supplying information at the outset which resulted in a false determination of indigency. The question is an ethical one and not easily answered. However, as a general rule, if an appointed attorney receives information of a change in financial condition he or she is obliged to advise the appointing judge and ask to be relieved of the assignment. However, if an attorney discovers that the defendant has provided erroneous information, he or she should request to be relieved of the appointment, but not be required to break the confidence of the attorney-client relationship. In any event, an attorney must make certain that the defendant's right to counsel remains protected until new counsel is available. U.S. Department of Justice, National Institute of Justice, *Containing the Cost of Indigent Defense Programs: Eligibility Screening and Cost Recovery Procedures* 28 (Sept. 1986).

This solution seems similar to that proposed by the Illinois Bar's opinion and to that taken by counsel in Arizona in *State v. Keswick*, discussed above.

Finally, Prof. John Burkoff has authored an excellent text that deals with issues of ethics for defense lawyers. John M. Burkoff, *Criminal Defense Ethics: Law and Liability* (1992). Prof. Burkoff's treatment, unfortunately, does not distinguish between the ethical duties of public defenders and privately retained counsel, except to note that they are generally "congruent" in the area of ineffective assistance of counsel since the decision in *Cuyler v. Sullivan*, 446 U.S. 343, 344-45 (1980). *Criminal Defense Ethics, supra,* at § 2.2.

Prof. Burkoff exhaustively discusses all of the interplay of the Model Code and Model Rules with regard to counsel's duties to reveal completed crimes, continuing crimes, or frauds upon the court. As to completed crimes, his answer is unequivocal; under any existing ethical standard an lawyer is not permitted to reveal confidential communications from her client relating to commission of past crimes. This conclusion, he asserts, is, if anything, strengthened by Sixth Amendment concerns. *Criminal Defense Ethics, supra,* § 6.5(e).

As to frauds, his analysis is similar to that offered above. He concludes that:

> [T]he primary . . . difference between the Model Rules and the ABA Code is that under the former an attorney must report a cli-

ent's fraud upon the court to the court if it is discovered any time prior to the conclusion of the proceeding (even if it is discovered after the fact). Under the ABA Code, in contrast, an attorney may—but need not—report a client's fraud upon the court to the court, but only if it is discovered before the fact. . . . *Criminal Defense Ethics, supra,* at § 6.5(g) (footnote omitted).

Prof. Burkoff also notes the disturbing dicta in *Nix v. Whiteside,* 475 U.S. 157, 168–70 (1986), which states that there is a "special duty of an attorney to prevent and disclose frauds upon the court."

As to continuing crimes, Prof. Burkoff cites to the commentary to Model Rule 1.2, set out above, and concludes that the Model Rules "imply that revelation of a client's continuing crime is ethically impermissible, but that a lawyer may do nothing to assist the client in engaging in such criminal activity." *Criminal Defense Ethics, supra,* at § 6.5(e) (footnote omitted). He suggests that when counsel is aware that the client intends to continue the criminal activity, counsel "should—or must—withdraw."

Taken together, these additional materials seem to suggest that appointed counsel has an absolute duty, under the Model Rules, to protect the revelation of false information by a client in a confidential communication, so long as that information constitutes a completed crime. However, if the false information is a fraud on the court, or if it constitutes an ongoing crime, a mandatory duty of revelation of the false information and eventual withdrawal from representation exists under the Model Rules, unlike the Model Code, which makes revelation optional, at most.

The Duty to Investigate and Its Relationship to High Caseloads in the Defender Office

The question presented here does not assume the existence of actual evidence of false information, but "information . . . which suggests" such evidence. It then asks what obligation the defender has to investigate the information further, and whether any such obligation is affected by the heavy caseloads that are typical of such offices. This discussion is saved for the final section because of this author's general opinion that the caseload of the defender office should not and, practically, will not enter into the determination whether to investigate, so long as recognized national standards are applied.

At the outset, it should be noted that the ethical provisions dealing with revelation of a fraud to the court, which seem to be the most relevant in this context, contain an introductory phrase in the Model

Code that states the lawyer must receive "information clearly establishing" a fraud before taking remedial action. DR 7-102(B). The Second Circuit Court of Appeals has interpreted this language to mean
that the lawyer must have "actual knowledge" of any covered fraud
before the duty to disclose is triggered. *In re Grievance Committee,* 847
F.2d 57, 63 (2d Cir. 1988). In this problem, the defender, who learns
information that suggests a fraud, does not yet seem to have reached
that level of knowledge, without further investigation.

Defenders and private appointed counsel are, unfortunately, more
often than not deprived of essential investigative resources to conduct
the most routine work involving the merits of the defendant's case, let
alone the collateral issue of the client's continued indigency. This is
true despite the existence of national standards calling for provision of
such services in such a manner that permits quality legal representation. ABA STANDARDS FOR CRIMINAL JUSTICE, *Providing Defense Services,*
Standard 5-1.4 (3d ed. 1992). As a resource matter, it would, in a great
many defender offices, border on malpractice or negligent misuse of
public funds to divert either the lawyer's or the investigator's time to
the issue of investigation of the client's assertion of the provision of
false financial information to obtain appointed counsel.

There is a suggestion in the ABA Standards that defenders and
assigned counsel generally have an interest in limiting caseloads and
will therefore not accept doubtful cases at the outset. ABA STANDARDS
FOR CRIMINAL JUSTICE, *Providing Defense Services,* Standard 5-7.3, Commentary at 99 (3d ed. 1992). The standard itself notes that "[i]f at any
subsequent stage in the proceedings new information concerning eligibility becomes available, eligibility should be redetermined." This, of
course, does not suggest that the response to new information should
be based on the fact that the defender's caseload is high.

In short, it does not seem to be a wise allocation of resources for
counsel to expend significant resources in the investigation of potential
fraud by the client. Factors that may affect the decision to conduct such
an investigation are the specificity of the client's identification of liquid
assets sufficient to permit retention of counsel; the point in the proceedings at which the revelation to counsel is made; and the extent to
which revelation of the false information may, in and of itself, directly
link the defendant to criminal activity (*see, e.g., In re Grand Jury Matter,*
969 F.2d 995 (11th Cir. 1992).

If the caseload of the defender office has increased to the point
where it is truly excessive, the office should take systematic steps to address the issue rather than concentrate on the presumably rare instances
presented in this hypothetical. The office or the individual defender
should consider either refusal of new cases or withdrawal from existing

cases, as is permitted by Standard 5-5.3 of the ABA Standards for Criminal Justice, *Providing Defense Services,* or the jurisdiction should consider litigation that will address more systematically the shortcomings in the delivery of defense services, which is provided for in Standard 5-5.4.

Conclusion

A key to the analysis of the question that begins this chapter is whether the initial provision of information to qualify for counsel is given on a sworn affidavit of indigency filed in open court or confidentially in a private interview with the defender office or a third-party agency. The more formal and public the initial representations by the client, the more likely that subsequent discovery of a crime or fraud by counsel will require disclosure.

If the false information is verified, the first course of action by counsel is to ask the client privately to voluntarily reveal the information to the tribunal. The most difficult situations arise when this course of action is recommended but the client refuses to take such action.

If the failure to reveal the false information constitutes a completed crime, both the ABA Model Code of Professional Responsibility and the Model Rules of Professional Conduct would seem to prohibit its revelation. If the information constitutes an ongoing crime, the Model Code permits but does not require revelation by counsel, while the Model Rules suggest that counsel should eventually withdraw without revealing the ongoing crime. In the event that the existence of false information constitutes a fraud upon the court, the Model Code makes revelation optional for the lawyer while the Model Rules make revelation mandatory. In the event that counsel determines that revelation is necessary and appropriate under state ethics provisions, the defender should ask to be relieved of the appointment without breaking confidences or revealing secrets, such as through a motion that calls for "redetermination of indigency." Appointed counsel should continue representation until new counsel is available.

The caseload of the defender office should not, in general, affect the decision to investigate the actual existence of the proffered false information or to withdraw from representation. Other, more systematic means exist to deal with a defender program's excessive caseload.[8]

Notes

1. *See also* Standard 4-3.1(b) (3d ed. 1993) ("To ensure the privacy essential for confidential communication between defense counsel and client, adequate facilities should be available for private discussions between counsel and accused in jails, prisons, courthouses, and other places where accused per-

sons must confer with counsel."). Standard 5-7.3 further provides that if, during proceedings, "new information concerning eligibility becomes available, eligibility should be redetermined."

2. The same language is used in Ohio, and resulted in suspension of a lawyer who failed to report a client's fraud. Office of Disciplinary Counsel v. Heffernan, 569 N.E.2d 1027 (Ohio 1991).

3. The Oregon analysis, in fact, reaches much the same conclusion through reliance on interpretations of these competing provisions in previous ethics opinions in that state, but concludes that the adoption of the "new" offense of theft of services, with its expanded definition of "deception" requires revelation to prevent participation by the lawyer in a "future" crime of the client under DR 4-101(C)(3).

4. Defenders in states whose version of DR 7-102(B) does *not* include the phrase "except when the information is protected as a privileged communication" may have a higher duty to take action to rectify the fraud, although ultimately that may result in revealing a privileged communication.

5. Cases such as this simply point to the difficulty of the defender's assessment of commission of a fraud. Here, obviously, the defender's conclusion was that the defendant maintained actual ownership of the property even though formal title had passed to other family members. Such a conclusion reasonably may not have been made by another defender.

6. The commentary suggests that the lawyer should "make disclosures of material facts known to the lawyer and that the lawyer reasonably believes are necessary to an informed decision." The defense lawyer, even in an ex parte hearing, has no duty to defend or advance interests adverse to his client's.

7. The National Association of Criminal Defense Lawyers offers a definitive and well-reasoned rejoinder to the Model Rules position. While written to deal with the more explicit issue of the defendant who proposes to commit perjury, the discussion is equally applicable here. In its Formal Opinion 92-2, the NACDL argues that "[t]he constitutional privilege against self-incrimination and the constitutional right to the effective assistance of counsel prohibit a lawyer from disclosing a client's perjury to the court, even though such conduct is in conflict with ethical rules, such as [Model] Rule 3.3(a)(2) and (4) . . . that call for disclosure." "The Ethics Advisory Committee of NACDL Formal Opinion 92-2," *The Champion* 23 (March 1993).

8. *See, e.g.,* ABA STANDARDS FOR CRIMINAL JUSTICE, PROVIDING DEFENSE SERVICES, Standard 5-5.3 (3d ed. 1992), which suggests solutions to excessive workload in defender offices. Commentary to the following standard, 5-5.4, notes that systematic attacks on excessive caseloads have been successful in a number of courts.

Bibliography

Articles, Reports, and Standards
ABA Committee on Professional Ethics and Professional Responsibility, Formal Opinions 287, 1314, 1137, 1141.

ABA MODEL CODE OF PROFESSIONAL RESPONSIBILITY, DR 4-101; 7-102 (1983).
ABA MODEL RULES OF PROFESSIONAL CONDUCT, Rules 1.2; 1.6; 3.3 (1991).
ABA STANDARDS FOR CRIMINAL JUSTICE, PROVIDING DEFENSE SERVICES §§ 5-1.4, 5-4.2, 5-5.3, 5-5.4, 5-7.2(a), 5-7.3 (3d ed. 1992).
ABA STANDARDS FOR CRIMINAL JUSTICE, PROVIDING DEFENSE SERVICES §§ 4-3.1(b), 5-7.3 (3d ed. 1993).
John M. Burkoff, *Criminal Defense Ethics: Law and Liability* §§ 2.2, 6.5(e), (f), (g) (1992).
Edward J. Cleary et al., *McCormick on Evidence* (3d ed. 1984).
John S. Dzienkowski, ed., *Selected Statutes, Rules, and Standards on the Legal Profession* (1992).
National Institute of Justice, U.S. Department of Justice, *Containing the Cost of Indigent Defense Programs: Eligibility Screening and Cost Recovery Procedures* 28 (1986).

Federal and State Codes, Statutes, and Opinions
18 U.S.C. § 3006A(c), (f) (1992).
National Association of Criminal Defense Lawyers Ethics Advisory Committee, Formal Op. 92-2 (1992).
Illinois Op. 533 (1976).
Michigan Syllabus CI-785 (June 23, 1982).
Michigan Syllabus CI-324 (June 30, 1977).
Michigan Op. 127 (1949).
NEBRASKA REV. STAT. § 29-3908 (Supp. 1990).
Nebraska Ethics Code, Op. 78-2.
OKLAHOMA MODEL RULES OF PROFESSIONAL CONDUCT Rule 1.6 (b)(2) (1988).
OR. REV. STAT. § 164.085(1)(b) (1991).
Oregon Bar Association, Op. No. 263 (May 11, 1974).

Cases
Cuyler v. Sullivan, 446 U.S. 343, 344–45 (1980).
Fuller v. Oregon, 417 U.S. 40 (1974).
In re Grand Jury Matter, 969 F.2d 995 (11th Cir. 1992).
In re Grievance Comm., 847 F.2d 57, 63 (2d Cir. 1988).
Nix v. Whiteside, 475 U.S. 157, 168–70 (1986).
Office of Disciplinary Counsel v. Heffernan, 569 N.E.2d 1027 (Ohio 1991).
State v. Keswick, 680 P.2d 182, 183–84 (Ariz. Ct. App. 1984).
United States v. Jimenez, 600 F.2d 1172 (5th Cir. 1979).

CHAPTER 📖 13

Disclosing Adverse Authority and Correcting Judicial Misunderstanding

Marilyn E. Bednarski

Does defense counsel have an ethical duty to advise the trial judge that she is relying on a misunderstanding of the law or overlooking settled law in handling her client's case?

Introduction

At a recent sentencing hearing in federal district court, a public defender argued for a sentence that the judge felt was too lenient. The judge demanded that the public defender tell the court as a "officer of the court" her personal opinion of the appropriate sentence. Any lawyer, civil or criminal, private or public defender, new or old, should have had an instinctive reaction that the court's demand was contrary to a criminal defense lawyer's obligations to the client. The court's inappropriate demand threatened the lawyer's loyalty to the client and the lawyer-client relationship. A defense lawyer may harbor the same instinctive negative reaction to the ethical rule that requires a lawyer who knows of legal authority directly adverse to a client's position to inform the court of its existence. This chapter explores the competing interests within the dual role of the defense lawyer as a zealous advocate and as an officer of the court in the context of answering the question presented above.

Discussion

As a zealous advocate, a criminal defense lawyer's instinctive reaction to having to disclose adverse authority is understandably negative. This predictable reaction is grounded in the harsh realities of the criminal justice system where, in the face of the government's greater resources and procedural advantages, defense counsel has meager resources to defend clients threatened with serious punishments. In light of this imbalance in the adversarial battle, why should a defense lawyer be required to depart from a strictly adversarial presentation by having to disclose adverse law? Why do the rules of ethics require a defense lawyer to give up any ground?

Before addressing defense counsel's duty, we need to understand the relationship between ethical rules and our adversarial system. As Stephen Landsman concludes, "because the highly competitive nature of adversary procedure may tend to promote a win-at-any-cost attitude, the adversary system employs a set of ethical rules to control the behavior of counsel. To ensure the integrity of the process, tactics designed to harass or intimidate an opponent, as well as those intended to mislead or prejudice the trier of fact, are forbidden."[1] At the same time, because vigorous advocacy assures the presentation of all available facts and theories, ethical rules were developed to assure zeal and to require lawyers to conduct themselves with undivided loyalty to their clients. Landsman, *supra* note 1, at 717.

In 1969, the American Bar Association adopted then existing ethical principals and codified them. The provisions in the ABA Code of Professional Responsibility (hereinafter Model Code) promoted the goal of lawyers being zealous advocates.[2] In its general canons, which are not binding, the Model Code articulates the specific responsibilities of undivided loyalty to clients: lawyers should preserve the confidences and secrets of their clients (Canon 4); exercise independent professional judgment on behalf of their clients (Canon 5); and represent their clients competently (Canon 6) and zealously (Canon 7). As Eugene Gaetke observes, the Disciplinary Rules, which are mandatory, go farther in defining the lawyer's obligations of zealous advocacy for the client. Gaetke, *supra* note 2, at 39, 50, n.66. These rules require that the lawyer represent the client the same as a client would represent himself, if the client were fully trained and skilled in law, thus limiting disclosure of client confidences (DR 4-101). Conflicts of interest also are restricted to assure that the lawyer has the same single-minded objectivity as the client (DR 5-101 to 5-107). In addition, the Disciplinary Rules mandate that the work done for the client must be as carefully and professionally done as if the client had been legally trained and had done it himself (DR 6-101) and that the full range of legal assistance available to the client be used (DR 7-101(A).

The ABA Model Rules of Professional Conduct (hereinafter Model Rules), adopted in 1983, are the ABA's latest articulation of ethical expectations. While the ABA reiterated the lawyer's obligation to the client, it expanded the lawyer's other role as an officer of the court. Gaetke, *supra* note 2, at 61–65. Nonetheless, as numerous commentators have observed, the present boundaries of the lawyer's role as an officer of the court are as murky as its origins.[3]

Eugene Gaetke points out that the lawyer, in addition to having duties as a zealous advocate, has historically had obligations to the judicial system that supersede the undivided fidelity and enthusiasm an agent owes to his principle. The lawyer, therefore, is an instrument that advances the ends of justice and in so doing must cooperate to some extent with the court. Gaetke, *supra* note 2, at 43, n. 20. Thus, the lawyer is required under limited circumstances to "subordinat[e] [the] interests of the client and the lawyer to those of the judicial system and the public." *Id.* at 48. Gaetke states that: "[the] duty to report adverse legal authority is the most noteworthy example of the Code's subordination of the interests of the client and the lawyer in favor of those of the judicial system." *Id.* at 57.

This obligation to disclose known adverse legal authority is contained in both the Model Code and the Model Rules. "The lawyer shall disclose: (1) legal authority in the controlling jurisdiction known to him to be directly adverse to the position of his client and which is not disclosed by opposing counsel." ABA MODEL CODE OF PROFESSIONAL RESPONSIBILITY, DR 7-106(B)(1) (1981). Model Rule 3.3(a)(3) (1990) is virtually identical.[4]

"The theory behind the rule [of disclosure of adverse legal authority] is that the purpose of litigation is to promote truth and justice. The lawyer is not required to advocate the controlling authority, and may argue that it should be distinguished or its application to the present case abandoned, but it still must be acknowledged so that an informed decision can be made." Robert H. Aronson, *An Overview of the Law of Professional Responsibility*, 61 Wash. L. Rev. 823, 864 (1986). The rule is designed to assist courts that, having limited staff resources, cannot be presumed to find all controlling authority, and to prevent errors of law that presumably will be corrected on appeal anyway. Geoffrey Hazard, Jr. and William Hodes, *The Law of Lawyering, A Handbook on the Model Rules of Professional Conduct*, 587 (2d. ed. 1990). Yet, the rule is clearly inconsistent with defense counsel's duty not to disclose adverse facts even though such nondisclosure may be more outcome determinative and hinder the search for truth. Charles Wolfram, *Modern Legal Ethics*, 681–82 (1986).

Another reason often propounded in support of the rule is that, unlike an adverse fact, adverse authority is not a confidence of the client, and because it does not belong to the client its disclosure is not considered to be damaging to the lawyer-client relationship. Hazard & Hodes, *supra* at 587. Similarly, in *United States v. Nobles*, 422 U.S. 225, 239 (1975), by putting the investigator on as a witness the defendant's lawyer waived his work-product privilege, which would have protected against disclosure of the defense investigator's notes. The work-product privilege "is not absolute" and "like other qualified privileges, it may be waived." *Id.* at 239. Critics of the rule, however, contend that prosecutors should be deemed to have waived a favorable legal argument if they failed to adequately research or brief the issue and that defense counsel should not have to compromise loyalty to the client to make up for a prosecutor's shortcomings.[5]

Nevertheless, because such disclosure rules have been adopted in most, but not all, states, defense counsel should check the ethical rules in her own jurisdiction to determine the specific duty required. The District of Columbia, for example, requires disclosure only if the adverse authority is "dispositive of a question at issue." DISTRICT OF COLUMBIA RULES OF PROFESSIONAL CONDUCT, Rule RPC 3.3(a)(3) (1989). California has not adopted a rule *requiring* disclosure of adverse law; its rule prohibits lawyers from misleading the judge by a false statement of law, from intentionally misquoting authority, and from citing authority that has been overruled, repealed, or declared unconstitutional. CALIFORNIA RULES OF PROFESSIONAL CONDUCT, RPC 5-200 (1989). The American Trial Lawyers Association's ethical guidelines require prosecutors but *not* defense lawyers to disclose adverse authority. AMERICAN TRIAL LAWYERS' CODE OF CONDUCT, Rule 9.10 (1990).

If the lawyer discloses adverse authority she is not required to disclose, she certainly hurts her client unnecessarily and may even be ineffective in doing so. Before taking a closer look at the rules, it is worth stopping to remind ourselves, as the Supreme Court noted in *Strickland v. Washington*, 466 U.S. 668, 688 (1983), that the ethical rules are "only guides" to determining what is reasonable. Counsel has an "overriding mission of vigorous advocacy of the client's cause". *Id.* at 689. This representation entails certain basic duties . . . to assist the defendant, and hence counsel owes a duty of loyalty, a duty to avoid conflicts of interest." *Id.* at 688.

The ethical rules on this subject, applicable in the lawyer's jurisdiction, should be carefully read. The terms "authority," "controlling jurisdiction," and "directly adverse" in the Model Rules and Model Code limit the defense lawyer's obligation to disclose adverse authority. "Authority" refers to legal authority and includes statutes, ordinances, regulations, administrative rulings, and case law. Hazard &

Hodes, *supra* at 587. "Controlling jurisdiction" means authority in a court having control over the trial court deciding the issue. For instance, in a state trial court "controlling jurisdiction" includes state statutes, regulations, and cases decided in that state's district, appellate court, and Supreme Court, as well as the United States Supreme Court. In a federal trial court, "controlling jurisdiction" includes federal statutes and regulations, as well as cases decided in that federal district or circuit and the United States Supreme Court. *Id.* A nonbinding 1949 American Bar Association Opinion suggests that when the legal question is new or novel, the obligation extends to disclosure of authorities that are directly adverse from other states and circuits. ABA Comm. on Ethics, Formal Op. 280 (1949).[6]

Clearly, when a case is "on all fours" against the client and is dispositive of the case, it is directly adverse. N.Y. Comm. on Ethics, Formal Op. 643 (1943). At least one ethics committee has supported a broader interpretation that includes "all decisions directly adverse to *any* proposition of law on which the lawyer is expressly relying". N.Y. Comm. on Ethics, Formal Op. 80-1 (emphasis added). The 1949 ABA opinion cited above went even farther than the New York opinion, suggesting that the proper interpretation of "directly adverse" might include authority that the judge might feel important or would clearly want to know. ABA Formal Op. 280, *supra*. *See also,* Hazard & Hodes, *supra* at 588. Like Monroe Freedman, I disagree with that subjective standard because it does not give the lawyer direction as to what might be important, or of interest, to the ruling judge. Therefore, this standard is difficult to apply and enforce.

A lawyer is prohibited from affirmatively representing or citing an overruled case or repealed statute or regulation. Similarly, a lawyer may not assert as law a particular proposition that has been completely or partially undermined by a recent case. Defense lawyers, especially public defenders, commonly confront situations where counsel must balance the lawyer's duty not to file a frivolous motion and the right to argue in good faith for reversal of law. Such situations require disclosure of adverse *controlling* authority.

Even if the nondisclosure is technically defensible, a lawyer may choose strategically to disclose authority that is applicable, but not directly on point or outside the controlling jurisdiction, and then distinguish the authority. This may be wise, especially if opposing counsel or the court is likely to bring up the authority and you will not be given a good opportunity to address it. However, this is a strategic choice, not an ethical one. Counsel should not make a disclosure detrimental to a present client to enhance her own reputation or aid a future client.

A lawyer may have a somewhat greater obligation to disclose adverse authority outside the controlling jurisdiction in an ex parte situation. Model Rule 3.3(d) requires the moving party to disclose all material facts to the court in such proceedings. This is so because the opposing party is not present. In most situations, the lawyer does not have a duty to disclose factual mistakes that she did not create. ABA Formal Op. 87-353 (1987) (the lawyer did not have a duty to correct the clerk who mistakenly advised the court the client had no criminal record).

In another situation, defense counsel was not obligated to tell the court it had overlooked a second criminal charge unless the client so requested. Virginia Formal Op. 1186 (2/13/89). In fact, as the opinion reasons, such a disclosure would be unethical since it would damage or prejudice the client.

Defense counsel should not be overly concerned with "disciplinary sanctions" by the state bar or court. To constitute a violation of professional conduct, a misrepresentation must be made with the "intent to mislead . . . negligence is not enough." In the Matter of Respondent K., 2 Cal. St. Bar Ct. Rptr. 335 (Review Dept. 1993); In the Matter of Farrell, 1 Cal. St. Bar Ct. Rptr. 490 (Review Dept. 1991) (the lawyer must "knowingly make a false, material statement of law or fact to the court with the intent to mislead"). Although disciplinary action is rare, sanctions have been assessed against lawyers who fail to disclose adverse authority.[7]

Hypotheticals

The following hypotheticals address examples of situations that may arise involving decisions to disclose adverse authority and suggest ways to handle the dilemma ethically and to the client's best advantage.

A Pretrial Motion to Suppress

A public defender in a district court in the Ninth Circuit moves to suppress her client's post-arrest statement based upon facts disclosed by the client. According to the client, during a Friday afternoon interrogation, after being Mirandized, the client asked the officer, "When will I be able to see a public defender?" The officer responded, "It will be quite a long time because it is too late to go to court today and your court appearance will be on Monday." The officer then asked the client "if she wanted to stop the interview until counsel is available," to which the client responded no. After signing the *Miranda* waiver form, the client provided a lengthy confession. The public defender files a

motion to suppress knowing at the time of filing about a case in the
Ninth Circuit that on indistinguishable facts holds that the officer's
follow-up questioning clarifying a client's equivocal request for counsel did not violate Fifth Amendment or *Miranda* requirements. Case
law involving similar factual situations reported in other circuits, however, *supports* suppression. Must the Ninth Circuit case be disclosed
and, if so, when?

Clearly the Ninth Circuit case is controlling adverse authority, and
ultimately must be disclosed before the court decides the issue.

Normally when a suppression motion is filed, the hearing is set for
a date weeks down the road. Before that time, the government is expected to respond in writing. Strategically, however, it may be better to
provide disclosure after seeing the government's opposition because
the government may state a different version of facts that may provide
grounds to distinguish the Ninth Circuit case. Thus, by delaying the
disclosure until the reply brief, or until the hearing, the public defender
may not tip off the prosecutor to the case that the prosecutor might use
in preparing her witnesses to testify. If the prosecutor discloses the case
in her opposition pleading, the public defender has no further obligation to disclose the authority. Clearly, if not yet disclosed, the public
defender must disclose the adverse authority before the court rules.

Nevertheless, the mere existence of this case does not preclude
counsel from filing the motion or mandate that the case be included in
counsel's initial motion. It could be argued that the motion filed is
frivolous and a violation of counsel's duty as an officer of the court. It
is not frivolous, however, to file an introductory motion to suppress
that shifts the burden to the prosecutor to put forward the officer's version of the facts. Whatever the situation, defense counsel must be able
to defend in good faith the steps taken. For instance, counsel may have
a good faith belief that a distinguishable set of facts will be revealed at
the hearing, thereby rendering the potentially adverse case irrelevant.
Even if the hearing shows that the Ninth Circuit case is squarely on
point, counsel may argue in light of the case law from other circuits
that the Ninth Circuit case should be reversed or modified. Additionally, since the initial pleading requesting suppression is merely introductory, a court would not be induced to rely on that pleading alone,
but would wait to learn the government's justification for the search
and seizure. This typical procedural scenario would support the lawyer initially holding back the adverse case. This would not be the case
in an ex parte proceeding where the court is expected to rule on the
moving papers. *See, e.g.,* Jorgenson v. Volusia County, 846 F.2d 1350 (11th
Cir. 1988) (involving an ex parte application for a restraining order).

A Sentencing Hearing

In federal court, the court must sentence within a range determined by the applicable Federal Sentencing Guidelines. The guidelines establish the range based upon the crime and its circumstances and the defendant's prior criminal history. In this hypothetical, the probation department in its presentence report takes the position that the crime of possession with intent to distribute narcotics involved a quantity that raised the crime to a level 32 offense. The probation department cited the applicable guideline section. When reading the report, defense counsel realizes that the probation department misapplied the guidelines and the amount of cocaine (not in dispute) actually raises the crime to a level 34 offense. What must defense counsel do at the sentencing hearing?

Since defense counsel did not create the mistake, he is not responsible for correcting it. Silence in such a situation is not unethical unless the court says something to indicate it believes the silence is an affirmation of the "fact." However, defense counsel is precluded by the rules of ethics (discussed in this chapter) from affirmatively arguing that this was a level 32 offense. Once realizing the error, defense counsel is barred from arguing it to advantage, although defense counsel may not disclose the error as that disclosure would result in a lengthier sentence for the client. Similarly, defense counsel cannot ethically argue that the probation department's level 32 calculation is correct. Moreover, counsel has no obligation to disclose the applicable guideline section; the probation department already did so. Defense counsel may argue that the court should sentence the client to the most lenient sentence within the applicable range, without affirmatively arguing an offense level or range. Even if asked directly, defense counsel should not disclose the error. Since counsel cannot make a false statement, the path advised is to divert the inquiry by advising the court to go to another source or to excuse counsel from answering the question. ABA Formal Op. 287.

Conclusion

Defense counsel has an ethical obligation not to affirmatively mislead or misadvise the trial court about controlling law. However, once the law is disclosed, defense counsel need not emphasize it, nor argue it. If the court has been presented the controlling law by the defense or the prosecution and has misunderstood or overlooked it in handling the case, then counsel has no ethical obligation to call it to the court's attention. Considerations of whether to do so are based on strategy and in maintaining credibility with the court. In summary, as with all ethical questions, if the problem is thought through and defense counsel feels that her position is defendable within the bounds of ethics, then the course of greatest possible benefit to the client should be followed.[8] The problem should be analyzed with the best interests of the current client in mind and not future clients or future appearances before the court. A criminal defense lawyer owes her absolute loyalty and best efforts to her client, a loyalty which should not be unduly comprised.

Notes

1. Stephen Landsman, *A Brief Survey of the Development of the Adversary System*, 44 OHIO STATE L.J. 713, 716–17 (1983).

2. Eugene R. Gaetke, *Lawyers as Officers of the Court*, 42 VANDERBILT L. REV. 39, 49–50 (1989). The Model Code was adopted in some form by virtually every state. *Id.* at 49. It has now been superseded in most states by the Model Rules of Professional Conduct.

3. *See, e.g.*, MONROE H. FREEDMAN, UNDERSTANDING LAWYERS' ETHICS (1990).

4. ABA STANDARDS FOR CRIMINAL JUSTICE DEFENSE FUNCTION Standard 4-1.2(g) (3d ed. 1991) includes a similar disclosure obligation.

5. *See, e.g.*, Monroe H. Freedman, *Arguing the Law in an Adversary System*, 16 GA. L. REV. 833 (1982).

6. *But see* FREEDMAN, *supra* note 3, at 106–7 (pointing out that in adopting Model Rule 3.3(a)(3) the ABA rejected a disclosure provision modeled on Formal Opinion 280 and criticizing Geoffrey Hazard, the reporter for the ABA, for looking to that opinion as authority).

7. *See* CHARLES W. WOLFRAM, MODERN LEGAL ETHICS, at 681. *See, e.g.*, Katris v. Immigration and Naturalization Service, 562 F.2d 866 (2d Cir. 1977); Jorgenson v. Volusia County, 846 F.2d 1350 (11th Cir. 1988).

8. As the Commentary to ABA Standard 4-1.2 states: "Included in defense counsel's obligation to the client is the responsibility of furthering the defendant's interest to the fullest extent that the law and the applicable standards of professional conduct permit."

Bibliography

Articles, Reports, and Standards

ABA Committee on Ethics and Professional Responsibility, Formal Opinion 87-353 (1987).

ABA Committee on Professional Ethics and Grievances, Formal Opinion 280 (1949).

ABA Committee on Professional Ethics and Grievances, Formal Opinion 287 (1953).

ABA MODEL CODE OF PROFESSIONAL RESPONSIBILITY, Canon 4, 5, 6, 7; DR 4-101, 5-101, 5-102, 5-103, 5-104, 5-105, 5-106, 5-107, 6-101, 7-101(A), 7-106(B)(1).

ABA MODEL RULES OF PROFESSIONAL CONDUCT, Rule 3.3(a)(3), 3.3(d).

ABA STANDARDS FOR CRIMINAL JUSTICE DEFENSE FUNCTION, 4-1.2, 4-1.2(g) and Cmt. (3d ed. 1991).

AMERICAN TRIAL LAWYERS' CODE OF CONDUCT, Rule 9.10 (1990).

Robert H. Aronson, *An Overview of the Law of Professional Responsibility*, 61 Wash. L Rev. 823 (1986).

CALIFORNIA RULES OF PROFESSIONAL CONDUCT, RPC 5-200 (1989).

Committee on Professional Ethics of the New York State Bar Association, Formal Opinion 80-1 (1943).

Committee on Professional Ethics of the New York State Bar Association, Formal Opinion 643 (1943).

DISTRICT OF COLUMBIA RULES OF PROFESSIONAL CONDUCT, Rule RPC 3.3(a)(3) (1989).

Monroe H. Freedman, *Arguing the Law in an Adversary System*, 16 Ga. L. Rev. 833 (1982).

Monroe H. Freedman, *Understanding Lawyers' Ethics* (1990).

Eugene R Gaetke, *Lawyers as Officers of the Court*, 42 Vand. L. Rev. 39 (1989).

Geoffrey C. Hazard & William W. Hodes, *The Law of Lawyering: A Handbook on the Model Rules of Professional Conduct* (2d ed. 1990).

Stephen Landsman, *A Brief Survey of the Development of the Adversary System*, 44 Ohio St. L.J. 713 (1983).

Standing Committee on Legal Ethics of the Virginia State Bar, Formal Opinion 1186 (1989).

Charles W. Wolfram, *Modern Legal Ethics* (1986).

Cases

In the Matter of Farrell, 1 Cal St. Bar Ct. Rptr. 490 (Review Dept. 1991).

In the Matter of Respondant K., 2 Cal. St. Bar Ct. Rptr. 335 (Review Dept. 1993).

Jorgenson v. Volusia County, 846 F.2d 1350 (11th Cir. 1988).

Katris v. Immigration and Naturalization Service, 562 F.2d 866 (2d Cir. 1977).

Strickland v. Washington, 466 U.S. 668 (1983).

United States v. Nobles, 422 U.S. 225 (1975).

CHAPTER 📖 14

Setting the Record Straight: The Client with Undisclosed Prior Convictions

William Talley, Jr.

Must defense counsel correct a trial judge who, in sentencing the defendant, indicates he is relying on the prosecutor's statement that the client has no prior record when counsel knows the defendant has a prior record? If, at a sentencing hearing, a defendant is asked by the court about a prior criminal record and denies having any record, does defense counsel have a duty to inform the court about the true state of the defendant's record? Must defense counsel divulge her client's criminal record if the judge specifically asks counsel whether her client has a criminal record?[1]

It is my opinion that under all circumstances the lawyer's first and primary duty is to protect the rights and confidential disclosures of her clients, even when this duty places the lawyer in direct conflict with an ethical duty of candor to the tribunal. Therefore, my answer to the question that begins this chapter is that the defense lawyer should not divulge, under any of the circumstances mentioned above, any information obtained as a result of the lawyer-client discussion.[2] Similarly, defense counsel should seek to avoid being placed in a situation where counsel's silence or refusal to answer a direct inquiry about her client's record would have the same effect as divulging the information.

These questions force defense counsel to balance conflicting duties. Counsel must safeguard the constitutional rights of her client without unduly compromising the procedural integrity of the judicial "truth finding" process. These questions raise issues about the client's constitutional rights and concerns about the client's ability to rely on the lawyer-client privilege with respect to confidential disclosures.

However, the current ABA Model Rules of Professional Responsibility, ABA Formal Opinions, and recent Supreme Court cases suggest that my position—client confidences should be kept or preserved at all cost—is a minority position. The majority view places the truth-finding process of the judiciary ahead of loyalty or allegiance to the client. Case law and ethics opinions tend to treat a client's lack of candor with the tribunal as fraud or perjury requiring the lawyer to withdraw or to reveal the client's falsehood to the court.[3] Most authorities suggest that the accused does not have the right to subvert the truth-finding process through perjury or fraudulent evidence and that counsel cannot assist the accused's perjury or fraud by her silence. Thus, the defense lawyer who finds herself facing these questions should always keep in mind that following the advice of this chapter, and by extension, Monroe Freedman, may have adverse consequences if detected by the court.

Before answering the questions presented, it is necessary to analyze the scope of the ethical and constitutional duties that the lawyer owes her client. A client is entitled to zealous and competent representation. Obviously, the lawyer cannot serve two masters at the same time. Thus, any lawyer who confronts any of the above-stated questions should be prepared to deal with both the state and federal constitutional ramifications of these questions in order to be able to argue that disclosure of client confidences is not required.

The United States Constitution, through the Fifth and Sixth Amendments, recognizes and mandates that the accused in a criminal proceeding has the right to rely on the advice of a zealous and competent counsel. Inherent in this right is the accused's ability to divulge personal and confidential information to his lawyer so that he may receive the best possible representation. A client's communications should remain confidential except in the most narrow of circumstances.[4] Any implication that the criminally accused could not fully rely on his lawyer to keep his confidences triggers serious constitutional ramifications. The defense lawyer's first responsibility is to her client.[5] She is duty bound to represent the client and she must now "champion against a hostile world"[6] the rights of that client and must do so zealously.[7]

Both the Model Code and the Model Rules expressly indicate that the lawyer should work to preserve a client's privileged communications[8] and should work zealously in the client's behalf.[9] The United States Supreme Court has held unanimously, in an opinion by Justice Rehnquist, that the lawyer's knowledge of all the facts is "essential to proper representation." *Upjohn v. United States*, 449 U.S. 387 (1981) (quoting MODEL CODE EC 4-1). If the client is apprehensive that his law-yer may be required to convey damaging information to the court, the client will be reluctant to confide in his lawyer. *Fisher v. United States,* 425 U.S. 391, 403 (1976). Speaking for the court in *Fisher,* Justice White explained: "[I]f the client knows the damaging information could more readily be obtained from the attorney following disclosure than from himself in the absence of disclosure, the client would be reluctant to confide in his lawyer and it would be difficult to obtain fully informed legal advice." *Fisher v. United States,* 425 U.S. at 403. Accordingly, Jus-tice White observed that the lawyer-client privilege protects those dis-closures that are necessary to obtain informed legal advice and that "might not" have been made absent the privilege. Thus, the privilege exists to protect the vast majority of lawyer-client communications. But more than just communicating information, "the privilege is intended to encourage parties to communicate harmful information to lawyers by reducing the risk lawyers will subsequently disclose that informa-tion to the tribunal."[10]

Moreover, as Justice White and others have noted:

> [T]he role of the defense counsel in the adversary system requires conduct that at times is at odds with the system's search for the truth. While law enforcement officers must be dedicated to mak-ing the criminal trial a procedure for the ascertainment of the true facts surrounding the commission of the crime[,] . . ., defense counsel has no comparable obligation to ascertain or present the truth. . . . Defense counsel need present nothing even if he knows what the truth is. He need not furnish any witnesses to the police, or reveal any confidences of his client, or furnish any other infor-mation to help the prosecution's case.[11]

There are commentators who believe a lawyer's primary alle-giance lies with the court since her obligations to the court began be-fore she ever had a client.[12] Many share the view that "[W]here the duties to his client to afford zealous representation conflict with his duties as an officer of the court to further the administration of justice, the private duty must yield to the public duty." *Fite v. Lee,* 521 P2d 964, 968 (Wash. App. 1974). Critics of the adversary system excoriate crimi-nal defense lawyers for failing to contribute to the truth seeking pro-cess, while doing everything they can for their client. Indeed, some advocate for full disclosure any time a lawyer learns of client false-hoods. The regime of absolute disclosure requires lawyers to disclose to the tribunal all relevant information and all information that might lead to the identification and presentation of relevant information. *See*

Marvin Frankel, *The Search for Truth: An Umpireal View*, 123 U. Pa. L. Rev. 1031, 1055–57 (1975). Many courts,[13] law review articles,[14] and some ethics opinions[15] emphasize the importance of candor to the tribunal in the context of client perjury and suggest that a failure to disclose a client's falsehood implies moral shortsightedness.

The right to a lawyer, however, is only meaningful if the client feels secure in disclosing all information to his lawyer, secure in the fact that such disclosures will not be used against him. As Monroe Freedman points out, "[i]t would be extremely unfair to put the burden on the client to decide what to hold back, separating the relevant from the irrelevant, and the incriminating from the exculpatory. If clients were able to do that, they wouldn't need lawyers."[16] The confidentiality of lawyer-client communications is a necessary part of the right to counsel. The lawyer is a vehicle by which a client may adequately assert his or her individual rights.

Clearly there is tension between the lawyer's duty, as expressed in the Model Code and Model Rules, to provide the client zealous and competent representation and the lawyer's allegiance to a tribunal, which does not necessarily have the client's best interest at heart. The Model Code and the Model Rules appear to require that the lawyer give final allegiance to the tribunal.[17] Nonetheless, the proper balance to be struck between the client's constitutional rights and the ethical commands that a lawyer should not subvert the truth-finding process is often difficult to ascertain.

The ethical rules adopted in a particular state impose certain constraints on the behavior of lawyers in that state. Yet in many situations, neither the Model Rules nor the Model Code provide clear guidance to the lawyer faced with the task of keeping a client's confidences while at the same time carrying out her responsibilities not to perpetrate or assist a fraud on the court. Even if the ethical rules do require that a lawyer take action contrary to a client's best interest, such rules still do not supersede the constitutional rights of a criminal defendant. (See Model Rule 3.3, Comment) Regardless of the apparent disclosures demanded by a state's ethical provisions, a lawyer's ethical obligations remain subordinate to a defendant's constitutional rights.

Ultimately, then, defense counsel must look to the U.S. Constitution as well as her state constitution to clarify counsel's responsibilities in representing her client. Unfortunately, unresolved constitutional issues leave defense lawyers in a precarious position. Lawyers should recognize, therefore, that while silence in the face of a client's misrepresentations may be golden for the client, it may also be deadly for counsel.[18]

What is the lawyer's duty to inform the court of her client's true criminal record where counsel knows that the prosecution is relying on an inaccurate criminal record but where neither the defendant nor defense counsel makes any affirmative statements regarding the nature of the client's prior criminal record?

This question envisions a scenario in which the court is relying on the prosecutor, the probation department, or the court clerk for information regarding the client's prior criminal record. Neither the lawyer nor the client is called upon to make any affirmative statements. This question manifests the tension between the ethical rules, which mandate that the lawyer protect his client's confidences, and those rules that govern the lawyer's duty of candor to the tribunal.

Both ABA Formal Opinions 287 and 87-353 agree that under the above circumstances the lawyer should do whatever she can to protect her client's confidences. Formal Opinion 287 stated that if the client communicates his criminal record to his counsel when seeking professional advice, Canon 37 would prevent its disclosure to the court.

Formal Opinion 287 evaluates the question in this fashion:

> If the client's criminal record was communicated by him to his counsel when seeking professional advice from him, Canon 37 would prevent its disclosure to the court unless the provisions of Canons 22, 29 and 41 require this. If the court asks the defendant whether he has a criminal record and he answers that he has none, this, although perhaps not technical perjury, for the purposes of the present question amounts to the same thing. Despite this, we do not believe the lawyer justified in violating his obligation under Canon 37. He should, in due course, endeavor to persuade the client to tell the court the truth and if he refuses to do so should sever his relations with the client, but should not violate the client's confidence.[19]

Opinion 287 goes on to say:

> Where the court is about to impose a sentence based on the misinformation that the defendant has no previous criminal record, if the attorney for the defendant learns of the previous record through his client's communications, he has no duty to correct the misinformation. But if he learned of the record independently of his client's communications and he has reason to believe that the court is relying on his silence as corroboration, he should inform the court not to rely on his silence as corroboration.

Formal Opinion 87-353 concludes that Formal Opinion 287 is still valid under the Model Rules, as long as there has been no client fraud or perjury. Therefore, if the probation department or prosecution misinforms the judge about the client's prior record and the client remains silent, the lawyer is prohibited, under Model Rule 1.6 and Model Code DR 4-101, from disclosing information relating to the representation.[20]

Of course, there are circumstances where a lawyer's silence may be viewed as an affirmative misrepresentation. *See* MODEL RULE 3.3, Comment. An affirmative act undertaken to perpetrate a fraud upon the court is not protected under the Constitution or the Model Rules.[21] Rarely will a lawyer be permitted to affirmatively state an untruth. (*But see* ATLA CODE 3.7 permitting a false statement to preserve a client's confidence). Defense counsel may not say, for example, that the court should adopt the prosecutor's recommendation because her client has no record, nor may she argue her client's clean record to the court as a reason to impose a light sentence.

Arguably, defense counsel may be able to relate to the court that the probation department indicates that the client has no prior record, but only if she is merely restating what the probation department has already reported. The lawyer should be very careful, however, to make sure that the statement she is making is not attributable as one she is making based on her personal knowledge of the client's record. It is safer to fashion a sentencing argument that avoids focusing on the client's record. Although the court may erroneously assume that the client has no record, counsel is not responsible for the failings of the prosecutor, the probation department, or the court clerk.

Even though defense counsel has not affirmatively offered false evidence to the court, she may be held responsible for the chain of events leading up to false information being presented at the court hearing. The prosecutor could be expected to relate some portion of his conversation with defense counsel to the court.[22] Defense counsel may be deemed to have perpetrated a fraud upon the court if at any time she made a false statement to a prosecutor or probation agent that she knew or believed the client had no criminal record and induced others to rely on that assertion. *See, Rohrback, supra* note 19.

Finally, if the lawyer does not learn about a client's true record until the sentencing hearing is over, it would appear that Formal Opinion 87-353 would allow the lawyer to continue to preserve the client's confidences by not requiring any disclosures to the court. A lawyer cannot reveal a client's past crimes and frauds. It follows, therefore, that a client's post-hearing disclosure that the judge was misinformed about the client's prior record cannot be revealed.

Defense counsel's role as a protector of the constitutional rights of her client also imposes a responsibility on the lawyer not to disclose her client's criminal record to the judge. Speaking through Chief Justice Warren E. Burger, the United States Supreme Court has noted that to compel a lawyer to disclose incriminating confidences would create "significant risks of unfair prejudice, especially when the disclosure is to a judge who may be called upon later to impose sentences on the attorney's clients." *Holloway v. Arkansas*, 435 U.S. 475, 487, n.11 (1978). It is rarely in a client's best interest that her lawyer inform the judge of that client's criminal record when the judge is about to pass sentence and the prosecutor has failed to alert the court to the client's prior record. In such a case, counsel's ethical and constitutional duties require that she remain silent.

> *What is the lawyer's duty at a sentencing hearing to his client where counsel knows of the client's prior criminal record, has confirmed the existence of the prior criminal record but upon examination by the court, the defendant, who is not under oath, falsely claims not to have a prior criminal record?*

The above situation often happens without the lawyer being fore-warned, consequently the lawyer may not have the benefit of research and reflection before having to respond to the court. Thus, the lawyer's response must be to make some decisions based on her interpretation of her role as a defense lawyer. If the lawyer truly sees her role as championing the client's cause, the conflict should be resolved in favor of protecting the client. The lawyer should recognize, however, that there is some risk in taking this approach.

As you will read, both the Model Rules and the Model Code, as well as the ABA Formal and Informal Opinions, while at least paying lip service to the client's right to have confidential discussions remain private, also advise the lawyer to withdraw from the case and disassociate herself from her client's false statements. This solution is not much of an option as far as the client is concerned. If the lawyer were to seek to withdraw immediately after a client tells the court at a sentencing hearing that he has no record, there is only one thing the court is likely to infer from such action: the client does in fact have a prior criminal record.

The question becomes, therefore, which part of the Model Code or the Model Rules the lawyer will choose to sacrifice: the obligation to hold inviolate the client's confidences and secrets[23] or the duty as an officer of the court not to engage in conduct that might mislead the tribunal. Monroe Freedman has stated that: "[If] . . . it is obvious that the very act of disassociation would have the effect of indirectly revealing the client's confidences"[24] the lawyer should not do so. ABA Formal Opinion 314 also warned against "waiving the red flag" when seeking to disassociate from a client.[25]

I would argue that under these circumstances the lawyer should attempt to keep her client from making any further fraudulent statements, but should not seek to withdraw as withdrawal would be tantamount to informing the court that the client has lied about his record. The lawyer will find some support for this position in the Model Code as well as in the ABA Formal and Informal Opinions, but less support in the Model Rules. My position echoes that taken by the ATLA Code. A look at the most significant ABA opinions may be helpful in determining what position counsel is willing to take.

In Formal Opinion 287, the ABA stated a preference for protecting a client's confidences even where there was some concern, as here, that the client may have made statements that while not technically perjury would amount to a fraud upon the court. The opinion stated:

> If the court asks the defendant whether he has a criminal record and he answers that he has none, this, although perhaps not technical perjury, for the purposes of the present question amounts to the same thing. Despite this, we do not believe the lawyer is justified in violating his obligation under Canon 37. He should, in due course endeavor to persuade the client to tell the court the truth and if he refuses to do so should sever his relations with the client, but should not violate the client's confidence.[26]

While the opinion does not call for the lawyer to violate the confidence of the client, it still counsels a lawyer to disassociate herself from any client who gives the appearance of perpetrating a fraud upon the tribunal. The real question, then, is how and when does one or should one withdraw from a case under such circumstances? The solution Formal Opinion 287 settles on is withdrawal. But the opinion goes on to say that the lawyer cannot even leave an impression by her silence that a statement by the client that he has no criminal record is a correct one.

> If under all the circumstances, the lawyer believes that the court relies on him as corroborating the correctness of the statement by the clerk or by the client that the client has no criminal record, the lawyer's duty of candor and fairness to the court requires him, in our opinion, to advise the court not to rely on counsel's personal knowledge as to the facts of the client's record.[27]

The upshot of the opinion is that while it claims to stand behind the lawyer's right to protect client confidences, it does not effectively deal with the situation that presents itself to the lawyer. If the lawyer feels obligated to follow the directives of Formal Opinion 287, she finds herself in the untenable position of having to tell the court that it should not rely on counsel's personal knowledge of the client's last statement. If the lawyer is not asked for her personal knowledge under these circumstances, it does not appear that Formal Opinion 287 absolutely requires the lawyer to refute the statements of the client. However, the implication of the opinion leads one to believe that if saying nothing results in the tribunal relying on the client's statement, then counsel has violated her duty to the tribunal.

If the lawyer knows before the sentencing hearing that the client intends to tell the court falsely that he has no criminal record, Formal Opinion 287 clearly directs the lawyer to at least attempt to persuade the client not to make such a statement. Discouraging client perjury is always a good idea. Assuming that there is ample time between the time the lawyer finds out about the client's intention to make false statements and the hearing, withdrawal may not be a problem. But clearly in many cases, defense counsel's attempt to withdraw will send a clear message to the court that counsel believes that her client is not telling the truth.

The ABA appeared to further expand the duty of the lawyer to keep the client's confidences under these circumstances when it promulgated Informal Opinion 1314, "Duty of a Lawyer Regarding Commission of Perjury by a Client" (1975). In this opinion the ABA stated that where the lawyer does not know in advance of the client's intention to make a false statement, she should continue to protect any privileged communication. "In other words, the confidential privilege, in our opinion, must be upheld over any obligation of the lawyer to betray the client's confidence in seeking rectification of any fraud that may have been perpetrated by his client upon a person or tribunal."[28]

Informal Opinion 1314 still admonishes the lawyer to encourage the client to rectify any fraudulent statements. It also instructs the lawyer to withdraw from the case at the time she determines that the client cannot or will not cease his fraudulent behavior. Thus, even with the stronger language encouraging the lawyer to protect the confidences of her client, the lawyer is still faced with the dilemma of exactly how to withdraw so that the client's confidences are in fact preserved.

In 1987 the ABA took a decidedly prodisclosure stance with its Formal Opinion 87-353, "Lawyer's Responsibility With Relation to Client Perjury." This opinion no longer appears to give counsel discretion of when and how to deal with the issue of client perjury. Instead, it suggests that the lawyer simply must turn the client in if the client refuses to rectify the fraudulent statements.

> If prior to the conclusion of the proceedings, a lawyer learns that the client has given testimony the lawyer knows is false, and the lawyer cannot persuade the client to rectify the perjury, the lawyer must disclose the client's perjury to the tribunal, notwithstanding the fact that the information to be disclosed is information relating to the representation.[29]

The only leeway given to the lawyer by this opinion appears to be the language that indicates the lawyer must turn in her client if she learns of the perjury *during* the course of representation. This indicates, consistent with Model Rule 3.3(b), that once the proceeding has ended, the lawyer's duty to disclose a client's false testimony also ceases.[30] The intent of the opinion appears to be to strengthen the lawyer's duty to the truth-finding process of the tribunal. Most chilling, however, is the apparent directive in Formal Opinion 87-353 that suggests that the lawyer must inform the client that if the client persists in his fraudulent behavior, she will be required to inform the tribunal. The lawyer becomes the system's lawyer rather than the client's.

> If the lawyer learns that the client intends to testify falsely before a tribunal, the lawyer must advise the client against such course of action, informing the client of the consequences of giving false testimony, including the lawyer's duty of disclosure to the tribunal.[31]

In contrast to the Model Rules, the Model Code seemingly affords greater protection to client confidences.[32] In 1969 the ABA adopted Model Code DR 7-102(B)(1), which required a lawyer to reveal to an affected person or tribunal any fraud perpetrated by the client in the course of the representation discovered by the lawyer. Because this provision was apparently inconsistent with the Model Code's directive in DR 4-101 that lawyers should not reveal confidences or secrets of their clients, DR 7-102(B)(1) was amended in 1974 to provide an exception to the duty to reveal a client's fraud when the information is protected as a privileged communication.[33]

According to Formal Opinion 87-353, this amendment severely limits the reach of DR 7-102(B) to those instances in which the information clearly establishing a fraud on a person or tribunal and committed by a client in the course of representation was obtained by the lawyer from a third party (but not in connection with his professional relationship with the client), because then the information would not be a confidence or secret of a client entitled to confidentiality. But even though the amended version of DR 7-102(B)(1) reflects the importance of preserving client confidentiality, the Model Code does not spell out clearly how the lawyer should proceed in the face of a client's falsehood.[34]

There is far less uncertainty under the Model Rules. Model Rules 3.3(a) and (b) mandate that a lawyer who knows the client has committed perjury must disclose this knowledge to the tribunal if the lawyer cannot persuade the client to rectify the perjury.[35] Formal Opinion 87-353 suggests that this disclosure provision represents a major policy change. Although the comment to Model Rule 3.3 mentions withdrawal as a possible remedy, the comment goes on to state that if withdrawal is impossible or not permitted, then disclosure is required.[36]

Monroe Freedman points out that such draconian answers to client perjury are simply not compatible with the adversary system and the development of effective lawyer-client relationships.[37] It would appear to be a fallacy that a defense lawyer can serve both the client and the tribunal in hierarchical fashion without one of her masters suffering. It should simply be acknowledged that this is not possible. While the court and the prosecutors are charged with finding the truth of charges against the accused, there is no such requirement placed on the function of defense lawyers. In fact, the client's constitutional right to remain silent has nothing whatsoever to do with the truth-finding process. Why then should the lawyer the system appoints to represent a criminal defendant have less incentive in protecting the client's rights than the client?

As already argued, I do not believe that defense counsel should function as the system's lawyer. Thus, I would rely on DR7-102(B)(1) as amended to permit me, if confronted with the problem of responding to my client's false statement about his criminal record, to maintain my client's confidences. Therefore, under the Model Code as amended, defense counsel is obligated not to disclose to the court the true state of her client's record. Under the Model Rules, however, defense counsel's decision not to reveal her client's false statement is certainly problematic.

Ultimately, defense counsel must look to the U.S. Constitution as well as her state constitution to clarify her responsibilities in representing her clients. Regardless of the apparent disclosure demanded by a state's ethical provisions, a lawyer's ethical obligations are subordinate to a defendant's constitutional rights. *See* MODEL RULE 3.3., Comment. In the aftermath of *Nix v. Whiteside*,[38] however, it is difficult to conclude that a client's false statements at a sentencing warrant constitutional protection.

What response should counsel make to the tribunal that makes direct inquiry about the personal knowledge that counsel has about her client's prior criminal record even though no affirmative statements have been made either by the defendant or the defense lawyer?

This situation may be the toughest of the three questions presented. It involves the right of the client to have his constitutional rights protected and the extent to which a defense lawyer should be required to go to protect those rights. It also calls into question how easily the rights of the client can be undermined by direct inquiry of the lawyer.

It is my opinion that it is unfair to abrogate a client's rights by simply bypassing the client and forcing his lawyer to give information against the client's interest. The right against self-incrimination means little if it can be circumvented so easily. To require counsel to disclose sensitive, confidential material at the whim of the court would effectively negate the right. From the outset it would undermine the lawyer's relationship with the client. A lawyer would be bound to warn her client at their first meeting that "anything you say to me could be used against you if the court makes direct inquiry of me." A lawyer can only be an effective advocate for her client if they develop a rapport that will allow an open investigation and exchange of information. *See* ABA STANDARD 4-3.7 and Commentary. The client's cooperation is essential to thorough preparation. "A client who cannot discuss his case fully and freely with his attorney cannot receive the effective assistance of counsel. And a client who confides in his lawyer, only to have those confidences betrayed, may suffer violation of his privilege against self-incrimination."[39] The client is not obliged to forfeit his Fifth Amendment right against self-incrimination to exercise his Sixth Amendment right to competent counsel.[40]

The American Trial Lawyers of America Code of Conduct 3.7 (ATLA Code) states: "A lawyer shall not knowingly file a materially false pleading, present materially false evidence or make a materially false representation to a court or other tribunal, except as required to do so by Rule 1.2,[41] which proscribes direct or indirect divulgence of a client's confidences." The ATLA Code has not been adopted by any jurisdiction nor, to my knowledge, has it been cited by any court decision. Yet this proposed code offers support for the proposition that in some instances a lawyer ought to be permitted to answer an inappropriate inquiry from a judge with a false statement in order to preserve a client's confidences.

Admittedly, however, a lawyer who responds to a direct inquiry from the bench as to the status of the client's criminal record by, in effect, telling the court that her client has no criminal record when she is aware of the fact that he does, runs a serious risk. It does not appear that the Model Code or the Model Rules directives to zealously represent one's clients and to keep client confidences will save the day. Rather, both the Model Code and the Model Rules forbid a lawyer from making a false statement thereby apparently requiring nothing less than immediate withdrawal or divulging client confidence. *See* MODEL RULE 3.3(a)(1); DR7-102(A)(5).

ABA Formal Opinion 287 indicates that if the court asks the lawyer whether the clerk's statement is correct, the lawyer is not bound by fidelity to the client to tell the court what he knows to be an untruth, and should ask the court to excuse him from answering the question and retire from the case, though this would doubtless put the court on further inquiry as to the truth.[42] This is a slightly easier case than the court asking the lawyer if the lawyer has any personal knowledge of the client's prior record.

Unfortunately, Formal Opinion 287 suggests that the lawyer should calculate what effect his claiming to rely on the clerk's statement has on the tribunal. If, in a particular case, the lawyer believes that the court relies on him as corroborating the correctness of the statement by the clerk or prosecutor that the client has no criminal record, the lawyer's duty of candor and fairness to the court requires him to advise the court not to rely on counsel's personal knowledge as to the facts of the client's record.[43]

Similarly, Formal Opinion 87-353 indicates that when the court puts a direct question to the lawyer, the lawyer may not reveal the client's confidences; but the lawyer also must not make any false statements of fact to the court. Formal Opinion 287 advised lawyers facing this dilemma to ask the court to excuse the lawyer from answering the question. The committee in Formal Opinion 87-353 conceded that it could offer no better guidance under the Model Rules, despite the fact it agreed that such a request by the lawyer most likely would put the court on further inquiry, as Formal Opinion 287 recognized.

Of course, had the question of his past criminal record been posed to the client directly, the accused would have been protected by the Fifth Amendment not to incriminate himself. He should expect no less protection from the lawyer who is now "championing" his cause. Accordingly, I agree with the drafters of the ATLA Code that a lawyer should not make a false representation to the court except where it is necessary to do so to avoid disclosing a client's confidence. I would fight to see to it that the judges in my jurisdiction were dissuaded from asking such an inappropriate question. If placed in the situation, however, I believe counsel is justified in responding to a judge's improper question in a manner that protects the client's constitutional rights, even if it means making a false statement.

Conclusion

The Commentary to ABA Standard 4-1.2 states that: "counsel's place in our adversary process of justice requires that counsel be guided constantly by the obligation to pursue the client's interest. Counsel must not be asked to limit his or her zeal in the pursuit of those interests except by definitive standards of professional conduct."

I believe that the lawyer should do everything in her power not to reveal client confidences in any of the circumstances discussed above. The client's constitutional right to a competent and zealous defense, not to mention the right against self-incrimination, should outweigh the ethical rules proscribed by any state association. To come to this conclusion, however, requires the reader to agree with me that defense counsel owes her primary duty to the client rather than to the court and that she should resolve ambiguities in her ethical obligations in favor of her client.

I am not arguing that the client has the *right* to perjure himself. But, if clients do not trust defense counsel and decide to perjure themselves without confiding in counsel, we have done little to advance the principle of truth or fair play in the judicial system. If instead the lawyer is permitted to preserve client confidences under any circumstances, we will increase the chances that lawyers will be able to talk their clients out of committing perjuring and thus reduce the amount of fraud on the court.

Given the present ethical rules in most jurisdictions and cases such as *Rohrback* and *Casby*, it may be unwise for a lawyer to do anything but ask to withdraw from representation in those instances where the court poses a direct inquiry to the lawyer about the client's prior record. Where no direct inquiry of the lawyer is made, the lawyer who remains silent finds herself on more solid ground. Nevertheless, I would urge the defense lawyer who represents a criminal defendant, above all, to champion the client's cause. One should remember that the very foundation of the U.S. Constitution mandates that the defendant need not assist in his own prosecution. Counsel should not assist in undermining one of our most important individual protections.

Notes

1. The reader should also assume that the client has informed the lawyer of his past criminal record, which differs materially with the record the court and the prosecutor possess.

2. My answer draws heavily from the writings of Monroe H. Freedman, especially his book Understanding Lawyers' Ethics (1990) and the Roscoe Pound-American Trial Lawyers Foundation, The American Lawyer's Code of Conduct (1982).

3. For the sake of brevity and argument, I will not debate the question of whether a client's statement at a sentencing hearing where the client was obviously not under oath constitutes perjury. In this chapter I will assume that any false statement by the client to a tribunal will be treated the same as testimony under oath, as regards its impact on the lawyer's duty to disclose.

4. A lawyer's duty of confidentiality extends beyond the lawyer-client privilege and is subject only to limited exceptions. See Charles W. Wolfram, Modern Legal Ethics § 7.6 (1986). The most significant exception involves information that, if not disclosed, could lead to the imminent death of or serious bodily harm to another. See, e.g., ABA Model Rules of Professional Conduct (hereinafter Model Rules), Rule 1.6(b)(1): "(b) A lawyer may reveal such information to the extent the lawyer reasonably believes necessary: (1) to prevent the client from committing a criminal act that the lawyer believes is likely to result in imminent death or substantial bodily harm . . . ."

5. See ABA Standards for Criminal Justice, Standard 4-1.2 (3d ed. 1993).

6. Monroe H. Freedman, Legal Ethics and the Suffering Client, 36 Cath. U. L. Rev. 331 (1987).

7. Model Rule 1.3, Cmt.; ABA Model Code of Professional Responsibility, Canon 7 (1969) (hereinafter Model Code).

8. Model Code DR 4-101; Model Rule 1.6(a).

9. See Model Rule 1.3. ("A lawyer shall act with reasonable diligence and promptness in representing a client."). The comment to Model Rule 1.3 states that "[a] lawyer should act with commitment and dedication to the interests of the client and with zeal in advocacy upon client's behalf." See also Model Code, Canon 7: "A lawyer should represent a client zealously within the bounds of the law."

10. Stephen McG. Bundy and Einer Richard Elhauge, Do Lawyers Improve the Adversary System? A General Theory of Litigation Advice and its Regulation, 79 Calif. L. Rev. 315 (1991). Communication is, however, a two way street. The lawyer is required to keep the client reasonably informed about the state of his case. Model Rules 1.2 and 1.4. Obviously, the lawyer is in no position to keep her client informed if she does not have the facts of the particular situation. The client does more harm to himself if he does not divulge sensitive information to his lawyer.

11. United States v. Wade, 388 U.S. 218, 256–57 (1976) (White, J., concurring in part and dissenting in part) (citing, among other sources, Monroe H. Freedman, Professional Responsibility of the Criminal Defense Lawyer: The Three Hardest Questions, 64 Mich. L. Rev. 1469 (1966)).

12. In re Integration of Nebraska State Bar Association, 275 N.W. 265 (Neb. 1937); State v. Kutchen, 417 P.2d 510 (Ariz. 1966) ("The duty of an attorney to a client . . . is subordinate to his responsibility for the due and proper administration of justice.").

13. *See, e.g.,* Nix v. Whiteside, 475 U.S. 157 (1986) ("both the Model Code and the Model Rules do not merely authorize disclosure of client perjury; they require such disclosure"); United States v. Henkel, 799 F.2d 369 (7th Cir. 1986); State v. Henderson, 468 P.2d 136 (Kan. 1970); State v. Robinson, 224 S.E.2d 174 (N.C. 1976). *See also* People v. Salquerro, 433 N.Y.2d 711 (N.Y. Supp. Ct. 1980) (counsel should inform court in jury trial of defendant's intention to commit perjury).

14. *See, e.g.,* Nathan M. Crystal, *Confidentiality Under the Model Rules of Professional Conduct,* 30 U. KAN. L. REV. 215 (1982); Stuart Watt, Note, *Confidentiality Under the Washington Rules of Professional Conduct,* 61 WASH. L. REV. 913 (1986).

15. *See, e.g.,* Comm. on Professional and Judicial Ethics of the State Bar of Michigan, Op. CI-789 (1982); Standing Comm. on Legal Ethics of the Virginia State Bar, Op. 506 (1983); Birmingham Bar Association, Op. 21 (1982).

16. Monroe H. Freedman, *Wrong? . . . Silence Is Right,* N.Y. TIMES, February 14, 1983.

17. Model Rule 3.3(b) specifically provides that the lawyer's duties as spelled out in Model Rule 3.3(a) apply "even if compliance requires disclosure of information otherwise protected by Rule 1.6." *But see* MODEL RULE 1.2(d), Comment suggesting that "[t]he lawyer is not permitted to reveal the client's wrong doing, except where permitted by Rule 1.6." Despite a 1974 amendment limiting disclosure when the "information is protected as a privileged information," DR 7-102(B)(1) has been interpreted to require that a lawyer disclose a client's falsehoods even though the information was gained as a client confidence. *See* MODEL RULE 3.3, MODEL CODE COMPARISON. *But see* MONROE H. FREEDMAN, UNDERSTANDING LAWYERS' ETHICS (1990).

18. *See, e.g.,* Attorney Grievance Committee of Maryland v. Rohrback, 591 A.2d 488 (Md. 1991) (defense counsel suspended for violating Model Rule 4.1 by failing to disclose his client's false identity); State v. Casby, 348 N.W.2d 736 (Minn. 1984) (defense lawyer convicted for failing to disclose client's use of false identity).

19. ABA Comm. on Professional Ethics and Grievances, Formal Op. 287 (1953).

20. *See* MODEL RULE 1.6(a) (". . . a lawyer shall not reveal information relating to representation of a client . . ."). *But see* MODEL RULE 1.6 Comment, which seems to allow lawyer to wave a red flag. *See also* DR 4-101.

21. Certainly there are bounds that constrain a lawyer's advocacy so as to ensure the integrity of the adversary process. "In our system the courts are almost wholly dependent on members of the bar to marshal and present the true facts . . . to enable the judge or jury to cook the adversary contentions in a crucible and draw off the . . . decisive facts to which the law may be applied. When an attorney adds or allows false testimony . . . he makes impure the product and it impossible for the scales to balance. No breach of professional ethics or of the law is more harmful to the administration of justice. . . ." Dodd v. Florida Bar, 118 So. 2d 17, 19 (Fla. 1960). *See also In re* Greenburg, 104 A.2d 46 (N.J. 1954); *In re* Carroll, 244 S.W.2d 474 (Ky. 1951). I suggest, however, that

there is a significant difference between advising clients or witnesses to perjure themselves or to present false evidence and remaining silent or refusing to divulge client confidences based on a belief that such conduct is constitutionally mandated. In the first instance the lawyer is assisting the client's fraud or criminal activity, while in the second the lawyer is struggling to reconcile incompatible duties.

22. *See* MODEL RULE 4.1 (counsel may not make false statements out of court).

23. MODEL CODE DR4-101, "Preservation of Confidences and Secrets of a Client," reads: "(B) Except when permitted under DR4-101(C), a lawyer shall not knowingly: (1) Reveal a confidence or secret of his client. (2) Use a confidence or secret of his client to the disadvantage of the client."

24. MONROE H. FREEDMAN, UNDERSTANDING LAWYERS' ETHICS 92 (1990).

25. *But see* ABA Comm. on Ethics and Professional Responsibility, Formal Op. 92-366 (1992) (taking the position that a "noisy" withdrawal is warranted if a lawyer's services are being used or are intended to be used to perpetrate a fraud).

26. ABA Comm. on Professional Ethics and Grievances, Formal Op. 287 (1953).

27. *Id.*

28. ABA Comm. on Ethics and Professional Responsibility, Informal Op. 1314 (1975).

29. ABA Comm. on Ethics and Professional Responsibility, Formal Op. 87-353 (1987).

30. Some jurisdictions have adopted their own version of Model Rule 3.3(b) and require a continuing duty on counsel to reveal a client's fraud even after the conclusion of the proceedings. *See, e.g.,* OKLAHOMA MODEL RULES OF PROFESSIONAL CONDUCT 3.3(b).

31. ABA Comm. on Ethics and Professional Responsibility, Formal Opinion 87-353 (1987).

32. The lawyer is reminded that a lawyer's disclosure obligations are predicated on the lawyer actually knowing the client is perpetrating a fraud on the tribunal. Merely suspecting fraud without more is not enough. *See, e.g.,* United States v. Long, 857 F.2d 436 (8th Cir. 1988); ABA Comm. on Ethics and Professional Responsibility, Formal Op. 87-353 (1987).

33. Not all jurisdictions have adopted the 1974 amendment to Dr 7-102(B)(1). *See, e.g.,* VIRGINIA CODE OF PROFESSIONAL RESPONSIBILITY, DR 7-102(B)(1).

34. *But see* Office of Disciplinary Counsel v. Heffernan, 569 N.E.2d 1027 (Ohio 1991) (where court suspended a lawyer from the practice of law for six months when the lawyer did not report a fraud upon the court even though the lawyer did not learn of the fraud until several months after the court proceedings). Ohio did not, however, adopt the amendment to DR 7-102(B)(1).

35. *See also* Nix v. Whiteside, 475 U.S. 157 (1986) (. . . a criminal defendant is not entitled to the assistance of counsel in giving false testimony and that a lawyer who refuses such assistance and who even threatens the client with

disclosure of the perjury to the court if the client does testify falsely, has not deprived the client of effective assistance of counsel).

36. *But see* the contradictory statement in the Comment to Rule 1.2(d) that a lawyer "is not permitted to reveal the client's wrongdoing, except where permitted by Rule 1.6."

37. For a detailed defense of the position that client confidentiality is essential to safeguarding the rights of the criminal accused, *see* MONROE H. FREEDMAN, UNDERSTANDING LAWYERS' ETHICS (1990). *See also* Monroe H. Freedman, *Professional Responsibility of the Criminal Defense Lawyer: The Three Hardest Questions,* 64 MICH. L. REV. 1469 (1966).

38. In *Nix v. Whiteside,* the lawyer representing the defendant, Mr. Whiteside, in a murder case was told by his client that he believed that although he had not seen a gun in the deceased's hands when he was stabbed, that he believed the deceased had a gun. Shortly before trial the defendant told the lawyer that he intended to testify that he had seen something metallic in the hand of the deceased shortly before his demise. Counsel told the defendant if he insisted on testifying falsely the lawyer would advise the court that he felt respondent was committing perjury and would seek to withdraw from representation. The defendant, thus, did not testify that he saw something metallic in the hands of the deceased and was convicted of murder. After the conviction, the respondent's appeal to the Iowa Supreme Court was denied. After seeking federal habeas corpus review, the United States Supreme Court held that the Sixth Amendment right of a criminal defendant to assistance of counsel is not violated when a lawyer refuses to cooperate with the defendant in presenting perjured testimony at his trial. The court determined that counsel's duty of loyalty to, and advocacy of, the defendant's cause is limited to legitimate, lawful conduct compatible with the very nature of a trial as a search for the truth. *See also, Rohrback, supra* note 18; *Casby, supra* note 18.

39. MONROE H. FREEDMAN, *supra* note 17.

40. Fisher v. United States, 428 U.S. 391 (1976). As Justice John Marshall Harlan wrote for the court ". . . it is intolerable that one constitutional right should have to be surrendered in order to assert another." Simmons v. United States, 390 U.S. 377, 394 (1968).

41. ATLA CODE Rule 1.2 directs that without client consent, a lawyer cannot divulge client confidences except as provided in the rules.

42. ABA Comm. on Professional Ethics and Grievances Formal Opinion 287 (1953).

43. ABA Comm. on Professional Ethics and Grievances Formal Opinion 287 (1953). *See also,* MODEL RULE 3.3, Comment; State v. Casby, 348 N.W.2d 736 (Minn 1984).

Bibliography

Articles, Reports, and Standards

ABA CANONS OF PROFESSIONAL RESPONSIBILITY, Canon 37.

ABA Committee on Professional Ethics and Grievances, Formal Opinion 287 (1953).

ABA Committee on Ethics and Professional Responsibility, Formal Opinion 87-353 (1987).

ABA Committee on Ethics and Professional Responsibility, Formal Opinion 92-366 (1992).

ABA Committee on Ethics and Professional Responsibility, Informal Opinion 1314 (1975).

ABA MODEL CODE OF PROFESSIONAL RESPONSIBILITY, Canon 7, DR 4-101, 4-101(C), 7-102(A)(5), 7-102(B), 7-102(B)(1), EC 4-1.

ABA MODEL RULES OF PROFESSIONAL CONDUCT, Rules 1.2, 1.2(d) & cmt., 1.3 & cmt., 1.4, 1.6, 1.6(b)(1), 3.3, 3.3(a), 3.3(a)(1), 3.3(b) & cmt., 4.1.

ABA STANDARDS FOR CRIMINAL JUSTICE, Standard 4-1.2, 4-3.7 & cmt. (3d ed. 1993).

AMERICAN TRIAL LAWYERS CODE OF CONDUCT, Rule 1.2 (1980).

Birmingham Bar Association, Opinion 21 (1982).

Stephen McG. Bundy and Einer Richard Elhauge, *Do Lawyers Improve the Adversary System? A General Theory of Litigation Advice and its Regulation*, 79 Cal. L. Rev. 315 (1991).

Committee on Professional and Judicial Ethics of the State Bar of Michigan, Opinion CI-789 (1982).

Nathan M. Crystal, *Confidentiality Under the Model Rules of Professional Conduct*, 30 U. Kan. L. Rev. 215 (1982).

Marvin Frankel, *The Search For Truth: An Umpireal View*, 123 U. Pa. L. Rev. 1031 (1975).

Monroe H. Freedman, *Legal Ethics and the Suffering Client*, 36 Cath. U. L. Rev. 331 (1987).

Monroe H. Freedman, *Professional Responsibility of the Criminal Defense Lawyer: The Three Hardest Questions*, 64 Mich. L. Rev. 1469 (1966).

Monroe H. Freedman, *Understanding Lawyers' Ethics* (1990).

Monroe H. Freedman, *Wrong? . . . Silence Is Right*, N.Y. Times, February 14, 1983.

OKLAHOMA MODEL RULES OF PROFESSIONAL CONDUCT, Rule 3.3(b) (1993).

Roscoe Pound–American Trial Lawyers Foundation, *The American Trial Lawyer's Code of Conduct* (1982).

Standing Committee on Legal Ethics of the Virginia State Bar, Opinion 506 (1983).

VIRGINIA CODE OF PROFESSIONAL RESPONSIBILITY, DR 7-102(B)(1) (1992).

Stuart Watt, Note, *Confidentiality Under the Washington Rules of Professional Conduct*, 61 Wash. L. Rev. 913 (1986).

Charles W. Wolfram, *Modern Legal Ethics* § 7.6 (1986).

Cases

Attorney Grievance Committee of Maryland v. Rohrback, 591 A.2d 488 (Md. 1991).

Dodd v. Florida Bar, 118 So. 2d 17 (Fla. 1960).

Fisher v. United States, 425 U.S. 391 (1976).

Fite v. Lee, 521 P.2d 964 (Wash. App. 1974).

Holloway v. Arkansas, 434 U.S. 475 (1978).

In re Carroll, 244 S.W.2d 474 (Ky. 1951).

In re Greenburg, 104 A.2d 46 (N.J. 1954).

In re Integration of Nebraska State Bar Association, 275 N.W. 265 (Neb. 1937).

Nix v. Whiteside, 475 U.S. 157 (1986).

Office of Disciplinary Counsel v. Heffernan, 569 N.E.2d 1027 (Ohio 1991).

People v. Salquerro, 433 N.Y.2d 711 (N.Y. Supp. Ct. 1980).

Simmons v. United States, 390 U.S. 377 (1968).

State v. Casby, 348 N.W.2d 736 (Minn. 1984).

State v. Henderson, 468 P.2d 136 (Kan. 1970).

State v. Kutchen, 417 P.2d 510 (Ariz. 1966).

State v. Robinson, 224 S.E.2d 174 (N.C. 1976).

United States v. Henkel, 799 F.2d 369 (7th Cir. 1986).

United States v. Long, 857 F.2d 436 (8th Cir. 1988).

United States v. Wade, 388 U.S. 218 (1976).

Upjohn v. United States, 449 U.S. 387 (1981).

CHAPTER 📖 15

Disclose or Not: The Client with a False Identity

Eva S. Nilsen

May defense counsel who learns that her client has been charged under a false name continue to represent that client without disclosing the client's true identity?

Introduction: The Problem in Context

It may come to defense counsel's attention that her client is charged under a false name. Counsel may learn this either from the client or a third party. This discussion assumes that defense counsel clearly knows that the client has intentionally given a false name. It is important to note that this problem is one of the most vexing because of counsel's competing duties to the client and the court. The most common reason for a client's misrepresentation of identity is that the client has a criminal record under the true name and would face serious consequences if charged or convicted again. These consequences may include ineligibility for release on personal recognizance or reasonable bail, arrest on outstanding warrants, probation and parole problems, unfavorable plea bargains, or harsh sentencing. Another reason for the client's use of an alias might be a fear that his immigration status would be jeopardized by a criminal charge. Also, the client may be in the midst of unrelated legal proceedings, for example, a family court matter, and his legal position could be compromised by a pending criminal matter. Giving a false name allows the client to come into the criminal justice system with a clean record.

214

Counsel's Dilemma

If defense counsel learns that her client is charged under the wrong name, she will have to address a difficult ethical dilemma. The obvious dilemma is how to resolve what appear to be conflicting loyalties to the client and the court. Counsel must adhere to her duties of loyalty and zealous representation while at the same time refrain from perpetrating a fraud on the court. The following questions may be useful in recognizing the problem and in determining the appropriate response: What is the source of the troubling information? (There may be more protection of the information if it comes directly from the client and could therefore be characterized as a "confidence," although both the Model Code and the Model Rules broadly define protected communication.) Is a false identity a material fact at issue in the case? Is it clear in the lawyer's jurisdiction that maintaining a false identity constitutes a future crime or fraudulent act? Does the answer to this question depend on whether the case will be resolved by plea and sentencing rather than a trial? Can the lawyer negotiate on behalf of a client using a false name? Does appearing on a case constitute making a false statement to the court? Does it matter whether or not the client will testify under the false identity? If counsel stands by silently during a guilty plea and does not give the client's name or criminal record during the sentencing argument, has counsel appropriately resolved the ethical problem?

Defense counsel can discern answers to some of these questions from the ABA Model Code of Professional Responsibility and the ABA Model Rules of Professional Conduct. Several ABA Formal Opinions and a few cases lend additional assistance. Moreover, just as with the perjury dilemma, defense counsel must wrestle with these ethical problems against a backdrop of unresolved constitutional concerns. This is not to say, however, that any of these sources provide a definitive set of answers to a series of perplexing ethical problems inherent in a lawyer being asked to serve two masters.

Differing Approaches of the Model Code and the Model Rules to the Issue of Confidentiality

Relevant provisions of the ABA Model Code of Professional Responsibility (hereinafter Model Code) include: DR 2-110(C) (withdrawal); DR 4-101 (duty of confidentiality); DR 7-101 (zealous advocacy); DR 7-101(A)(4) (no perjury); DR 7-102(A)(5) (no false statements); and DR 7-102(B)(1) (reveal fraud unless privileged).

Under the Model Code, defense counsel's duty to protect client confidentiality usually takes precedence over her duty of candor to the court.[1] The Model Code trumpets the importance of the lawyer as zealous advocate who should maintain inviolate the client's confidences and secrets. Among the limited exceptions to this duty of confidentiality are (1) when the client intends to commit a crime and it is necessary to reveal the confidence or secret to prevent the crime,[2] and (2) when allowed under other Disciplinary Rules or required by law or court order.[3] But even in such an exceptional case, the Model Code grants the lawyer discretion to disclose. Nonetheless, failure to disclose client crimes or continuing wrongful acts may subject counsel to disciplinary action.[4]

The problem for defense counsel turns, in part, on whether a defendant's continued use of a false name constitutes a crime.[5] When a client has already been charged under a false name it may be difficult for the lawyer to ascertain whether the client intends to commit a crime. If the client plans to testify under oath, he may or may not be committing perjury. The continued use of a false name may subject the client to a lesser crime than perjury, such as lying under oath, filing papers containing a false statement made under penalties of perjury, or criminal contempt. Or, for example, the defendant's use of a false name when responding to a probation officer's questions may constitute obstructing justice. Yet, the Model Code's "future crime" exception may be intended to protect the public against totally distinct future crimes, such as crimes against the person. If this is so, then counsel might not be permitted to break confidentiality. It is clear, however, that the Model Code prohibits counsel from disclosing a client's past falsehood, whether or not it constitutes a crime, unless the act constitutes part of a continuing or future crime.[6]

Historical Basis of Present Model Code Protection

The importance of confidentiality protection cannot be overemphasized. It is linked to a conception of justice that encourages clients to be candid with lawyers so that lawyers may advise clients wisely. Formal Opinion 287, which the ABA issued in 1953, focused on three situations involving the sentencing of a lawyer's client: (1) the judge is erroneously informed by a records custodian that the defendant has no prior criminal record and the lawyer knows that his client has a prior record; (2) the judge asks the defendant about his record and the defendant falsely answers he has none; and (3) the judge asks the lawyer whether his client has a prior record. Formal Opinion 287 declared that a lawyer's duty not to reveal a client's confidence prohibited the disclosure

of a client's past perjury to the court and barred a lawyer from disclosing the client's actual record in the three situations described above.
Thus, Formal Opinion 287 concluded that under the ABA Canons of
Professional Ethics, the duty to maintain confidentiality prevailed over
the duty to reveal fraud or deception to the court and over the duty to
come forward with knowledge of past perjury.[7]

When the Model Code was first promulgated in 1969, the issue of
how a lawyer was to reconcile the conflict of loyalties between the client and the court in a case of client fraud appeared unresolved. DR
7-102(B)(1) required the lawyer to try to persuade the client to rectify
the fraud and, if unsuccessful, to reveal the fraud to the court. This
disclosure obligation, however, directly clashed with the duty to hold
inviolate client confidences and secrets as stated in Canon 4. Recognizing this impasse for lawyers, the ABA amended DR 7-102(B)(1) to
require disclosure to the court "except when the information is protected as a privileged communication."[8] Moreover, Formal Opinion
341 (1975) interpreted privileged communications to include both confidences and secrets protected under Canon 4. Accordingly, the Model
Code appears to forbid a lawyer from disclosing client fraud or false
statements to the court.[9]

The issue, however, is further complicated by the fact that generally a client's identity is not considered to be protected by the lawyer-
client privilege. There are several exceptions to this general rule. For
instance, a client's name or identity may be protected from disclosure
as confidential information where revealing the client's name would
implicate him in the crime for which he sought the lawyers advice in
the first place.[10] But cases such as *Baltes v. Doe*, 4 Law. Man. Prof. Conduct 356 (Fla. Cir. Ct. 1988), a highly publicized Florida case in which
the trial court approved of a lawyer's refusal to disclose the identity of
his client who had been involved in a hit-and-run accident, address a
different problem from that facing the lawyer with a client who has
given a false name. Those cases extend the protection of the lawyer-
client privilege to a client who wishes to remain anonymous and out of
the reach of authorities. Information relating to a continuing or future
crime or fraud, however, is not protected by the lawyer-client privilege.
See, e.g., In re Grand Jury Proceeding, 680 F.2d 1026 (5th Cir. 1982). Thus,
despite the language of Formal Opinion 87-353, the amendment to DR
7-102(B)(1) may not relieve defense counsel of the obligation to inform
the court of a client's continuing fraud.

Case law and state ethics opinions offer uneven and at times conflicting advice to defense counsel who confronts a situation where a
criminal defendant is not who he initially claims to be. Courts seem

more inclined to resolve this ethical dilemma in favor of candor to the court rather than protection of the client's confidences.[11] In *State v. Casby*, 348 N.W.2d 736 (Minn. 1984), for example, the Minnesota Supreme Court affirmed a lawyer's conviction for the misdemeanor of committing deceit or collusion with intent to deceive a court or any party. The court rejected the lawyer's justification for refusing to disclose her client's true identity, finding that the client's false identity was not protected by the lawyer-client privilege or the Fifth or Sixth Amendments. Rather, the court described the lawyer's knowingly undertaking plea bargaining as actively assisting her client's fraud. Although the court stressed that the lawyer made no effort to dissuade the client from persisting in misrepresenting his identity, it does not appear that anything short of withdrawal or disclosure would have satisfied the court. Indeed, the court observed that under the circumstances, "it is difficult to see how Ms. Casby could have continued to represent Peter, even under the most passive conditions, without the danger of assisting the client's fraudulent conduct and preserving false evidence in violation of DR 7-102(A)." *Casby*, at 739.

In two other examples, *Office of Disciplinary Counsel v. Hazelkorn*, 480 N.E.2d 1116 (Ohio 1985) and *Office of Disciplinary Counsel v. Heffernan*, 569 N.E.2d 1027 (Ohio 1991), the Ohio Supreme Court disciplined defense lawyers who failed to disclose the true identity of their clients. The court did not discuss any constitutional issues or the lawyer's justifications for nondisclosure in either case. In *Hazelkorn*, the court affirmed the disciplinary board's findings that the lawyer knew the client's true identity and that the client was trying to avoid disclosure of his prior record. Counsel's actions misled the prosecutor and the court and thereby assisted the client in illegal and fraudulent conduct in violation of various provisions of DR 7 and DR 1. In *Heffernan*, counsel did not discover the fraud until after the plea hearing. Nonetheless, the court found that counsel violated DR 7-102(B)(1) by not revealing the fraud.

Similarly, in a controversial opinion by the Ethics Committee of the Massachusetts Bar Association, Opinion 89-1 (1989), the committee concluded, in a *civil* case where perjury had been committed at a deposition, that the lawyer may disclose a client's past deposition perjury in order to prevent the client from committing intended future perjury. The Massachusetts opinion protects the confidentiality of the initial fraudulent act unless the client intends to commit a new crime, such as giving perjured testimony at trial. The committee looked at DR 4-101(C)(3), which it assumed gave the lawyer discretion to reveal his client's intention to commit a crime and the information necessary to prevent the crime even if it meant disclosing a past crime. This Model

Code provision was read in conjunction with DR 7-102(B) "A lawyer who receives information clearly establishing that (1) His client has, in the course of representation, perpetrated a fraud upon a person or tribunal shall promptly call upon his client to rectify the same, and if his client refuses or is unable to do so, he shall reveal the fraud to the affected person or tribunal, except when the information is protected as a privileged communication." As already discussed, this provision seems to prevent the lawyer from disclosing the fraud since it is protected by Canon 4. Nonetheless, Opinion 89-1 takes the position that if the client intends to repeat his perjury at trial or commit another crime, then the lawyer has discretion under DR 4-101(C)(3) to reveal his client's intention. It follows, according to the committee, that because future crime information is not a "privileged communication" covered by the exception to DR 7-102(B)(1), the lawyer in such a case has a mandatory duty to disclose.[12]

Defense counsel still must decide whether the continued use of, or failure to correct, a false name constitutes a future crime or a continuing fraud. Unquestionably, the Ethics Committee of the Massachusetts Bar Association would treat a lawyer's protection of a client's false identity as assisting a fraud on the court. Certainly that is the position suggested by a second opinion of that ethics committee, Opinion 914 (1991). In Opinion 914, the committee considered the obligations of defense counsel representing a defendant who lies about his identity to a probation officer during a presentence investigation. The committee opined that the lawyer's duty turns on whether the false statement constitutes a crime. If it is a crime, then the lawyer must advise the client to rectify the situation and, if the client refuses, disclose the falsehood to the court. The committee suggests that the falsehood does not warrant the protection of the lawyer-client privilege because it will be used to perpetuate a fraud in a future sentencing proceeding. But even if the false statement does not constitute a crime (and the opinion indicates it cannot take a position on this point), then the committee suggests the lawyer should seek to withdraw, but offers no guidance as to what the lawyer should do if that motion is unsuccessful. Opinion 914 reaffirms the Opinion 89-1 conclusion that client's lies are not protected by the lawyer-client privilege, but expresses no conclusion as to whether the client's privilege against self-incrimination affects the lawyer's duty. Although these ethics opinions were harshly criticized by bar counsel (the head of the Massachusetts Board of Bar Overseers) for their omission of the Model Code alternative response of withdrawal when faced with client fraud,[13] these opinions undoubtedly reflect the prevailing attitude of state ethics boards toward this issue. *See, e.g.,* Virginia Opinion 1331 (1990), *supra* note 8.

Relevant provisions of the ABA Model Rules of Professional Responsibility (hereinafter Model Rules) include: Rule 1.2(d) (may not assist fraud); Rules 1.6 and 3.3(b) (confidentiality); Rule 1.16(b) (withdrawal); Rule 3.3(a)(1) (must not make false statement); Rule 3.3(a)(2) (must disclose crime or fraud); and Rule 3.3(a)(4) (must correct false evidence).

The Model Rules clearly subordinate the protection of client confidences to the obligation of candor to the court. *See* ABA Formal Opinion 87-353. Lawyers practicing under the Model Rules, therefore, have less leeway when representing a client who has used a false identity than lawyers governed by the Model Code. This appears most explicitly in Model Rule 3.3(a)(4), stating that a lawyer must take remedial measures if she has offered material false evidence in a court proceeding even if doing so would force her to reveal information otherwise protected by Model Rule 1.6.[14] Other Model Rules that govern the lawyer faced with a problem of false identity are Rule 3.3(a)(1), prohibiting a lawyer from making a false statement to the court, and Rule 1.2, prohibiting a lawyer from assisting a client in what the lawyer knows is criminal or fraudulent conduct. Defense counsel faced with an issue of false identity must determine whether false identity is a material fact in the case and whether she can find a way to continue on the case without making a false statement or perpetuating a fraud.

Arguably, identity is not material in some circumstances, for example, whether or not *A* assaulted *B* in self-defense. Nevertheless, even in such a case, identity may still be material where *A*, under his true name, has impeachable offenses, or where the issue before the court is bail, probation or parole revocation, or sentencing.[15] Even in the unusual case where the client's identity does not appear to be material, it is not clear that a lawyer is free to argue the client's *credibility*, knowing that the client testified falsely about his name. This is particularly problematic if the client has a criminal record under his true name and would be subject to impeachment at trial if this were known.

How certain must the lawyer be before a duty to act is triggered? There should be no doubt in counsel's mind that the client is proceeding under a false identity. This level of certainty can be achieved only when the information about the fraud comes from the client.[16] Is the timing of counsel's knowledge important in determining the proper action? For instance, if defense counsel argued for personal recognizance at the client's arraignment based in part on his apparent lack of a criminal record, must counsel disclose the client's true name during the next court proceeding? Was the decision to release the client on personal recognizance tainted and, therefore, in need of correction? If counsel learns of the fraud only after the case is finished, must she go back before the court to disclose this?[17]

If counsel decides that the client's false identity is material and that continued representation constitutes a continuing fraud or crime, unquestionably the lawyer's first duty is to seek to persuade the client to disclose his true identity to the court.[18] Counsel who is unsuccessful is advised to take "reasonable remedial measures."[19] These measures differ for civil and criminal clients, with greater protection for the latter. Nonetheless, in a jurisdiction governed by the Model Rules, defense counsel appears to have only limited options if the client chooses not to rectify the false information. The Model Rules do not allow the lawyer to make false statements or fail to disclose a material fact if failure to do so assists in the client in defrauding the court or in the commission of a crime.[20]

Even if the Model Rules mandate disclosure, however, counsel's obligations may still be qualified by constitutional considerations.[21] Indeed, some states specifically recognize that a criminal defense lawyer may have an obligation different than other lawyers with respect to disclosing a client's falsehoods. In Maryland, for example, Model Rule 3.3(c) has been modified to read "notwithstanding paragraphs (a) through (d), a lawyer for an accused in a criminal case need not disclose that the accused intends to testify falsely or has testified falsely if the lawyer reasonably believes that the disclosure would jeopardize any constitutional right of the accused."[22]

How I Handle This Problem

I have faced this problem many times as a lawyer and clinical teacher. Usually I become aware of the false identity after the client has been arraigned and released.[23] I have always learned about the misrepresentation from the client, sometimes in response to my efforts to gather information.[24] My first response has been to find out why the client gave a false name and to counsel him about alternative ways to meet his concerns about using his true identity. My approach is to advise him to correct the information and to allow me to help him minimize whatever problems he foresees. For example, if he fears deportation based on this state court case, my advice may include such issues as whether this is a deportable offense, whether there is a defense to the charge, or whether we can work out a "no record" disposition of the case such as a dismissal. Moreover, it is possible that the federal authorities will never learn of the state court case, though I cannot promise this.

Typically, the client's concern is that his prior record under his true name will assure a harsher sentence if he is found guilty of the current charge. (This is becoming an even greater fear under state and federal "three-strikes" statutes.) Again, I counsel him about the likelihood of winning the new case, leaving him to decide whether to face the court under his true name. I advise the client that I cannot continue to represent him under a false name because to do so would be to engage in defrauding the court. I explain that I cannot even try to negotiate a favorable disposition for him because, in misrepresenting his identity (and record) to the district attorney, I may be assisting him in committing a fraud against the court.[25] I further advise the client that if he does not correct the problem I will try to withdraw from the case and help him get another lawyer without disclosing his true identity.

Whether to Move to Withdraw

Withdrawal may be possible in the early stages of representation but may become increasingly difficult as the trial date approaches. In deciding what to do, counsel should consider the following questions: What was the reason for the client's use of a false identity? What will happen to the client if he reveals his true identity to the court? What are the implications of counsel's withdrawal from the case? Will other lawyers be available? Will a motion to withdraw signal "perjury" to the court and hurt the client? Will the court grant a continuance for successor counsel to prepare adequately? Is withdrawal and appointment of new counsel sufficient to get recusal?

In answering these questions one cannot avoid the possibility that the client may be harmed by counsel's withdrawal, particularly where counsel has done considerable trial preparation.[26] There is a risk that successor counsel will not have adequate time to prepare the case. Alternatively, the court may deny counsel's motion to withdraw or ask for reasons. Counsel need not give the actual reason, relying on the confidentiality of the client communications.[27] However, there is no escaping that this proceeding may tip off the judge that there is something questionable about the client.[28] If the court denies the request to withdraw, there are two possible courses of action. Counsel may continue to zealously represent the accused while at the same time protecting herself as best as possible from any criminal or disciplinary action. See NACDL Formal Opinion 90-2. Conversely, counsel may decide to disclose the fraud.

The lawyer who continues to represent a client who she knows is charged under a false name should recognize that the ABA ethics provisions, especially the Model Rules, do not provide much of a safe harbor. Even the lawyer in a Model Code jurisdiction who relies on ABA Opinion 287 and declines to disclose the client's true identity walks an unsteady tightrope. Counsel in either a Model Code or Model Rules jurisdiction may not make an affirmative misstatement to the court. Will counsel be able to continue to represent the client with a false name without making a false representation or assisting the client's fraud? If the case is not triable and the client is considering a guilty plea, it is hard to imagine a plea proceeding where counsel would not risk participating in a fraud on the court. The client may be under oath during the plea colloquy, and in many jurisdictions the lawyer is required to actively participate in plea proceedings. Certainly, if the client's reason for giving the false name is to avoid the consequences of his actual criminal record, the lawyer who protects the client's false identity may well have assisted the client in furthering a fraud upon the court.[29]

If the case goes to trial, the client may elect not to testify. This at least eliminates the issue of perjured testimony. If the client testifies and withdrawal is not possible, counsel's options are to (1) let the client testify in narrative form without lawyer guidance; (2) take the position that a criminal defense counsel is excused from a duty to reveal a client's falsehoods, particularly when, as in the case of false identity, the information may not be material to the factual issues before the court; or (3) reveal the perjury to the court. Although the first and last options may raise Fifth and Sixth Amendment problems, as well as state constitutional equivalents, some courts have taken the position that these rights are not implicated when the client commits perjury.[30] Other jurisdictions have modified their ethical provisions to acknowledge that a criminal defendant's constitutional rights may override the normal responsibilities a lawyer has as an officer of the court.[31] The comment to Model Rule 3.3 expressly recognizes that "in some jurisdictions these provisions have been construed to require that counsel present an accused as a witness if the accused wishes to testify, even if counsel knows the testimony will be false. The obligation of the advocate under these Rules is subordinate to such a constitutional requirement." Although counsel can point to constitutional considerations as justification for nondisclosure of a client's true identity, cases such as *Casby, Heffernan, Hazelkorn,* and *Rohrback* make it clear that continued representation of a client with a false name presents potentially serious problems for defense counsel.

> *May counsel act at a stage of the proceedings where representation will not constitute fraud on the tribunal?*

It is possible that counsel may continue to represent the client during the pretrial phase of a case without running afoul of the ethics rules.

Since these proceedings are primarily "legal" in nature and do not rely on testimony of the client or representation about his identity and criminal record, it may be possible to postpone withdrawal while trying to persuade the client to correct the misinformation. This course of action should be considered because some motions need prompt resolution to protect the client's rights. The ethics rules call for consideration of the client's interests even when withdrawal is contemplated. *See* MODEL RULE 1.16(b). It is also worthwhile to consider that in a case unlikely to advance due to weaknesses in the state's evidence, withdrawal may be unnecessary as there will be no occasion for misrepresentations to the court.

What I Would Do

In those instances where I have had a client with a false name, I usually try to resolve the problem early. I begin by trying to find a way with the client's consent to correct the problem without adversely affecting the client. If the client is not interested in correcting the problem, it is easier on the client, and more likely to be favorably received by the judge, if withdrawal is attempted early in the representation. However, if I thought that the case was likely to be dismissed or that it would be resolved by motions, I might continue the representation past the resolution of these issues. During this period I would continue to advise the client to correct his identity with the court. If the client refused to correct the problem and I was not allowed to withdraw from the case, then I would continue with the case, being careful to make no misrepresentations to any court personnel. I would continue to advise the client to correct the problem, explaining to him that the problem was hindering my ability to represent him effectively. No client with a false identity has pushed me to the point of a trial or a plea. Clients have either corrected the problem or failed to appear for trial, leaving the problem for another lawyer at another time (and undoubtedly teaching the client a lesson about the limits of confidentiality). My main concerns are that I not unduly compromise my client's rights or needs while at the same time I protect my reputation and license to practice. Because Massachusetts is still, albeit probably not for long, a Model Code state, confidentiality continues to hold a slight edge over candor to the court.[32]

If I discovered after the case was over that my client had used a false name throughout the proceedings, I would not disclose the fraud, nor do I think it is required in most Model Code or Model Rules jurisdictions.[33] The fraud would then be a completed or past fraud or crime and, thus, protected.[34]

Disclosure

As many authorities recognize, disclosure of a client's confidences can wreak havoc on the client, leaving him feeling betrayed by a lawyer who began the relationship with what now seems like an empty promise of loyalty. Both the Model Code and the Model Rules point out the benefits that our legal system derives from rules that vigorously protect confidentiality. Clients are encouraged to tell their secrets to lawyers because of this protection. Moreover, the consequences of disclosure may be extremely harsh, including loss of the case and a prosecution for perjury. But these grave effects of required disclosures are weighed against the deleterious effects to the adversary system of both the presentation of false evidence to the court and the perception that the client made the lawyer a party to the fraud.[35] It is important to remember, however, that the comment to Model Rule 3.3 does not recommend disclosure except as a last resort. Ultimately, counsel must decide the proper course to follow based on the specific facts of the case, the implications for the client, and the state's law on the subject.

Conclusion

The National Association of Criminal Defense Lawyers (NACDL) Ethics Advisory Committee, in Opinion 90-2, recently addressed the issue of whether a lawyer representing a client who has given a false name to avoid deportation is obligated to disclose the client's true identity. The opinion assumes that the client specifically instructs the lawyer not to disclose his true identity and that the client's use of a false identity is a felony. Moreover, the opinion suggests that the defendant may be committing a continuing crime each time he appears in court under the false identity. Although the opinion notes that the lawyer-client privilege does not cover future or ongoing crimes or frauds, it argues that in the underlying drug case under consideration, the use of the false name is not material or relevant. The committee concludes, therefore, that nondisclosure will not foster a fraud on the court. Alternatively, the committee concludes that the privilege against self-incrimination mandates nondisclosure because, even if the ethical rules require disclosure, "ethical rules must, at least in this instance, give way to constitutional guarantees." No authority, however, is cited for this proposition and, in fact, in a footnote, the committee acknowledges that *State v. Casby* cuts the other way.

NACDL Opinion 90-2 also observes that the problem is exacerbated if the defendant is called as a witness, because then "the problem of client perjury, fraud on the court, and the lawyer's complicity

therein will be implicated." The committee again recommends the lawyer seek to withdraw if the client refuses to rectify the situation, but the
opinion does not clearly spell out what the lawyer should do if that
motion to withdraw is denied. The opinion does offer steps lawyers
might want to take to protect themselves from accusations of misconduct when dealing with a client who is using a false name. The lawyer
should document:

> (1) the fact the client made a privileged communication revealing
> an arguably ongoing crime; (2) that the lawyer clearly asked the
> client to reveal and discontinue the crime (with full advice of the
> risks of doing so); (3) that the lawyer clearly and unmistakably has
> advised the client that he or she will not participate in any acts
> which further the client's crime or fraud; (4) that the client pro-
> hibits the lawyer from disclosing the true facts; (5) that the lawyer
> believes the privilege against self-incrimination prohibits him or
> her from disclosing the ongoing crime; and (6) that the lawyer told
> the client he or she may have to withdraw (without disclosing the
> facts to the court) to avoid furthering a fraud on the court.

While no concise answer to our question can be stated, lawyers
need to exercise great care. To do nothing upon learning of the client's
false identity is to risk sanction by the court or the state ethics board.
In some jurisdictions, case law imposes a clear duty upon defense
counsel to disclose client fraud while in others, counsel's ethical obligations are less clear. In some instances, a sanction might reasonably be
preferred to the dire consequences to the client of disclosure or even
withdrawal. A full documentation of the issue should appear in defense counsel's file, including defense counsel's thought processes, advice to the client, and any measures taken to minimize the problem.

Notes

1. *But see* In the Matter of Neitlich, 597 N.E.2d 425 (Mass. 1992) (client's
interests must yield to lawyer's duty to the court where conflict exists).
2. DR 4-101(C)(3)
3. DR 4-101(C)(2)
4. ABA Comm. on Professional Ethics and Grievances, Formal Op. 155
and 156 (1936) and ABA Comm. on Professional Ethics, Formal Op. 314 (1965).
But see Attorney Grievance Comm. of Maryland v. Rohrback, 591 A.2d 488, 496
(Md. 1991) ("Failure to reveal that which may be revealed, as opposed to that
which must be revealed, is not a basis for disciplinary action.").
5. *See* Nat'l Ass'n of Crim. Defense Lawyers Ethics Advisory Comm.,
Formal Op. 90-2 (1990) in THE CHAMPION 40 (Mar. 1991) (hereinafter NACDL

Opinion 90-2), noting that in most jurisdictions it is a crime to knowingly assume a false identity with intent to secure a unlawful benefit. The opinion also suggests that the defendant may be committing a continuing crime every time he appears in court under a false identity.

6. *See Rohrback, supra* note 4, at 494–96. *See also* ABA Comm. on Professional Ethics and Grievances, Formal Op. 287 (1953); Ethics Comm. of the Massachusetts Bar Association, Op. 89-1 (1989).

7. *See also* AMERICAN LAWYER'S CODE OF CONDUCT (1982) [hereinafter ATLA Code] (an alternative set of rules produced by the American Trial Lawyers' Association). The Comment to Ch. 1 of the ATLA Code, "The Client's Trust and Confidences," elaborates on the paramount role of confidentiality in the adversary system. The ATLA Code is more protective of confidentiality than either the Model Code or the Model Rules and permits but does not require divulgence of a client's confidences in circumstances in which the other codes mandate disclosure.

8. *See* DR 7-102(B)(1), amended in 1974. Many states, however, did not adopt this amendment. *See, e.g.,* VIRGINIA CODE OF PROFESSIONAL RESPONSIBILITY, DR 7-102(B)(1). Thus, the Standing Committee on Legal Ethics of the Virginia State Bar in Op. 1331 (1990) stated that a lawyer could not stand silent at a sentencing when the client was using a false name to hide his prior record. In the committee's view, the lawyer would be assisting in the perpetration of a fraud on the court. If the client will not reveal his true identity, the lawyer has an obligation to do so.

9. *See* ABA Comm. on Ethics and Professional Responsibility, Formal Op. 87-353 (1987) (stating that DR 7-102(B)(1) as amended requires lawyers to protect their clients' confidences just as called for by ABA Formal Opinion 287). *But see* MODEL RULE 3.3, "Model Code Comparison," contending that because the lawyer-client privilege has been construed to exclude communications that further a crime, including perjury, DR 7-102(B)(1), even as amended, may be interpreted to require disclosure of client perjury.

10. *See, e.g.,* U.S. v. Jones, 517 F.2d 666 (5th Cir. 1975) and *In re* Grand Jury Proceedings 899 F.2d 1039 (11th Cir. 1990) (client's identity generally not privileged unless to reveal true identity would reveal other privileged communications). For further discussion of the issue of whether the client's identity is privileged, *see* John R. Przypyszny, Note, *Public Assault on the Attorney-Client Privilege: Ramifications of* Baltes v. Doe, 3 GEO. J. LEGAL ETHICS 351 (1989). *See generally* JOHN M. BURKOFF, CRIMINAL DEFENSE ETHICS, § 6.5(a), 58–67 (1993) (discussing cases where counsel seeks to keep client's identity confidential against orders to disclose); Diane M. Allen, Annotation, *Attorney's Disclosure, in Federal Proceedings, of Identity of Client as Violating Attorney-Client Privilege*, 84 A.L.R. FED. 852 (1987).

11. *See, e.g.,* Nix v. Whiteside, 475 U.S. 157, 174 (1986). *See also* In the Matter of Neitlich, 597 N.E.2d 425, 428 (Mass. 1992) insisting that the lawyer is duty bound "to uphold the integrity of that system by being truthful to the court and opposing counsel. Where this duty is in seeming conflict with the client's

interest in zealous representation, the latter's interest must yield. Were we to condone any action to the contrary, the integrity of the judicial process would be vitiated." *Cf.* Office of Disciplinary Counsel v. Hazelkorn, 480 N.E.2d 1116 (Ohio 1985) (a previously reprimanded lawyer who negotiated with a prosecutor and appeared before a judge without revealing client's true identity was indefinitely suspended from law practice).

12. If the client perjury was complete and no future crime intended, however, the exception to DR 7-102(B)(1) would apply and bar disclosure. It should be noted that the committee acknowledged that it was not addressing a criminal case or expressing any view on Fifth Amendment issues. In addition, bar counsel of the state ethics board filed a vigorous dissent to the position that DR 7-102(B)(1) overrides the client confidentiality of DR 4-101. *See* Arnold Rosenfeld, *Bar Counsel Comments,* 17 MASS. LAWYERS WEEKLY 977 (1989).

13. *See* Arnold Rosenfeld, *Bar Counsel Comments,* 20 MASS. LAWYERS WEEKLY 2107 (1992); *See also* Rosenfeld, *supra* note 12.

14. Model Rule 3.3(a)(2) states that a lawyer shall not knowingly "fail to disclose a material fact to a tribunal when disclosure is necessary to avoid assisting a criminal or fraudulent act by the client." It is important to note that some jurisdictions have modified Model Rule 3.3 to eliminate the word "material" so that any false statement violates Model Rule 3.3. *See, e.g.,* OKLAHOMA MODEL RULES OF PROFESSIONAL CONDUCT, Rule 3.3(a)(2).

15. *See* Attorney Grievance Comm. of Maryland v. Rohrback, 591 A.2d 488 (Md. 1991), where the defense attorney was held to have violated Model Rule 4.1 by assisting his client's use of a false identity when he accompanied the client to a meeting with a probation officer preparing a presentence report and failed to disclose the client's true identity. The court found that the client was concealing his identity to hide his prior record and that the lawyer breached his duty to disclose material facts to avoid assisting a fraud. The court looked to U.S. v. Thoreen, 653 F.2d 1332 (9th Cir. 1981) where counsel was held in contempt for substituting someone else at counsel's table for the defendant without the court's permission. The court in *Rohrback* also suggested in dicta that if the lawyer had actively participated in the bail hearing knowing his client was using a false name the lawyer would also be in violation of Model Rule 1.2(d). It should be noted that Maryland has a specific exception to Model Rule 1.6 that provides that a lawyer may reveal information "to rectify the consequences of a client's criminal or fraudulent act in the furtherance of which the lawyer's services were used." Ultimately, however, the court held that counsel's conduct knowingly and actively assisted his client's fraud in violation of Model Rule 4.1 thereby warranting a 45-day suspension. For further discussion about the materiality of the client's identity, *see generally* JOHN M. BURKOFF, CRIMINAL DEFENSE ETHICS, § 6.5(a), 58–67 (1993) (discussing cases where counsel seeks to keep client's identity confidential against orders to disclose).

16. It makes sense to adopt the same level of certainty as has been recommended for ascertaining whether a client intends to commit perjury. Thus, "it is absolutely essential that a lawyer have a firm factual basis before adopt-

ing a belief of impending perjury." United States v. Long, 857 F.2d 436, 445 (1988). *See also* Nat'l Ass'n of Crim. Defense Lawyers Ethics Advisory Comm., Formal Op. 92-2 (1992), in THE CHAMPION 23, 27 (Mar. 1993) ("If the lawyer believes that the client intends to commit perjury, the lawyer should not act on that belief unless it is clear beyond a reasonable doubt.")

17. *See* MODEL RULE 3.3, Comment 13, "Duration of Obligation" (counsel's obligation ends when case is over); ABA Formal Opinion 87-353. *But see infra* note 33; Office of Disciplinary Counsel v. Heffernan, 569 N.E.2d 1027 (Ohio 1991), where the court suspended a lawyer from practice for six months because he did not report fraud to the court even though he learned about it several months after the court hearing. The court specifically found that DR 7-102(B)(1) imposed a duty to reveal the fraud. It should be noted that Ohio's version of DR 7-102(B)(1) does not contain the clause "except when the information is protected as a privileged communication."

18. *See* MODEL RULE 3.3, Comment 5; NACDL Opinion 90-2.

19. MODEL RULE 3.3(a)(4). The remedial measures suggested by the comment to this rule include confidential remonstrations, withdrawal, and disclosure.

20. MODEL RULE 3.3(a)(1)–(4). *See also* ABA Comm. on Ethics and Professional Responsibility, Formal Opinion 87-353 (1987).

21. *See* MODEL RULE 3.3, Comment 12; NACDL Opinion 90-2.

22. *But see Rohrback, supra* note 4, where the court looked to this provision and found that it did not justify counsel's failure to disclose his client's use of a false name because the lawyer could not reasonably believe his client's constitutional right to effective assistance of counsel would be jeopardized by counsel's disclosure. The opinion makes no mention of the client's compromised Fifth Amendment right.

23. The prearraignment contact with the client is brief, and if the probation department notes the absence of a criminal record, and the client has demonstrated sufficient identification or ties to the community, the issue of his identity doesn't arise. If there are questions noted by the probation department, I pursue these questions with the client to facilitate his release. Sometimes this brings to light a false identity situation that can be corrected prior to the case being called.

24. I have encountered situations where the client has said "this is not my complete record." When asked whether his record could be under another name, he has responded "not to my knowledge." In such a case I believe that I am not obligated to find the record or the other name, if there is one. I represent him under his true name and, therefore, I am making no misrepresentations as to identity to the court.

25. Essentially, my advice tracks the positions taken in ABA Comm. on Ethics and Professional Responsibility, Formal Opinion 87-353 (1987). Under some circumstances a lawyer may be prohibited from disclosing confidential information to correct a mistake, but generally she must, at least under the Model Rules, correct a client's lie and not make an affirmative false statement. *See also* Ethics Comm. of the North Carolina State Bar Assoc., Op. 33 (1987), a

North Carolina ethics opinion contending that prior to trial a lawyer may not disclose the client's true identity because doing so would reveal his prior record and result in additional charges. At trial, however, the lawyer cannot permit the client to present perjured testimony, and if the client persists the lawyer must seek to withdraw. The opinion also insists that the lawyer may not misrepresent the client's identity or record to the court in response to a direct question posed to the lawyer from the judge. Nevertheless, the lawyer is under no obligation to answer the question and, apparently, under no obligation to inform the court of the client's true identity if the accused doesn't testify and the judge makes no direct inquiry.

26. DR 2-110(A) states that "a lawyer shall not withdraw from employment until he has taken reasonable steps to avoid foreseeable prejudice to the right of his client. . . ." *See also* Canon 4 (stressing importance of preserving client's confidences and secrets); JOHN M. BURKOFF, CRIMINAL DEFENSE ETHICS § 5.2 (1993). These concerns are echoed in the Model Rules. *See* MODEL RULE 1.16. Cases such as *State v. Casby, supra,* demonstrate that counsel's desire to avoid harm to a client does not necessarily obviate counsel's disclosure obligations.

27. Model Rule 1.16, Comment 3, addresses this issue: "[t]he lawyer's statement that professional considerations require termination of the representation ordinarily should be accepted as sufficient." Unfortunately, some judges will insist upon more information before ruling on the motion thereby further complicating counsel's dilemma.

28. In discussing the problem with the client, the client should be warned about this possibility.

29. *See* State v. Casby, 348 N.W.2d 736, 739 (Minn. 1984).

30. *Id.*

31. *See* MARYLAND LAWYERS RULES OF PROFESSIONAL CONDUCT 4.1 and 3.3(e). Rule 3.3(e) states that "a lawyer for an accused in a criminal case need not disclose that the accused intends to testify falsely or has testified falsely if the lawyer reasonably believes that the disclosure would jeopardize any constitutional right of the accused."

32. *But see* Massachusetts opinions to the contrary, *supra* notes 1, 12, and 13 and *infra* note 35.

33. Model Rule 3.3(b) provides that counsel's obligation to rectify terminates at the conclusion of the proceedings. Some states, however, have modified this provision to extend counsel's duty beyond the conclusion of the proceeding. *See, e.g.,* FLORIDA RULES OF PROFESSIONAL CONDUCT 3.3(b) and OKLAHOMA MODEL RULES OF PROFESSIONAL CONDUCT 3.3(b).

34. *See Rohrback, supra* note 4, at 496; ABA Comm. on Ethics and Professional Responsibility, Formal Op. 87-353. *But see* Office of Disciplinary Counsel v. Heffernan, 569 N.E.2d 1027 (Ohio 1991), where the court suspended a lawyer from practice for six months for failing to reveal his client's use of a false identity at a plea hearing even though he did not discover the fraud until months after the hearing.

35. The prevailing judicial attitude toward issues involving possible fraud on the court is reflected in the opinion of a Massachusetts justice who stated "the more persuasive judicial decisions require a lawyer to bring material facts to the attention of the court when ignorance by the court is likely to produce an erroneous decision and not just when his opponent is and will remain ignorant." *In re* Mahlowitz, 1 Mass. Atty. Disc. Rep. 189, 194–95 (1979). *See also supra* note 11.

Bibliography

Articles, Reports, and Standards

ABA Committee on Professional Ethics, Formal Opinion 314 (1965).

ABA Committee on Professional Ethics and Grievances, Formal Opinion 155 (1936).

ABA Committee on Professional Ethics and Grievances, Formal Opinion 156 (1936).

ABA Committee on Professional Ethics and Grievances, Formal Opinion 287 (1953).

ABA Committee on Ethics and Professional Responsibility, Formal Opinion 341 (1975).

ABA Committee on Ethics and Professional Responsibility, Formal Opinion 87-353 (1987).

ABA MODEL CODE OF PROFESSIONAL RESPONSIBILITY, Canon 4, DR 2-110(C); 4-101(C)(2); 4-101(C)(3); 7-101; 7-101(A)(4); 7-102(A)(5); 7-102(B)(1) (1980).

ABA MODEL RULES OF PROFESSIONAL CONDUCT, Rules 1.2(d), 1.6, 1.16(b), 3.3(a)(1), 3.3(a)(2), 3.3(a)(3), 3.3(b), 3.3(c) and cmt. 5, 11, and 12, 4.1 (1983).

Diane M. Allen, Annotation, *Disclosure, in Federal Proceedings, of Identity of Client as Violating Attorney-Client Privilege,* 84 A. L. R. Fed. (1987).

AMERICAN LAWYER'S CODE OF CONDUCT (1982).

John M. Burkoff, *Criminal Defense Ethics* §§ 5.2, 6.5(a) (1993).

Ethics Committee of the Massachusetts Bar Association, Opinion 89-1 (1989).

Ethics Committee of the Massachusetts Bar Association, Opinion 91-4 (1991).

Ethics Committee of the North Carolina State Bar Association, Opinion 33 (1987).

FLORIDA RULES OF PROFESSIONAL CONDUCT, Rule 3.3(b) (1992).

MARYLAND LAWYERS RULES OF PROFESSIONAL CONDUCT, 3.3(E); 4.1 (1993).

National Association of Criminal Defense Lawyers Ethics Advisory Committee, Formal Opinion 90-2, in THE CHAMPION 40 (Mar. 1991).

National Association of Criminal Defense Lawyers Ethics Advisory Committee, Formal Opinion 92-2 (1992), in THE CHAMPION 23 (Mar. 1993).

OKLAHOMA MODEL RULES OF PROFESSIONAL CONDUCT, Rules 3.3(a)(2), 3.3(b) (1993).

John R. Przypyszny, Note, *Public Assault on the Attorney-Client Privilege: Ramifications of* Baltes v. Doe, 3 Geo. J. Legal Ethics 351 (1989).

Arnold R. Rosenfeld, *Bar Counsel Comments*, 17 Mass. Lawyers Weekly 977 (1989).

Arnold R. Rosenfeld, *Bar Counsel Comments*, 20 Mass. Lawyers Weekly 2107 (1992).

Standing Committee on Legal Ethics of the Virginia State Bar, Opinion 1331 (1990).

VIRGINIA CODE OF RESPONSIBILITY, DR 7102(B)(1) (1992).

Cases

Attorney Grievance Committee of Maryland v. Rohrback, 591 A.2d 496 (Md. 1991).

Baltes v. Doe, 4 Law. Man. Prof. Conduct 356 (Fla. Cir. Ct. 1988).

In re Grand Jury Proceedings, 899 F.2d 1039 (11th Cir. 1990).

In re Grand Jury Proceedings, 680 F.2d 1026 (5th Cir. 1982).

In re Mahlowitz, 1 Mass. Atty. Disc. Rep. 189 (1979).

In the Matter of Neitlich, 597 N.E.2d 425 (Mass. 1992).

Nix v. Whiteside, 475 U.S. 157 (1986).

Office of Disciplinary Counsel v. Hazelkorn, 480 N.E.2d 1116 (Ohio 1985).

Office of Disciplinary Counsel v. Heffernan, 569 N.E.2d 1027 (Ohio 1991).

United States v. Jones, 517 F.2d 666 (5th Cir. 1975).

United States v. Long, 857 F.2d 436 (1988).

United States v. Thoreen, 653 F.2d 1332 (9th Cir. 1981).

PART III

Conflicts of Interest

In theory, the criminal defense lawyer is called upon to represent a client with single-minded devotion and undivided loyalty. In practice, however, a defense lawyer must allocate limited time and energy to serve a number of different clients whose cases necessarily compete with each other for attention. Moreover, in every criminal case, the defense lawyer finds that representation is affected to varying degrees by a host of factors such as the lawyer's relationship with the judge and prosecutor assigned to the case, the time the lawyer has available to work on the case, and the lawyer's other interests and responsibilities. The question becomes whether the defense lawyer's representation is affected to such an extent or in such a way that it generates a conflict-of-interest problem.

It is not surprising, then, that conflict-of-interest issues bedevil lawyers more frequently than any other issue of professional responsibility. In a variety of different situations, the defense lawyer may find that competing interests and conflicting responsibilities seemingly mandate declining or withdrawing from representing a client or at least securing informed consent to continued—and conflicted—representation. For many lawyers, it is difficult to sort out this maze of ethical rules, a difficulty compounded by unclear constitutional concerns. The next six chapters focus on some common conflict-of-interest questions that trouble criminal defense lawyers and offer guidance to lawyers confronting tricky conflict-of-interest questions.

In Chapter 16, Nancy Shaw addresses the question of whether lawyers from the same public defender office should represent codefendants. Shaw concludes that dual representation not only poses insurmountable practical difficulties, but also discourages the development of healthy lawyer-client relationships. Except in the rare case, Shaw recommends against dual representation and against securing waivers permitting such representation. Finally, Shaw argues that even provisionally or limited dual representation serves to undermine client confidence and should be avoided.

Both Shaw and Phyllis Goldfarb review a number of appellate cases in which courts have looked at conflict-of-interest problems in the context of ineffective assistance of counsel claims. It is clear, however, that a court's unwillingness to overturn a conviction on appeal because the defendant was unable to establish actual prejudice flowing from an apparent conflict of interest says little about the ethical propriety of the lawyer's conduct. Sound ethical lawyering may compel a defense lawyer to avoid cases in which prior representation or current relationships compromise or even appear to compromise client loyalty or the preservation of client confidences.

Goldfarb in Chapter 17 and Judy Clarke in Chapter 18 examine instances in which the defense lawyer's prior work—as a prosecutor in a related case—or present relationships—the lawyer's spouse is a prosecutor—raise real concerns about the lawyer's zeal as well the client's perception of his lawyer's zeal and loyalty. Certainly the defense lawyer should not be involved in a case in which the lawyer's ability to provide zealous representation is adversely affected by other professional or personal interests. Indeed, in some instances, a lawyer's entire office may be disqualified because of one lawyer's conflicted position.

Nonetheless, all of the authors in Part III recognize that in many situations, a conflict of interest can be waived. That waiver, of course, must be an informed one. The task of seeking an informed waiver, however, may be inextricably linked to the underlying conflict itself. Thus, as Nicholas Chiarkas demonstrates in Chapter 19, certain conflicts cannot be waived. In fact, some conflict situations involving multiple clients are so interwoven that the lawyer may find it necessary to withdraw from several cases and to do so without jeopardizing either client or revealing any client confidence.

Finally, Chapter 20 by Barbara Schwartz and Chapter 21 by Graham Strong address the impact of the defense lawyer's personal relationships on counsel's ability to provide conflict-free representation. As in the case of the spouse-prosecutor conflict discussed in Chapter 18, Schwartz observes that a defense lawyer's intimate personal relationships with a police officer, prosecutor, or judge may create an actual conflict or at least the appearance of a conflict of interest. As with other conflicts, the defense lawyer's response, including the wisdom of seeking a waiver or the effect of the conflict on the ability of other lawyers in the firm to handle the case, turns on specific aspects of the particular relationship and on whether the lawyer is in a Model Code or Model Rules jurisdiction. Finally, in Chapter 21, Graham Strong explores the dangers confronting the defense lawyer interested in a sexual relationship with a client. Strong's discussion of the waiver issue highlights how difficult it is to ensure that a criminal client, especially an indigent one, is truly making an informed waiver.

CHAPTER 📖 16

Representing Codefendants Out of the Same Office

Nancy Shaw

Should two lawyers from the same public defender office represent codefendants? To what extent is it ethically proper for a public defender to provide some representation to both codefendants before and at the initial appearance knowing that one codefendant will be assigned outside counsel?

The centerpiece of the multiple representation analysis is the lawyer's duty of loyalty to his client. A public defender's judgment, strategy, and candor with his client cannot be restrained by concern for another client, the defender's own interest, or the welfare of his coworkers. Whether a lawyer's representation is conflict-free is determined in the first instance by the lawyer himself. If a conflict with another client is possible or certain to exist, the lawyer in a Model Code jurisdiction must find it "obvious" that he can adequately represent the interest of each of the affected clients before committing to joint representation.[1] The Model Rules require a "reasonable belief" that the representation "will not adversely affect the relationship with the other client."[2] The ABA Standards for Criminal Justice are more explicit and more conservative: representing codefendants is condemned except when it is clear there will be "no conflict" or that joint representation will be advantageous.[3] If a lawyer or public defender office undertakes to represent codefendants, all three formulations require that the clients expressly consent and that the lawyer or lawyers believe, notwithstanding the potential for adversity, that adequate representation will be provided. The ABA Standards for Criminal Justice, in addition, mandate a waiver on the record.

236

Obtaining a client's consent is itself problematic. The lawyer must fairly disclose to the client the facts and legal issues that create the difficulty. The explanation must include discussion of the lack of a lawyer-client privilege among members of the defense group and the lawyer's obligation to withdraw altogether if a conflict that is not waived by any party is later discovered.

The lawyer may not be able to predict accurately the posture of the case throughout a prosecution. If the evidence against the clients or the charges against them cause them to be situated quite differently, there may be a conflict in the desirable style of representation. The client's perception of his self-interest and his relationship to any codefendant may change unpredictably. Moreover, the prosecutor may inject an unanticipated conflict through a favorable settlement offer, a grant of immunity, or a "package" plea proposal.

The careful view, therefore, is that the consent to multiple representation should be requested only after the risks of joint representation have been scrupulously assessed by the lawyer, and thoroughly explained to each client. Even then, an invitation should be made to each to seek independent counsel for advice on whether the shared representation will adequately protect each of them. If there is a risk of improper dominance of one client by another, or if the defenses could not be coordinated in a manner fair to both, the duty of loyalty imposes an additional ethical restraint on the lawyer. Despite the willingness of the clients to consent to joint representation, "[w]hen a disinterested lawyer would conclude that the client should not agree to the representation under the circumstances, the lawyer involved cannot properly ask for such agreement or provide representation on the basis of the client's consent."[4]

Vicarious Conflicts/Imputed Disqualification

Under both the Model Code and the Model Rules, if a lawyer is barred ethically from the representation of codefendants, then the other members of that lawyer's firm are also prohibited from being involved.[5] There is disagreement, however, about whether a public defender office is a "firm" governed by these imputed disqualification rules. The comment to Model Rule 1.10 suggests that "lawyers employed in the same unit of a legal service organization constitute a firm, but not necessarily those employed in separate units." If a local defender office does constitute a firm, then the lawyers in that office may represent codefendants only in cases where a single lawyer could represent the codefendants without violating Model Rule 1.7. As already indicated, however, such cases are rare.

A 1978 American Bar Association Informal Opinion (No. 1418) confirms that a public defender office is a law firm, its staff lawyers confined to accepting multiple representation only under circumstances in which one lawyer might do so. Some state courts agree. *See,* for example, *Commonwealth v. Green,* 550 A.2d 1011 (Pa. 1988); *Commonwealth v. Westbrook,* 400 A.2d 160 (Pa. 1979); *State v. Stenger,* 754 P.2d 136 (Wa. 1988); *Okeani v. Superior Court,* 871 P. 2d 727 (Az. App. 1993); *State v. Dillman,* 591 N.E.2d 849 (Ohio App. 1990); *Rodriguez v. State,* 628 P.2d 950, 955 (Az. 1981); *Townsend v. State,* 533 N.E.2d 1215, 1231 (Ind. 1989).

The Fourth Circuit Court of Appeals for the State of Louisiana disagrees. Without elaboration it found public defenders to be public employees, not members of a law firm, and, therefore, exempt from the application of Model Rule 1.10. *Louisiana v. McNeal,* 593 So.2d 729 (La. App. 1992). Similarly, Utah and Missouri reject a per se rule prohibiting public defenders from representing codefendants. *State v. Humphrey,* 793 P.2d 918 (Ut. 1990); *Utah v. Barella,* 714 P.2d 287 (Ut. 1986); *Shaw v. State,* 766 S.W.2d 676, 680 (Mo. 1989). Nor does New York extend the rule that knowledge of one member of a law firm will be imputed to all members of the firm to defenders in the New York Legal Aid Society. *People v. Wilkins,* 268 N.E.2d 756 (N.Y. 1971).

While not going as far as Louisiana or New York, New Jersey will not presume conflict where the public defender office represents codefendants, but the assignment of codefendants to outside counsel "shall be the norm." *State v. Bell,* 447 A.2d 525 (N.J. 1982). Illinois requires a case-by-case examination of the circumstances of codefendant representation by a defender office to determine "whether any facts peculiar to the case preclude the representation of competing interests by separate members of the public defender's office." *People v. Banks,* 520 N.E.2d 617, 620 (Ill. 1987); *People v. Miller,* 404 N.E.2d 199 (Ill. 1980); *People v. Robinson,* 402 N.E.2d 147 (Ill. 1979). Approaching the question somewhat differently, Maryland requires a case-by-case analysis of the structure of the particular defender office, which includes consideration of the degree of separation of the practices of the lawyers assigned to represent codefendants and the structural modifications that could be implemented to protect the confidences of the clients without withdrawal. *Graves v. State,* 619 A.2d 123, *rev'd on other grounds,* 637 A.2d 1197 (Md. 1993).

Ethical Walls

In certain limited situations, courts have recognized the use of a screening procedure called an "ethical wall," or "Chinese wall," to insulate disqualified individuals within a firm from privileged material. These screening procedures were developed primarily to minimize disqualification of firms hiring lawyers who left public service to enter private practice. There is, however, no language in either the Model Code or the Model Rules that suggests these screening procedures should be extended to cover the situation in which the lawyers seeking to represent clients with conflicting interests are both presently employed by the same firm.[6] Nevertheless, an advocate for joint representation may propose that ethical walls be implemented so that a defender office could absorb codefendant cases.

It is questionable whether a defender office can provide competent representation to any individual when it segregates its resources to avoid conflicts. The first question is a practical one. Administratively, can the office manage to segregate the support staff, mail, files, and lawyers so that no exchange of information will take place? The small office may be incapable of making the necessary arrangements. Even when legal and secretarial services can be rendered separately, there may be functions performed by individuals on lower or higher rungs of the organizational ladder that are less easily divided. For example, a single receptionist may acquire confidential information while learning the identity of callers and taking messages. The person who opens and stamps the mail will receive correspondence relating to all clients. Accounting duties, which reveal the identities of experts and the direction of the defense strategy, may be performed for all lawyers by a single individual or department whose commitment to the delicacy of the lawyer-client relationship may be somewhat less than that shared by the professional staff. While the lawyers may function separately, their supervision and administration ultimately will be joint at the management level. Decisions will be made about lawyer performance, counseling and supervision will be provided, and requests for the use of agency resources will be received. Although the lawyers and files may be separated from each other, competent supervision will require that some individual have access to confidential information about all the affected clients, and, under some circumstances, such individuals will employ this information to approve agency expenditures or invest other office resources.

The defender organization's obligation to preserve confidentiality will grow in complexity and administrative burden as the number of in-house conflicts increases. The procedures necessary to protect codefendants represented by intersecting pairs of lawyers may defeat the largest office.

The office that accepts codefendant representations also may have cause to regret the cost in office collegiality. The artificial divisions between staff members will inhibit exchange and the ability of staff members to assist one another. The likelihood that clients will testify against one another, or take adversarial positions in the litigation, and that their lawyers may be perceived to thereby undermine the success of their coworkers, may jeopardize the work environment. In offices where employees share car pools, enjoy a congenial work relationship, and "brainstorm" cases, such benefits could be lost if the office preserves separate secrets and defense plans of its codefendant clients. The Maryland Court of Appeals recognized just this difficulty in a trial judge's effort to save codefendants' relationships with their lawyers, who were partners, by imposing a "gag order" between the two. "What Judge Angeletti chose to do was to reach an improper compromise. He, in effect, discharged one-half of Mr. Austin's defense team." By imposing the gag order, Judge Angeletti "did not reduce the conflict; he reduced the defense team." *Austin v. State*, 609 A.2d 728, 736–37 (Md. App. 1992).

Ineffective Assistance of Counsel

In addition to looking at the ethical parameters of the problem of multiple representation, it is important to consider also the constitutional implications of such representation. Beginning with *Glasser v. United States*, 315 U.S. 60 (1942), the Court recognized that the appointment of defense counsel to represent codefendants with conflicting interests may be constitutionally offensive. The Sixth Amendment right to assistance of counsel incorporates the assurance that the lawyer-client relationship be "untrammeled and unimpaired by a court order requiring that one lawyer shall simultaneously represent conflicting interests."[7] While waiver of the right was recognized to be permissible constitutionally in *Glasser*, the apparent acquiescence of the defendants did not serve as intelligent and competent waivers. The Supreme Court found that Glasser's representation was compromised because of the conflicts, but also cautioned the courts against attempts to quantify the prejudice flowing from a Sixth Amendment violation of this order. "The right to have the assistance of counsel is too fundamental and absolute to allow courts to indulge in nice calculations as to the amount of prejudice arising from its denial."[8] Since *Glasser*, courts have increasingly engaged in such calculations to determine if the Sixth Amendment or its state constitutional counterparts mandate reversal in cases where defendants are jointly represented.

While *Glasser* appeared to hold that multiple representation is never harmless, the next benchmark case acknowledged that the existence of nominal conflicts can be without constitutional significance. The focus in *Holloway v. Arkansas*, 435 U.S. 475, 98 S. Ct. 1173, 55 L.

Ed.2d. 426 (1978), was on the court's obligation to conduct a hearing on the propriety of multiple representation when an appropriate objection is made. The trial court is required, in this event, to either appoint separate counsel or to make findings that the risk of conflict is too remote to require separate representation.

In *Cuyler v. Sullivan*, 446 U.S. 335, 100 S. Ct. 1708, 64 L. Ed.2d 333 (1980), the Court limited the trial judge's duty to inquire, in the absence of an objection, to cases in which the judge knows or should know that a possible conflict of interest exists. Multiple representation in severed trials was not thought by the court to be sufficient to alert the trial court to the possibility of conflict. Moving away from the *Glasser-Holloway* concerns, the Court in *Cuyler* placed the burden on the defendant to prove in postconviction proceedings that "an actual conflict of interest adversely affected his lawyer's performance."[9] The hoped-for per se rule prohibiting multiple representation was firmly rejected, despite an acknowledgment that a "possible conflict inheres in almost every instance of multiple representation."[10] The Sixth Amendment right to zealous representation by an advocate unrestrained by a conflict may be reduced in the federal courts to the opportunity to be heard on whether multiple representation will actually affect the defense or, on a post-conviction motion, whether it can be proved to have done so.

The right to conflict-free counsel was reaffirmed in *Wood v. Georgia*, 450 U.S. 261, 171, 101 S. Ct. 1097, 1103, 67 L. Ed. 2d 220, 230 (1981), and endorsed once again by the Supreme Court in *Strickland v. Washington*, 466 U.S. 668, 692, 104 S. Ct. 2052, 2067, 80 L. Ed. 2d 674, 696 (1984), which fashioned a "fairly rigid rule of presumed prejudice" in which the applicant must demonstrate that the performance of his lawyer was less effective than it might have been absent the conflict. That presumption has been undercut, however, by the Court's willingness to tolerate multiple representation in light of the practical difficulties of providing conflict-free counsel. The Court acknowledged in *Burger v. Kemp*, 483 U.S. 776, 107 S. Ct. 3114 (1987) that a conflict existed in representation of codefendants by law partners, but balanced the potential problems against the expectation that each lawyer would be motivated by an overarching duty of loyalty to his client.

> In smaller communities where the supply of qualified lawyers willing to accept the demanding and unrewarding work of representing capital prisoners is extremely limited, the defendants may actually benefit from the joint efforts of partners who supplement one another in their preparation. In many cases a "common defense . . . gives strength against a common attack."[11]

The court moved further from a per se rule by finding it inappropriate to speculate that a defense strategy was "tainted by a lawyer's improper motivation."[12]

The states have not uniformly followed the line of federal cases, which have upheld convictions, despite conflict problems, in the absence of specific provable prejudice. Two recent cases that reinforce more traditional notions of complete relief for such constitutional violations are *Littlejohn v. State*, 593 So. 2d 20 (Miss. 1992) and *Shongutsie v. State*, 827 P.2d 361 (Wyo. 1992). In both cases, convictions were reversed because of the lawyer's representation of codefendants. The Mississippi Supreme Court conspicuously relied upon pre–1980 federal case law, but the opinion may be otherwise unremarkable because actual prejudice was easily identified in the case's factual setting.[13] Montana directly rejected federal precedent and the "highly speculative task" of a reviewing court to "search the record to identify actual conflicts of interest and some corresponding effect on representation."[14]

Waivers

A valid waiver of the defects in multiple defendant representation bars a later attack on a conviction premised on the assertion of a conflict. The waiver will be deemed to be knowing and intelligent if made with "sufficient awareness of the relevant circumstances and likely consequences." *Brady v. United States*, 397 U.S. 742, 748, 90 S. Ct. 1463, 1469, 25 L. Ed. 2d 747 (1970). "The question is whether the defendant knew enough to make the choice an informed one—a rational reconciliation of risks and gains that are in the main understood." *United States v. Roth*, 860 F.2d 1382, 1387 (7th Cir. 1988). The waiver proceeding will examine the facts and circumstances of the case, as well as the "background experience and conduct of the accused." *Johnson v. Zerbst*, 304 U.S. 458, 464, 58 S. Ct. 1019, 1023, 82 L. Ed. 2d 1461 (1938). Thus, if counsel believes it is appropriate in a particular case to seek a client's waiver to allow counsel's office to represent codefendants, counsel should clearly inform the client of the ramifications of that waiver, including the client's inability to raise the conflict issue on appeal.

A caution is in order: a waiver on the record that is likely to be upheld on appeal may not be well-reasoned in fact. The battered woman, the gang member, or, simply, an individual whose trust in his confederates is misplaced, may be willing to waive the opportunity to have independent counsel because of fear or bad judgment. The presence of the codefendants in the defender's office may cause the intimidated client to deal with his counsel only as he would in a setting in which the strength and integrity of the codefendant is endorsed; he may feel powerless to distance himself, legally or otherwise, from his associates. Joint representation in this instance may be harmful or dangerous to the client, and the joint representation itself may preclude the lawyer from learning the facts necessary to identify the conflict and provide competent advice to the client.

Provisional Representation

In some jurisdictions, provisional representation of codefendants at arraignment and bail hearings may allow for orderly movement of the court calendar and early pretrial release of some individuals. General concern for the accused and familiarity with court routine may move an institutional defender to assist an individual in the early stages of the proceedings, even when he or she appreciates a conflict that would prevent the lawyer from representing the person at trial.

It makes sense to keep in mind the consequence for the defendant that the public defender has been appointed to represent if the lawyer establishes a conflicting relationship with a second individual. Withdrawal from both cases will be required if the lawyer acquires information in confidence from the provisionally represented person that he can neither disclose to his client nor exploit to his client's benefit. Once the nonclient has opened a conversation about the arraignment or bail with an admission or a comment on the relative culpability of the client, it will be difficult to find an ethically comfortable position with the client.

A lawyer-client relationship irrevocably begins with the client's offer of information to the lawyer that the lawyer would ordinarily treat as confidential, whether or not the lawyer has solicited sensitive material. And the individual's protestations that he doesn't care if the codefendant possesses the information or if the facts are disclosed in a public forum will not change the character of the lawyer-client exchange; for the lawyer might persuade the client that he would be disadvantaged by disclosure in a way the client did not anticipate or that disclosure of the matters should be delayed.

Care to avoid a conflict may cause the lawyer to refrain from putting to her client—or to the provisionally represented party—questions that she would ordinarily ask to competently represent the client in the early stages. Moreover, the effort to maintain a neutral posture may delay an investigation or preclude the defender from taking other early measures to protect the interests of the client that the lawyer proposes to represent throughout the litigation. Simply stated, the primary duty of loyalty to each represented person prohibits the lawyer's well-intentioned efforts to be of service to another client to adversely affect the representation of a present client.

If it is possible to contrive a situation where the lawyer commands the attention of a client's codefendant so that he may provide unilateral advice on neutral topics—the right to counsel, the procedure for requesting appointment of counsel, the nature of court hearings, and the like—then a lawyer-client relationship will not have formed. A telephone call to a friend or lawyer made as a courtesy to the unrepresented individual may be of assistance. Newly arrested individuals and those under investigation likely will be anxious and quick to discuss the merits of the charges, however clear the explanation of the limits of a provisional relationship. The lawyer who initiates these unilateral conversations will not always avoid disqualification.

The lawyer who offers assistance to an unrepresented codefendant risks the confidence of her client, particularly if she is known to have conferred privately with the codefendant. The provisional representation may also benefit an individual that the client deems hateful or frightening. If loyalty and the appearance of loyalty are the primary objectives in the lawyer-client relationship, the effort to assist a codefendant may seriously compromise that relationship.

Provisional assistance to a codefendant may be only microscopically less harmful to the lawyer-client relationship when an associate of the defender takes the part of the codefendant. The explanation to the client that the defender office proposes to advance the cause of his tormentor "for a short time" will rarely be sufficient to establish the climate of confidence necessary to a competent defense.

Conclusion

Providing a secure atmosphere in which the client may discuss criminal charges with the promise of confidentiality is the ethical obligation of the lawyer and the prerequisite to the delivery of high-quality legal service. It is doubtful that a busy defender office can construct an effective "ethical wall," or a cross-hatch of such barriers that will reliably insulate the activities of one defense team from the other. The administrative difficulties are formidable, and the disruptions of the office culture predictable. Of greater concern is the inability of an office hospitable to codefendants to encourage the confidence of its clients. In short, lawyers would be wise to follow the position advocated by the ABA Standards for Criminal Justice. That is, that the potential for conflict is "so grave" that defense counsel should decline to act for codefendants unless it is "clear" that no conflict will develop and the clients consent to multiple representation on the record.

The caution against acceptance of codefendants is no less appropriate when considering nominal or provisional representation at initial appearances and bail hearings. Unilateral advice about the nature of upcoming proceedings, the manner in which a request for counsel is presented to the court, or advice to consult an attorney is unobjectionable. A limited exchange with a recently charged individual, however, carries with it no less likelihood for conflict than a more mature relationship. If the lawyer's relationship turns on his loyalty to the client and the fostering of mutual trust and confidence, he must endeavor from the outset to serve that client alone. When the lawyer attempts to serve two or more jointly charged individuals, the risk of acquiring information that will occasion a genuine conflict is substantial; the divided loyalty and effort may forever scar the lawyer's relationship with his client.

Notes

1. *See* ABA MODEL CODE OF PROFESSIONAL RESPONSIBILITY, DR 5-105(C).
2. *See* ABA MODEL RULES OF PROFESSIONAL CONDUCT, Rule 1.7(b).
3. *See* ABA STANDARDS FOR CRIMINAL JUSTICE, 4-3.5(C) (3d ed. 1993).
4. *See* ABA MODEL RULE 1.7, Comment.
5. *See* DR 5-105 and MODEL RULE 1.10.
6. *See* G.C. HAZARD, JR. & W.W. HODES, THE LAW OF LAWYERING, 333–35 (2d ed. 1990).
7. Glasser v. United States, 315 U.S. at 70.
8. *Id.* at 75.
9. Cuyler v. Sullivan, 446 U.S. at 348.
10. *Id.*
11. Burger v. Kemp, 483 U.S. at 783.
12. *Id.* at 785.
13. The lawyer in *Littlejohn* assisted the first client in reaching a plea agreement that required him to testify against the second client, who went to trial.
14. Shongutsie v. State, 827 P.2d 361, 365 (Wyo. 1992).

Bibliography

Standards

ABA Committee on Ethics and Professional Responsibility, Informal Opinion 1418 (1978).

ABA MODEL CODE OF PROFESSIONAL RESPONSIBILITY, Canon 9, DR 5-105, 5-105(C).

ABA MODEL RULES OF PROFESSIONAL CONDUCT, Rules 1.7(b), 1.10.
ABA STANDARDS FOR CRIMINAL JUSTICE, 4-3.5(C) (3d ed. 1993).

Cases

Ailen v. Dist. Ct., 579 P.2d 351 (Colo. 1974).

Austin v. State, 609 A.2d 728 (Md. App. 1992).

Brady v. United States, 397 U.S. 742, 90 S. Ct. 1463, 25 L. Ed.2d 747 (1970).

Burger v. Kemp, 483 U.S. 776, 107 S. Ct. 3114, 97 L. Ed.2d 638 (1987).

Commonwealth v. Green, 550 A.2d 110 (Pa. 1988).

Commonwealth v. Westbrook, 400 A.2d 160 (Pa. 1979).

Cuyler v. Sullivan, 446 U.S. 335, 100 S. Ct. 1708, 64 L. Ed.2d 333 (1980).

Glasser v. United States, 315 U.S. 60, 62 S. Ct. 457, 86 L. Ed. 680 (1942).

Graves v. State, 619 A.2d. 123, *rev'd on other grounds,* 637 A.2d 1197 (Md. 1993).

Holloway v. Arkansas, 435 U.S. 475, 98 S. Ct. 1173, 55 L. Ed.2d 426 (1978).

Johnson v. Zerbst, 304 U.S. 458, 58 S. Ct. 1019, 82 L. Ed.2d 1461 (1938).

Littlejohn v. State, 593 So. 2d 20 (Miss. 1992).

Louisiana v. McNeal, 593 So. 2d 729 (La. App. 1992).

Okeani v. Superior Court, 871 P.2d 727 (Az. App. 1993).

People v. Banks, 520 N.E.2d 617, 620 (Ill. 1987).

People v. Miller, 404 N.E.2d 199 (Ill. 1980).

People v. Robinson, 402 N.E.2d 147 (Ill. 1979).

People v. Wilkins, 268 N.E.2d 756 (N.Y. 1971).

Rodriguez v. State, 628 P.2d 950 (Ariz. 1981).

Shaw v. State, 766 S.W.2d 676, 680 (Mo. 1989).

Shongutsie v. State, 827 P.2d 361 (Wyo. 1992).

State v. Bell, 447 A.2d 525 (N.J. 1982).

State v. Dillman, 591 N.E.2d 849 (Ohio App. 1990).

State v. Humphrey, 793 P.2d 918 (Ut. 1990).

State v. Stenger, 754 P.2d 136 (Wa. 1988).

Strickland v. Washington, 466 U.S. 668, 104 S. Ct. 2052, 80 L. Ed.2d 696 (1984).

Townsend v. State, 533 N.E.2d 1215, 1231 (Ind. 1989).

United States v. Roth, 860 F.2d 1382 (7th Cir. 1988).

Utah v. Barella, 714 P.2d 287 (Ut. 1986).

Wood v. Georgia, 450 U.S. 261, 101 S. Ct. 1097, 67 L. Ed.2d 220 (1981).

CHAPTER 📖 17

Defense Counsel with a Spouse Who Prosecutes

Judy Clarke

May a public defender represent an indigent client when her husband is employed by the prosecutor's office? What if her husband is prosecuting a case she is defending? If she is disqualified, is her entire office disqualified? May the conflict be waived?

Several potential problems arise with spouses representing conflicting client interests—a potential breach of confidentiality, an actual conflict of interest, an appearance of impropriety, and the right of the accused to the effective assistance of counsel. These issues are addressed in several ABA Rules and Canons, as well as in the ABA Defense Function Standards. All of the following discussion assumes that the spouses would not directly breach confidentiality or knowingly create a conflict of interest.

Considerations of Confidentiality

One of the basic tenets of the lawyer-client relationship is the obligation of the lawyer to hold "inviolate" the confidences and secrets of the client. The purpose of this basic tenet, which is contained in most state bar codes of professional responsibility, is to facilitate the full development of facts necessary to competent representation and to encourage people to seek early assistance of counsel.

The ABA Model Code of Professional Responsibility and the ABA Model Rules of Professional Conduct specify this most basic obligation in Model Rule 1.6 and Canon 4 of the Model Code. Model Rule 1.6 provides that:

a lawyer shall not reveal information relating to representation of
a client unless the client consents after consultation, except for disclosures that are impliedly authorized in order to carry out the
representation, and except as stated in paragraph (b) . . . [preven-
tion of crime or resolution of dispute between client and lawyer].

Canon 4 of the Model Code provides that "a lawyer should preserve
the confidences and secrets of a client." With limited exceptions, Disciplinary Rule 4-101(B) prohibits a lawyer from knowingly revealing a
client's confidences or secrets, using the confidence or secret to the disadvantage of the client or, absent consent, from using the confidence or
secret to the advantage of the lawyer or a third person.

More on point, Model Rule 1.8(i) provides that:

[a] lawyer related to another lawyer as parent, child, sibling or
spouse shall not represent a client in a representation directly adverse to a person who the lawyer knows is represented by the
other lawyer except upon consent by the client after consultation
regarding the relationship.

Formal Opinion No. 340 (1975) issued by the ABA Commission on
Professional Ethics provided that:

It is our opinion that the representation of defendants in criminal
matters in a county in which one's wife is assistant prosecutor
would be improper in that the relationship of the attorneys would
place an undue, and perhaps impossible burden upon each attorney's duty to guard the confidence of his clients. . . .

The marriage relationship may be conducive to inadvertent
breaches of confidentiality. A spouse may have knowledge of out-of-
town investigative trips at or around the time of preparation for a particular case; clients and witnesses may contact the lawyer at home or
leave messages on the home answering machine that may reveal a tac-
tic or a confidence. Working papers left at home or work performed at
home may reveal confidences of a client. The needs of a lawyer to work
early or late or on weekends may give rise to the need for explanation
in a marriage relationship that could inadvertently reveal client confidences or secrets.

Potential for Actual Conflict

ABA Model Code Canon 5 mandates that "a lawyer should exercise
independent professional judgment on behalf of a client." Ethical considerations following Canon 5 require that the lawyer's professional

judgment be exercised solely for the benefit of the client (EC 5-1) and that the lawyer not accept employment if personal interests will adversely affect the advice to be given (EC 5-2).

Disciplinary Rule 5-101 requires a lawyer to refuse employment when the interest of the lawyer may impair the lawyer's independent professional judgment. Subsection (A) of DR 5-101 provides that:

> Except with the consent of his client after full disclosure, a lawyer shall not accept employment if the exercise of his professional judgment on behalf of his client will be or reasonably may be affected by his own financial, business, property, or personal interests.

ABA Standards for Criminal Justice Standard 4-3.5(a) (3d. ed. 1993) provides that the client's interests are paramount to the lawyer's by stating that:

> Defense counsel should not permit his or her professional judgment or obligations to be affected by his or her own political, financial, business, property, or personal interests.

The potential conflict of interest that may arise can be financial or personal. A district attorney or public defender may have a special interest in the outcome of a case based on a concern for a promotion or political benefit for one's spouse. A lawyer's loyalty to a client may be impaired by a personal interest in the success of a spouse or the emotional difficulties of competing against a spouse in a hotly contested trial.

Problems with the Appearance of Impropriety

Canon 9 of the ABA Model Code provides that "a lawyer should avoid even the appearance of professional impropriety." The Ethical Considerations provide in part that "a lawyer should promote public confidence in our system and in the legal profession" (EC 9-1) and that "when explicit ethical guidance does not exist, a lawyer should determine his conduct by acting in a manner that promotes public confidence in the integrity and efficiency of the legal system and the legal profession." (EC 9-2). The Disciplinary Rules supporting Canon 9 refer to restrictions on employment where the lawyer has previously acted as a judge or had prior substantial involvement as a public employee. The disciplinary rules also discuss the handling of client funds.

There is a real likelihood of an appearance of impropriety when spouses are charged with the defense and the prosecution of the same person. The public perception could be that confidences are shared and that neither the state nor the defendant would be treated according to the law. Depending upon the relationship of the spouses, either the defendant or the state may have a perceived advantage.

Similar concerns over the appearance of impropriety are raised when a prosecutor and a defense lawyer, although not married, are dating, engaged, or living together.[1] A California Court of Appeals addressed this issue in a case in which appointed counsel failed to inform the defendant that he had an ongoing dating relationship with the prosecutor. *People v. Jackson,* 167 Cal. App. 3d 829 (1985). In reversing the defendant's conviction the court noted:

> as distinct to casual social contacts those who are involved in a sustained dating relationship over a period of months are normally perceived, if not in fact, as sharing a strong emotional or romantic bond. Such an apparently close relationship between counsel directly opposing each other gives rise to speculation that the professional judgment of counsel as well as the zealous representation to which an accused is entitled has been compromised. *Id.* at 833.[2]

Unlike the Model Code, the Model Rules do not apply the appearance of impropriety standard. The commentary to Model Rule 1.9 criticizes the appearance of impropriety standard as a "general concept," "undefined," and "question-begging." The drafters of the Model Rules opted to include Model Rule 1.8(i) and leave out the appearance of impropriety language from Canon 9. Model Rule 1.8(i) prohibits the spouses from representing directly adverse clients, unless the client consents after consultation.

So, How Should These "Rules" Apply?

Five different scenarios can exist when a public defender is married to a district-attorney spouse:

1. The public defender is representing a client prosecuted by her spouse.
2. The public defender is representing a client prosecuted by her spouse's colleague in the district attorney's office.
3. The public defender's colleague is representing a client prosecuted by the spouse.
4. The public defender's colleague is representing a client prosecuted by the spouse's colleague.
5. The public defender is the head of the office (or a supervisor responsible for case-related supervision).

Proposition #1:
A public defender should not represent a client prosecuted by her district-attorney husband.

This situation is fraught with danger, particularly given the number of ways that client confidences can be breached inadvertently. Certainly if a public defender represents a client prosecuted by her district-attorney husband, adequate precautions must be taken to ensure that there will not be any breach of confidentiality. The spouses must be sensitive to their ethical obligations and the potential for inadvertent disclosures. Given the nature of a criminal law practice and the typically close bond of the marital relationship, it is unlikely that adequate precautions can be enforced.

Can a client consent to representation by a public defender whose spouse is prosecuting the client? ABA Model Rule 1.8(i) provides:

> A lawyer related to another lawyer as parent, child, sibling or spouse shall not represent a client in a representation directly adverse to a person who the lawyer knows is represented by the other lawyer except upon consent by the client after consultation regarding the relationship.

In addition, Formal Opinion No. 340 provides in part that:

> In any situation where a client or potential client might question the loyalty of the lawyer representing him, the situation should be fully explained to the client and the question of acceptance of continuance of representation left to the client for decision.

Thus, under the Model Rules consent is a clear alternative for continued representation when the prosecutor and public defender are married. Absent consent, Model Rule 1.8(i) mandates disqualification. A number of states have not adopted the Model Rules and still follow the Model Code of Professional Responsibility. The Model Code does not specifically address the issue of consent. Canon 9 of the Model Code requires that the lawyer should avoid even the appearance of professional impropriety.[3] Presumably, the appearance of impropriety continues to exist even if the client consents after consultation.

The Court of Appeals in Texas addressed the question of consent of an indigent defendant in the context of appointed counsel whose law partner was married to the district attorney. *See Haley v. Boles*, 824 S.W.2d 796 (1992). The court held that the appointed counsel for the criminal defendant was required to withdraw due to the conflict of interest created by the fact that one of his law partners was married to the prosecutor assigned to the case. Important to the decision was the court's determination that (a) the client did not participate in the selection of the lawyer assigned by the trial court; (b) the sixth amendment assures conflict-free representation; (c) the cornerstone of the legal system is effective, independent representation of the respective litigants by counsel; (d) the close personal relationship of the adversaries' lawyers created an appearance of impropriety; and (e) the lawyers had a financial interest in each other. The court then noted that even if the defendant had consented to the representation, the above concerns would not have been cured:

> An indigent defendant is assigned the lawyer who will represent him. The indigent defendant's consent to continued representation . . . [under the consent rules] does not embody the same degree of free choice as that of the paying client. Therefore, for purposes of the Sixth Amendment right to conflict-free representation, the solution provided by . . . [the consent rules] will not suffice to alleviate a conflict of interest where the defendant is indigent. *Haley*, 824 S.W.2d at 798.

In so holding, the court distinguished between "paying clients" and "indigent defendants." Those who pay are free to accept or reject representation by a lawyer after having been informed of a conflict of interest.

The Texas case makes a good point—an indigent defendant's consent may not be free and voluntary given the lack of choice presented. The Texas case did not appear to recognize the interest an indigent defendant may have in being represented by a public defender she knows or whom she would otherwise select as counsel. In such situations, this delicate consent issue may be resolved by the court thoroughly advising the indigent defendant of the right to receive conflict-free appointed counsel.

California would answer the question differently. In Formal Opinion No. 1984-83, the state bar's Standing Committee on Professional Responsibility and Conduct concluded that a public defender could, with full disclosure and the consent of the client, represent a client prosecuted by his or her spouse district attorney. The opinion noted the lawyer's duty of complete fidelity and concluded that if the lawyer believes the nature or quality of the representation would be adversely affected by the relationship, the lawyer should not accept employment on that matter. However, assuming the lawyer believes that she could effectively represent the client (the accused or the people), the client should be advised of the relationship and given an opportunity to consent.

In *People v. Jackson,* 167 Cal. App. 3d 829 (1985), the court of appeal reversed a conviction on the ground of ineffective assistance of counsel based on the lawyer's failure to inform the defendant of counsel's sustained dating relationship with the prosecutor during the course of the case. The court held that counsel involved in a potential conflict situation such as a sustained dating relationship with the prosecutor should fully explain the relationship to the client and afford the client the opportunity to secure conflict-free counsel.

Several other states apparently disagree with the California interpretation. *See* fn. 2 to Formal Opinion 1984-83, *citing* Arizona Op. No. 73-6 (1973); New Jersey Op. No. 288 (1974) (impermissible for wife to practice criminal law in county where husband is assistant prosecutor); New York Op. No. 409 (1975) (impermissible for assistant district attorney and assistant public defender married to one another to work on same case; they may otherwise handle cases not in direct opposition to one another); Oregon Op. No. 281 (1975) (same as New York). The California Formal Opinion distinguished itself because California had not adopted an "appearance of impropriety" standard with respect to its disciplinary rule on conflicts of interest.

Even with the consent possibilities, given the pressures on an indigent defendant to "please" the judge or to conform to the apparent requirements of the system and given the appearance of impropriety as well as a real potential for inadvertent breaches of confidentiality, it is recommended that a public defender not represent a client prosecuted by her district-attorney husband.

Proposition #2:
With appropriate established protections, a public defender can represent a client prosecuted by a colleague of her district-attorney husband.

There is less opportunity for inadvertent breaches of confidentiality, reduced financial incentives (if they exist at all) and reduced appearance of impropriety in this situation. However, appropriate steps must be taken by both the public defender and the district-attorney spouse to avoid the potential for impropriety or inadvertent breaches of confidentiality. The district-attorney spouse should avoid discussions with others in the prosecuting office who are involved in the prosecution and should not participate in any preparation sessions regarding the case. Disclosure should be made to the client and the client given an opportunity to have other counsel assigned upon request.

Proposition #3:
With appropriate established protections, the colleagues
of a public defender can represent clients prosecuted by
the public defender's district-attorney spouse.

Under DR 5-105 (D) of the ABA Model Code, if a lawyer is required to decline employment in a particular case by virtue of a disciplinary rule, then the lawyer's partners or associates must also decline such employment. Under this theory, the colleagues of the public defender would be precluded from representing clients prosecuted by the district-attorney spouse. However, because the disqualification is a voluntary one, made in favor of the appearance of impropriety and to avoid the potential for conflict, arguably the colleagues should not automatically be disqualified.

The comment to Model Rule 1.8(i) clarifies that disqualification should be personal and not imputed to other members of the firm.[4] The commentary in the ABA Standards for Criminal Justice Standard 4-3.5 also indicates that the "conflict should not be imposed vicariously upon other lawyers in defense counsel's law firm." Even though the entire firm should not be disqualified, a Chinese wall (limitation on access to information or discussions) should be erected around the public-defender spouse.

Proposition #4:
Colleagues of the public defender can represent clients
prosecuted by colleagues of the district-attorney spouse.

At this point the marital relationship is substantially removed from the issue and the reality of any potential conflict greatly diminished. As always, both spouses must continue to be guided by the principles set forth above and hold inviolate all confidences of their clients and the clients represented by their colleagues.

Proposition #5:
Supervisors in the public defender's office
should not be married to a district attorney.

Supervisors in a public defender office who are actively involved in supervision of lawyers or participation in the brainstorming and preparation of cases handled by assistant public defenders should not be married to prosecutors. Considerations of inadvertent breach of confidentiality, the appearance of impropriety, and DR 5-105(D) would conflict other defenders off of cases. A Chinese wall around a supervisor would weaken the leadership of the office and render the supervisor almost useless as an advisor and trainer. The Sixth Amendment considerations raised in *Haley* would be exaggerated, making it difficult for a client's consent to be meaningful if the entire public defender's office is conflicted.

Conclusion

There are no easy answers to these questions. At issue is the right of the indigent accused to the effective assistance of counsel, including conflict-free representation, and the societal interest in having married couples pursue their desired careers. The easiest answer is that spouses should not be public defenders and prosecutors at the same time in opposing offices (or at least in the criminal divisions of those offices). In an attempt to balance the two interests, respecting the privacy and association interests of the lawyers and in consideration of potential conflicts, including actual financial or personal conflicts, breach of confidentiality, the appearance of impropriety, and the Sixth Amendment, the following conclusions are suggested:

1. A public defender should not represent a client prosecuted by his or her district-attorney spouse, even with the consent of the client.
2. The public defender should be able to represent clients prosecuted by the spouse's colleagues in the district attorney's office, but established precautions should be taken to avoid any appearance of impropriety or actual conflict.
3. Colleagues of both spouses should be able to oppose each other on cases, again with established precautions taken to prevent any conflict of interest.
4. A supervisory public defender with responsibilities for case-related assistance to other defenders in the office should not be married to a prosecutor.

While many potential conflicts ordinarily can be resolved by the consent of the client, the restrictions suggested above limiting public defender and prosecutor spouses are guided by Sixth Amendment considerations. There can always be a question as to the adequacy of the client's consent. An indigent defendant's consent to continued representation may not be the same free choice as that of a client who retains counsel. The appearance of impropriety of law partners representing conflicting interests compels the suggestion that appropriate precautions be taken to prevent any conflict of interest.

In any questionable case, the lawyer should make full disclosure to the client and the court and a hearing should be held on the propriety of the continued representation. *See Wheat v. United States*, 486

U.S. 153 (1988) (court can decide conflict issue even with client's waiver). In weighing whether a public defender can be married to a district attorney in offices that are constantly opposing each other, the leadership of the office must consider the inevitable danger of the institutional defender being seen as a fungible advocate lacking the true interest of the client.

Notes

1. Some guidance on this issue is provided in the ABA Standards for Criminal Justice Defense Function (3d ed. 1993). Defense Function Standard 4-3.5(i) provides that a defense counsel who has a significant personal relationship with the prosecutor should not represent the client in a criminal matter where defense counsel knows the government is represented in the matter by such prosecutor, except upon consent by the client after consultation regarding the relationship.

2. *See* Cohn v. Rosenfeld, 733 F.2d 625, 631 (9th Cir. 1984), where a mere social relationship between defendant and a member of the plaintiff's law firm was insufficient to disqualify the law firm from representing the plaintiff.

3. The courts have split in determining when the appearance of impropriety requires disqualification. *Compare* Board of Ed. of City of New York v. Nyquist, 590 F.2d 1241, 1247 (2d Cir. 1979) (when there is no claim that the trial will be tainted, the appearance of impropriety is simply too slender a reed on which to rest a disqualification order except in the rarest of cases); Blumenfeld v. Borenstein, 276 S.E.2d 607, 609 (1981) (no per se disqualification of a lawyer on the basis of an appearance of impropriety alone); and Woods v. Covington County Bank, 537 F.2d 804, 819 (5th Cir. 1976) ("inasmuch as attempts to disqualify opposing counsel are becoming increasingly frequent, we cannot permit Canon 9 to be manipulated for strategic advantage on the account of an impropriety which exists only in the minds of an imaginative lawyer") *with* Richardson v. Hamilton International Corp., 469 F.2d 1382, 1386 (3d Cir. 1972) ("a court may disqualify an attorney not only for acting improperly but also for failing to avoid the appearance of impropriety").

4. In Haley v. Boles, 824 S.W.2d 796 (1992), the disqualification was imputed to the entire firm. It should be noted, the Texas version of the Model Rules do not include 1.8(i) and its commentary.

Bibliography

Articles, Reports, and Standards

ABA Committee on Ethics and Professional Responsibility, Formal Opinion 340 (1975).

ABA MODEL CODE OF PROFESSIONAL RESPONSIBILITY, Canons 4, 5, and 9; DR 4-101, 5-101, 5-101(A), 5-105(D); EC 5-1, 5-2, 9-1, 9-2 (1980).

ABA MODEL RULES OF PROFESSIONAL CONDUCT, Rules 1.6, 1.8, 1.8(i), 1.9 and Cmt. (1983).

ABA STANDARDS FOR CRIMINAL JUSTICE, Standards 4-3.5(a), 4-3.5(i) and Cmt. (3d ed. 1993).

Nancy B. Calvin, Note, *Legal Ethics—Representation of Differing Interests by Husband and Wife: Appearances of Impropriety and Unavoidable Conflicts of Interest?* 52 Denv. L. J. 735 (1975).

Committee on Professional Ethics of the New York State Bar Association, Opinion 409 (1975).

Committee on Rules of Professional Conduct of the State Bar of Arizona, Opinion 73-6 (1973).

John J. Cross, III, *Ethical Issues Facing Lawyer-Spouses and Their Employers*, 34 Vand. L. Rev. 1435 (1981).

Legal Ethics Committee of the Oregon State Bar, Opinion 281 (1975).

New Jersey Advisory Committee on Professional Ethics, Opinion 288 (1974).

Helen Rives-Hendricks, Comment, *Ethical Concerns of Lawyers Who Are Related by Kinship or Marriage*, Or. L. Rev. 399 (1981).

Standing Committee on Professional Responsibility and Conduct of the State Bar of California, Formal Opinion 1984-83 (1984).

Developments in Law: Conflict of Interest in the Legal Profession, 94 Harv. L. Rev. 1244 (1981).

Cases

Blumenfeld v. Borenstein, 276 S.E.2d 607 (Ga. 1981).

Board of Education of City of New York v. Nyquist, 590 F.2d 1241 (2d Cir. 1979).

Cohn v. Rosenfeld, 733 F.2d 625 (9th Cir. 1984).

Haley v. Boles, 824 S.W.2d 796 (Tex. 1992).

People v. Jackson, 167 Cal. App. 3d 829 (Cal. 1985).

Richardson v. Hamilton International Corp., 469 F.2d 1382 (3d Cir. 1972).

Wheat v. United States, 486 U.S. 153 (1988).

Woods v. Covington County Bank, 537 F.2d 804 (5th Cir. 1976).

CHAPTER 📖 18

Switching Hats: The Ex-Prosecutor as Defense Counsel

Phyllis Goldfarb

Is it ethically proper for a public defender to represent a defendant when that public defender previously prosecuted the defendant on an unrelated case?

Introduction

The right to effective assistance of counsel, protected by the Sixth Amendment to the United States Constitution, entitles a criminal defendant to the undivided loyalty of counsel. *Glasser v. United States*, 315 U.S. 60, 69 (1942). Most court decisions concerning potential violations of this principle that arise from a lawyer's conflict of interest involve situations where a single lawyer represents codefendants or otherwise potentially adverse clients.

Although a defense lawyer's representation of a defendant whom she previously prosecuted differs from the typical multiple defendant paradigm, the two situations are analogous in their potential to compromise a lawyer's loyalty. In either case, the lawyer may feel a competing loyalty that leads to representation of interests in conflict with the client's interest. Therefore, a careful resolution of the question presented requires an understanding of both the pertinent case law on ineffective assistance of counsel arising from conflicts of interest and the prevailing ethical guidelines concerning such matters.

Ethical Guidelines

Model Rules of Professional Conduct

MODEL RULE 1.7. The provisions of the ABA Model Rules of Professional Conduct (hereinafter "Model Rules") are particularly relevant to the question presented. The first relevant provision is Rule 1.7, which establishes general proscriptions regarding attorney-client conflicts of interest. Rule 1.7(b) states in pertinent part: "A lawyer shall not represent a client if the representation of that client may be materially limited by the lawyer's responsibilities . . . or by the lawyer's own interests."

Subsections b(1) and b(2), however, establish exceptions to Rule 1.7's general prohibition of representation where "the lawyer reasonably believes the representation will not be adversely affected," and where the client consents after informed consultation. The implication of these exceptions is that the Model Rules would permit a public defender to represent a defendant whom she has previously prosecuted if the public defender has (1) determined that the past role of prosecutor will not impair her representation in any manner, and (2) apprised the client of the full implications of a potential ethical conflict and received the client's consent to continued representation.

MODEL RULE 1.11. Model Rule 1.11, "Successive Government and Private Employment," does not appear to alter this conclusion. Rule 1.11(a) states that "[a] lawyer shall not represent a private client in connection with a matter in which the lawyer participated personally and substantially as a public officer or employee." This prohibition, by its terms, appears to refer only to representation in the very same case with which the lawyer was involved as a public officer. Consequently, it does not apply to the instant scenario and offers no assistance in analyzing the ethical implications of a public defender's representation of a client whom she has previously prosecuted only in an unrelated case.

MODEL RULE 6.2. Model Rule 6.2 poses ethical limits on the acceptance of court appointments. Rule 6.2(a) prohibits a lawyer from seeking to avoid a court's appointment to represent a client except for good cause, such as "[when] representing the client is likely to result in violation of the rules of professional conduct or other law." Clearly, Rule 6.2 can be understood only by reference to ethical guideposts provided by other rules and cases. The comment accompanying Rule 6.2 refers to Rule 1.7's prohibition against a lawyer representing a client when conflicting interests of the lawyer might impair that representation. Nothing in the language of Rule 6.2 or its commentary contributes to a deeper under-standing than that provided by Rule 1.7 regarding the nature of the con-flicts of interest that preclude ethically proper representation.

Model Code of Professional Responsibility

Canon 9 of the Model Code of Professional Responsibility (hereinafter "the Model Code") indicates that "a lawyer should avoid even the ap-pearance of impropriety." Ethical Consideration 9-3 (EC 9-3), subsumed under the admonition of Canon 9, further indicates that "[a]fter a lawyer leaves judicial office or other public employment, he should not accept employment in connection with any matter in which he had substantial responsibility prior to his leaving, since to accept employment would give the appearance of impropriety even if none existed." Disciplinary Rule 9-101(B) (DR-101(B)), also subsumed under Canon 9, states: "A lawyer shall not accept private employment in a matter in which he had substantial responsibility while he was a public employee."

EC 9-3 and DR 9-101(B) should be interpreted literally. Like Model Rule 1.11, these two provisions prohibit a former government lawyer from participating on both sides of a single legal matter. This literal interpretation was adopted in *State v. Sparkman*, 443 So. 2d 700, 701 (La. Ct. App. 1983), in which the court invoked DR 9-101(B) to disqualify cocounsel for the defendant, when cocounsel had acted in the same criminal matter while employed by the state as an assistant district at-torney. Consequently, EC 9-3 and DR 9-101(B) cannot help in address-ing the ethical propriety of a lawyer's representation of a person whom he or she formerly prosecuted in an unrelated case.

The language of Canon 9, on the other hand, sweeps broadly enough that it could be read to prohibit a lawyer's representation of her former prosecutee. This prohibition would derive from the possible appearance of impropriety inherent in this situation, even where no such impropriety exists. Although many federal courts have turned ex-pressly to Canon 9 in resolving the myriad ethical issues that surface throughout a lawyer's professional life, few courts have read Canon 9 so expansively. For example, in *Woods v. Covington County Bank*, 537 F.2d 804, 813 (5th Cir. 1976), the Fifth Circuit reversed the district court's disqualification of plaintiffs' privately retained counsel in a se-curities fraud case where the plaintiffs were former prisoners of war and their lawyer had previously investigated the same matter pursu-ant to his responsibilities as a naval reserve officer in the Judge Ad-vocate General Corps. While conceding that this representation may have created the appearance of impropriety, the Fifth Circuit found that:

Canon 9 does not require the disqualification of every attorney who has been privately retained in a matter for which he had substantial responsibility while associated with the Government.... Such an inflexible application of Canon 9 would frequently defeat important social interests including the client's right to counsel of his choice, the lawyer's right to freely practice his profession, and the government's need to attract skilled lawyers. *Id.* at 813.

The implication of this passage in *Woods* is that, according to the Fifth Circuit, courts should undertake a balancing approach to determine whether a public defender's representation of a client whom he or she previously prosecuted is ethically proper. The Fifth Circuit identifies three policy considerations that should be weighed in the balance against the ethical concern with the appearance of impropriety expressed in Canon 9. When the competing considerations trump Canon 9, then the representation of a client whom the lawyer has previously prosecuted would be ethically proper unless the client suffered prejudice as a consequence.

ABA Standards for Criminal Justice

Chapter 4 of the ABA Standards for Criminal Justice (hereinafter "the Standards"), "The Defense Function," concerns the specific duties and obligations of individual defense lawyers and supplements the other general ABA codes of professional conduct. The language of Standard 4-3.5, which covers conflict of interest issues, does not explicitly prohibit the representation of a client whom the attorney once prosecuted. Standard 4-3.5 does, however, speak to certain matters that bear to some extent on the resolution of the question presented.

Subsection (b) of Standard 4-3.5 requires a defense lawyer to "disclose to the defendant any interest in or connection with the case or any other matter that might be relevant to the defendant's selection of counsel to represent him or her or counsel's continuing representation." This mandate is consistent with the large number of cases that hold a defense lawyer to a duty to inform the client at the earliest possible moment of a potential conflict of interest.

Subsection (f) of Standard 4-3.5 reads: "Defense counsel should not defend a criminal case in which counsel's partner or other professional associate is or has been the prosecutor in the same case." Subsection (h) reads: "Defense counsel who formerly participated personally and substantially in the prosecution of the defendant should not thereafter represent any person in the same or substantially related matter. . . ." These subsections refer only to representing clients in matters related to a former prosecution. Standard 4-3.5 makes no mention of the propriety of defending a client whom one had previously prosecuted in an unrelated matter. Since both these subsections are fairly new, there has been no mention of them in the case law addressing this question. Moreover, the cases do not mention any earlier version of Standard 4-3.5.

Application of Ethical Codes in State and Federal Courts

Federal courts have explicitly incorporated ABA codes, rules, and considerations into decisions regarding ethical conduct at the federal bar, but have left to state courts and legislatures all decisions concerning the application and enforcement of these standards in the states. For example, in *Goodson v. Peyton*, 351 F. 2d 905, 907 (4th Cir. 1965), a state prisoner's appeal from the denial of a habeas corpus petition, the Fourth Circuit declined to rule on the propriety of a court-appointed defense lawyer's concurrent service as a prosecutor in a neighboring county. The court hinted that "decided possibilities of conflicts of interest [were] inherent" in such a situation, and "it may well be that the only workable rule of the future will be a *per se* one, in which it would be presumed that one involuntarily represented by a public prosecutor in a criminal trial has not had the fair trial to which he is constitutionally entitled." *Id.* at 909–10. Nevertheless, in declining to decide the issue the Fourth Circuit stated:

> Enforcement of ethical standards is the primary concern of the state courts and of state associations of lawyers and judges. Transgressions of professional standards in the federal courts are subject to federal control, but conduct which is arguably unethical in the courts of a state is a matter of state concern. *Id.* at 907.

A majority of states, however, have incorporated into their state ethical codes a version of the ABA Model Rules of Professional Conduct adopted in 1983. Some states have incorporated a version of the Model Code of Professional Responsibility into the state's code. In any event, both state and federal courts frequently analyze constitutionally based ethical issues by reference to the codes promulgated by the ABA. Consequently, the ABA standards and the cases construing them are the appropriate ethical guides when analyzing the question that opens this chapter.

Judicial Guidance

Supreme Court Cases

The Supreme Court's opinion in *Strickland v. Washington*, 466 U.S. 668, 687, *rehearing denied*, 467 U.S. 1267 (1984) established a two-tiered analysis of claims of ineffective assistance of counsel. In reversing the Fifth Circuit's decision to overturn the defendant's conviction and death sentence by granting his Sixth Amendment claim, the Court held:

> First, the defendant must show that counsel's performance was deficient. This requires showing that counsel made errors so serious that counsel was not functioning as the 'counsel' guaranteed the defendant by the Sixth Amendment. Second, the defendant must show that the deficient performance prejudiced the defense. *Id.* at 687.

Strickland heightened the threshold that defendants had to cross before their claims to ineffective assistance would be granted.

The Supreme Court has also considered claims of ineffective assistance of counsel based on a lawyer's conflict of interest. In the pre-*Strickland* case of *Holloway v. Arkansas*, 435 U.S. 475 (1978), the Court held that a trial judge should have made a diligent inquiry into a possible conflict of interest raised by defendant's pretrial request for separate counsel. A judge, having made such an inquiry, would have found that a public defender could not provide effective assistance for each of three codefendants in a rape and armed robbery case without the risk of representing conflicting interests. Two years later, *Cuyler v. Sullivan*, 446 U. S. 335 (1980) modified *Holloway*, finding that a defendant, in order to prevail on a claim of ineffective assistance, must show that an actual conflict of interest adversely affected his lawyer's performance.

Burger v. Kemp, 483 U.S. 776, 783, *rehearing denied*, 483 U.S. 1056 (1987) applied the updated law of ineffective assistance to the holding of *Cuyler*. In the *Burger* case, the Court found that the appointment of two partners in the same law firm to represent coindictees in their respective trials did not create an actual conflict of interest that prejudiced either or both clients, and, therefore, the defendant's claim of ineffective assistance of counsel was denied. The *Burger* court rejected "the adoption of an inflexible rule that would presume prejudice in all such cases" in favor of *Strickland's* required showing of actual prejudice. *Id.* at 783.

Burger is significant in that it uses the two-tiered *Strickland* standard to refuse to presume prejudice in a situation in which the lawyer's loyalty may be compromised by a conflicting interest. Therefore, when a lawyer represents a defendant whom he has previously prosecuted, the arrangement does not violate federal constitutional standards unless the defendant can establish actual prejudice resulting from the potential conflict. This is the approach followed by most state courts, although a few jurisdictions retain a per se proscription against defense lawyer's representation of a client whom she once prosecuted.

Lower Court Cases

THE MINORITY POSITION. Illinois and Oklahoma would prohibit a lawyer's representation of her former prosecutee, based on strict adherence to a Canon 9-style concern with avoidance of even the appearance of impropriety. In *People v. Franklin*, 387 N.E.2d 685, 686 (Ill. 1979), the Illinois Supreme Court describes its rationale:

> In furtherance of this fundamental right [to effective assistance of counsel], this court has adopted a *per se* rule which provides essentially that where defense counsel is involved in an actual or potential conflict of interest, it is unnecessary for the defendant to establish actual prejudice, as prejudice is presumed by law. *Id.* at 686.

Despite this presumption, the *Franklin* court held that a defendant was not denied effective assistance of counsel where the public defender, formerly an assistant state's attorney, had prosecuted the defendant almost five years earlier on an unrelated matter. In reaching this holding, the court emphasized the peculiar circumstance that the defendant had led the defense lawyer to believe that the defendant was not the person whom the lawyer had convicted of a prior burglary charge. Although the court did not indicate that the lawyer's failure of independent recollection was determinative of the outcome, it noted that the lawyer's lack of awareness of the prior prosecution dispelled some of the "subliminal effects" and "subtle influences," that characterize a presumptive conflict of interest. *Id.* at 687. Moreover, the defendant's conflict of interest claim was not timely, having been made as a post-trial motion for a new trial. In the court's words:

> The logical inferences from this record are that had defendant not denied that it was he who was the subject of the [earlier] prosecution and conviction, defense counsel would have realized prior to trial, as he did after the trial, that he had prosecuted the [earlier] case against defendant. The question of a conflict, if one was thought to exist, could then have been explored in timely fashion. To now reward defendant's deceit with a new trial would make a mockery of the truth-seeking process upon which our system of justice is founded. *Id.* at 688.

Apparently, then, the holding of *Franklin* turns, at least in part, on the court's disapproval of the defendant's perceived procedural manipulations. Dicta in *People v. Simmons*, 409 N.E.2d 99, 100 (Ill. App. Ct. 1980) supports such a reading. In that case, the defendant claimed that his right to waive a conflict of interest had been violated where the court automatically replaced the assigned public defender once it was disclosed that the public defender had previously prosecuted the defendant on another matter. Before addressing whether defendants have a right to waive a potential conflict of interest in these circumstances, the court remarked that "had the trial court failed to replace original counsel and had defendant been convicted, he would now be claiming reversible error because of conflict of interest on the part of his counsel." *Id.* at 100. If the defendant had had a right to waive this potential conflict of interest, the right was forfeited by his failure to raise it prior to trial. Clearly the Illinois courts are concerned with setting up a system that defendants can abuse.

Simmons then goes on to suggest that even in the absence of concerns about manipulation of waiver procedures, no such waiver would have been permitted in these circumstances. This suggestion comports with two prior state cases, *People v. Moore*, 389 N.E.2d 944, 946 (Ill. App. Ct. 1979) and *People v. Stoval*, 239 N.E.2d 441, 444 (Ill. 1968). The former case, involving two public defenders from the same office representing a defendant and his brother, a codefendant, asserts that it is difficult to obtain a valid waiver of a conflict of interest. The latter case indicates that trial courts should presume against even knowing waivers by defendants in conflict-of-interest matters.

Even more explicitly, Oklahoma courts have forbidden waivers by defendants of the potential conflicts of interest of their lawyers. In *Worthen v. State*, 715 P.2d 81 (Okla. Crim. App. 1986), the court unequivocally condemned representation of a defendant by a lawyer who had previously served as an assistant district attorney and had convicted the defendant on two prior charges. In broad language reminiscent of Canon 9, the court stated that defense counsel had an ethical obligation to avoid potential conflicts such as these and to advise the court promptly when they arise. This language implies that defendants cannot waive potential conflicts of interest by their lawyers, since lawyers have an independent ethical obligation to avoid such representation.

This interpretation is supported by *Skelton v. State*, 672 P.2d 671 (Okla. Crim. App. 1983), in which the court invoked DR 9-101(B) to reverse the conviction of a defendant who had been represented at trial by the lawyer who had prosecuted him at arraignment. *Skelton* held that reversal was required in this situation notwithstanding the defendant's waiver of objection to the lawyer's representation. According to the Oklahoma courts, a strict reading of Canon 9's admonition to avoid the appearance of impropriety outweighs a defendant's limited Sixth Amendment interest, recognized in *Glasser v. United States*, 315 U.S. at 75, to a lawyer of one's choice.

Howerton v. State, 640 P.2d 566 (Okla. Crim. App. 1982) reinforces this reading. *Howerton* held that a part-time district attorney could not be appointed to represent defendants either within or outside his jurisdiction. In so holding, the court noted:

> The public has a right to absolute confidence in the integrity and impartiality of the administration of justice. The conflicts presented in [these types of] case[s], at the very minimum, give the proceeding an appearance of being unjust and prejudicial. In [these] situation[s], it is difficult if not impossible to determine whether the defendant's representation was affected by the conflict. *Id.* at 568.

Given a judge's difficulty in determining whether representation is affected by a conflict, the *Howerton* court thought it illogical, especially in light of the high ethical stakes involved, to entrust a defendant with making such a determination through a waiver procedure.

Although the holdings in these Illinois and Oklahoma cases are not required by federal constitutional standards for ineffective assistance of counsel, they may rest on the states' interpretations of their own ethical guidelines and constitutional law. Nevertheless, since the federal constitutional trend, as exemplified in *Strickland* and *Burger,* is toward requiring actual prejudice to establish a claim of ineffective assistance of counsel on the basis of conflict of interest, rulings such as those cited in this section may be vulnerable to challenge. If challenged, state courts might assert more precisely the sources of authority upon which their rulings rest.

THE MAJORITY POSITION. Most lower courts that have ruled on the issue find no impropriety in a public defender's representation of a client whom he or she has previously prosecuted in an unrelated case. For example, *Stigars v. State of Delaware,* 577 A.2d 755 (Del. 1990), held that "the mere fact that a [public defender] prosecuted the defendant many years ago in an unrelated case is not a basis for disqualification nor does it establish a conflict of interest." The court found the potential for conflict irrelevant without a showing of actual prejudice to the defendant's Sixth Amendment rights. See also *State v. King,* 447 So. 2d 395, 396 (Fla. Dist. Ct. App. 1984); *State v. Martz,* 760 P.2d 65, 68 (Mont. 1988).

In cases such as these, the burden of establishing prejudice rests on the defendant. In *Stigars,* the necessary showing, similar to that required in federal constitutional law, was that the lawyer actively represented conflicting interests and that the conflict adversely affected the lawyer's performance. With such a steep standard of proof, most courts in most circumstances would not find a lawyer's representation of a client whom she previously prosecuted in another matter to be improper.

In these jurisdictions, defendants are permitted to waive any potential conflict of interest that their lawyers might appear to represent. On occasion, a prosecutor may object to defense representation by a lawyer who previously prosecuted the defendant. In *United States v. Smith*, 653 F.2d 126, 128 (4th Cir. 1981), the prosecutor sought to have the defendant's waiver disallowed on the grounds that the defense lawyer, who as a former assistant U.S. attorney had supervised the investigation and trial of his client on an unrelated charge, might make "unfair use of information gained in public employment . . . to the detriment of the government." *See also State v. King*, 447 So. 2d 395, 396 (Fla. Dist. App. Ct. 1984).

These cases hold that a defendant's waiver of a lawyer's potential conflict of interest will not be disallowed unless the prosecutor is able to demonstrate actual prejudice to the government as a result of the defense representation. As the Fourth Circuit observed, "[The standard] cannot be a fanciful, unrealistic or purely subjective suspicion of impropriety that requires disqualification." *Smith*, 653 F.2d at 128. This requirement is symmetrical to that imposed on a defendant who seeks to challenge the propriety of such representation after conviction. According to *Smith*, such a requirement indicates that, in this context, a defendant's choice of a lawyer is weightier than concerns about inconvenience to the government or even the public image of lawyers.

Both *Smith* and *King* involved a prosecutor's attempt to disqualify privately retained lawyers, not public defenders, on conflict-of-interest grounds, although this distinction is not evident in either opinion. In reality, public defenders may be more likely to withdraw voluntarily when faced with a potential conflict. See, for example, *Seay v. State*, 550 N.E.2d 1284, 1286 (Ind. 1990), in which the defendant's three court-appointed lawyers withdrew in succession, one on the grounds that he had formerly prosecuted a case involving the defendant. Nevertheless, a defendant's waiver of a potential conflict of interest would logically hold whether a lawyer is privately retained, court appointed, or employed by the local public defender agency.

On the other hand, a defendant's attempt to waive a lawyer's conflict of interest would likely fail if the lawyer had previously prosecuted the defendant on the same case or a related case. For example, in *State v. King*, 447 So. 2d at 396, the court implies that it found no actual conflict of interest requiring a defense lawyer's disqualification because "[It had] . . . not been shown that counsel had any substantial involvement on behalf of the state in *the same action*" (emphasis in original). *Accord State v. Martz*, 760 P.2d 65, 68 ("[The former prosecution was] a completely separate case from the one at issue"); *In re Pepperling*, 508 P.2d 569, 570 (Mont. 1975) ("separate and distinct criminal charge").

In *People v. Kester*, 361 N.E.2d 569 (Ill. 1977) the court found a conflict of interest, even in the face of a client's apparent waiver, where a court-appointed defense lawyer had previously appeared on behalf of the prosecution in the same criminal proceeding. The court explained its rationale for this ruling:

> [A] potential conflict of interest nevertheless exists in a situation such as this when a prosecutor who personally has been involved in the prosecution of a defendant in a particular criminal proceeding later assumes the duties of court-appointed defense counsel for that defendant in the same proceeding. . . . [T]he untenable situation which results . . . is one which can and should be avoided in the interests of the sound administration of criminal justice. *Id.* at 571–72.

The court in *Kester* then went on to explain that if such representation were allowed, then the defendant could later contend that "the advice and performance of court-appointed counsel was affected by a subliminal reluctance to attack pleadings or other actions and decisions by the prosecution which he may have been personally involved with or responsible for." *Id.* at 572.

Other courts have indicated that the public interest is advanced when criminal laws are enforced free of unnecessary suspicion or distrust of the judiciary and the prosecution. *United States v. Kitchin*, 592 F.2d 900 (5th Cir. 1979), involved an associate of the defendant's lawyer who had been actively involved on behalf of the government in an earlier stage of the same matter. In disapproving these representation arrangements, the court stated, "[S]ociety's interest in fair but unimpeded prosecution of the criminal law outweighs the defendant's right to counsel of his choice under the circumstances of this case." *Id.* at 905.

Clearly, representation is improper where the defense lawyer has previously prosecuted the defendant on the same case or a related case. Occasionally, however, a problem arises in determining whether a particular case is related to a prior case. In *People v. Hoskins*, 392 N.E.2d 405 (Ill. App. Ct. 1979), a lawyer who had been involved in the prosecution of burglary charges against a defendant was subsequently appointed to represent the defendant on motions to withdraw guilty pleas to later forgery charges. In finding the two proceedings to be related, the court reasoned, that "[a] relationship arises because the conviction on the forgery offenses resulted in the revocation of the defendant's sentence of probation which he received when convicted on the burglary charge." *Id.* at 407

According to this approach, cases may be deemed related where the earlier disposition affects the later one. In *United States v. Smith*, 653 F.2d 126, 128 (4th Cir. 1981), the Fourth Circuit struck a compromise to blunt the impact of such an approach. In the *Smith* case, the defendant's former prosecutor was permitted to represent the defendant at the trial of other charges but not at the subsequent probation violation proceedings, the sort of proceedings where the outcome can be most affected by the earlier prosecution. The court in *Smith* found that such a compromise permitted the defendant to be represented by a lawyer of his choice while still adhering to prevailing ethical and constitutional standards.

At the other end of the spectrum are two Michigan cases that found past and present proceedings to be unrelated despite a relatively substantial nexus between them. In *People v. Gorzen*, 337 N.W.2d 359 (Mich. Ct. App. 1983), the defendant was represented at sentencing by a lawyer who previously had been an assistant prosecutor on the same cases. These proceedings were found not sufficiently related to require the case to be remanded for resentencing. Likewise, in *People v. Young*, 450 N.W.2d 43 (Mich. Ct. App. 1989), the court found that no conflict inhered in a court-appointed lawyer's representation of the defendant at probation violation proceedings although the lawyer had prosecuted the defendant for the original offense.

Conclusion

In a majority of jurisdictions, no actual conflict of interest arises when a public defender represents a client who that defender previously prosecuted on an unrelated case unless the defendant can show that he suffered prejudice as a result of the representation. In these jurisdictions, defendants are permitted to waive potential conflicts of interest, although prosecutors may sometimes object to the attempted waiver. A prosecutor's objection will be upheld only in the rare event that the prosecutor can show that representation of the defendant by the defense lawyer would betray the public trust invested in that lawyer when she was a prosecutor.

A few jurisdictions presume that a public defender's representation of a client whom she formerly prosecuted is a conflict of interest and, therefore, ethically improper. Even in those numerous jurisdictions that refuse to indulge such a presumption in the absence of prejudice, a public defender's representation of her former prosecutee may be deemed improper if the present and past proceedings are found to be related. In some jurisdictions, "related" cases comprise not only earlier stages of the same criminal proceeding but also prior proceedings that can affect the disposition and sentence in the current case.

A public defender who previously prosecuted her client on another case would be well-advised to check the prevailing law of the relevant jurisdiction to determine whether this case may be found to be related to the present matter. Under the current law in every state, continued representation in this case would likely be considered ethically improper. In these circumstances, the public defender should not seek the client's informed consent to the representation but should move to withdraw.[1] If, however, under the prevailing law of the jurisdiction the current case appears to be wholly unrelated to the prior prosecution, the public defender, in accordance with ethical standards, may secure in writing the client's informed consent to the representation after a full discussion of the issue with the client. Public defenders in Oklahoma and Illinois should not seek the client's waiver of the potential conflict of interest, as such representation is always considered ethically improper in these jurisdictions.

Notes

The author is grateful for the excellent research assistance of Neil Mooney and John Sheridan, law students at Boston College Law School.

1. Under Model Rule 1.11, the disqualification under ethical standards of one public defender does not automatically disqualify the entire public defender office. Another public defender in the same office may undertake the representation as long as the client consents and the lawyer has no communication about the case with the colleague who formerly prosecuted the client. Where the size of the office permits, assigning the defendant's case to a public defender other than his former prosecutor would be generally advisable.

Bibliography

Articles

Marshall Breger, *Disqualification for Conflicts of Interest and the Legal Aid Attorney*, 62 B.U. L. Rev. 1115 (1982).

Developments in the Law—Conflicts of Interest in the Legal Profession, 94 Harv. L. Rev. 1244 (1981).

Developments in the Law—Public Employment, 97 Harv. L. Rev. 1611 (1984).

Margo L. Frasier, *Disqualification of Criminal Defense Attorneys Due to Prior Government Service*, Fla. St. U. L. Rev. 95 (1984).

Gary F. Lowenthal, *Successive Representation by Criminal Lawyers*, 93 Yale L.J. 1 (1983).

Richard H. Underwood, *Part-Time Prosecutors and Conflicts of Interest: A Survey and Some Proposals*, 81 Ky. L.J. 1 (1993).

Federal Cases

Burger v. Kemp, 483 U.S. 776, *rehearing denied*, 483 U.S. 1056 (1987).

Cuyler v. Sullivan, 446 U.S. 335 (1980).

Glasser v. United States, 315 U.S. 60 (1942).

Goodson v. Peyton, 351 F. 2d 905 (4th Cir. 1965).

Holloway v. Arkansas, 435 U.S. 475 (1978).

Strickland v. Washington, 466 U.S. 668, *rehearing denied*, 467 U.S. 1267 (1984).

Woods v. Covington County Bank, 537 F.2d 804 (5th Cir. 1976).

United States v. Kitchin, 592 F.2d 900 (5th Cir. 1979).

United States v. Smith, 653 F.2d 126 (4th Cir. 1981).

State Cases

Howerton v. State, 640 P.2d 566 (Okla. Crim. App. 1982).

People v. Franklin, 387 N.E.2d 685 (Ill. 1979).

People v. Gorzen, 337 N.W.2d 359 (Mich. Ct. Ap. 1983).

People v. Hoskins, 392 N.E.2d 405 (Ill. App. Ct. 1979).

People v. Kester, 361 N.E.2d 569 (Ill. 1977).

People v. Moore, 389 N.E.2d 944 (Ill. Ap. Ct. 1979).

People v. Simmons, 409 N.E.2d 99 (Ill. App. Ct. 1980).

People v. Stoval, 239 N.E.2d 441 (Ill. 1968).

People v. Young, 450 N.W.2d 43 (Mich Ct. App. 1989).

In re Pepperling, 508 P.2d 569 (Mont. 1975).

Seay v. State, 550 N.E.2d 1284 (Ind. 1990).

Skelton v. State, 672 P.2d 671 (Okla. Crim. App. 1983).

State v. King, 447 So. 2d 395 (Fla. Dist. Ct. App. 1984).

State v. Martz, 760 P.2d 65 (Mont. 1988).

State v. Sparkman, 443 So. 2d 700 (La. Ct. App. 1983).

Stigars v. State of Delaware, 577 A.2d 755 (Del. 1990).

CHAPTER 📖 19

Simultaneous Representation of the "Innocent" Client and the Real Culprit

Nicholas L. Chiarkas

What is the proper ethical response for a public defender when a client (Mr. Jones) discloses to that defender that he committed a crime for which another one of the defender's clients (Mr. Smith) has been charged? Can any other lawyer in the public defender office represent Mr. Smith?

Client Smith

Under various provisions of the ABA Model Rules of Professional Conduct and the ABA Model Code of Professional Responsibility, the defender must withdraw from representing client Smith. First, the defender cannot use the information from client Jones in her representation of client Smith because it would clearly violate the rule of client confidentiality. Model Rule 1.6(a) states that "[a] lawyer shall not reveal information relating to representation of a client unless a client consents after consultation . . . ."[1] Likewise, Model Code DR 4-101(B) prohibits a lawyer from knowingly revealing a confidence or secret of her client. As a consequence of the defender's ethical obligations to keep confidential the information disclosed by client Jones, she cannot fulfill her duty to zealously represent client Smith under Canon 7 of the Model Code. *See also* MODEL RULE 1.3, Comment. Obviously, the information received from client Jones would exonerate client Smith. But to reveal this information in the course of representing client Smith would breach the lawyer's duty to client Jones and may lead to another criminal charge being brought against client Jones. On the other hand, by ignoring or concealing this exculpatory information, counsel may not be able to zealously defend client Smith.

Second, Model Rule 1.7(a) and (b) state, in pertinent part, that "[a] lawyer shall not represent a client if the representation of that client will be directly adverse to another client. . . . . [and] a lawyer shall not represent a client if the representation of that client may be materially limited by the lawyer's responsibilities to another client . . . ." These rules also require the defender to withdraw from representing client Smith. In order for the defender to represent client Smith adequately, she would need to figure out a way to utilize the exculpatory information given to her by client Jones. It is obvious that use of this information would be directly adverse to client Jones because it would implicate him in another crime. Furthermore, by not using the exculpatory information because of the duty to preserve another client's confidences, the defender's representation of client Smith would be materially and severely limited. Indeed, it would be extremely difficult to construct a defense of client Smith untainted by the confidential information received from client Jones.

Third, Model Code DR 5-105(B) states that "[a] lawyer shall not continue multiple employment if the exercise of his independent professional judgment in behalf of a client will be or is likely to be adversely affected by the representation of another client, or if it would be likely to involve him in representing differing interests. . . ." In the present case, the defender must withdraw from the representation of client Smith because any judgment she exercises in representing client Smith is likely to be materially affected by the confidential information she gained from client Jones that he committed the crime for which client Smith is charged. Once again, it would be virtually impossible to separate the privileged information counsel received from client Jones from any untainted information she discovered independently through her case investigation. Moreover, if counsel stayed on client Smith's case and her "independent investigation" uncovered evidence that led to charges being brought against client Jones, Jones surely would complain that his undoing was the result of the defender's unethical use of confidential communications.

Finally, the Model Code of Professional Conduct at EC 5-14, states that "[m]aintaining the independence of professional judgment required of a lawyer precludes his acceptance or continuation of employment that will adversely affect his judgment on behalf of or dilute his loyalty to a client. This problem arises whenever a lawyer is asked to represent two or more clients who may have differing interests, [footnote omitted] whether such interest be conflicting, inconsistent, diverse, or otherwise discordant." Clients Jones and Smith certainly have diverse interests; Smith needs Jones's confession for an acquittal, and Jones doesn't want to face another criminal charge. The defender cannot maintain independent judgment in such a classic example of ". . . conflicting, inconsistent, diverse, or otherwise discordant" interests. In this situation, counsel simply cannot zealously pursue each client's best interests and remain loyal to both clients.

Problems may arise in the attempt to withdraw from representing client Smith. Certainly the defender must attempt to withdraw from the Smith case without having to explain why and without damaging either client. Client Smith simply should be told that it is the defender's ethical duty to withdraw. An interesting question is how far the defender can go if the judge insists on more information before granting the motion to withdraw. If pressed the defender should file an affidavit in support of the motion, noting that a conflict exists because of the duty owed to another client.[2]

The defender does not have the option of transferring Jones's case to another lawyer in the office as a way of maintaining her representation of Smith. Model Rule 1.10(a) states that "[w]hile lawyers are associated in a firm, none of them shall knowingly represent a client when any one of them practicing alone would be prohibited from doing so. . . ." Under the Model Code, DR 5-105(D) states that "[i]f a lawyer is required to decline employment or to withdraw from employment under a Disciplinary Rule, no partner, or associate, or any other lawyer affiliated with him or his firm may accept or continue such employment."

Client Jones

Assuming that the defender is permitted to withdraw from the Smith case, the question remains as to whether she must withdraw from the Jones case. If it is in any way a related case, then Model Rule 1.9(a) would mandate withdrawal from the Jones case.[3] If the Jones case is unrelated to the Smith case, then there is no conflict and no need to withdraw. However, it would be advisable for the defender to notify client Jones of her former representation of Smith, the person falsely accused of the crime Jones admitted committing. She should also inform Jones that his confession to her will be held in confidence. Finally, the defender should also tell client Jones that if he were ever charged with the crime to which he confessed, she would not be able to represent him.

Notes

1. The defender faces a conflict that cannot be waived because her duty to maintain each client's confidences prevents her from even seeking to obtain an informed waiver of the conflict. Under Model Rule 1.7(a) and (b) a lawyer would be unreasonable in concluding that her zealous representation of client Smith would not affect her relationship with or not adversely affect her representation of client Jones. Moreover, it would be unreasonable to believe that the defender could fully explain the potential problems in a way that allows for informed consent or that the relationship or representation of client Jones would not be adversely affected as she tried to exonerate client Smith.

2. *See* MODEL RULE 1.16, Comment, "[t]he court may wish an explanation for the withdrawal, while the lawyer may be bound to keep confidential the facts that would constitute such an explanation. The lawyer's statement that professional considerations require termination of the representation ordinarily should be accepted as sufficient."

3. MODEL RULE 1.9(a) states that "[a] lawyer who has formerly represented a client in a matter shall not thereafter represent another person in the same or a substantially related matter in which that person's interests are materially adverse to the interests of the former client unless the former client consents after consultation."

Bibliography

ABA MODEL CODE OF PROFESSIONAL RESPONSIBILITY, Canon 7; DR 4-101(B), 5-105(B), 5-105(D); EC 5-14 (1980).

ABA MODEL RULES OF PROFESSIONAL CONDUCT, Rules 1.3, Cmt., 1.6(a), 1.7(a), 1.7(b), 1.9(a), 1.10(a), 1.16, Cmt. (1983).

CHAPTER 📖 20

The Limits of Defense Counsel's Intimate Relationships with Others in the System

Barbara A. Schwartz

Does criminal defense counsel's ongoing sexual relationship with a police officer, prosecutor, or judge ethically bar counsel from handling cases involving that police officer, prosecutor, or judge? If she is disqualified, is her entire office disqualified? Must defense counsel advise the client if he is sexually involved with a prosecutor, police officer, or judge?

This chapter seeks to address the type of relationships that are likely to become more common as the ranks of defense lawyers, prosecutors, police officers, and judges become more diverse. My analysis assumes that the close relationships this essay deals with (those that go beyond those ordinary friendships that have always developed among lawyers and other actors in the criminal justice system) are noncoercive, and do not otherwise raise issues of sex discrimination or sexual harassment. My analysis also assumes that the relationship has not been initiated by one of the parties as a means to gain some professional advantage on behalf of a client, such as that alleged in *Gregori v. Bank of America*, 207 Cal. App. 3d 291, 254 Cal. Rptr. 853 (1989).

This chapter is organized to analyze defense counsel's personal relationships with prosecutors and police officers separately from relationships with judges. It treats prosecutors and police officers together because, while the recent literature focuses on relationships between opposing counsel and not between lawyers and nonlawyers otherwise associated with litigation, there is no reason to think the analysis should be any different. Whatever concerns are created by intimate personal

276

relationships between opposing counsel would exist where a police officer, rather than the prosecutor, is a party to the relationship. As for judges, the analysis is different because a different source of law—the Code of Judicial Conduct or its equivalent—is implicated.

Personal Relationships with Prosecutors and Police Officers

A single case is widely cited for the proposition that a defense lawyer's dating relationship with the prosecutor personally responsible for a prosecution (or, by analogy, a police officer associated with the case) raises serious questions about the effectiveness of counsel. Because there is so little other judicial authority on point, it is probably useful to start with this case.

In *People v. Jackson*, 167 Cal. App. 3d 829 (Cal. App. 3d Dist. 1985), the defendant appealed from a jury-based conviction of assault with intent to commit rape. Following the verdict, but before sentencing, the defendant discharged his court-appointed counsel. Through retained counsel he moved for a new trial, alleging that he had learned only after the trial that his counsel and the prosecutor were engaged in an ongoing "dating" relationship.

There was not much dispute about the nature of the relationship between defense counsel and the prosecutor. The two lawyers had been dating about eight months at the time Mr. Jackson was charged; they continued to date "on a regular basis" during the entire period Mr. Jackson was represented by his assigned counsel; they appeared as counsel in directly adverse roles at a preliminary examination, pretrial conferences, and trial; they were never married, engaged to each other, or living together. (The court is silent on whether the lawyers were sexually intimate; one can conclude either that the court considered that irrelevant to its analysis or that it assumed, without stating it, that the relationship was sexual in nature.) Neither the defendant nor the court was aware of the relationship; however, no confidential information was disclosed by defense counsel to the prosecution.

In analyzing whether Mr. Jackson was denied effective assistance of counsel as a result of a conflict of interest, the court found it unnecessary to determine whether the relationship between defense counsel and the prosecutor created an *actual* or a *potential* conflict.[1] Relying on case law interpreting the California constitution, which provided that "even a potential conflict may require reversal if the record supports 'an informed speculation' that appellant's right to effective representation was prejudicially affected," 167 Cal. App. 3d at 832 (citations omitted), the court granted Mr. Jackson a new trial.

The court cited two grounds for determining that the relationship presented at least a potential for conflict of interest. The first was a concern that defense counsel's emotional stake in the dating relationship might affect his zealousness in pursuing the client's interest. "No matter how well intentioned defense counsel is in carrying out his responsibilities to the accused, he may be subject to subtle influences manifested, for example, in a reluctance to engage in abrasive confrontation with opposing counsel during settlement negotiations and trial advocacy." *Id.* at 833. The second was a concern that the relationship might lead the client or others to question the impartiality and integrity of the system—in other words, the *appearance* of impropriety. Once these potential problems were identified, the court reasoned, then the client, rather than counsel, was the proper one to decide whether the lawyer-client relationship could continue or whether he would prefer to secure counsel unencumbered by potential divided loyalties. Since such a decision could only be made by the client after being adequately informed, at the very least counsel should have made full disclosure.

In relying on the failure to disclose as a basis for reversal, the court did not have to decide if the relationship might have required withdrawal whether or not the client requested it. Additionally, the court expressly declined to comment on whether defense counsel's conduct might have constituted an ethical violation. *Id.*, at 833, note 1.[2]

While *Jackson* provides a good starting point for analysis, it leaves a lot of questions unanswered. What types of social relationships trigger a duty to disclose to the client, or further, a duty to decline or withdraw from the representation? Do the concerns expressed by the *Jackson* court apply as well to lawyers who have supervisory responsibilities for the defense and/or the prosecution? If defense counsel has a conflict as a result of a dating relationship, and cannot represent a client, is the conflict imputed to other members of the firm or organization? Do the answers to these questions depend on whether defense counsel practices in a Model Code or a Model Rules jurisdiction? While the dearth of authority makes definite answers unlikely, a general framework is useful for analysis on a case-by-case basis.

General Analytic Framework

While their terminology may differ, legal authorities identify three fundamental ethical values at stake in conflict-of-interest analysis. The first fundamental concern is that when counsel represents differing interests—whether it be differing interests among multiple clients or interests of a client that differ from the personal, political, or economic interests of the lawyer—counsel's ability to represent his or her client(s) zealously will be compromised. This concern is frequently articulated as the requirement that counsel exercise independent legal judgment on behalf of the client. The paradigm example of a situation where differing interests may interfere with the exercise of independent legal judgment is the simultaneous representation of jointly charged codefendants.

The second fundamental ethical concern in conflict-of-interest analysis is counsel's duty of confidentiality. In this regard, the rules are prophylactic in nature in identifying those situations where a lawyer's ability to maintain client confidences might be so impaired that disclosure and/or withdrawal are required. A common example in criminal defense practice is the representation of a client against whom a former client is expected to give adverse testimony. While the duty of zealous representation of the current client may not be compromised, the duty of maintaining the confidences of the former client may be; therefore, where the former representation and the current representation are "related," disclosure to both clients and their consent are required.

The third fundamental ethical concern in conflict-of-interest analysis is an appearance of impropriety that undermines public confidence in the judicial system. Commentators are less in agreement about this concern.[3] This ambivalence about the appearance of impropriety, at least where judges and other tribunals are not involved, is reflected, for example, in differences between the Model Code and the Model Rules. The Model Code considers the appearance of impropriety to warrant its own canon (Canon 9), while the Model Rules, which address the substance of Rules contained in Canon 9, do not ascribe to the rubric of "appearance of impropriety." Indeed the Comment to Model Rule 1.9 rejects the term as "question-begging."

In tension with these three ethical concerns are practical concerns that arise where conflict-of-interest regulations are applied inflexibly. One concern in tension with inflexible regulation is the restriction on access to counsel, particularly interference with a client's ability to choose counsel. An inflexible application of disqualification requirements, for instance, interferes with a client's ability to retain or otherwise select counsel of his or her own choosing; in a rural or otherwise underserved area, access to any lawyer may be impaired.

Another practical concern raised by inflexible regulation of conflicts of interest is the ability of counsel to obtain employment. Inflexible application of disqualification requirements, particularly imputation requirements, will render some lawyers unemployable. Potential employers may decline to hire lawyers simply out of a concern that they may bring the grounds for their disqualification with them and that the grounds for that disqualification will apply to the entire firm or organization. Just such a concern that government lawyers would be unemployable in the private sector were they to bring the grounds for their disqualification with them and thus disqualify the entire firm, gave rise to the judicially created "screening" device as an alternative to imputation. Those judicially created screening devices (formerly known as "Chinese walls") are now expressly approved in the Model Rules. *See* MODEL RULE 1.11(a)(1).

Where defense counsel and prosecutor are involved in an ongoing personal relationship, but one or both of them has only supervisory responsibility for a particular prosecution, these competing values should be kept in mind when attempting to determine whether disclosure and/or withdrawal is called for. If one's connection to a charged client is not direct, only administrative, with no meaningful access to confidential information from that client and no participation in the conduct of the representation, then there may be no need to engage in the foregoing inquiry. Support for this position exists in the commentary to California Rule 3-320, which provides that it does not apply to "circumstances in which a member fails to advise the client of a relationship with another member who is merely a partner or associate in the same law firm as the adverse party's counsel, and who has no direct involvement in the matter." However, if the connection to the charged client is direct—with access to confidential communications and/or responsibility in some meaningful way for the conduct of the defense, then defense counsel should evaluate whether disclosure or more is appropriate. Similarly, if defense counsel's involvement with the representation of the charged client is direct, but the member of the prosecutor's office with whom he or she is having the relationship is not the "on-line" lawyer in charge of that particular prosecution, defense counsel should evaluate the nature of the supervisory or administrative relationship between the prosecutors to determine whether the foregoing inquiry and analysis should be initiated.

In the absence of a bright-line rule, such as that in California, defense lawyers ought to analyze a situation where there is a romantic relationship with a prosecutor or a police officer with these factors in mind, along with attention to the particular rules in effect in their jurisdiction.[4]

Model Rules Jurisdictions

For defense lawyers practicing in one of the thirty-nine or so jurisdictions in which the ABA Model Rules of Professional Conduct apply, reference should be made to Model Rules 1.7, 1.8, and 1.9. Model Rule 1.7 is the general rule applying to conflicts of interest and states in relevant part:

> (b) A lawyer shall not represent a client if the representation of that client may be materially limited by the lawyer's responsibilities to another client *or to a third person or by the lawyer's own interests* unless: (1) the lawyer reasonably believes the representation will not be adversely affected and (2) the client consents after consultation.

Model Rule 1.8 (i), which supplements but does not replace Model Rule 1.7, states that a lawyer related to another lawyer as a spouse shall not represent a client in a representation adverse to that of a person represented by that other lawyer except upon consent by the client after consultation regarding the relationship. One should keep in mind that Model Rule 1.8(i) is only one step of the analysis. Lawyers married to opposing counsel must still consult Model Rule 1.7(b), and decline representation altogether unless they reasonably believe that the representation will not be adversely affected.[5]

While Model Rule 1.8 (i) does not extend to nonmarital relationships, it provides a basis for analyzing a problem under Model Rule 1.7(b). The more a relationship resembles a marriage, the more appropriate to treat the relationship, for conflict-of-interest purposes, the same way one would treat a marriage—as a per se basis upon which to disclose and consult. The objectifiable factors one should consider in the relationship might be whether the lawyers are cohabiting; whether they are in any respect an economic unit; sharing of income or expenses; length of the relationship; frequency and nature of the time spent together; exclusivity of the relationship; existence of long-term plans; and whether there is a sexual relationship. Even in the absence of objectifiable factors that indicate an intimate personal relationship, the lawyer must also decide subjectively if his or her emotional stake in the relationship is such that it might either affect the ability to represent one's client zealously or compromise one's duty to maintain client confidences.

Of the above-mentioned factors in determining if a personal relationship triggers a duty to disclose and/or withdraw, whether the relationship is sexual in nature is the most volatile. On the one hand, it may be seen by some—including the client—as the crucial factor; on the other hand, it is the factor people may be most reluctant to disclose. While the facts in *Jackson* made it unnecessary to inquire into whether the lawyers' relationship was sexual, in the absence of a reasonably long-term, relatively intense dating relationship, one can assume that courts would be interested in whether the relationship in question was sexual. While sex may not be the sine qua non of every intimate relationship, and while intimacy may not be the sine qua non of every sexual relationship, it more than likely will be considered a major factor in the analysis. For example, in *Gregori v. Bank of America*, 207 Cal. App. 3d 291, 254 Cal. Rptr. 853 (1989), where defendants sought the disqualification of plaintiff's counsel on the grounds that he had initiated a social relationship with defense counsel's legal secretary, the court was unwilling to credit hearsay evidence that counsel and the secretary had intercourse following a dinner date. But the court sent the matter back to the trial court to take the testimony of the secretary, leaving the distinct impression that if there was reliable evidence of a sexual relationship it would play an important role in the analysis.

Realistically, a conscientious defense lawyer should probably resolve questions about whether his or her relationship with the prosecutor triggers the disclosure and consent requirement of Model Rule 1.7(b) in favor of disclosure.[6] From that initial conclusion several things can happen. Counsel can decide, for any number of perfectly understandable reasons, that he or she would rather withdraw from or decline representation than disclose to the client the existence of a personal relationship with the prosecutor or officer in charge. Counsel may also decide that disclosure and consent is not an adequate remedy because the relationship is such that he or she cannot reasonably conclude that the representation will not be adversely affected. Or, the client may decide after disclosure and consultation, that he or she wants other counsel. What then?

The lawyer who would rather decline or withdraw from representation than disclose the existence of an intimate relationship to his or her client should consider whether it is possible to resolve the ethical dilemma without telling someone. Is the firm or defender office set up to provide for a reassignment of the case to another lawyer, without disclosing to someone the reason why the reassignment is necessary? If defense counsel involved in the intimate relationship has filed an appearance, local rules might require him or her to obtain the court's permission to withdraw, and some judges may want to know the reasons for withdrawal. It may be impossible both to be properly ethical and completely discrete about one's personal relationships. The bottom line is that if for any reason defense counsel wants to keep an intimate relationship secret from clients and professional colleagues, he or she should avoid establishing such relationships with anyone who is likely to be on the opposing side in a case, as either a prosecutor or police officer.[7]

If total secrecy is not a concern, the implications of declining representation are not as substantial in a Model Rules jurisdiction as they might be in a Model Code jurisdiction. The Model Rules are more flexible with matters of imputation, or disqualification of the disqualified lawyer's entire law firm or organization, recognizing that some factors that mandate the disqualification of one lawyer in an office do not also taint his or her colleagues. For instance, the commentary to Model Rule 1.8(i) expressly provides that if a married lawyer is disqualified from representation because, after disclosure, the client does not consent, then the disqualification is personal only, and not imputed to the firm. The limited imputation under this provision results from a practical concern that lawyers married to other lawyers will not be able to obtain professional employment for fear that a firm or organization would be prohibited from accepting clients. Therefore, if the only basis for disqualification is the per se conflict created by Model Rule 1.8 (i), and there is no actual or potential conflict that will compromise the other lawyers in the married lawyer's organization, good policy calls for flexible application of imputation.

The issue of imputation is not so easy, however, if under Model Rule 1.7(b) the defense lawyer involved in a relationship must decline representation. Under Model Rule 1.10(a), if a lawyer is disqualified under any of the provisions of Model Rule 1.7, then all of the lawyers associated with him or her are also disqualified. However, the harshness of Model Rule 1.10(a) is ameliorated somewhat by Model Rule 1.10(c), which provides that imputation is waivable by the affected client after disclosure and consultation.

If, under the Model Rules, imputation to the entire office is required, and hardship would result because of the unavailability of alternative counsel, then defense counsel should determine whether, under the law of the relevant jurisdiction, one can argue some exceptions to the imputation requirement. For instance, the case law in some jurisdictions has approved the construction of screening devices in situations where Model Rule 1.11(a)(1) would not apply.[8] Additionally, some jurisdictions have a "rule of necessity," whereby imputation will be waived when there is no other counsel reasonably available to provide the representation if the entire organization is disqualified.[9]

Model Code Jurisdictions

Lawyers practicing in the minority of jurisdictions still regulated by the ABA Model Code of Professional Responsibility should review the section of this chapter dealing with the Model Rules, because much of the analysis is the same in Model Code jurisdictions. The Model Code, first drafted in 1968, does not take into account the changing demographics of the bar, and simply contains no analogue to Model Rule 1.8(i), dealing with lawyers who have lawyer spouses, much less a rule analogous to California Model Rule 3-320, which takes into account a broad range of intimate relationships. Moreover, the Model Code contains no conflict provisions, such as Model Rules 1.8(f), 1.9, 1.10(b), 1.11 (a), (b), recognizing the interest in confidentiality; it relies instead on Canon 4, the general rule dealing with client confidences and secrets. Nonetheless, the decision about whether defense counsel should disclose and/or decline representation may not be substantially different.

DR 5-101(A) of the Model Code states:

> Except with the consent of his client after full disclosure, a lawyer shall not accept employment if the exercise of his professional judgment on behalf of his client will be or reasonably may be affected by his own financial, business, property, or personal interests.

Additionally, EC 9-1, 9-2, and 9-6 impose a general duty on counsel, at least in those Model Code jurisdictions where the Ethical Considerations are binding, to avoid the appearance of impropriety and refrain from conduct that might undermine public confidence in the justice system.

In some respects, the Model Code may be broader than the Model Rules in its regulation of intimate personal relationships, because it might be construed—especially if read in conjunction with *Jackson*—to require disclosure and consent where the relationship presents merely an appearance of conflict of interest. (The Model Rules, on the other hand, are expressly concerned with actual and potential conflicts, but not the appearance of conflict.) What this could mean is that more relationships, even those that do not create even a potential threat to zealousness or confidentiality but might create an appearance of impropriety, would raise a duty of disclosure. Even though the Model Code seems to require disclosure when there is merely an appearance of impropriety, the weight of authority seems to be that withdrawal or disqualification is not required in the absence of an actual conflict.[10]

On the other hand, in at least one respect the Model Code is less protective of the client's interests. Under Model Rule 1.7(b), if defense counsel involved in a relationship cannot reasonably conclude that his or her representation will not be adversely affected, then representation is prohibited, even if the client is informed and consents. However, under DR 5-101 (A), a fully informed client can waive an actual conflict.

One could reasonably conclude, then, that the Model Code does not require disqualification under any circumstances arising from a personal intimate relationship, as long as a fully informed client consents. If disqualification is required, however, what about the rest of the firm or organization? Again, the Model Code is somewhat different than the Model Rules. Its provisions for imputation do not take into account the competing values in tension with imputation as do those of the Model Rules. DR 5-105 (D) states:

> If a lawyer is required to decline employment or to withdraw from employment under a Disciplinary Rule, no partner or associate, or any other lawyer affiliated with him or his firm may accept or continue such employment.

There are no express exceptions to DR 5-105(D); moreover, there are no provisions that permit a client to waive imputation, even after disclosure. Defense lawyers in Model Code jurisdictions, nonetheless, should research the law of that jurisdiction for judicially created exceptions, approval of screening devices, or adoption of a "rule of necessity."[11]

Personal Relationships with a Judge Presiding over the Prosecution of a Client

In evaluating the ethical and constitutional obligations of a defense lawyer involved in a romantic relationship with a judge assigned to preside in any manner over the prosecution of a client's case, the analysis is basically the same as used in the first section of this chapter. However, the ethical and constitutional duties of the judge also come into play. Under prevailing standards, a judge has a duty to inform the litigants of the relationship, whether or not it is raised by either lawyer.

In most jurisdictions, the ABA Model Code of Judicial Conduct has been adopted as the regulatory scheme for judges. The majority of those jurisdictions use the 1972 version; gradually, jurisdictions are adopting the 1990 version. For purposes of this discussion, there is not a significant difference in the substance of the applicable provisions, but the numbering is different. This essay will refer to the 1972 provisions, with the 1990 provisions in square brackets, where different.

In Canons 1 and 2 of both versions, judges are exhorted to "uphold the integrity and independence of the judiciary" and to avoid "impropriety and the appearance of impropriety" in all of the judge's activities. (The language is mandatory in the 1990 version, hortatory in the 1972 version.) Canon 3, and in particular Rule 3.C [3.E], deals with disclosure and recusal, as follows:

C [E]. Disqualification.

(1) [1]. A judge should [shall] disqualify himself [or herself] in a proceeding in which his impartiality might reasonably be questioned, including but not limited to instances where:

(a) he has a personal bias or prejudice concerning a party [or a party's lawyer], or personal knowledge of disputed evidentiary facts concerning the proceeding;

* * *

(c) he knows that he, individually or as a fiduciary, or his spouse [or parent] or minor child [whether or not] residing in his household, [or any other member of his family residing in the judge's household] has a financial interest in the subject matter in controversy or in a party to the proceeding, or any other [more than de minimus] interest that could be substantially affected by the outcome of the proceeding;

(d) he or his spouse, or a person within the third degree of relationship to either of them, or the spouse of such a person:

* * *

(ii) is acting as a lawyer in the proceeding;

* * *

D [F]. Remittal of Disqualification.

A judge disqualified by the terms of Canon 3C(1)(c) or Canon 3C(1)(d) [Section 3E] may, instead of withdrawing from the proceeding, disclose on the record the basis of his disqualification. If, based on such disclosure [of any basis for disqualification other than personal bias or prejudice concerning a party] the parties and lawyers, independently of the judge's participation, all agree in writing that the judge's relationship is immaterial or that his financial interest is insubstantial, the judge is no longer disqualified, and may participate in the proceeding. The agreement, signed by all parties and lawyers, shall be incorporated in the record of the proceeding.

Defense counsel involved in a personal relationship with a judge should also consult the court rules and statutes of the relevant jurisdiction to determine if there is another source of law dealing with judicial conduct. For instance, 28 U.S.C. § 455 applies in all federal proceedings, and substantially tracks the language of Canon 3.C. and 3.D. [3.E. and 3.F.] One major difference is that under § 455, waiver by the parties of recusal is impermissible where the disqualification arises under any of the enumerated grounds. Waiver is permissible only where the basis for disqualification is required for any nonenumerated reason where the judge's impartiality might reasonably be questioned. Since an amatory relationship with counsel does not come within the enumerated reasons for mandatory recusal, then recusal is probably waivable if the relationship has been properly disclosed by the judge.

Notwithstanding this significant difference between § 455 and the Codes of Judicial Conduct, federal case law interpreting 28 U.S.C. § 455 is persuasive authority in interpreting the meaning of Canon 3.C.[3.E.]. One commonly cited federal case interpreting § 455 is *United States v. Murphy*, 768 F.2d 1518 (7th Cir. 1985), which was a political corruption prosecution against a state trial judge arising out of Operation Greylord in Chicago. It was personally prosecuted by Dan Webb, who was the U.S. Attorney, and presided over by Judge Kocoras. Following sentence and judgment, the defendant filed a § 455 motion, raising for the first time that the personal relationship between Webb and the judge required recusal. The judge and Webb were described as "the best of friends." They had been colleagues early in their careers in the U.S. Attorney's office and their families remained close. The families had traveled on vacation together. Of greatest concern to the court was that the judge and Webb left immediately after Murphy's sentencing for a planned vacation to a resort, where the families rented adjoining cottages. The court's discussion is interesting:

> In today's legal culture friendships among judges and lawyers are common. They are more than common; they are desirable. A judge need not cut himself off from the rest of the legal community. Social as well as official communications among judges and lawyers may improve the quality of legal decisions. Social interactions also make service on the bench, quite isolated as a rule, more tolerable to judges. Many well-qualified people would hesitate to become judges if they knew that wearing the robe meant either discharging one's friends or risking disqualification in substantial numbers of cases. Many courts therefore have held that a judge need not disqualify himself just because a friend—even a close friend—appears as a lawyer. (Citations omitted.)
>
> These cases also suggest, however, that when the association exceeds "what might reasonably be expected" in light of the associational activities of an ordinary judge, the unusual aspects of a social relation may give rise to a reasonable question about the judge's impartiality. The relation between Judge Kocoras and U.S. Attorney Webb was unusual. These close friends had made arrangements before the trial began to go off to a vacation hideaway immediately after sentencing. *Id.*, at 1537–38.

Applying "'[t]he twofold test . . . of whether the judge feels capable of disregarding the relationship and whether others can reasonably be expected to believe that the relationship is disregarded,' Advisory Opinion No. 11, Interim Advisory Committee on Judicial Activities (1970)," *id.*, the court held that the judge should have disclosed these circumstances on his own. The court further held that since there was no evidence that the court was actually not impartial, this was a case where only the appearance of impartiality might be in question and, upon proper disclosure, the parties could waive recusal.

Because judicial ethics require judges to avoid even the appearance of impropriety to a much greater extent than lawyers acting as advocates, it is quite likely that the analysis triggered under *Murphy* encompasses more personal relationships than that compelled under the analysis set forth in the first section of this chapter, applying to personal relationships between a defense lawyer and a prosecutor or police officer. It may be reasonable to conclude that most people would consider any sexual relationship, no matter how casual or transitory, and most dating relationships, even in the absence of sex, between a judge and one of the lawyers, as an association that exceeds "what might reasonably be expected in light of the associational activities of an ordinary judge." Criminal defense lawyers should be wary of continuing the representation of a client appearing before a judge with whom they are having a personal relationship in the absence of an acknowledgment from the court to both parties of the existence of the relationship. Disclosing to one's own client may be adequate to discharge one's own duty to the client, but it is not adequate to discharge the judge's duty to all the parties.

Notes

1. *Cf.* Cuyler v. Sullivan, 446 U.S. 335 (1980) (Defendant alleging Sixth Amendment violation warranting new trial must establish an actual conflict of interest.).

2. This issue is no longer in dispute in California. Under the current version of the California Rules of Professional Conduct, which became effective in 1989, Rule 3-320 provides: "A member shall not represent a client in a matter in which another party's lawyer is a spouse, parent, child, or sibling of the member, lives with the member, is a client of the member, or has an intimate personal relationship with the member, unless the member informs the client in writing of the relationship."

3. CHARLES W. WOLFRAM, MODERN LEGAL ETHICS, § 7.1.4 (1986).

4. For instance, in Texas the court has constructed a two-tier analysis depending on whether the defense counsel is appointed to represent an indigent client or is retained to represent a client capable of paying a fee. In Haley v. Boles, 824 S.W.2d 796 (Tex. App. 1992), the court, relying on the Sixth Amendment guarantee of counsel, held that a lawyer appointed to represent an indigent accused should have been allowed to withdraw because his partner was married to the prosecutor. It rejected disclosure and consent as adequate, even though permitted under Texas' ethical rules, because of the lack of "real choice" by the indigent client. It would find disclosure and consent of the client adequate in the case of an accused who has chosen to retain counsel.

5. For a more thorough analysis of conflicts of interest among married lawyers, see Chapter 19.

6. Standard 4-3.5 ("Conflicts of Interest") of the ABA Standards for Criminal Justice Defense Function (3d. ed. 1993) [hereinafter ABA STANDARD 4-3.5] provides that defense counsel should disclose to the client at the earliest feasible opportunity "any interest in or connection with the case or any other matter that might be relevant in or connection with the case or any other matter that might be relevant to the defendant's selection of counsel . . . or counsel's continuing representation." ABA STANDARD 4-3.5(b). The ABA Standards then proceed to expand upon Model Rule 1.8(i) by prohibiting defense counsel who has a subsequent "personal relationship with a prosecutor from representation of a client in a criminal matter unless the client consents after disclosure." ABA STANDARD 4-3.5(i). The comments to the ABA Standard suggest that where a conflict exists warranting prohibition of representation, the conflict is not imputed to other lawyers in defense counsel's firm, nor does the prohibition apply where the relationship is with a prosecutor who is not "directly involved in the particular prosecution." *Id.*

7. The conflict between privacy and disclosure can be especially acute for gay and lesbian lawyers for whom disclosure of the existence of an intimate personal relationship might entail personal and/or professional risk.

8. *See, e.g.,* Nemous Foundation v. Gilbane, Aetna, Federal Ins. Co., 632 F. Supp. 418 (D. Del. 1986). *See also* ABA Comm. on Ethics and Professional Responsibility, Formal Opinion 90-358 (Sept. 13, 1990), reprinted in ABA/BNA LAWYER'S MANUAL ON PROFESSIONAL CONDUCT, 901: 132, 136–37, n.12; RESTATEMENT 3D OF THE LAW GOVERNING LAWYERS (Tentative Draft No. 4, April 10, 1991), § 204(2).

9. *See, e.g.,* Sapienza v Hayashi, 57 Haw. 289, 554 P.2d 1131 (1976) (A prosecuting attorney appointed by a municipality's chief executive should be disqualified from investigating possible criminal conduct of that chief executive, provided, however, that disqualification is not imputed to every lawyer in the office if imputation left office with no one to conduct the investigation.).

10. *See, e.g.,* Gregori v. Bank of America 207 Cal. App. 3d 291, 254 Cal. Rptr. 853 (1989) and authorities cited therein.

11. *See* notes 7, 8, *supra.*

Bibliography

Standards and Books

ABA Committee on Ethics and Professional Responsibility, Formal Opinion 90-358 (1990).

ABA MODEL CODE OF JUDICIAL CONDUCT, Canons 1, 2, 3 (1972).

ABA MODEL CODE OF PROFESSIONAL RESPONSIBILITY, Canons 4, 9; DR 5-101(A), 5-105(D); EC 9-1, 9-2, 9-6 (1980).

ABA MODEL RULES OF PROFESSIONAL CONDUCT, Rules 1.7, 1.7(b), 1.8, 1.8(f), 1.8(i), 1.9 and Cmt., 1.10(a), 1.10(b), 1.10(c), 1.11(a), 1.11(a)(1), 1.11(b) (1983).

ABA STANDARDS FOR CRIMINAL JUSTICE DEFENSE FUNCTION 4-3.5, 4-3.5(b), 4-3.5(i) (3d ed. 1993).

Interim Advisory Committee on Judicial Activities, Advisory Opinion 11 (1970).

RESTATEMENT (THIRD) OF THE LAW GOVERNING LAWYERS § 204(2) (Tentative Draft No. 4, 1991).

RULES OF PROFESSIONAL CONDUCT OF THE STATE BAR OF CALIFORNIA, Rule 3-320.

Charles W. Wolfram, *Modern Legal Ethics,* § 7.1.4 (1986).

28 U.S.C. § 455 (1988).

Cases

Cuyler v. Sullivan, 446 U.S. 335 (1980).

Gregori v. Bank of America, 207 Cal. App. 3d 291, 254 Cal. Rptr. 853 (1989).

Haley v. Boles, 824 S.W.2d 796 (Tex. App. 1992).

Nemous Foundation v. Gilbane, Aetna, Federal Ins. Co., 632 F. Supp. 418 (D. Del. 1986).

People v. Jackson, 167 Cal. App. 3d 829 (Cal. App. 3d Dist. 1985).

Sapienza v. Hayashi, 57 Haw. 289, 554 P.2d 1131 (1976)

United States v. Murphy, 768 F.2d 1518 (7th Cir. 1985).

CHAPTER 📖 21

Sex and the Criminal Defense Lawyer: The Ethical Limits of Intimacy in the Lawyer-Client Relationship

Graham B. Strong

Is it ethically proper for an appointed criminal defense lawyer to be sexually involved with a client? Is it ethically proper for such a lawyer to begin a sexual relationship with a client after the client's criminal case has been completed?

Introduction

The relationship between a lawyer and client is often, by necessity, one of sudden and extraordinary intimacy between strangers. This is especially true of the relationship between the appointed criminal defense lawyer and the indigent criminal defendant, who, at a time of special emotional vulnerability, is very quickly called upon to share the most intimate personal information with an appointed professional confidant. It should come as no surprise that on occasion the line between professional and personal intimacy is breached and a sexual relationship between lawyer and client develops. This has been, as one judge put it, the legal profession's "dirty little secret." *In re the Marriage of Kantar,* 581 N.E.2d 6, 12 (Ill. App. Ct. 1991) (Greiman, J., specially concurring). Although reliable data on the subject is understandably scarce, it has been suggested on the basis of available evidence that sexual contact with clients occurs "fairly frequently," and that after divorce lawyers criminal defense lawyers appear to be among those most likely to have sexual relations with their clients.[1]

After a prolonged period of national inattention to the subject, recently there has been a relative explosion of interest in the ethics of lawyer-client sex. In 1991, the American Academy of Matrimonial

Lawyers (AAML) adopted an aspirational ethical standard flatly condemning lawyer-client sexual relationships during representation. AAML, *Bounds of Advocacy: Standards of Conduct*, Rule 2.16 (1991). The following year, the ethics committee of American Bar Association issued a formal opinion concluding that a sexual relationship between lawyer and client may violate both the ABA Model Rules of Professional Conduct (hereinafter Model Rules) and the ABA Model Code of Professional Responsibility (hereinafter Model Code). ABA Comm. on Ethics and Professional Responsibility, Formal Op. 92-364 (July 6, 1992). Shortly thereafter, California took the lead among the states in adopting the nation's first ethics rule and ethics legislation specifically addressing the matter of lawyer-client sex. CAL. RULES OF PROFESSIONAL CONDUCT 3-120; CAL. BUS. & PROF. CODE § 6109.9 (1992). Oregon and New York have since followed with new ethics rules of their own on the subject, and other states have considered proposed rules changes as well.[2] A flurry of scholarly articles on the subject have appeared in legal journals. *See* bibliography, *infra*. Even comedian Jay Leno has joked about the topic on the "Tonight Show" (suggesting that lawyers should be banned from ever having sex in order to prevent them from reproducing). Jorgenson & Sutherland, *supra* note 1, at 462 n.4. The legal profession's "dirty little secret" is out.

Neither the Model Code nor the Model Rules make any specific mention of the ethical propriety of sexual entanglement with a client. That is not to say, however, that existing general provisions of the ethics codes do not provide a solid basis, at least in theory, to regulate such conduct. Although there are disturbing indications that clients' complaints regarding sexual misconduct by their lawyers have been systematically discounted by some bar disciplinary authorities in the investigation stage,[3] courts have routinely imposed discipline upon lawyers once there is a factual finding of sexual involvement with a client. The practice contexts and factual circumstances have varied, and the courts have drawn upon a variety of ethics provisions as the basis for decision, but the emerging trend has been steady: in recent years, most reported disciplinary cases involving lawyer-client sex have resulted in the imposition of some form of discipline. 8 Law. Man. on Prof. Conduct (ABA/BNA) No. 10, at 171 (June 17, 1992).

The trend of recent decisions and other recent developments is a clear warning signal of increasing volume to the appointed criminal defense lawyer who is considering a sexual relationship with a client. In fact, a number of criminal defense lawyers have already been disciplined for unethical sexual involvement with their clients. The next section of this chapter summarizes the range of circumstances in which, and the rules under which, courts have imposed discipline upon criminal defense lawyers in such cases. The third section of this chapter analyzes the degree to which conflict of interest may be an inherent feature of all cases of sex, clients, and the appointed criminal defender. It suggests that a sexual relationship with an indigent client in a criminal case presents an intractable potential for conflict between the interests of the client and the personal interests of the lawyer. Due primarily to the uneven balance of power between lawyer and client in such cases, moreover, it would ordinarily not be possible to "cure" the potential conflict through a process of consultation and consent. Section four of this chapter explores the ethics of sexual intimacy between a criminal defender and a former client, and the concluding section examines the emerging trend of opinion regarding cases of sexual intimacy within the lawyer-client relationship generally.

The Criminal Defense Lawyer at the Bar

The most extreme of the reported cases imposing discipline upon a criminal defense lawyer for sexual intimacy with a client are those where a criminal lawyer is truly a *criminal* lawyer; that is, where the lawyer's sexual involvement with a client takes the form of a sexual assault or other criminal offense.[4] In such egregious cases, courts have relied especially upon the broadest "catch-all" misconduct provisions of the ethics codes, sometimes employing them in redundant clusters and often with little discussion. In Model Code jurisdictions, these have included the general rules prohibiting a lawyer from engaging in illegal conduct involving moral turpitude (DR 1-102(A)(3)); from engaging in other conduct that adversely reflects on the lawyer's fitness to practice law (DR 1-102(A)(6)); and from intentionally prejudicing or damaging a client during the course of the professional relationship (DR 7-101(A)(3)). In Model Rules jurisdictions, where general misconduct provisions are drafted in slightly narrower terms, the rules of choice have been 8.4(b) and (d), which provide that it is professional misconduct for a lawyer to "commit a criminal act that reflects adversely upon the lawyer's honesty, trustworthiness or fitness as a lawyer in other respects," or to "engage in conduct that is prejudicial to the administration of justice."

Other cases, less extreme but perhaps no less troubling, involve no criminally assaultive behavior but rather the sexual exploitation of an especially vulnerable client without the use of physical force.[5] Discipline has also been imposed upon a criminal defense lawyer in at least one case where there was no indication of assaultive or coercive conduct by the lawyer or unusual vulnerability on the part of the client.[6] In these cases of nonassaultive sexual intimacy between lawyer and client, the courts have grounded discipline upon elastic "catch-all" provisions (such as Model Code DR 1-102(A)(6) and DR 7-101(A)(3)), or, with little elaboration, upon a finding of conflict between the interests of lawyer and client under Model Rule 1.7(b) or Model Code DR 5-101(A).

Thus, it appears that criminal defense lawyers who choose to become sexually involved with their clients are, at the least, "living on the edge." *Kantar,* 581 N.E.2d at 14. In fact, the broad range of circumstances in which criminal defense lawyers have been disciplined in such cases suggests that the interesting question no longer is whether sexual relationships between defenders and their clients *can* be a violation of existing standards of professional ethics but, rather, whether they are *always* a violation of such standards.

The Nature of the Problem

In extreme cases of assaultive conduct or of overtly coercive sexual blackmail by a criminal defense lawyer, there can be little question that the bounds of ethical propriety have been reached and breached. These are the easy cases, and fall well within the general misconduct provisions of the ethical codes. But what of the case, more difficult and surely more common, where there appears to be a genuine mutual attraction between lawyer and client? Is it always unethical for two willing adults to act upon their mutual attraction in the context of a lawyer-client relationship? Are there special considerations at work when the lawyer is a criminal defense lawyer and the apparently willing client is an indigent charged with a crime?

Although a variety of ethical obligations can be implicated in cases of sexual intimacy between lawyer and client, the problem associated with such cases is probably best understood, at its root, as a problem of conflict of interest. The problem has two primary aspects. The first has to do with the predictable vulnerabilities of a lawyer who wishes to act upon a sexual attraction to a client, and the second has to do with the predictable vulnerabilities of the client who is the object of that attraction.

The Lawyer's Predictable Vulnerabilities:
The Problem of Impaired Judgment and Diluted Loyalty

A lawyer, of course, has a general duty to exercise professional judgment for the sole benefit of the client, free from compromising influences, including the influence of personal interests that undermine single-minded devotion to the interests of the client. *See* MODEL CODE EC 5-1; ABA STANDARDS FOR CRIMINAL JUSTICE DEFENSE FUNCTION, Standard 4-3.5(a) (3d ed. 1993) [hereinafter DEFENSE FUNCTION]. Model Rule 1.7(b) forbids representation of a client if the representation "may be materially limited" by the lawyer's own interests, unless the lawyer reasonably believes that the representation will not in fact be adversely affected and the client consents after consultation. The Model Code formulation, in DR 5-101(A), requires a lawyer not to accept employment if the exercise of the lawyer's judgment on behalf of the client "will be or reasonably may be affected" by the lawyer's personal interests, unless the client consents after full disclosure. This provision has been interpreted to apply both to the acceptance and the continuation of employment, and the phrase "personal interest" has been specifically interpreted to include a lawyer's sexual interest in a client. *In re Wolf*, 826 P.2d 628 (Or. 1992).

Sex is a natural drive of such force that it always carries the potential to exert an influence, and perhaps an extremely distorting influence, upon the judgment and motivations of a lawyer who becomes sexually involved with a client. It may seem, at first blush, as though sexual intimacy with a client would simply tend to enhance the devotion of the lawyer to the service of the client's interests, to add special zest and passion to the warm zeal expected of the advocate. While it is surely true that the fervor of advocacy may in some cases be enhanced to the client's advantage, it is also true that passion may undermine objectivity in judgment to the long-term disadvantage of a client.[7] Moreover, there are common and predictable circumstances where a lawyer's own interest in the personal relationship with the client may be directly at odds with the client's case-related interests. In such circumstances there is always a residual risk that the lawyer's fidelity to the interests of the client will be compromised and that the quality of representation can thereby be undermined. Consider the ways that these general propositions can play out in the specialized context of the relationship between the defense lawyer and the indigent criminal defendant.

Imagine the competition of incentives in the heart of a criminal defense lawyer who is engaged in a budding sexual relationship with an apparently willing client. If it is uncertain whether the developing romance will survive the professional association, the lawyer will have a personal incentive to prolong the criminal case so as to extend regular contact with the client. Trial dates may be set farther into the future, motions delayed, continuances sought (or not opposed), statutory time limits waived. It cannot be gainsaid that delay can sometimes work to the tactical advantage of a criminal defendant. But, as has been recognized especially in the context of speedy trial claims, it can also prejudice a defendant's interest severely: not only will the defendant predictably suffer anxiety and concern during the pendency of a criminal charge, but also the defense can be impaired, especially by the fading memories of witnesses or by their death or disappearance. *See Barker v. Wingo*, 407 U.S. 514 (1972). If the client's case is delayed unnecessarily for personal reasons, the ethical concern rooted in conflict of interest may branch to implicate the distinct ethical duties to act with reasonable promptness in the representation of a client and to avoid practices that have no substantial purpose other than delay. *See* MODEL RULES 1.3, 3.2, 3.2 comment; MODEL CODE DR 7-102(A)(1).

The influence of sexual or romantic interest in the client may also undercut the lawyer's ability to function as a dispassionate counselor in assisting the client to make case-related decisions, especially the decision to accept or reject a plea offer. Suppose, for example, that the client is faced with a choice between a certain three-year term in the penitentiary upon a plea of guilty or the uncertain prospect of a trial on a charge that could carry a much longer sentence. Suppose also that a three-year sentence would be, on balance, a good case result for the client. The defense lawyer, in such a circumstance, may be more inclined toward a go-for-broke trial strategy than would otherwise be the case due to an urgent and selfish personal desire to keep the client free and available for the immediate continuation of the sexual relationship. That inclination could skew the objectivity with which the lawyer discussed the plea offer with the client, and thereby impair the client's decision-making process. At the extreme, an underselling of the risks of the trial process, or other intentional manipulation of the client's choices, could run afoul of the lawyer's duty to assist the client to make an informed decision regarding the plea to be entered in a criminal case. *See* MODEL RULES 1.2(a), 1.4(b); MODEL CODE EC 7-7, 7-8; DEFENSE FUNCTION, Standard 4-5.1.

If the sexual relationship thrives and the lawyer spends a good deal of private time with the client, information gained in the personal relationship may well have a bearing upon the criminal case. Suppose, for example, that the client is charged with a violation of the conditions of pretrial release and the lawyer, purely as a result of the personal relationship with the client, is aware of facts relevant to the claimed violation. Such information may be held to be unprotected by the lawyer-client privilege, even if communicated directly from the client and intended to be confidential, because it was not communicated to one who was at the time functioning in the capacity of a lawyer.[8] A lawyer forced to disclose such information testimonially would have failed to act in a manner that preserves the lawyer-client privilege and would in addition be faced with the dual—and ordinarily incompatible—roles of witness and advocate. *See* MODEL RULE 3.7; MODEL CODE EC 4-4, DR 5-102.

Inherent in any intimate relationship, however sweet may have been its tender beginnings, is the prospect that it can unexpectedly turn sour with age. That prospect alters, but scarcely reduces, the potential for competition of motivations within the heart of the criminal defense lawyer, or the potential for damage to the quality of representation. Suppose, for example, that a sexual liaison with a client has ended in bitter acrimony. Now, rather than an incentive to prolong the case to extend the personal relationship, the lawyer may have a special incentive to minimize contact with the client by expediting the case or by curtailing consultation time (implicating the duty to maintain adequate communication under Model Rule 1.4). The consultations that do occur, moreover, may become combative, and a loss of trust in the personal relationship may undermine the client's faith in the professional relationship with the lawyer. At the extreme there may be a temptation for the lawyer to pay back personal dissatisfactions within the professional relationship, where the lawyer's power is especially great and the stakes for the client are especially high.

Thus, whether the sexual relationship with the client thrives or withers, there are a variety of ways that it can routinely be expected to exert an untoward influence upon the judgment and loyalty of the criminal defense lawyer and threaten to produce an unwholesome effect upon the quality of representation. Although neither the Model Code nor the Model Rules contemplate that any possibility of conflict, however slight, will preclude representation, here the risk is palpable that personal desires may interfere significantly with the lawyer's professional judgment in considering, recommending, and carrying out alternative courses of action on behalf of the client. *See* MODEL RULE 1.7(b), 1.7 comment; MODEL CODE DR 5-101(a), EC 5-2. In the typical case, therefore, it is prudent to conclude that the criminal defense lawyer who wishes to become sexually involved with a client during the course of representation may not ethically do so, absent fully informed consent by the client.

Even if the client consents after consultation, there are circumstances where that consent will be ineffective: consent is not after all a "universal solvent that dissolves all conflicts." Charles W. Wolfram, *Modern Legal Ethics* § 7.2.2 at 339 (1986). First, under the Model Rules, a personal-interest conflict is, in effect, "nonconsentable" whenever the conflict is so severe that a disinterested lawyer would conclude that the client should not agree to the representation under the circumstances. Only if the lawyer reasonably believes that the potential adverse affect upon the representation will not actually materialize can consent properly be sought from the client or acted upon if obtained. MODEL RULE 1.7(b)(1); 1.7 comment; *see also* MODEL CODE EC 5-2. Because such a belief seems possible in some cases of proposed sexual intimacy between lawyer and client, this first hurdle to effective consent, though significant, may not be insurmountable. A second hurdle, however, remains. Nominal consent, even if otherwise adequate, is of course ineffective if it is not voluntary, and "courts have generally insisted that the lawyer be aware that the client's consent is voluntarily given . . . ." Charles W. Wolfram, *supra*, § 7.2.4 at 347. As the next section will suggest, the dependent and vulnerable position of the indigent criminal defendant draws sharply into question whether it is ever safe for an appointed criminal defense lawyer to conclude that nominal consent to the combination of sexual intimacy and legal representation is truly the product of free choice.

The Client's Predictable Vulnerabilities:
The Problem of Coerced or Induced Consent

The professional relationship between a criminal defense lawyer and an indigent client is ordinarily, and perhaps inevitably, characterized by a radical disparity in power. The indigent criminal defendant typically enters the relationship in a position of exceptional weakness and vulnerability. The pending criminal charge—and the attendant prospect of incarceration—predictably will be the source of significant stress and anxiety. *Gibbons, supra* note 4, 685 P.2d at 175. Poverty will have deprived the client of an initial choice of counsel and of the power to express displeasure with the representation by substituting counsel at will. *See Morris v. Slappy*, 461 U.S. 1 (1983) (the Sixth Amendment right to counsel does not include a right to the appointment of a particular lawyer). Although the client may have some familiarity with law and the legal system, that knowledge will ordinarily be slight in comparison to the practiced legal sophistication of the criminal defense lawyer. Therefore, self-representation is rarely a realistic option and the client ordinarily will be forced into a position of dependence upon the appointed counsel for critical aid in a time of great need. These near-universal sources of client vulnerability will often be accompanied by others: youth, drug or alcohol dependency, psychological disorder. And although lawyer-client sex can of course occur in any gender permutation, the reported cases overwhelmingly involve male lawyers and their female clients, thus introducing gender-based power disparities into the mix. *See* Caroline Forell, *Lawyers, Clients and Sex: Breaking the Silence on the Ethical and Liability Issues,* 22 Golden Gate U. L. Rev. 611 (1992).

In a relationship where power is so unevenly balanced, there is cause for special concern that a sexual overture by the lawyer may induce an acquiescence that may be mistaken for free consent. It has been argued convincingly that consent to sexual intimacy in a "power dependency" relationship of this sort "is inherently suspect and should be legally ineffective."[9] It is theoretically possible, of course, even in the face of power disparity, for a client who fully understands the risks involved to agree very sincerely to the sexualization of an ongoing professional relationship. The difficulty is that it is hard—and perhaps impossible—for the self-interested criminal defender to distinguish free consent from induced acquiescence in a relationship that carries intrinsic coercive power and perhaps a seductive potential as well.

The coercive power of the relationship is derived from the natural fear of a vulnerable client, with much at stake and nowhere else to turn for assistance, that refusal to consent to sexual activity with the lawyer may have an adverse effect on the lawyer's performance in the representation. Thus, sex can function in effect as a kind of currency with which the client purchases adequate representation. An explicit statement by a lawyer linking legal services to sexual cooperation is the most obvious kind of exploitation of this coercive power, and has been routinely condemned by the courts.[10] Even in the absence of overt threats or promises, however, the client may feel compelled to respond affirmatively to a sexual overture from the lawyer out of fear that the choice is encumbered by an implicit linkage to the legal representation.[11]

It has been suggested that the relationship carries a special seductive potential as well, based upon an aspect of the recognized psychological phenomenon known as "transference." Transference occurs when there is an unconscious displacement of feelings associated with one figure of authority in a person's life to another, especially to a professional upon whom the person is dependent in a time of crisis. *See* Jorgenson & Sutherland, *supra* note 1, at 483. For this reason, "a frequent consequence of power dependency relationships may be a sexual desire, the source of which is the relationship itself rather than the powerful person. The dependent person's consent to sex is no more than a predictable response to the feelings aroused by the underlying relationship. Thus, 'consent' may actually be transference masquerading as love."[12]

Thus, for the appointed criminal defense lawyer seeking a sexual relationship with a client, informed consent appears to be a solution that is more theoretical than actual. The very process of detailing the potential deleterious effects that a sexual relationship could have upon the representation, of course, could function "as the legal equivalent of a cold shower." *See Kantar*, 581 N.E.2d at 13 n.4. And if it did not, it would be difficult or impossible for the appointed counsel to be confident that any apparent consent obtained was in fact the product of a choice that was neither coerced nor unfairly induced.

Is there nevertheless limited room for consent as a mechanism to "cure" the potential conflict inherent in a sexualized relationship between the lawyer and an indigent client in a criminal case? Any factor that reduces client vulnerability would also reduce the likelihood of sexual exploitation and increase the chance that effective consent could be obtained. It has been suggested, for example, that if it is the client who initiates or suggests the idea of a sexual relationship, there may be less cause for concern that the client's consent may not be truly voluntary, and that such variables as the client's sophistication, maturity, and degree of passivity will affect the likelihood that consent has been obtained through undue influence. Cal. Ethics Op. 1987-92 (1987). Ongoing consensual sexual relationships that predate the representation are also less likely to have been the product of undue influence by the lawyer. Such pre-existing relationships have been specifically excluded from the scope of California's legislation and Oregon's ethics rule on lawyer-client sex, and from a variety of other formulations on the subject as well.[13] In most circumstances, however, it is prudent to conclude that the predictable vulnerabilities of the indigent client in a criminal case will render informed consent effectively unavailable as a solution to the problem of conflict of interest posed by sexual intimacy between lawyer and client.

Intimate Relationships after Representation Is Complete

After representation is complete, however, the ethical risks associated with sexual intimacy between an appointed criminal defense lawyer and a client (who has now become a former client) are dramatically reduced. Lingering fiduciary responsibilities, particularly with regard to the preservation and use of confidential information, do survive the termination of the representation. MODEL RULES 1.6, 1.6 comment, 1.9(c); MODEL CODE DR 4-101, EC 4-6. These responsibilities, however, are much less likely to be inconsistent with romance than are the lawyer's broader obligations during the course of the representation. Moreover, once the criminal case is completed there will ordinarily be a significant reduction of the client's vulnerability to implicit or explicit coercion from the lawyer. *See* Coleman, *supra* note 1, at 134–35. Therefore, a consensual sexual relationship begun after an appointed criminal defense lawyer has fully completed the representation of a client, and not illegal for other reasons, should not be considered ethically improper so long as there is no misuse of client confidences. Even the most stringent of the proposed or adopted formulas for restricting lawyer-client sex do not extend the prohibition beyond the completion of the representation.[14]

Beyond the Criminal Context: The Emerging Trend of Opinion

The foregoing analysis suggests that due to the predictable vulnerabilities of both the lawyer and the client it would, in most circumstances, be ethically improper for an appointed criminal defense lawyer to become sexually involved with a client in the course of the representation. The potential for significant conflict between the interests of the lawyer and the client is foreseeable, and informed consent is suspect as a cure.

It would, however, be too strong a statement to assert that there is yet a clear national consensus that existing ethical standards effectively prohibit lawyer-client sexual intimacy generally. The positions of commentators, ethics committees, legislatures, and courts have been less than unanimous, but the emerging trend of opinion clearly disfavors lawyer-client sexual intimacy, not only in criminal cases but in all practice settings.

A number of commentators have suggested that existing rules of professional conduct should ordinarily function to bar sexual intimacy between lawyers and clients generally.[15] Others have questioned the adequacy of existing rules and have proposed that the matter be dealt with through a specifically tailored new ethics rule.[16] No sentiment has been expressed in the scholarly journals, however, that lawyer-client sex, as a general matter, is ethically proper.

The ABA Committee on Ethics and Professional Responsibility has taken the position that although neither the Model Code nor the Model Rules expressly prohibit a sexual relationship with a client, such a relationship does pose a significant danger that the lawyer's ability to represent the client adequately may be impaired in violation of both sets of model standards. ABA Comm. on Ethics and Professional Responsibility, Formal Op. 92-364 (1992). The committee concludes that lawyer-client sexual liaisons may breach the lawyer's fiduciary obligations to the client, may affect the independence of the lawyer's judgment, may create a prohibited conflict of interest, and may undermine the protection of client confidences. Therefore, the committee suggests that lawyers in all fields of practice "would be well advised to refrain from such a relationship." *Id.* State bar ethics opinions on the subject have sometimes given advice that is more strongly worded than the ABA formal opinion.[17]

Those few states that have actually adopted ethical standards specifically addressing the matter have taken disparate approaches. Oregon's new ethics rule flatly bans sexual relations between a lawyer and a current client absent a pre-existing sexual relationship. OR. CODE OF PROFESSIONAL RESPONSIBILITY DR 5-110. New York has adopted a new rule that similarly forbids a lawyer from beginning a sexual relationship with a client during the representation, but its reach is limited to lawyers in domestic relations cases. 9 Law. Man. on Prof. Conduct (ABA/BNA) No. 21, at 336 (Nov. 17, 1993). California's recent legislation (which trumps its corresponding ethic rule) falls well short of a general prohibition, focusing its restrictions primarily upon situations in which there is undue influence or a demonstrable risk of harm to a client's case. *See* CAL. BUS. & PROF. CODE § 6109.9 (1992).

The courts, while routinely willing to impose discipline upon lawyers who engage in sexual activity with their clients, have been less than uniform in their choice of disciplinary theory and more than reluctant to announce general rules on the subject. Some judges have employed sweeping language that does suggest a flat prohibition of lawyer-client sex, at least within a particular field of practice.[18] Other judges have intimated in dicta that upon different facts than those presented, lawyer-client sex might not be improper.[19] Most courts, however, as might be expected, leave the matter to case-by-case adjudication, imposing discipline upon the facts before them but leaving unresolved whether there may be other circumstances where sexual intimacy in the lawyer-client relationship would be ethically proper.

Despite the lack of unanimity among commentators, bar ethics committees, legislatures, and courts concerning the ethics of sexual intimacy within the lawyer-client relationship, it is fair to say that the emerging trend of opinion sharply condemns the practice, regardless of the field of law in which it occurs, with few exceptions. Against this general background, the special ethical risks associated with a sexual relationship between lawyer and client in appointed criminal cases stand out even more clearly.

Conclusion

In the context of the defense of the indigent criminal defendant, the case for ethical proscription of sexual intimacy between lawyer and client is especially strong due to the predictable vulnerabilities of both the lawyer and the typical client in such cases. Though a variety of ethical restrictions are implicated, at the root of the problem is an intractable, and ordinarily incurable, potential for conflict between the interests of the client and the personal interests of the lawyer. Intimacy is an inevitable, and, indeed, an indispensable aspect of the relationship between a criminal defense lawyer and an indigent client charged with crime. Professional intimacy, however, must have a safe environment in which to flourish, and not be threatened or exploited by the intrusion of physical intimacy into the professional sphere.

Notes

I wish to express my special thanks to Charles W. Wolfram, my former colleague at Cornell Law School, for sharing helpful thoughts, information, and prepublication materials on the topic with me; to Beverly Grace Strong, for research assistance; and to the office of California State Senator Tom Hayden, for helpful information concerning California legislation.

1. Linda Mabus Jorgenson & Pamela K. Sutherland, *Fiduciary Theory Applied to Personal Dealings: Attorney-Client Sexual Contact*, 45 ARK. L. REV. 459, 471 (1992). *See also* Dan S. Murrell, J. L. Bernard, Lisa K. Coleman, Deborah L. O'Laughlin & Robert B. Gaia, *Loose Canons—A National Survey of Attorney-Client Sexual Involvement: Are There Ethical Concerns?* 23 MEM. ST. U. L. REV. 483, 488–91 (1993) (7 percent of practitioners responding to a nationwide survey reported having engaged in a sexual relationship with a client, and 32 percent reported knowing of at least one lawyer who at some time had engaged in sex with a client); *California Lawyer Fax Poll: The Results from July*, CALIFORNIA LAWYER 120 (Oct. 1992) (18 percent of respondents reported having had sex with a client); Phyllis Coleman, *Sex in Power Dependency Relationships: Taking Unfair Advantage of the Fair Sex*, 53 ALB. L. REV. 95, 127 (1988) (divorce and criminal law clients appear to be the most vulnerable to sexual exploitation).

2. *See* OR. CODE OF PROFESSIONAL RESPONSIBILITY DR 5-110; *New York Imposes New Rules on Divorce Lawyers' Conduct*, 9 LAW. MAN. ON PROF. CONDUCT (ABA/BNA) No. 16, at 252 (Sept. 8, 1993); *Florida Bar Panel Considers Ethics Rule on Sexual Conduct*, 9 LAW. MAN. ON PROF. CONDUCT (ABA/BNA) No. 2, at 32 (Feb. 24, 1993); McQueen, Comment, *Regulating Attorney-Client Sex: The Need for an Express Rule*, 29 GONZ. L. REV. 405, 412 (1993/94) (reporting the rejection of a proposed sexual misconduct rule in Washington State); *Sexual Relations with*

Client: Problem with No Clear Answer, 8 LAW. MAN. ON PROF. CONDUCT (ABA/ BNA) No. 10, at 171 (June 17, 1992) (reporting a proposed sexual misconduct rule in Illinois).

3. *See* Chicago Bar Ass'n Comm. on Professional Responsibility, *Report of the Subcommittee on Attorney-Client Sexual Misconduct* 12 (Oct. 18, 1991) (most such complaints in Illinois do not result in charges because uncorroborated client testimony is regarded as insufficient evidence).

4. *See, e.g., In re* Wells, 572 N.E.2d 1290 (Ind. 1991) (male criminal defense lawyer touched the genitals of young male clients without their consent); *In re* Littleton, 719 S.W.2d 772 (Mo. 1986) (criminal defense lawyer brushed his hand across his client's breasts and made other unwelcome advances toward her); *In re* Stanton, 708 P.2d 325 (N.M. 1985) (public defender entered a plea of nolo contendere to a charge of attempted criminal sexual contact with one of his female clients, and made similar advances toward a second); Oklahoma *ex rel.* Oklahoma Bar Ass'n v. Sopher, 852 P.2d 707 (Okla. 1993) (criminal defense lawyer put his arm around his client, pulled her blouse out and looked down it); *In re* Howard, 681 P.2d 775 (Or. 1984) (criminal defense lawyer, representing a woman charged with prostitution, committed the crime of prostitution himself by performing legal services in exchange for sex with his client).

5. *See* People v. Gibbons, 685 P.2d 168 (Colo. 1984) (66-year-old criminal defense lawyer engaged in a covert sexual relationship with a 23-year-old female client with a ninth-grade education); *In re* Ridgeway, 462 N.W.2d 671 (Wis. 1990) (public defender initiated sexual contact with an alcoholic female client after giving her beer in violation of the terms of her probation).

6. *See* Committee on Professional Ethics and Conduct of the Iowa State Bar Association v. Durham, 279 N.W.2d 280 (Iowa 1979) (kissing, embracing, and occasional caressing or fondling between lawyer and her male client during visits to the penitentiary).

7. In the words of a resolution of the Illinois State Senate, "emotional detachment is essential to the lawyer's ability to render competent legal services, yet it is extremely difficult to separate sound judgment from the emotion or bias that may result from a sexual relationship between a lawyer and his or her client . . . ." S.Res. 361, 87th General Assembly, Illinois Senate (July 2, 1991) (urging the Illinois Supreme Court to adopt a specific rule prohibiting most lawyer-client sex). *See also* People v. Zeilinger, 814 P.2d 808 (Colo. 1991) (a sexual relationship with a client in a divorce case may "blind the attorney to the proper exercise of independent judgment"); *In re* Bowen, 542 N.Y.S.2d 45, 47 (it is "obvious" that a sexual relationship with a divorce client "is likely to compromise the good judgment and legal advocacy of the attorney"); Standing Comm. on Professional Responsibility and Conduct of the State Bar of California, Op. 1987-92 (1987) ("emotions triggered by sex with a client could impact the objectivity or emotional detachment essential to the lawyer's ability to render competent legal services").

8. *See* 8 J. WIGMORE, EVIDENCE § 2292 at 554 (J. McNaughton rev. 1961); G. LILLY, AN INTRODUCTION TO THE LAW OF EVIDENCE § 9.6 at 397 (1987) ("the privi-

lege does not arise when a client speaks with a lawyer in the latter's capacity as a . . . friend, even if legal matters are discussed").

9. Coleman, *supra* note 1, at 96–97; *see also* Or. Ethics Op. 475 (1982) (due to the client dependency fostered by the fiduciary relationship between lawyer and client, even if the lawyer in a divorce case were able to explain the consequences of sexual involvement to a client "it is doubtful that the client's consent to the attorney's continued representation could ever be deemed informed and voluntary").

10. *See, e.g.,* McDaniel v. Gile, 230 Cal. 3d 363, 281 Cal. Rptr. 242 (1991) (lawyer in a divorce case withheld or threatened to withhold legal services if sexual favors were not granted by his female client); People v. Crossman, 850 P.2d 708 (Colo. 1993) (lawyer solicited sexual favors in exchange for legal fees on three separate occasions); In re Wood, 489 N.E.2d 1189 (Ind. 1986) (lawyer in a criminal case convinced his young female client to engage in oral sex in exchange for legal services); In re Rudnick, 581 N.Y.S.2d 206 (1992) (lawyer threatened client that if she ended an undesired sexual relationship with him he could abandon her case and she would lose custody of her child).

11. *See* Standing Comm. on Professional Responsibility and Conduct of the State Bar of California, Op. 1987-92 (1987) ("Would the client's consent be truly voluntary, or would it be based on a fear of retaliation that the lawyer may withdraw from the case or may compromise his or her efforts because he or she is angry with the client for refusing?").

12. Coleman, *supra* note 1, at 97; *see also* Watson, *The Lawyer as Counselor,* 5 J. FAM. L. 7, 16 (1965) ("Due to the psychological tendency on the part of the client to invest the counselor with all sorts of power, authority, and a nearly magical belief in their helplessness, there will also be a powerful tendency to bestow affection").

13. *See* CAL. BUS. & PROF. CODE § 6106.9 (1992); OR. CODE OF PROFESSIONAL RESPONSIBILITY DR 5-110; Alaska Ethics Op. 88-1 (1988); Note, *supra* note 14, at 916–17. *But see, e.g.,* Lawrence Dubin, *Sex and the Divorce Lawyer: Is the Client Off Limits?* 1 GEO. J. LEGAL ETHICS 585, 618 (1988); AAML, BOUNDS OF ADVOCACY: STANDARDS OF CONDUCT, Rule 2.16 (1991).

14. *See, e.g.,* THE ROSCOE POUND-AMERICAN TRIAL LAWYERS FOUNDATION, THE AMERICAN LAWYER'S CODE OF CONDUCT, Rule 8.8 (Revised Draft 1982) ("A lawyer shall not commence having sexual relations with a client during the lawyer-client relationship"); AAML, BOUNDS OF ADVOCACY: STANDARDS OF CONDUCT, Rule 2.16 (1991) ("An attorney should never have a sexual relationship with a client . . . during the time of the representation"); OR. CODE OF PROFESSIONAL RESPONSIBILITY DR 5-110(A) ("A lawyer shall not have sexual relations with a current client of the lawyer unless a consensual sexual relationship existed between them before the lawyer/client relationship commenced").

15. *See, e.g.,* Geoffrey C. Hazard, *Lawyer-Client Sex Relations Are Taboo,* NAT'L L.J., Apr. 15, 1991, at 13, 14 ("In my opinion, having a sexual relationship with a client is prohibited by the present rules against conflict of interest between lawyer and client"); Charles W. Wolfram and B. Hill, Remarks at Panel

on "Sex, Power, and the Profession," ABA National Conference on Professional Responsibility (June 3–6, 1992), as reported in 8 LAW. MAN. ON PROF. CONDUCT (ABA/BNA) No. 10, at 171, 173 (June 17, 1992) (existing ethics rules on conflicts of interest are adequate to meet the problem in most circumstances).

16. *See, e.g.*, Dubin, *supra* note 13; Forell, *supra*; Jorgenson & Sutherland, *supra* note 1; Note, *Keeping Sex Out of the Attorney-Client Relationship: A Proposed Rule*, 92 COLUM. L. REV. 887 (1992); Anthony E. Davis & Judith Grimaldi, *Sexual Confusion: Attorney-Client Sex and the Need for a Clear Ethical Rule*, 7 NOTRE DAME J.L. ETHICS & PUB. POL'Y 57 (1993); Murell et al, *supra* note 1.

17. An Oregon ethics opinion, first issued in 1982, represented a virtual per se prohibition of lawyer-client sex in the divorce context, but its language was softened somewhat (to allow for the possibility of client consent) when the opinion was renumbered and reissued nine years later. *See* Legal Ethics Committee of the Oregon State Bar, Op. 475 (1982); Legal Ethics Committee of the Oregon State Bar, Op. 1991-99 (1991). A Maryland ethics opinion required a lawyer to withdraw from employment when sexually involved with a client in a case involving a possible divorce and related property issues. *See* Committee on Ethics of the Maryland State Bar Association, Op. 84-9 (1983). In California, the bar ethics committee issued a lengthy formal opinion that eschewed a per se prohibition of lawyer-client sex while noting multiple situations where the practice would run afoul of ethical proscriptions that predated the California legislation on the subject. *See* Standing Committee on Professional Responsibility and Conduct of the State Bar of California, Op. 1987-92 (1987). An Alaska ethics opinion announced a presumption that it is unethical for a lawyer to have a sexual relationship with a client in cases of a type that "can be viewed objectively as emotionally traumatic," including divorce and criminal cases. Ethics Committee of the Alaska Bar Association, Op. 92-6 (1992); *see also* Ethics Committee of the Alaska Bar Association, Op. 88-1 (1988).

18. *See, e.g.*, Kantar, 481 N.E.2d at 13 (Greiman, J., specially concurring) ("a divorce lawyer who has sexual intercourse with his client has engaged in a per se violation of the rules governing conflict of interest"); *In re* Lewis, 415 S.E.2d 173 (Ga. 1992) (a sexual relationship with a client in a contested divorce and custody case constitutes, in se, a violation of conflict-of-interest standards).

19. *See, e.g.*, Durham, *supra* note 6, 279 N.W.2d at 284–85 (suggesting that there would have been no ethics violation had the lawyer's sexual contact with the client occurred while she was meeting her client in a personal rather than a professional capacity); *In re* Bourdon, 565 A.2d 1052, 1057 (N.H. 1989) (suggesting that warning the client of the potential effects that a sexual relationship could have upon her case could have cured the conflict).

Bibliography

Articles

Jeffrey A. Barker, *Professional-Client Sex: Is Criminal Liability an Appropriate Means of Enforcing Professional Responsibility?* 40 UCLA L. Rev. 1275 (1993).

Phyllis Coleman, *Sex in Power Dependency Relationships: Taking Unfair Advantage of the Fair Sex*, 53 Alb. L. Rev. 95, 127 (1988).

Jill M. Crumpacker, *Regulation of Lawyer-Client Sex: Codifying the "Cold Shower" or a "Fatal Attraction" Per Se?* 32 Washburn L.J. 379 (1993).

Anthony E. Davis & Judith Grimaldi, *Sexual Confusion: Attorney-Client Sex and the Need for a Clear Ethical Rule*, 7 Notre Dame J.L. Ethics & Pub. Pol'y 57 (1993).

Lawrence Dubin, *Sex and the Divorce Lawyer: Is the Client Off Limits?* 1 Geo. J. Legal Ethics 585 (1988).

Caroline Forell, *Lawyers, Clients and Sex: Breaking the Silence on the Ethical and Liability Issues*, 22 Golden Gate U. L. Rev. 611 (1992).

Caroline Forell, *Oregon's "Hands-Off" Rule: Ethical and Liability Issues Presented by Attorney-Client Sexual Contact*, 29 Willamette L. Rev. 711 (1993).

Linda Mabus Jorgenson & Pamela K. Sutherland, *Fiduciary Theory Applied to Personal Dealings: Attorney-Client Sexual Contact*, 45 Ark. L. Rev. 459, 471 (1992).

Margit Livingston, *When Libido Subverts Credo: Regulation of Attorney-Client Sexual Relations*, 62 Fordham L. Rev. 5–63 (1993).

Lyon, *Sexual Exploitation of Divorce Clients: The Lawyer's Prerogative?* 10 Harv. Women's L.J. 159 (1987).

McQueen, Comment, *Regulating Attorney-Client Sex: The Need for an Express Rule*, 29 Gonz. L. Rev. 405 (1993–94).

Dan S. Murrell, J. L. Bernard, Lisa K. Coleman, Deborah L. O'Laughlin & Robert B. Gaia, *Loose Canons—A National Survey of Attorney-Client Sexual Involvement: Are There Ethical Concerns?* 23 Mem. St. U. L. Rev. 483 (1993).

John M. O'Connell, Note, *Keeping Sex Out of the Attorney-Client Relationship: A Proposed Rule*, 92 Colum. L. Rev. 887 (1992).

Robert M. Muriel, Note, *Suppressed v. Suppressed: A Court's Refusal to Remedy the Legal Profession's "Dirty Little Secret," Attorney-Client Sexual Exploitation*, 23 Loy. U. Chi. L.J. 309 (1992)

Cases

Barbara A. v. John G., 145 Cal. App. 3d 369, 193 Cal. Rptr. 422 (1983).

Committee on Professional and Ethics and Conduct of the Iowa State Bar Association v. Durham, 279 N.W.2d 280 (Iowa 1979).

Committee on Professional and Ethics and Conduct of the Iowa State Bar Association v. Hill, 436 N.W.2d 57 (Iowa 1989).

Committee on Professional and Ethics and Conduct of the Iowa State Bar Association v. Durham, 279 N.W.2d 280 (Iowa 1979).

In re Bergren, 455 N.W.2d 856 (S.D. 1990).

In re Bourdon, 565 A.2d 1052 (N.H. 1989).

In re Bowen, 542 N.Y.S.2d 45 (1989).

In re Drucker, 577 A.2d 1198 (N.H. 1990).

In re Gibson, 369 N.W.2d 695 (Wis. 1985).

In re Howard, 681 P.2d 775 (Or. 1984).

In re Lewis, 415 S.E.2d 173 (Ga. 1992).

In re Liebowitz, 516 A.2d 246 (N.J. 1985).

In re Littleton, 719 S.W.2d 772 (Mo. 1986).

In re Ridgeway, 462 N.W.2d 671 (Wis. 1990).

In re Rudnick, 581 N.Y.S.2d 206 (1992).

In re Stanton, 708 P.2d 325 (N.M. 1985).

In re the Marriage of Kantar, 581 N.E.2d 6 (Ill. App. Ct. 1991).

In re Wells, 572 N.E.2d 1290 (Ind. 1991).

In re Wolf, 826 P.2d 628 (Or. 1992).

In re Wood, 358 N.E.2d 128 (Ind. 1976).

In re Wood, 489 N.E.2d 1189 (Ind. 1986).

In re Woodmansee, 434 N.W.2d 94 (Wis. 1989).

McDaniel v. Gile, 230 Cal. 3d 363, 281 Cal. Rptr. 242 (Ct. App. 1991).

Office of Disciplinary Counsel v. Paxton, 610 N.E.2d 979 (Ohio 1993).

Oklahoma ex. rel. Oklahoma Bar Ass'n v. Sopher, 852 P.2d 707 (Okl. 1993).

People v. Crossman, 850 P.2d 708 (Colo. 1993).

People v. Gibbons, 685 P.2d 168 (Colo. 1984).

People v. Zeilinger, 814 P. 2d 808 (Colo. 1991).

State v. Heilprin, 207 N.W.2d 878 (Wis. 1973).

Suppressed v. Suppressed, 565 N.E.2d 101 (Ill. App. Ct. 1990).

United States v. Babbitt, 22 M.J. 672 (ACMR 1986).

Ethics Opinions

ABA Committee on Ethics and Professional Responsibility, Formal Opinion 92-364 (July 6, 1992).

Committee on Ethics of the Maryland State Bar Association, Opinion 84-9 (1983).

Ethics Committee of the Alaska Bar Association, Opinion 88-1 (1988).

Ethics Committee of the Alaska Bar Association, Opinion 92-6 (1992).

Legal Ethics Committee of the Oregon State Bar, Opinion 475 (1982).

Legal Ethics Committee of the Oregon State Bar, Opinion 1991-99 (1991).

Standing Committee on Professional Responsibility and Conduct of the State Bar of California, Opinion 1987-92 (1987).

PART IV

Providing Defense Services

Most criminal defense lawyers, especially public defenders and assigned lawyers, find themselves at a serious disadvantage when preparing the defense of a criminal case. Few defense lawyers can match resources with the prosecution. The defense lawyer's limited access to investigative assistance and expert witnesses is exacerbated by the fact that the lawyer is attempting to construct a defense days, weeks, or even years after the events leading to a criminal charge have occurred. The defense lawyer's ability to investigate and prepare a defense is also hampered by the reluctance of many witnesses to cooperate with the defense. It is not surprising, then, that criminal defense lawyers and their investigators find that their efforts to persuade and cajole reluctant or belligerent witnesses to cooperate may put them in an ethically vulnerable position.

In Chapter 22, Robert Baum explores one aspect of the problem of dealing with witnesses—the extent to which witnesses can be compensated. As Baum makes clear, certain payments to lay witnesses or experts are improper. But Chapter 22 also delineates the types of payments the defense lawyer can safely make.

In the book's final chapter, Chapter 23, Edward Monahan tackles a different kind of resource problem—the public defender or public defender program with a staggering caseload. Monahan's discussion of this crucial issue also highlights one of the underlying themes of this book: A criminal defense lawyer who believes she is confronting an ethical problem must first determine if the problem can be resolved by modifying some aspect of her own behavior. It may be appropriate then for the lawyer to look to one's colleagues and supervisors for assistance before deciding whether to involve a client or the court. Finally, Monahan points out, as others have done throughout this book, that a public defender ultimately may discover that there is no viable way out of an ethical bind. Thus, the defender facing an ethical impasse may be compelled to make a hard moral choice with direct personal consequences for the defender. In the end, hard choices demand lawyers with courage and commitment.

CHAPTER 📖 22

Compensating Defense Witnesses

Robert M. Baum

Is it ethically proper for a public defender or a public defender agency to compensate a lay witness or to advance funds to cover expenses incurred by a lay witness? Is it ethically proper for a public defender or a public defender agency to compensate an expert witness or to retain an expert witness on a contingent basis?

Payments to Lay Witnesses

Witnesses play an essential role at trials. To state the obvious, live evidence is the critical determinant in the fact-finding process. Witnesses breathe life into the evidence and their testimony usually is the effective cause of the court's verdict. Yet, witnesses are often unpredictable and, at least occasionally, malleable and corruptible. Because of the importance of witnesses in a trial's search for truth and because of human susceptibility to corruption, courts, legislative bodies, and ethicists universally condemn compensation to lay witnesses. Unlike many rules that are vague or subject to qualification and interpretation, the prohibition against compensating lay witnesses unqualifiedly and flatly interdicts all payments except statutory witness fees and the reimbursement of actual expenses. Plainly put, a lay witness may not be hired to tell the truth. *In re O'Keffe*, 142 P. 638, 641 (Mont. 1914). As a New York court explained over eighty years ago, "... payment to [induce] a witness to testify in a particular way ... payment to prevent a witness' attendance ... [and] payment to make him 'sympathetic' ... are payments which are absolutely indefensible." *In re Robinson*, 151 A.D. 584, 600 (1st Dept.), *aff'd*, 209 N.Y. 354, 103 N.E. 160 (1912).

In keeping with the foregoing policy considerations, the ABA
Model Code of Professional Responsibility (1969 as amended) (hereinafter Model Code) and the ABA Model Rules of Professional Conduct (1992) (hereinafter Model Rules) instruct against compensating
lay witness. DR-7-109(C) of the Model Code provides that:

> A lawyer shall not pay, offer to pay, or acquiesce in the payment
> of compensation to a witness contingent upon the content of his or
> her testimony or the outcome of the case. But a lawyer may ad-
> vance, guarantee, or acquiesce in the payment of: 1. Expenses rea-
> sonably incurred by a witness in attending or testifying; 2.
> Reasonable compensation to a witness for the loss of time in at-
> tending or testifying.

Model Rule 3.4(b) contains a similar prohibition: "A lawyer shall
not . . . offer an inducement to a witness that is prohibited by law." In
addition to the Model Code and the Model Rules, the ABA Standards
for Criminal Justice (3d ed. 1993) (hereinafter ABA Standards) and the
American Trial Lawyers Association Draft of *The American Lawyer's
Code of Conduct* (1980) (hereinafter ATLA Code)[1] echo the injunction
against remuneration of fact witnesses. A useful restatement of the
ethical prohibition and its rationale is found in the Commentary to
Standard 4-4.3 of the ABA Standards:[2]

> Because of the risk of encouraging perjury, or appearing to do so,
> witnesses may not be compensated by the parties for their testi-
> mony, though they may be paid ordinary witness fees. However,
> it is well accepted that the prohibition against paying for testi-
> mony does not forbid reimbursement of witnesses for their actual
> expenses and reasonable payment for loss of income.

Since, at a minimum, compensation is an invitation to perjury, the
ethical codes and the judicial authorities make it black letter clear that
any payment to a lay witness, except for statutory fees, expenses, and
demonstrable financial loss proximately caused by testifying, is per se
forbidden. *In re O'Keefe*, 142 P. 641 (Mont. 1914); *In re Howard*, 372
N.E.2d 371 (Ill. 1977); *In re Robinson*, 136 N.Y.S. 548, *aff'd*, 209 N.Y. 354,
103 N.E. 160 (1913); *see also Annotated Model Rules of Professional Conduct*, Offering an Illegal Inducement to a Witness, 356 (2d ed. 1992).
Even the sacrifice of truth does not justify a relaxation of the prohibition. *In re Howard, supra*; G.C. Hazard & W.W. Hodes, *The Law of Lawyering*, 376 (2d ed. 1990). And, not surprisingly, neither the mechanism

of a loan nor de minimis consideration evade the reach of the rule. *Matter of Shamy*, 282 A.2d 401 (N.J. 1971) (prohibiting a loan to a witness); *Matter of Simmons*, 757 P.2d 519 (Wash. 1988) (finding that giving two bottles of whisky to adverse witness compromises the administration of justice).

In addition to the ethical prohibitions, compensating a lay witness could trigger charges under state bribery, subornation of perjury, or obstruction of justice statutes. Since payments to lay witnesses are forbidden by the criminal law in every jurisdiction, no comfort can be drawn from the Model Rules provision that forbids only inducements that are "prohibited by law." *See, e.g.,* 12 *Am Jur 2d*, Bribery §§ 4, 5, 8, 12; *Am Jur 2d*, Obstruction of Justice § 13; G.C. Hazard & W.W. Hodes, *supra*, 376.

It is interesting to note that the realm of ethics and the underlying law are not evenhanded in allowing prosecutors to influence witnesses by accepting lesser pleas, recommending leniency, granting witness protection, providing immunity, and even making naked cash payments. Ethicists and judges who condemn nominal remuneration to a defense witness, turn a blind eye to these much greater inducements routinely furnished by the government. M. H. Freedman, *Lawyers' Ethics in an Adversary System*, 88–89 (1975); C.W. Wolfram, *Modern Legal Ethics*, 651 (1986). Indeed, payments to witnesses of several thousands of dollars by prosecutors have been judicially approved. For example, in *United States v. Gray*, 626 F.2d 494 (5th Cir. 1980), *cert. denied*, 449 U.S. 1091 (1981), the Court found payments of $37,000 and $25,000 to cooperating witnesses were not inappropriate.

Despite the unanimous hostility to lay witness compensation, all authorities agree that it is permissible to reimburse a fact witness for actual and reasonable expenses incurred. The Model Rules and the commentary to the ABA Standards extend reimbursement to expenses for attendance at depositions and pretrial interviews. It is reasonable to assume that the broad language of the Model Code, Model Rules, and ATLA Code also embraces expenses related to attendance for pretrial discovery and interviews. Also, advancing expenses prior to a witness's appearance is permitted specifically by the Model Code and is approved implicitly by the Model Rules.[3]

The Model Code, ABA Standards, and ATLA Code also allow reimbursement for "loss of time," "loss of income," and "reasonable financial losses," respectively. These varying formulations are intended to keep the witness whole with respect to workplace losses occasioned by testifying, in addition to out-of-pocket expenditures. It is not clear, however, whether "loss of time," "loss of income," or "reasonable financial loss" cover the following hypotheticals:

1. The witness's salary is not affected by absence, i.e., her employer does not charge her salary for absence from work occasioned by her testimony.
2. The witness's salary is not affected, but she is charged for vacation time.
3. The witness is self-employed and tracing financial loss is difficult.

There is no bright-line rule to resolve the above examples. On one hand, it can be asserted that, since expenses were not actually incurred, reimbursement is disguised compensation. On the other hand, it can be urged with equal force that such payments constitute reimbursement consistent with traditional formulations of the collateral source rule in civil damage awards. The collateral source rule permits recovery for loss of income even though a claimant did not incur real out-of-pocket diminution of income. *See, e.g.,* Mincer, Nates, Kimball, Axelrod and Goldstein, *Damages in Tort Actions,* (1993).

In the above hypotheticals, then, defense counsel is unlikely to risk disciplinary action or sanctions for providing defense witnesses a reasonable reimbursement for their time. The Model Code, ABA Standards, and ATLA Code explicitly require, however, that the expenses be reasonable. Here too, there is little guidance beyond common sense as may be affected by community standards and a judge's notion of fairness. Thus, while more expensive options are not automatically foreclosed (e.g., limousine vs. public transportation, luxury vs. standard hotel, first class vs. coach air travel), more costly alternatives naturally attract attention and may increase susceptibility to attack. For most public defender programs, tight budgets and the desire to treat similarly situated defense witnesses evenhandedly—not ethical prohibitions—restrict a defender's ability to reimburse the reasonable expenses of defense witnesses.

Expert Witnesses

Philosophically, the policy against compensating witnesses to avoid the appearance of bribery should apply equally to expert witnesses. Like all witnesses, experts are bound to tell the truth and "should be free from financial inducements that might tempt them to do otherwise." Model Code, Ethical Consideration EC-7-28. However, ethicists and lawmakers recognize that to require professionals to testify for free is hopelessly Utopian. Thus, in acknowledgment of these real work practicalities, the ethical rules and the substantive law permit litigants to pay expert witnesses. However, the license to compensate experts is not unbridled. Obviously, the expert's fee must be reasonable. An excessive fee, like compensation to a fact witness, gives rise to the appearance of payment for tainted testimony. Wolfram, *Modern Legal Ethics* § 12.4.6 (1986).

In line with this rule of moderation, the Model Code expressly limits payment for opinion evidence to "a reasonable fee for the professional services of an expert witness." DR 7-109(C)3.[4] Though the divide between reasonable and excessive compensation, like the distinction between reasonable and excessive expenses, cannot be calibrated precisely, defense counsel must reckon with the reality of the limitation. Adhering to prevailing hourly compensation standards for the area of expertise involved, together with documentation of the hours expended by the expert, should provide a practical safe harbor.

Making an expert witness a stakeholder in the litigation by keying her fee to the substance of her testimony or the result of the lawsuit is viewed as a potential corruption of her integrity. Thus, in line with the policy of avoiding the temptation of witnesses, the Model Code precludes expert compensation that is "contingent upon the content of his or her testimony or the outcome of the case." DR 7-109. Similarly, the commentary to the Model Rules leaves little doubt that conditional fees to experts are ethically and legally disfavored, if not foreclosed: "[t]he common law rule in most jurisdictions is that it is improper . . . to pay an expert witness a contingent fee." MODEL RULES, Comment to Rule 3.4.[5] The ATLA Code stands alone in not explicitly proscribing contingent fees to experts. ATLA CODE, Rule 3.1. The ambiguous silence of the ATLA Code aside, the overwhelming weight of authority prohibits content based or result-oriented compensation to expert witnesses. *See, e.g.,* J.M. Burkoff, *Criminal Defense Ethics and Liability,* § 9.3(a) n.74.

To complete the circle, it should be noted that the wisdom of prohibiting contingent fees has been questioned since, like lawyers' contingent fees in civil cases, contingent compensation of experts would better advance the interest of litigants of modest means. J.M. Burkoff, *supra,* § 9.24 (1990); Wolfram, *supra,* § 17.4.6. Despite the persuasive argument that the rule against contingent fees to experts does more harm than good, such fees are beyond the ethical pale. Burkoff, *supra,* § 9.3(b)(2). The legality of the restriction against contingent compensation of experts was laid to rest in New York in a case that attacked the constitutionality of DR-7-109(C) on the grounds that the prohibition irrationally disfavors indigent litigants in contravention of the Fourteenth Amendment to the U.S. Constitution. In reversing the trial court, the Second Circuit held that DR 7-109(C) was a permissible regulation of the legal profession. *Person v. Association of the Bar of New York,* 554 F.2d 534 (2d Cir.), *cert. denied,* 434 U.S. (1977).

Notes

1. While the ATLA Code has not been adopted in a single jurisdiction it may have persuasive value in clarifying, extending, or interpreting the Model Code or Model Rules. The persuasive value of the ATLA Code is probably enhanced because it was commissioned to express the dissatisfaction of a significant segment of the trial bar with the Model Code and Model Rules. The ATLA Code formulation of this rule is: "A lawyer shall not give a witness money or anything of substantial value, or threaten a witness with harm, in order to induce the witness to testify or dissuade the witness from testifying. However, a lawyer may pay a fee to an expert witness; a lawyer may reimburse a witness' actual, reasonable financial losses and expenses of appearing; a lawyer may give a witness protection against physical harm; and a prosecutor may immunize a witness from prosecution in order to avoid an assertion of the constitutional privilege against self-incrimination." *See also* ABA STANDARDS FOR CRIMINAL JUSTICE, DEFENSE FUNCTION, 4-4.3(b) (3d ed. 1993).

2. The parallel formulation in the Model Code provides: "Witnesses should always testify truthfully and should be free from any financial inducements that might tempt them to do otherwise. A lawyer should not pay or agree to pay a non-expert witness an amount in excess of reimbursement for expenses and financial loss incident to being a witness; however, a lawyer may pay or agree to pay an expert witness a reasonable fee for services as an expert. But in no event should a lawyer pay or agree to pay a contingent fee to any witness. A lawyer should exercise reasonable diligence to see that the client and lay associates conform to their standards." EC 7-28.

3. The broad language of the ATLA Code and the ABA Standards also suggest that advances are appropriate.

4. So, too, the commentary to the Model Code provides that an expert's compensation may not exceed "terms permitted by law." Comment to Model Rule 3.4 and the ATLA Code approves of "a fee to an expert."

5. The commentary to Standard 4-4.4 of the ABA Standards also admonishes the avoidance of contingent and excessive compensation to experts: "[I]t is important that the fee paid to an expert not serve to influence the substance of the expert's testimony. To avoid both the existence and the appearance of influence, the fee should not be made contingent on a favorable opinion or result in the case, and the amount of the fee should be reasonable."

Bibliography

Books and Standards

ABA MODEL CODE OF PROFESSIONAL RESPONSIBILITY (1969 as amended), DR-7-109(C), DR 7-109(C)(3), DR 7-109, EC-7-28.

ABA MODEL RULES OF PROFESSIONAL CONDUCT, Rule 3.4(b), (1983).

ABA STANDARDS FOR CRIMINAL JUSTICE, 4-4.3(b), 4-4.4 (3d ed. 1993).

AMERICAN TRIAL LAWYER'S CODE OF CONDUCT, Rule 3.1 (1980).

ANNOTATED RULES OF PROFESSIONAL CONDUCT (2d ed. 1992).

John M. Burkoff, *Criminal Defense Ethics and Liability*, (1990).

Geoffrey C. Hazard & William W. Hodes, *The Law of Lawyering*, (2d ed. 1990).

Mincer, Nates, Kimball, Axelrod and Goldstein, *Damages in Tort Actions*, (1993).

Monroe H. Freedman, *Lawyer's Ethics in an Adversary System*, (1975).

Charles W. Wolfram, *Modern Legal Ethics*, (1986).

12 *Am. Jur. 2d*, Bribery § 4, 5, 8, 12; Obstruction of Justice § 13.

Cases

In re Howard, 372 N.E.2d 371 (Ill. 1977).

In re O'Keffe, 142 P. 638 (Mont. 1914).

In re Robinson, 151 A.D. 584, 600 (1st Dept.), *aff'd*, 209 N.Y. 354, 103 N.E. 160 (1912).

In re Robinson, 136 N.Y.S. 548, *aff'd*, 209 N.Y. 354, 103 N.E. 160 (1913).

In the Matter of Shamy, 282 A.2d 401 (N.J. 1971).

In the Matter of Simmons, 757 P.2d 519 (Wash. 1988).

Person v. Association of the Bar of New York, 554 F.2d 534 (2d Cir.), *cert. denied*, 434 U.S. (1977).

United States v. Grey, 626 F.2d 494 (5th Cir. 1980), *cert. denied*, 449 U.S. 1091 (1981).

CHAPTER 📖 23

Coping with Excessive Workload

Edward C. Monahan and James Clark

What must a full-time public defender or appointed counsel do if the defender believes that she cannot competently handle any larger workload if assigned more cases or other work by a supervisor or if appointed to cases by a judge? What must a defender do if she has more work than she can handle in a competent, quality manner? What must a public defender supervisor do when a subordinate lawyer refuses additional cases or other work because of an inability to do any additional work competently? If there is disagreement between the supervisor and subordinate about the ability of the subordinate to assume additional work, how is that difference of opinion resolved? Who, the supervisor or subordinate, is responsible if incompetent representation by the subordinate is afforded a client because of too large of a workload? What must the chief defender do with additional cases coming into the office if the defender's staff cannot handle additional work in a competent, quality manner?

Work, Not Cases

Every person representing indigents accused or convicted of a crime eventually confronts the harsh reality of whether competent representation is provided given the number of clients, the demands of the cases, and the necessity of other work. The core of this perennial defender issue centers on the point at which a lawyer's *workload* exceeds ethical limits. It would be naive to translate this issue into the question, "When does a lawyer's *caseload* exceed ethical limits?" The ethical lawyer has work beyond cases. To limit the question to caseloads is to ignore the full reality of legal representation of indigent criminal defendants at a professional level.

A defender's work includes more than her cases. She must consult with others about her cases, engage in review processes to assure quality of her cases, and handle other work, for example, brainstorming, case or peer review, mock presentations, post-case critiques, and performance evaluations. An ethical defender maintains and advances her knowledge by reading newly decided cases and newly enacted laws and rules, and by attending training sessions. She must support others in her office by doing case consultation for colleagues. Defenders must perform administrative and office duties. She must supervise support staff to ensure that their work is at the requisite standard.[1]

Principles, Standards, Case Law, and Capacity for Work

To determine what a defender must do about excessive workload, it is necessary to answer three questions: (1) What ethical principles and benchmark standards must a lawyer meet? (2) How does a lawyer meet those principles and standards in criminal cases? (3) What influences a lawyer's capacity to perform assigned work effectively? A look at these three areas provides the basis for analysis and conclusions.

ABA Ethical Principles and ABA Standards

The ABA has pronounced substantial ethical commands in its previous Model Code of Professional Responsibility (1969) and its current Model Rules of Professional Conduct (1983), and has significant standards in its current Standards for Criminal Justice on the duties of lawyers in the representation of a criminal client, the standard of representation, and the limitations of workload. These principles and standards reveal the responsibilities of a lawyer who assigns work as a supervisor or who faces excessive work as a subordinate.

THE ETHICAL MINIMUM IS COMPETENT LEGAL REPRESENTATION. Competence and our understanding of its meaning has evolved as an ethical standard for legal representation of the client. Its evolution continues. For some time, many courts have viewed competence as coextensive with legal representation.[2] The legal profession was much slower to recognize and impose competence as an ethical command. The ABA Canons of Professional Ethics (1908) did not detail competence as an ethical requirement. This absence led various authorities to conclude that competence was not an ethical mandate for a lawyer.[3] Such superficial thinking has been supplanted.

The ABA Model Code established a duty of competence. While stated positively as Canon 6, "[a] lawyer should represent a client competently," the duty of competence was unfortunately stated in the negative in the mandatory disciplinary portion of the Model Code. Disciplinary Rule 6-101(A)(1), "Failing to Act Competently," prohibited a lawyer from doing work on a matter "which he knows or should know that he is not competent to handle, without associating himself with a lawyer who is competent to handle it." The defining of competence in the Model Code was minimal. Disciplinary Rule 6-101(A)(2) required "preparation adequate in the circumstances." DR 6-101(A)(3) prohibited "neglect" of a legal matter.

The ABA Model Rules affirmatively identified competence as the mandatory standard of professional duty to a client and embarked on a more deliberate definition of its dimensions. Model Rule 1.1, the *first* ethical rule, states, "[a] lawyer shall provide competent representation to a client." Model Rule 1.3 requires that a lawyer "act with reasonable diligence and promptness." Model Rule 1.4 mandates that a lawyer communicate promptly and effectively with her clients.

THE NATIONAL PROFESSIONAL BENCHMARK IS QUALITY LEGAL REPRESENTATION. Both the ABA Standards for Criminal Justice, *Providing Defense Services* (3d ed. 1992) and *The Defense Function* (3d ed. 1993) set quality legal representation as the national benchmark for criminal defense lawyers. Standard 4-1.2, "The Function of Defense Counsel," declares that "[t]he basic duty defense counsel owes to the administration of justice and as an officer of the court is to . . . render effective, quality representation." Standard 5-1.1 echoes the principle that "[t]he objective in providing counsel should be to assure that quality legal representation is afforded. . . . "

The Dimensions of Competence and Quality
for Criminal Defense Lawyers

Both the 1983 Model Rules and the latest ABA Criminal Justice Standards go far in explaining what competence[4] and quality[5] entail for lawyers generally and for criminal defense lawyers specifically. The magnitude of the duties necessary for competent, quality representation of a criminal defendant is prodigious. The breadth of the responsibilities as defined in the Model Rules and the ABA Standards include the following eleven substantial areas.[6]

LEGAL KNOWLEDGE AND SKILL. Model Rule 1.1 defines competence as requiring "the legal knowledge, skill, thoroughness and preparation reasonably necessary for representation." The comment[7] to the Model Rule expands on this definition. Every legal problem, according to the Comment to Model Rule 1.1, involves certain significant legal skills such as "analysis of precedent, the evaluation of evidence and legal drafting." However, the most fundamental legal skill is identified as "determining what kind of legal problems a situation may involve."

According to the Comment to Model Rule 1.1, factors determining whether a lawyer has the necessary legal knowledge and skill include the relative complexity of the matter; the specialized nature of the matter; the general experience of the lawyer; the training and experience of the lawyer in the area; the preparation and study the lawyer can give the problem; and the ability to obtain the assistance of a lawyer who is knowledgeable and skilled in the area.

Inexperience is not a defense to incompetence. *In re Deardorff*, 426 P.2d 689, 692 (Col. 1981). Being too busy with cases is not an acceptable excuse to avoid discipline for lack of knowledge of the law. *Nebraska State Bar Association v. Holscher*, 230 N.W.2d 75, 80 (Neb. 1975).

TIMELINESS OF REPRESENTATION. Attorneys must act promptly to protect the rights of the accused, including informing the client of those rights, seeking pretrial release, obtaining mental health assistance, requesting a different venue, seeking a continuance, moving to suppress illegal evidence, asking for severance of counts or defendants, and requesting dismissal. *See* ABA STANDARD 4-3.6, "Prompt Action to Protect the Accused"; ABA STANDARD 4-1.3, "Delays; Punctuality; Workload"; MODEL RULE 1.3, "Diligence"; MODEL RULE 3.2, "Expediting Litigation."

THOROUGHNESS AND PREPARATION. In explaining this dimension of competence, the Comment to Model Rule 1.1 sets out the following aspects included in this concept: (1) inquiry into the legal and factual elements of the problem; (2) analysis of the legal and factual elements of the problem; (3) adequate attention and preparation; (4) the attention and preparation necessary are partly determined by "what is at stake"; the greater the complexity or consequences, the greater the attention and preparation needed; and (5) use of methods and procedures which meet "the standards of competent practitioners."

For proper preparation, a lawyer must conduct basic research to discover readily ascertainable law, *Baird v. Pace*, 752 P.2d 507 (Ariz. App. 1988), or risk disbarment. *State ex rel Oklahoma Bar Ass'n v. Hensley*, 661 P.2d 527 (Okl. 1983). Ignorance of the "rules of procedure, constitutional law, the relationship between state and federal proceedings, and federal rules of evidence" caused the suspension of a lawyer handling a criminal case in federal court. *Matter of Dempsey*, 632 F. Supp. 908 (N.D. Cal. 1986).

CLIENT RELATIONSHIP AND INTERVIEWING. Attorneys are not technicians. Rather, a lawyer must seek to develop a relationship with the client. The relationship should be characterized by honesty, trust, and confidence. Axiomatically, a relationship of honesty, trust, and confidence necessarily involves a commitment of time. An initial interview of the accused should take place as soon as possible. Defense counsel must discuss the objectives of the lawyer's representation, explain the meaning of confidentiality, and "probe for all legally relevant information" known to the accused. *See* ABA STANDARD 4-3.1, "Establishment of Relationship"; ABA STANDARD 4-3.2, "Interviewing the Client."

Unfortunately, client interviewing and client relationship are frequently dealt with inadequately by the overworked defender. Defenders who have too much to do are unable to spend sufficient time with their clients to obtain all necessary information in a timely manner, much less develop the honesty, trust, and confidence that is essential to an effective working relationship.[8]

COMMUNICATING WITH THE ACCUSED. No relationship is successful without communication. The lawyer is required to communicate with the client, informing him about "developments in the case"; advising him about "the progress of preparing the defense"; explaining matters so that he can "make informed decisions regarding the representation"; and "promptly comply[ing] with reasonable requests for information from the client." *See* ABA STANDARD 4-3.8, "Duty to Keep Client Informed"; MODEL RULE 1.1, "Communication."

"The overloaded defender frequently is placed in the situation where there is insufficient time to properly communicate with clients."[9] But too much work is not an acceptable excuse for a failure to communicate. Effective performance or an excellent outcome do not excuse inadequate communication. A lawyer who failed to adequately communicate with his client was disciplined by the Nevada Supreme Court with the court observing, "[i]t cannot be overemphasized that communication with a client is, in many respects, at the center of all services. The failure to communicate creates the impression of a 'neglectful' attorney and leads to client discontent, even if the case is competently and expeditiously handled." *State Bar v. Schreiber*, 653 P.2d 151 (Nev. 1982).

Jonathan Casper, in his empirical study *Criminal Courts: The Defendant's Perspective* (1978), found that defendants represented by public defenders fared no worse than defendants represented by retained counsel in terms of sentences imposed. Nonetheless, the defendants had a significantly lower opinion of the service provided by their public defender. Casper found that defenders spent appreciably less time consulting with their clients. Casper, therefore, concluded that many clients' poor opinion of their public defender is caused by defenders' failure to spend time interviewing and consulting with their clients.

ADVISING THE ACCUSED. Once counsel obtains the facts, understands the applicable law, and interviews the client, she must advise the accused "with complete candor concerning all aspects of the case, including a candid estimate of the probable outcome." ABA STANDARD 4-5.1. That candid assessment must include the risks, hazards, and prospects of the case. Moreover, the defender must advise in such a way that ensures that *the client* makes the decision. Also, the lawyer must caution the accused to avoid communication with witnesses, jurors, family, friends, or cellmates.

When a case warrants, a lawyer must explore alternative resolutions. Plea discussions with the prosecutor must be promptly communicated and explained to the accused. *See* ABA STANDARD 4-6.1, "Duty to Explore Disposition without Trial"; ABA STANDARD 4-6.2, "Plea Discussions."

INVESTIGATION. Prompt, thorough, focused investigation is essential to competent, quality representation. There must be an investigation into all facts relevant to the merits of the case and to possible penalties. The defender must look to all available sources, including the client, the police, and the prosecution. Lack of time or investigative staff does not excuse a defender's failure to conduct an adequate investigation. Many defenders labor in programs without adequate investigative staff. Defenders often do their own investigation. In such cases, interviews of witnesses should take place in the presence of another defender or a member of the defender's staff to allow effective impeachment. "The duty to investigate exists regardless of the accused's admissions or statements to defense counsel of facts constituting guilt or the accused's stated desire to plead guilty." *See* ABA STANDARD 4-4.1, "Duty to Investigate."

"Under no circumstances should defense counsel recommend to a defendant acceptance of a plea unless appropriate investigation and study of the case has been completed, including an analysis of controlling law and the evidence likely to be introduced at trial." *See* ABA STANDARD 4-6.1, "Duty to Explore Disposition without Trial."

In *Collins on Behalf of Collins v. Perrine*, 778 P.2d 912 (N.M. App. 1989), the Court upheld a $2,958,789 award in a legal malpractice case where the lawyer negligently prepared the medical malpractice case and recommended settlement. The lawyer did not do the minimum level of discovery required in this complex case.

The U.S. Supreme Court has not hesitated to find a constitutional violation when a lawyer failed to request discovery to learn about information actually or constructively possessed by the prosecutor. Such a discovery request would have revealed inculpatory evidence that would have necessitated a suppression motion. *Kimmelman v. Morrison*, 477 U.S. 365, 368–69, 385 (1986).

The less significant the charges, the more likely it is for a defender to ignore the duty to adequately investigate the case. The overworked defender often rationalizes waiver of the necessary investigation by claiming it is a logical causality of triage. Too often defenders efficiently lead clients to take the deal rather than delay disposition pending full investigation. The defender is able to live with herself because she's merely doing what the client wants or demands. Unfortunately for both the client and the defender, these rationalizations cheat the client.

A lawyer with three years experience joined the Wisconsin public defender staff and was assigned a complex homicide case the first day on the job. The case was tried and the client was convicted of second degree murder of her husband. The case was reversed because the new defender was ignorant of the defense of sudden heat of passion. The defender never educated his expert on that defense or the defense of insanity. The defender initially entered a plea of insanity and then withdrew it without discussion of the legal consequences with his client. The court in *State v. Felton*, 329 N.W.2d 161 (Wis. 1983) determined that the defender was ineffective for failing to inform himself of the law, to adequately advise his client on the defenses, and to adequately investigate the case through his expert and the state's expert as required under ABA Standard 4.1, 5.1(a), and 5.2. The novice defender recognized his probable incompetence to handle a case of this significance, and he "attempted to get experienced private counsel appointed, but his superiors encouraged him to undertake the defense. The administrators of the public defender's program provided him with the assistance of a more experienced attorney; but according to the trial attorney, he had only limited opportunity to consult with that attorney until just before the time of trial." *Id.* at 166.

When an inexperienced lawyer is not competent to handle a serious criminal case, does not seek help from a competent lawyer, and does little investigation, research, or preparation, substantial ethical sanctions are appropriate. *See, e.g., Office of Disciplinary Counsel v. Henry,* 664 S.W.2d 62 (Tn. 1983). Moreover, as the concurrence in Felton warns, defender supervisors also must ensure that cases are assigned with care to lawyers capable of handling them. *Felton,* 329 N.W.2d at 177.

TRIAL COURT REPRESENTATION. Much is required of the defender when the case proceeds to trial. Preparation must be conducted to select and challenge jurors effectively. Effective opening statements, cross-examinations, direct examinations, and closings must be given, and appropriate jury instructions be offered. A competent defender must make and respond to prosecution objections promptly and effectively. No lawyer will be effective without an adequate understanding of the rules of evidence and the relevant case law interpreting those rules and any constitutional dimensions. *See* ABA STANDARDS 4-7.1 through 4-7.9.

SENTENCING. Defense counsel must be familiar with and consider all sentencing alternatives that would be appropriate in a given case. The lawyer must understand parole consequences and other practical or collateral consequences of a sentence and explain these to the client. The judge's sentencing practices must be discussed with the client. The lawyer is required to present any facts or legal grounds to the sentencers to urge the most favorable disposition for the defendant. *See* ABA STANDARD 4-8.1, "Sentencing."

Attorneys must be present at presentence investigation interviews conducted by probation and parole officers to ensure the convicted client is fully advised at this critical stage of the proceedings.[10] Lawyers should verify information in the presentence report and supplement the report when this in the interest of the defendant. Appropriate post-trial motions must be factually investigated, legally researched, and presented when in the convicted defendant's interest. *See* ABA STANDARD 4-7.9, "Post-Trial Motions."

APPELLATE REPRESENTATION. Trial defense counsel must explain to the convicted client the right to appeal, the consequences of an appeal, the grounds available for appellate review, and the advantages as well as disadvantages of an appeal. Defense counsel must take all steps necessary to ensure perfection of the appeal if the client chooses to challenge the conviction or sentence. *See* ABA STANDARD 4-7.9, "Post-Trial Motions"; ABA STANDARD 4-8.2, "Appeal."

Appellate counsel must read or view the entire appellate record, consider all potential appellate guilt or penalty issues, do appropriate research, and present all pleadings in the interest of the client. ABA STANDARD 4-8.3, "Counsel on Appeal."

MAINTAINING COMPETENCE AND ASSURING QUALITY. Competence and quality require continuous learning. The Comment to Model Rule 1.1 explicitly recognizes a duty to maintain competence, and it provides mandatory and discretionary methods to achieve this maintenance: 1) "A lawyer should engage in continuing study and education," and 2) a lawyer should consider accessing "a system of peer review" in appropriate circumstances.

Although the Comment to Model Rule 1.1 devotes only a single paragraph to the obligation to maintain the requisite level of competence, this duty will increase in a professional environment that is constantly changing.[11] As quality is increasingly defined by the customer, a defender cannot render quality representation without staying abreast of recent developments.

In the information revolution age, the necessity for continuous learning is inescapable. "The 'half-life' of knowledge in any given profession may now be as little as two to three years. The degree, in short, is today the beginning of the education of a professional."[12] To avoid obsolescence the professional must constantly integrate new knowledge and learn new skills.[13] Training for public defenders, as for all lawyers, is essential. Continual training "plays a significant role in supporting and driving a continuous improvement culture."[14] Simply put, professionals who do not regularly enhance their competencies will not have the abilities to provide competent, quality representation for the criminal defendant.[15]

Most states now mandate that lawyers annually participate in continuing legal education programs. Similarly, the ABA recognizes that lawyers representing indigent defendants need specialized training. Thus, ABA Standard 5-1.5, "Training and Professional Development," recommends that all plans or programs providing indigent defense services include "effective training, professional development and continuing education of all counsel and staff . . . [c]ontinuing education programs should be provided to enable all counsel and staff to attend such programs."[16]

Total quality management (TQM) is emerging as a standard management method in law firms and defender offices.[17] "Total quality is a marriage of business strategy and human resource development at the altar of customer satisfaction."[18]

In a TQM defender environment, "staff training must be given the greatest organizational priority. The more staff learns, the better and more efficiently they can perform. Training must be done intensively at all levels of the organization; lawyers, support staff and supervisors must be included. Training! Training! Training!"[19] Quality mandates deliberate employment of quality assurance processes.[20] Quality legal processes include thinking expansively and creatively at the beginning of the case representation process (brainstorming with others);[21] supervisory coaching throughout case representation (pretrial, case review, or peer review);[22] mock practices with feedback; observation in court or during other parts of the case representation with coaching; random case-file review; evaluation by the customers; and performance evaluations.[23]

The Model Rules place substantial responsibility on supervising lawyers to ensure that subordinates comply with all of the Model Rules. MODEL RULE 5.1. A supervisor, therefore, has significant responsibility to have processes in place to enable subordinates to perform competently in all eleven areas discussed above without interfering with the subordinate's ethical duty to provide the client with independent representation. This has momentous consequences for defender offices with their fierce culture of unsupervised representation.

Lisa McIntyre notes that the public defender supervisor plays only a ceremonial role that gives the organization some trappings of bureaucratic structure. This lack of effective supervision has traditionally bolstered important cultural myths in defender organizations: "The myth of competency embraces public defenders the moment they are appointed to the office. Although there is a hierarchical structure in place, it is treated as if for purposes of show only: supervisors are believed to be redundant; public defenders work as a company of equals. Even when supervision or teaching and the like do occur, they are carefully done in a way that nurtures the myth and allows it to go unchallenged."[24] She further suggests that the lack of supervision protects defenders from unethical interference by superiors. Unfortunately this exacts a high price: "[I]n the absence of any meaningful supervisory structure there are no institutional guarantees that public defenders will provide quality representation. . . ."[25]

In *Matter of Yacavino*, 494 A.2d 801 (N.J. 1985), a lawyer became an associate of a firm of twenty lawyers with offices in three cities. In handling cases, this new lawyer was "left virtually alone and unsupervised. . . . The office was lacking in the essential tools of legal practice. Partners rarely attended the office; no member of the firm inquired as to the status of the office matters." *Id.* at 803. In *Yacavino*, the court strongly disapproved of the practice of allowing new lawyers to sink or swim. The court pronounced a need for "collegial support and guidance" by supervisors for subordinates, and a need for "a systematic organized routine for periodic review of a newly admitted attorney's files." *Id.*

These eleven performance areas add up to a substantial volume of duties. They require a demanding level of work for defenders. Too often they are not being performed by the overworked defender.

Capacity for Work

Persons' capacity for work vary. Some workers have the natural or trained strength to lift a certain weight, the capability to engineer certain results, or the ability to serve the needs of numerous clients. A defense lawyer's capacity for work is dependent on several factors, including available staff and resources; personal management skills; personally destructive consequences of excessive work; available work hours; and caseload standards.

AVAILABLE STAFF AND RESOURCES. A lawyer who has the regular assistance of competently performing staff and adequate resources is able to handle substantially more work than one who has inadequate resources and limited staff support. Theoretically, the greater the resources and staff available to and used by a lawyer, the larger the quantity of work the lawyer can handle. For instance, a lawyer who has an investigator to obtain records, to interview witnesses, and to assist in marshaling evidence will be able to achieve more objectives than a lawyer who has no investigative help. Other staff who will influence the amount of work a lawyer can do include legal secretaries, law clerks or paralegals, mental health experts, sentencing specialists, librarians, and supervisors. A lawyer who has efficient access to a library of carefully selected and maintained resources with a professional providing help will be equipped to perform more work than a lawyer who has less access to such information sources. A lawyer who has word processing and computer support will be capable of performing more work.[26]

Effective assistance of counsel means "that the lawyer not only possesses adequate skill and knowledge, but also that he has the time and resources to apply his skill and knowledge to the task of defending each of his individual clients." *State v. Peart,* 621 So. 2d 780, 789 (La. 1993).

PERSONAL MANAGEMENT SKILLS. Today's technology-driven, information-overloaded, complex work environment presents most professionals with a volume of work that is impossible to complete well without effective management of time, people, and most importantly, one's self. Court systems, jails and prisons, probation and parole and clerk's offices are often significant wasters of defender's time. Too often defenders do not use their time well.

A defender who is unable to handle additional work because she manages time,[27] people, or herself poorly cannot continue to refuse additional work without first directly addressing and improving her personal management skills to increase her capacity for work. A lawyer cannot continue inefficient work habits and ethically refuse additional work. A lawyer cannot refuse to delegate appropriate portions of her work to support staff, while refusing to take additional cases.

The fourth generation of time management is upon us. The "essence of effective time and life management is to organize and execute around balanced priorities."[28] As Stephen Covey persuasively argues, "[e]ffective management is putting first things first."[29] Covey identifies four activities that are essential to effective self-management: identifying your key roles; selecting several goals for a week at a time; scheduling to achieve those goals; and adapting on a daily basis.[30] These commonsense habits often are not common practices of defenders.

An unrealistic approach to time-management problems begins early in the careers of most lawyers: "Law school does appear to inoculate in students an expectation that they will lead time-pressured lives regardless of personal and societal costs. . . . [T]he time management issue, as shown by the current study, also affects law students and alumni long after the first year of law school ends. Law school may be training lawyers to contend with the harsh realities of professional practice. Yet excessive workload and time management difficulties appear to set into motion an unfortunate cycle; lawyers may find that too much work and too little time make it difficult to cope with their work (or their lives), which distresses them. This experience of failure and/or hassles leads to even less adequate coping and greater distress.[31]

PERSONALLY DESTRUCTIVE CONSEQUENCES OF EXCESSIVE WORK. Recent empirical studies of career lawyers reveal startling facts. Lawyers suffer depression at a rate of two to four times that of the general population, and significantly higher rates than most other professions. Eighteen percent of lawyers are problem drinkers and the rate of alcohol abuse significantly increases with the number of years of practice, moving to a rate of 25 percent for lawyers practicing more than twenty years. Disturbingly high rates of lawyer experimentation with drugs (especially cocaine) were found.[32] While researchers cannot definitively blame one source for these problems, they claim that while "the deteriorating work environment has not led to a mass exodus from the profession, it has affected the lawyers' quality of work and productivity, their firms, their clients, their satisfaction with the profession, and their families."[33] When too much work results in lawyer burnout, discipline for neglect of a client is still the consequence. *In re Conduct of Loew*, 642 P.2d 1174 (Or. 1982).

AVAILABLE WORK HOURS. It takes time to perform the many dimensions of competent, quality work. The time available for defenders—and for all lawyers—is limited. Billable hours in private firms range from 1,750 to 1,900 hours, with 45 percent of lawyers in private practice billing 1,920 or more hours per year. Half of private lawyers are working 2,400 hours or more each year.[34]

In *Case Weighing Systems for the Public Defender* (1985), Joan Jacoby defined available hours for work by a full-time employee at 2,080.[35] Subtracting annual, holiday and sick leave, she assumed 1,792 to 1,816 work hours per lawyer per year depending on the level of the lawyer. Supervisors must recognize the outer limits of available lawyer hours.

CASELOAD STANDARDS. "The most widely visible benchmark in the effort to describe maximum caseload limits for a defender staff lawyer are the caseload standards adopted by the National Advisory Commission on Criminal Justice Standards and Goals (NAC) in 1973. The Commission, appointed by the administrator of the Law Enforcement Assistance Administration, was composed of elected officials, law enforcement officers, community leaders, prosecutors, judges, corrections officials, and defenders."[36] The NAC established the following standards:

> The caseload of a public defender office should not exceed the following: felonies per attorney per year: not more than 150; misdemeanors (excluding traffic) per attorney per year: not more than 400; juvenile court cases per attorney per year: not more than 200; Mental Health Act cases per attorney per year: not more than 200; and appeals per attorney per year: not more than 25.[37]

These caseload standards did not include capital cases. NLADA standards for the Appointment and Performance of Counsel in Death Penalty Cases (1988) prohibit counsel from accepting capital workloads that by reason of their excessive size interfere with the rendering of quality representation.

Courts have relied on national caseload standards in determining the competence of the lawyer's performance for all of her clients. *See, e.g., State v. Smith,* 681 P.2d 1374 (Ariz. 1984). "The insidiousness of overburdening defense counsel is that it can result in concealing from the courts, and particularly the appellate courts, the nature and extent of damage that is done to defendants by their attorneys' excessive caseloads." *Id.* at 1381.

Precise caseload standards can be helpful in providing the subordinate lawyer and supervisory lawyer with a national context for evaluating what an individual lawyer can handle under the circumstances of her practice, experience, and capacities. Indeed, some states have proscribed statutory caseload caps for defenders. *See, e.g.,* Sec. 977.08(5)(b), Wisconsin statutes; Sec. 611.215(2)(c)(2), Minnesota statutes.

Caseload standards can only provide a rough measure or context for evaluation since numbers do not offer total insight on quality, the ultimate criteria for defender work.

Assigning or Accepting Excessive Workload Is Legally and Ethically Prohibited

While neither the Model Code nor the Model Rules directly address defender workloads, both effectively prohibit a lawyer from accepting an amount of work that prevents competent representation. Model Rule 6.2, "Accepting Appointments," does not allow a lawyer to take a case if it would likely result in an unreasonable financial burden or would likely cause a violation of any ethical rule. Model Rule 8.3, "Misconduct," identifies a violation of any other ethical rule as professional misconduct. A lawyer who represents another client when she already has more work than she can competently handle violates Model Rule 1.7(b), which commands that "[a] lawyer shall not represent a client if the representation of that client may be materially limited by the lawyer's responsibility to another client or to a third person, or by the lawyer's own interests. . . ." A lawyer who has so much work, so many cases, so many other clients that she is materially limited in her ability to effectively represent another client has an impermissible personal conflict of interest and cannot assume responsibility for an additional client.

These rules clearly establish that a lawyer cannot ethically accept another case or other work when she has so much work that accepting another case will preclude her from competently representing the new client or performing any of the other ethical requirements, for example, communicating fully and promptly with the client, fully and promptly interviewing the client, or investigating the case and adequately advising the client.

The ABA reiterated these ethical principles when formulating the standards for criminal defense work in *The Defense Function*. ABA Standard 4-1.3(e), "Workload," states: "[d]efense counsel should not carry a workload that, by reason of its excessive size, interferes with the rendering of quality representation, endangers the client's interest in the speedy disposition of charges, or may lead to the breach of professional obligations." It is significant that this standard speaks in terms of *workload*, not just *caseload*. This standard applies not only to the individual defense lawyer but also to defense organizations, appointed counsel, and contract counsel. ABA STANDARD 5-5.3, "Workload."

The eleven areas of competent representation cannot be neglected by a defender because she is overworked. Nor can nonperformance in any of these areas be justified by too much work. Failure to keep caseload within manageable limits does not excuse failure to perform ethically. *See, e.g., Matter of Klipstine*, 775 P.2d 247 (N.M. 1989) ("While the members of this Court are well aware of the demands of sole practice, a failure to keep one's caseload within manageable proportions cannot and does not excuse the type of blatant neglect exhibited by Klipstine.").

Within this substantial context, the preeminent defender question—what to do about too much work—can be reliably answered. In theory, the answer is easy: A defender cannot take on more work than can be competently handled. In practice, however, it is difficult to apply this concept to legal work, which has subtle factual nuances entangled with complex and competing principles and standards and which is performed in the real world of power, funding, and politics.

Issue #1: A lawyer must refuse to handle additional cases when unable to do so competently and in a quality manner.

"[T]he duty of loyalty [is] perhaps the most basic of counsel's duties." *Strickland v. Washington*, 466 U.S. 668, 692 (1984). "When faced with a workload that makes it impossible for a lawyer to prepare adequately for cases and to represent clients competently, the staff lawyer should, except in extreme or urgent cases, decline new legal matters and should continue representation in pending matters only to the extent that the duty of competent, nonneglectful representation can be fulfilled." Wisconsin Formal Opinion E-84-11, reaffirmed in Wisconsin Formal Opinion E-91-3.[38] "There can be no question that taking on more work than an attorney can handle adequately is a violation of a lawyer's ethical obligations. . . . No one seriously questions that a lawyer's staggering caseloads can result in a breach of the lawyer's duty of competence." Arizona Opinion 90-10.

There are practical reasons to avoid excessive workloads. "As licensed professionals, attorneys are expected to develop procedures which are adequate to assume that they will handle their cases in a proficient fashion and that they will not accept more cases than they can manage effectively. When an attorney fails to do this, he or she may be disciplined even where there is no showing of malicious intent or dishonesty. The purpose of attorney discipline is not to punish the attorney but to ensure that members of the public can safely assume that the attorney to whom they entrust their cases is worthy of that trust." *In re Martinez*, 717 P.2d 1121, 1122 (1986). The fact that the unethical conduct was a prevalent or customary practice among other lawyers is not sufficient to excuse unprofessional conduct. *KBA v. Hammond*, 619 S.W.2d 696, 699 (Ky. 1981).

The most meaningful reason for this ethical mandate is that too much work prevents competent representation for someone whose liberty is at risk. Incompetent performance has its most dramatic consequences in capital cases, and is often due to overwork. It is a deadly problem across the United States.[39]

A defender who resolves having too much work by deferring a right of one client in order to serve another client is providing unethical representation to the client who forfeits his rights. "Effectiveness . . . is not a matter of professional competence alone. It also includes the requirement that the services of the attorney be devoted solely to the interest of his client undiminished by conflicting considerations."[40] In *People v. Johnson*, 606 P.2d 738, 744 (Cal. 1980), the court found that a public defender who, "burdened by the conflicting rights of clients entitled to a speedy trial, seeks to waive one client's right, that conduct cannot be justified on the basis of counsel's right to control judicial proceedings. The public defender's decision under these circumstances is not a matter of defense strategy at all; it is an attempt to resolve a conflict of interest by preferring one client over another. As a matter of principle, such a decision requires the approval of the disfavored client. (*Cf.* ABA CODE OF PROF. RESPONSIBILITY, E.C. 5-16.) We conclude that the consent of appointed counsel to a postponement of trial beyond the statutory period, if given solely to resolve a calendar conflict and not to promote the best interests of his client, cannot stand unless supported by the express or implied consent of the client himself."

DISCIPLINARY AND MALPRACTICE CONSEQUENCES OF EXCESSIVE WORK. A defender who accepts "more cases than can be properly handled may result not only in reversals for failing to adequately represent clients, but in disciplinary action for violation of the Code of Professional Responsibility." *State v. Joe U. Smith*, 681 P.2d 1374, 1382 (Ariz. 1984).

Excessive trial or appellate cases is not viewed as a defense to failing to fulfill ethical duties of representation regardless of the intention of the lawyer, since the bar's obligation is to protect the public from incompetent service.[41] "The lack of time available to a public defender for the preparation of each case and the resulting failure to exercise the requisite diligence can subject the attorney to civil liability in a malpractice action. Even though the Code and Model Rules disclaim any setting of standards to be used in judging an attorney's conduct in a malpractice suit, a recent trend is to use the Code as the proper standard."[42]

"The ABA Standing Committee on Lawyers' Professional Liability and its National Legal Malpractice Data Center has found that a disproportionate number of lawyers that have been in practice more than ten years are the subject of malpractice claims. Younger lawyers account for fewer claims, which suggests that failure to maintain knowledge and skills is an important component of malpractice risk."[43]

Issue #2: If the workload of a defender is currently more than can be competently performed in a quality manner, she must withdraw from sufficient cases to enable ethical representation.
A defender "should withdraw from a sufficient number of matters to permit proper handling of the remaining matters." Wisconsin Formal Opinion E-84-11, *reaffirmed,* Wisconsin Formal Opinion E-91-3; *State v. Alvey,* 524 P.2d 747 (1974); *State v. Gasen,* 356 N.E.2d 505 (1976).

The reasons for this conclusion are obvious. The eleven substantial areas discussed above must be performed by the defender. Those dimensions of representation are substantial; they take time. A defender's time to work on cases has an upper limit. When a lawyer fails to make full use of discovery procedures, fails to adequately investigate or interview or subpoena favorable witness, fails to perfect an appeal, or fails to file appropriate motions, that defender faces substantial disciplinary consequences, including disbarment. *See, e.g., The Florida Bar v. Morales,* 366 So. 2d 431 (Fla. 1978); *Matter of Lewis,* 445 N.E.2d 987 (Ind. 1983).

However, if the motion to withdraw made to the court is denied, a lawyer has no legal or ethical choice but to continue representing the client. Model Rule 1.16(a), "Declining or Terminating Representation," states ". . . a lawyer . . . shall withdraw from the representation of a client if: 1) the representation will result in violation of the Rules of Professional Conduct or other law; 2) the lawyer's physical or mental condition materially impairs the lawyer's ability to represent the client. . . ." However, Section (c) of Model Rule 1.16 instructs that ". . . when ordered to do so by a tribunal, a lawyer shall continue representation notwithstanding good cause for terminating the representation." DR 2-110 of the Model Code is substantially the same in its requirements.

As the protested representation proceeds, the defender must continue to object and pursue appropriate additional judicial review. A defender "ordered by a court to engage in action which is believed by the lawyer to be an ethical violation, should continue to object on ethical grounds and to seek whatever judicial review in his or her independent judgment is reasonably available and necessary, although complying in the meantime with any court order." Arizona Opinion 90-10.

The requirement to proceed presents a defender with real dilemmas that must be realistically hurdled. For instance, the defender must do voir dire, an opening statement, a closing argument, and, when appropriate, direct and cross-examinations, even though the lawyer has had insufficient preparation time to perform in a way that reflects competence and quality. Standing mute is not acceptable ethical conduct despite the inability to perform at an appropriate level.

If a lawyer is required to proceed despite being unprepared because of too many cases, the lawyer should consider an extraordinary writ as an appropriate challenge to the court's forced representation.[44] Ironically, the writ will further increase the workload of the defender.[45]

Issue #3: A supervising lawyer cannot assign additional work to a subordinate lawyer if the volume of work would cause the defender to perform incompetently.

If a supervising lawyer orders a subordinate lawyer to assume additional work, including additional casework, the subordinate lawyer is ethically required to refuse that additional work as long as the subordinate lawyer is unable to comply with the required ethical duties and criminal justice standards. Model Rule 5.2, "Responsibilities of a Subordinate Lawyer," rejects the notion that a lawyer is not ethically responsible for her conduct simply because she acted at the direction of another person, the so-called Nuremberg defense. The logic is simple and compelling. It is wrong to act unethically even if ordered to do so by a supervisor. Although the principle is clear in theory, it is often difficult to follow in practice, especially when there are substantially negative consequences from following it. *See Attorney Grievance Commonwealth v. Kahn*, 431 A.2d 1336 (Md. 1981) (lawyer's conduct not excused merely because employer directed the conduct on pain of dismissal.). However, a defender does not violate the Model Rules if she acts in accordance with a supervisor's "reasonable resolution of an arguable question of professional duty." MODEL RULE 5.2(b).

Consistent with these directives, Model Rule 5.1, "Responsibilities of a Partner or Supervising Lawyer," prevents a supervisor from ordering a subordinate lawyer to do something that would cause a violation of the ethical rules. Thus, "supervisors in a state public defender office may not ethically increase the workloads of subordinate lawyers to the point where the lawyer cannot, even at personal sacrifice, handle each of his or her clients' matters competently and in a non-neglectful manner." Wisconsin Formal Opinion E-84-11, *reaffirmed*, Wisconsin Formal Opinion E-91-3. A supervisor who does so, or a chief defender who permits it, acts unethically.

Issue #4: Who ultimately decides when there is a difference in judgment between the supervisor and subordinate over the ability of the subordinate to handle additional work?

This is a difficult issue that has no easy solution since both the supervisor and subordinate have ethical and employment duties. Practically, how is the conclusion reached that one more case is excessive work? Is the subordinate lawyer the sole determiner of this? If not, is the supervising lawyer the final arbiter? In cases assigned by a judge, is the court the final arbiter?

Substantial but not complete deference must be given to the staff lawyer's judgment since that lawyer has significant, independent ethical duties, and is most informed about her work duties. When a supervisor is fully apprised of the work the defender is doing, the capacity for work of the defender, and is convinced that the lawyer can perform additional work, the supervisor can assign the additional work and the lawyer must accept it.

In determining what constitutes an excessive caseload, reliance on caseload standards, such as the NLADA standards, provide a context. The caseload of a defender represents only a rough measure of the workload of that lawyer. A caseload number provides little information to a supervisor, judge, or funding authority about the quality or competence of the work. Before a defender can seek to decline or withdraw from additional work, the defender must substantiate she is working at her capacity. If other public-sector employees, for example, prosecutors, are required to work only forty hours or are paid overtime or are given compensatory time for all extra hours, then a defender should not be expected to handle the work above the normal workweek for "free." While extra hours for lawyers are to be expected, there are limits. At some point, a defender cannot be compelled to do all work in excess of a normal workweek under compulsion of disciplinary action for incompetence or dismissal by her employer. A defender must refuse additional work when unable to perform the tasks necessary to meet the eleven areas identified by the Model Rules and the ABA Standards, and maintain a balanced life.

In assigning this work, the supervisor bears significant responsibility to assist the lawyer in understanding how she can handle this additional work. This can include increased coaching by the supervisor, more support staff, and additional training. If the staff lawyer remains convinced that despite such efforts the additional work cannot be done effectively, the lawyer can ask the court for permission to withdraw from appropriate case(s) and make a record in appropriate cases that the representation is not competent.

A lawyer who refuses work because she remains convinced of her inability to do more work competently places her continued employment at risk. This potential harsh employment consequence is all the more reason for supervisors to defer substantially to staff who indicate an inability to do more.

Issue #5: Both the supervisor and the subordinate are ethically culpable when the subordinate performs incompetently due to excessive workload.

Under Model Rules 1.7(b), 5.2, 6.2, and 8.3, a lawyer cannot accept work if it would likely result in the lawyer's violation of an ethical rule, including the rule to provide competent representation. The staff lawyer cannot rely on the defense that she was ordered to do it.

A supervising lawyer cannot, under Model Rule 5.1, require a staff lawyer to do anything that would cause a violation of an ethical rule, including handling more cases than can be done competently. A supervisor cannot rely on the defense that she did not know about the excessiveness of the work assigned the staff lawyer.

Issue #6: When a defender office has reached or exceeded its limit in the number of clients it can competently represent in a quality manner, the chief defender must decline additional clients or move to withdraw from cases causing excessive workload.

Under ABA Standard 5-5.3, "Workload," a defender organization cannot handle more cases than it has the human capacity to handle competently. Courts likewise conclude that defender systems cannot accept work in excess of a load that can be performed competently and with quality. There are distinct realities, however, that deter a chief defender from refusing to take additional cases or moving to withdraw from cases: political ramifications to the chief defender's employment, future funding reductions, and inability to muster the necessary proof of the overwork of the staff.[46]

Despite compelling reasons for a chief defender's reluctance to decline appointment to additional cases or move to withdraw from excessive cases, ethical and professional standards leave the chief defender no choice. The cases must be declined or turned back. This procedure is recognized as the legal and ethical mandate of defender offices.[47] When funding or staffing is reduced to the level that new or existing clients cannot be represented competently throughout their case, the defender office must decline new cases or withdraw from existing cases. The Model Code "creates a primary duty to existing clients of the lawyer. Acceptance of new clients, with a concomitant greater overload of work, is ethically improper. Once it is apparent that staffing reductions caused by loss of funding will make it impossible to serve even the existing clientele of a legal services office, no new matters should be accepted, absent extraordinary circumstances." ABA Formal Opinion 347, *Ethical Obligations of Lawyer to Clients of Legal Services Offices When Those Offices Lose Funding* (1981). DR 6-101(A)(2) and (3) are violated by the lawyer who represents more clients than can be handled competently. *Id.*

While this discussion of the public defender's ethical duties may seem esoteric to some observers, it is clear that the ethical duties of the individual defender are often severely compromised by systemic, organizational pathology. Current analyses in the areas of organizational management and ethics increasingly point to moving away from Kantian models of individual duty to postmodern models examining the political and moral responsibilities of organizations where individuals face intractable ethical dilemmas.[48] While there is not enough space to discuss fully the ramifications of this for public defenders, it is clear that the "overwork" dilemmas under discussion are primarily generated by macrosystems rather than merely the product of the deficits of individual lawyers. Therefore, it seems fitting to look toward future discussions of such ethical problems using analyses that embrace larger systems.

Conclusion

There are immutable realities facing today's defender:

1. Every client whose life or liberty is at risk must be afforded quality representation, even if poor.

2. There are a limited number of hours available for a lawyer to do work.
3. The competent, quality representation of a criminal client has many significant dimensions that require time to perform.
4. It takes time for a lawyer to remain current in legal knowledge and skills.
5. Different people have varying capacities for work based on their personality, available staff support, and their particular life stressors.
6. The pressure to accept whatever workload is assigned by a supervisor or appointing judge is immense.
7. Many public defenders suffer from denial of their forced ineffectiveness and the battering of constant overwork.

Forced ineffectiveness due to too much work is the most pernicious reality facing defenders today. Incompetent work that does not meet quality standards, even on behalf of the guilty, undermines the integrity of our criminal justice process and the reliability of its results, which necessarily depend on effective performance by prosecutor, judge, and defender. Unfortunately, too many defenders take on all work assigned and thus provide incompetent or marginal representation that falls short of national quality performance standards. That conduct also directly discourages improvement of the system. This is serious misconduct that all too often is tolerated silently in a dysfunctional manner. Public defenders must provide zealous, ethical representation and must advocate for the necessary time and tools to do so.

Accordingly, public defenders facing the questions presented in this chapter should respond as follows:

1. A public defender cannot ethically accept work beyond a quantity she can competently perform in a quality manner.
2. If the workload of a defender is currently more than can be done in a competent, quality manner, the defender must decline to accept additional cases and withdraw from sufficient work to enable effective representation for the defender's remaining clients. However, if the motion to withdraw from case(s) is denied by the court, the public defender must continue to represent the client(s), objecting to the continued representation and seeking further judicial review as appropriate.
3. A public defender supervisor cannot assign work to a subordinate above an amount the subordinate lawyer can competently handle in a quality manner based on the nature of the other cases and other work already assigned, other staff sup-

port available or not available to the supervisor or subordinate lawyer, and the subordinate lawyer's current capacity for work.

4. When the subordinate and the supervisor disagree over the ability of the subordinate to handle additional work, substantial but not complete deference should be afforded the subordinate lawyer who bears independent ethical responsibilities and who is most knowledgeable about the nature and extent of her workload. When the supervising lawyer strongly believes the subordinate lawyer can competently render quality service with the additional work, the supervising lawyer can assign the work but must affirmatively assist the subordinate lawyer in understanding how the additional work can be effectively performed. The subordinate lawyer who continues to believe she is incapable of ethically handling the additional work must move the court to withdraw from the additional case(s), knowing that her continued employment is separate from her ethical duties.

5. When a subordinate lawyer's work is incompetently performed due to excessive workload, both the subordinate lawyer and supervising lawyer are responsible for the unethical conduct.

6. If the office's lawyers cannot competently render quality representation for the additional work, the chief defender must decline acceptance of additional incoming cases or move to withdraw from cases causing excessive workload.

Notes

1. *See* MODEL RULE 5.3.

2. *See, e.g.*, Gambert v. Heat, 44 Cal. 542 (1872).

3. *See, e.g.*, Friday v. State Bar, 144 P.2d 564 (Cal. 1943). The lawyer in Friday was suspended for six months for solicitation of business. The court discussed its ability to also discipline a lawyer for incompetent performance. "There is nothing in the State Bar Act conferring authority upon the board of governors to recommend a discipline for lack of legal learning, as a general charge. Nor does the board have power to recommend the discipline of an attorney for a deficiency in legal knowledge when such deficiency is the gravamen of the charge of specific misconduct with relation to a client. The only cause for discipline which would appear to be a basis for such a charge is a violation of the oath taken by the attorney, or of his duties as such attorney." BUSINESS AND PROFESSIONS CODE, *see* 6103, St. 1939, p. 357. The oath of a lawyer pledges him "faithfully to discharge the duties of any attorney at law to the best of his knowledge and ability. . . . In other words, he must perform his duties to the best of his individual ability, not the standard of ability required of lawyers generally in the community. Mere ignorance of the law in conducting the affairs of his client in good faith is not a cause for discipline. . . . Some spe-

cific act of immoral conduct must be the basis of discipline. In respect to legal learning it is assumed that once he is found to possess it he continues to have it. As we have seen, no mere charge of an act or a series of acts showing ignorance of the law is ground for discipline." *Id.* at 567, 568. *See also* Gaudineer, *Ethics and Malpractice*, 26 DRAKE L. REV. 88, 96 (1977).

4. *Competent* is defined in *Webster's Third New International Dictionary* as "possessed of or characterized by marked or sufficient aptitude, skill, strength, or knowledge . . . possessed of knowledge, judgment, strength, or skill needed to perform an indicated action. . . ."

5. *Quality* is defined in *Webster's Third New International Dictionary* as "a degree of excellence . . . degree of conformance to a standard. . . ."

6. Legal competence has also been defined by the ALI-ABA Committee on Continuing Legal Education, *A Model Peer Review System* (1980). An evaluation process was proposed that was aimed at improving lawyers' performance, and it was developed with reference to accounting and medical peer review programs. "[C]ompetence (subjective) and performance (objective) . . . are inextricably related. In fact, performance is probably the best indicator of underlying knowledge and skill." *Id.* at 12. Aspects of competent performance by a lawyer identified in *A Model Peer Review System* are: 1) identifying legal competence, 2) information gathering, 3) legal analysis, 4) strategy formation, 5) strategy execution, 6) following through, 7) practice management, 8) professional responsibility, 9) practice evaluation, 10) training and supervising support personnel, 11) continuing lawyer self-education. *Id.* at 11–25.

7. Importantly, the comment to the Model Rule is clear in explaining that it is providing thinking on the dimensions included in the concept of competence, and is not providing an exhaustive listing of all aspects of competence. Prompt action varies depending on the case and the nature of the action. Nevertheless, it is not proper to delay or fail to perform tasks necessary to render effective representation to a client because of other legal work.

8. Prof. Charles Ogletree argues that those activities are essential to developing empathy with clients. Avoiding intense client contact not only leads to inadequate lawyering, it robs the lawyer of self-enhancing and sustaining experiences in the practice of law. Charles Ogletree, *Beyond Justifications: Seeking Motivations to Sustain Public Defenders*, 106 HARV. L. REV. 1239–94 (1993).

9. Richard Klein, *Legal Malpractice, Professional Discipline, and Representation of the Indigent Defendant*, 61 TEMPLE L. REV. 1171, 1182 (1988).

10. While neither the Model Rules nor the ABA Standards refer to this obligation, courts are increasingly requiring this in light of the substantial harm to defendants who reveal harmful information during these interviews. The federal sentencing guidelines criteria have dramatically focused this reality. United States v. Herrera-Figueroa, 918 F.2d 1430 (9th Cir. 1990); United States v. Davis, 919 F.2d 1181 (6th Cir. 1990).

11. "In almost every sphere of law, developments are rapid and constant. Consider some of the changes that have taken place in the past 50 years: . . . changes in criminal procedure which have altered it to the point of being

virtually unrecognizable to pre-World War II students of the subject. Changes in the next 50 years—the likely span of many new lawyers' practices—are likely to be no less great. Even where such changes have not taken place, there is a need to hone one's skills and gain new perspectives on the same subject matter. . . ." *In the Spirit of Public Service: A Blueprint for the Rekindling of Lawyer Professionalism*, 112 F.R.D. 243, 273 (1986).

12. FRANDSON, "Continuing Education for the Professions," SERVING PERSONAL AND COMMUNITY NEEDS THROUGH ADULT EDUCATION (1980).

13. Livneh, *Characteristics of Lifelong Learners in the Human Service Professions*, 38 ADULT EDUC. QTRLY 149 (1988).

14. Ferketish & Hayden, *HRD and Quality: The Chicken or the Egg*, TRAINING AND DEVELOPMENT (January 1992) at 39.

15. The "TQM Revolution" is sweeping all the human service professions. The effective lawyer at least must understand the language and values of TQM to work collaboratively with professionals from other disciplines such as medicine, social work, and public administration. A hidden advantage for the informed lawyer is that more effective collaboration across disciplines yields more powerful case advocacy and, in the long-run, better investment of limited time and resources. *See* L.M. MARTIN, TOTAL QUALITY MANAGEMENT IN HUMAN SERVICE ORGANIZATIONS (Sage 1993).

16. The ABA Criminal Justice Mental Health Standards (1989) require continuing education of "advanced instruction on mental health and mental retardation law. . . ." ABA STANDARD 7-1.3.

17. Anne Melissa Rossheim, "Putting Clients' Needs First: Law Firms Get Trained in Total Quality Management," *Lawyer Hiring and Training Report*, Vol. 12 No. 6 (June 1992) at 1; Joel F. Henning, "TQM Doesn't Just Happen Unless Your Firm Invests in Training," *Lawyer Hiring and Training Report*, Vol. 12 No. 6 (June 1992) at 4; ALI-ABA, *A Practical Guide to Achieving Excellence in the Practice of Law.*

18. Dodson, *Speeding the Way to Total Quality*, TRAINING AND DEVELOPMENT (June 1991) at 35.

19. David Meyer, *Toward the Total Quality Law Office: New Approaches to Defender Management*, NLADA CORNERSTONE, Vol. 13 No. 4 (1991) at 14.

20. *See generally* Edward C. Monahan, *Deciding to Train for Quality Service: Quality is the Only Acceptable Standard*, NLADA CORNERSTONE, Vol. 14, No. 3 (1992) at 11.

21. *See, e.g.*, Stephen Rench, *Building the Powerfully Personal Criminal Defense*, 42 MERCER L. REV. 569 (1991). Defenders' culture has lionized and rewarded Lone Rangers. Teamwork and consultation have never been hallmarks of the criminal defense lawyers' culture.

22. Peer review can be introduced through various methodologies. Its "proven way of enhancing performances, its various formats, and its lethargic acceptance by attorneys" is reviewed by Edmund B. Spaeth, Jr., in *To What Extent Can a Disciplinary Code Assure the Competence of Lawyers?* 61 TEMPLE L. REV. 1211 (1988). Colorado defenders employ a pretrial review process. Ken-

tucky defenders use a similar process identified as case review. The National Legal Aid and Defender Association has provided training on these quality assurance processes at its Defender Management Conferences.

23. Leon R. Kass observes that the ethical practice of the novice professional probably will not develop as the result of reading codes and manuals. Profound ethical understanding and praxis is the result of novices working closely with ethical mentors and supervisors. The death of institutionalized novice-mentor relationships, therefore, has profound implications for the young professional's grasp of crucial ethical principles in the practice of law, especially in defender organizations. *See* L.R. Kass, *Practicing Ethics: Where's the Action?* HASTINGS CENTER REPORT (Jan./Feb. 1990) 5–12.

24. LISA J. MCINTYRE, THE PUBLIC DEFENDER: THE PRACTICE OF LAW IN THE SHADOWS OF REPUTE (University of Chicago Press 1987) at 115.

25. *Id.* at 118.

26. A recent random sampling of lawyers in this country reveals that dissatisfaction with the profession is rampant. All of the above resources have been in rapid decline in the belt-tightening environment of most law firms and agencies, and the loss of key resources as well as the resulting "time famine" leads to high rates (23 percent) of intense dissatisfaction. D. Mochogrosso, Proceedings of the ABA Commission of Impaired Attorneys, ABA Midyear Convention (1991). This study is cited at length in Benjamin & Sales, "Lawyer Psychopathology," *infra* note 31, at 295.

27. In its fourth generation "time management" is "really a misnomer—the challenge is not to manage time, but to manage ourselves." STEPHEN R. COVEY, THE SEVEN HABITS OF HIGHLY EFFECTIVE PEOPLE (1989) at 150.

28. *Id.* at 157; Stephen R. Covey, in *First Things First* (1994), describes the four generations as follows: The first generation involves reminders, notes, checklists. The second generation is characterized by planning and preparation with calendars and planning devices with goal setting. The third generation is planning, prioritizing and controlling with long and short-term goals with detailed daily planning. The fourth generation moves "beyond time management to life leadership—to a fourth generation based on paradigms that will create quality-of-life results." *Id.* at 22–31.

29. *Id.* at 148.

30. *Id.* at 162–65.

31. G.A.H. Benjamin and B.D. Sales, "Lawyer Psychopathology: Development, Prevalence, and Intervention," in J.R.P. OLGOFF, LAW AND PSYCHOLOGY: THE BROADENING OF THE DISCIPLINE (Carolina Academic Press 1992) at 288.

32. Benjamin and Sales, *supra* note 31, at 291–92.

33. *Id.* at 295.

34. ABA, At The Breaking Point: A National Conference on the Emerging Crisis in the Quality of Lawyers' Health and Lives—Its Impact on Law Firms and Client Services (1991).

35. Forty hours per week for fifty-two weeks.

36. NLADA, *Indigent Defense Caseloads and Common Sense: An Update* (1992) at 6. This work extensively discusses caseload caps for capital and non-

capital cases, for full-time and contract public defenders, and it details, among other things, methodologies and case weighting.

37. National Advisory Commission on Criminal Justice Standards and Goals, *Courts,* Standard 13.12, "Workload of Public Defenders," (1973) at 276.

38. The ethics opinions of the ABA and state bars that address workload are uniform in their conclusions.

39. Stephen B. Bright, *Counsel for the Poor: The Death Sentence Not for the Worst Crime But for the Worst Lawyer,* 103 YALE L.J. 1835 (1994). Stephen Bright identifies the political and systematic horrors that propel the continued underfunding of defenders who have too much work. "Despite abundant documentation of the enormity of the need for substantive changes, some continue to suggest that the burden of providing counsel to the poor—even in capital cases—may be satisfied by the conscription of members of the legal profession. However, it is the constitutional duty of the state, not of members of the legal profession, to provide indigent defendants with counsel. Responses to the problems posed by ineffective assistance of counsel should be conceived in a way that gives effect to this principle. Georgia, a state in which there have been numerous egregious examples of deficient representation, has no difficulty coming up with local, state, and federal money to prepare for the Olympic Games, but it does not secure or appropriate funding to assure competent representation and equal justice in its courts." *Id.* at 1869.

40. People v. Corona, 145 Cal. Rptr. 894, 915 (1978).

41. *See generally* Richard Klein, *Legal Malpractice, Professional Discipline, and Representation of the Indigent Defendant,* 61 TEMPLE L. REV. 1171, 1185–86 (1988).

42. *Id.* at 1190–91.

43. *In the Spirit of Public Service: A Blueprint for the Rekindling of Lawyer Professionalism,* 112 FRD 243, 273 n.83 (1986).

44. *Cf., e.g.,* Brothers v. Burt, 265 N.E.2d 922 (N.Y. 1970); Brown v. Pa. Railroad, 255 A.2d 554 (1969); Cardot v. Luff, 262 S.E.2d 889 (W.Va. 1980).

45. There is a real and present danger that a half-baked job may survive the constitutional requirement of *Strickland.* A defender may want to consider fully informing the defendant of counsel's incompetence, per Easley v. State, 334 So. 2d 630 (Fla. Dist. Ct. App. 1976), so the client can complain and seek the defender's removal. Making a clear record is critical. *In Re* Sherlock, 525 N.E.2d 572 (Ohio App. 1987).

46. *See generally* Suzanne Mounts, *Public Defender Program: Professional Responsibility and Competent Representation,* 1982 WISC. L. REV. 473, 503–7.

47. *See, e.g., In re* Prosecution of Criminal Appeals by the Tenth Judicial Public Defender, 561 So. 2d 1130 (Fla. 1990) In this case, the public defender office had 1,700 appeals waiting to be briefed. Briefs for nonindigents were filed at least one year sooner than briefs for indigents. The court held that "the lengthy delay in filing initial briefs in appeals by indigents is a clear violation of the indigent state defendant's constitutional right to effective assistance of counsel on appeal." *Id.* at 1132. The court identified the cause of the problem as "woefully inadequate funding of the public defender's office despite re-

peated appeals to the legislature for assistance." *Id.* When the "backlog of cases in the public defender's office is so excessive that there is no possible way he can timely handle these cases, it is his responsibility to move the court to withdraw," and the court will appoint other counsel. *Id.* at 1138. *See also* Hattern v. State, 561 So. 2d 562 (Fla. 1990); State v. Pitner, 582 A.2d 163 (Vt. 1990); Schwarz v. Cianca, 495 So. 2d 1208 (Fla. App. 1986).

48. *See, e.g.,* R. Hardin, *The Artificial Duties of Contemporary Professionals,* 64 SOCIAL SERVICE REV. 528–41 (1990). For further discussion of organizational pathology and ethics, *see* K.G. Denhardt, "Organizational Structure as a Context for Administrative Ethics," in T.L. COOPER (ED.) HANDBOOK OF ADMINISTRATIVE ETHICS (Dekker 1994).

Bibliography

Books and Standards

ABA/BNA LAWYERS MANUAL ON PROFESSIONAL CONDUCT (1984).

ABA CANONS OF PROFESSIONAL ETHICS (1908).

ABA MODEL CODE OF PROFESSIONAL RESPONSIBILITY (1969 as amended through 1980).

ABA MODEL RULES OF PROFESSIONAL CONDUCT (1983 as amended through 1992).

ABA STANDARDS FOR CRIMINAL JUSTICE DEFENSE FUNCTION (3d ed. 1993).

ABA STANDARDS FOR CRIMINAL JUSTICE PROVIDING DEFENSE SERVICES (3d ed. 1992).

Burke, Broderick, Walko, *Indigent Defense Caseloads and Common Sense: An Update* (1992).

Ethics Opinions

ABA Comm. on Ethics and Professional Responsibility, Formal Opinion 347 (1981) *Ethical Obligations of Lawyers to Clients of Legal Services Offices When Those Offices Lost Funding.*

ABA Comm. on Ethics and Professional Responsibility, Informal Opinion 1359 (1976) *Use of Waiting Lists or Priorities by Legal Service Office.*

Arizona Opinion No. 90-10 (1990).

Wisconsin Formal Opinion E-84-11 (1984) *Ethical Obligations with Heavy Workload in State Public Defender Office.*

Wisconsin Formal Opinion E-91-3 (1991) *State Public Defender Office Workload.*

Cases

State v. Joe U. Smith, 681 P.2d 1374 (Ariz. 1984).

In re Prosecution of Criminal Appeals by the Tenth Judicial Public Defender, 561 S.W.2d 1130 (Ala. 1990).

APPENDIX

List of Specific Questions Presented in Each Chapter

Chapter One

May a public defender be found in contempt for refusing to accept a criminal appointment because she believes that she is ethically barred from representing a defendant? What should a public defender do if a judge or her supervisor orders her to proceed or to continue representing a defendant when the defender believes she cannot ethically do so?

Chapter Two

Should an individual public defender be permitted to refuse to represent certain categories of clients for moral or ideological reasons? Does the public defender supervisor or agency have the right to limit a defender's ability to "opt out" of certain cases?

Chapter Three

Does defense counsel with doubts about a client's competence have an ethical duty to raise the competency issue even though doing so is contrary to the defendant's best interests or wishes?

Chapter Four

Does counsel have an ethical duty to disregard the client's wishes and assert the insanity defense when counsel believes that raising the defense is in the client's best interest?

347

Chapter Five

Is defense counsel obligated to pursue a suppression motion requested by her client if she feels that the motion is strategically damaging to the defendant's case? If counsel wants to pursue a legal issue in a pretrial motion, but defendant does not, may counsel still go forward?

Chapter Six

Is it ethically proper for defense counsel to call a defense witness to testify, when the defendant insists, if counsel knows the witness will testify falsely? Is it ethically proper for defense counsel to call a defense witness to testify, when the defendant insists, if counsel believes the witness' testimony will be detrimental to the client's case? Is it ethically proper for defense counsel to call a defense witness if counsel believes that the witness' testimony will be helpful, but the client objects to calling that witness?

Chapter Seven

Is defense counsel ethically required to communicate every plea bargain offered to a client even if counsel feels that the offer is unacceptable?

Chapter Eight

When, if ever, is it appropriate in a juvenile delinquency proceeding for a lawyer to ignore a judgment or decision made by a child client and substitute her own judgment or that of the child's parent?

Chapter Nine

What is the role, if any, of the parent or guardian of an accused juvenile delinquent in making decisions during the course of legal representation of the juvenile? Is this role affected in any way by the fact that the parent or guardian has retained counsel for an accused juvenile delinquent or is obligated by law or court order to pay for the cost of assigned counsel or public defender services for the juvenile? What, if any, impact do laws or precedents requiring parental involvement in waivers of their child's rights, parental contributions to the costs of placements or other dispositions, or parental participation in counseling or other juvenile dispositional programs have upon counsel's representation of an accused juvenile?

Chapter Ten

When does a criminal defense lawyer know that a defendant or defense witness intends to commit or has committed perjury?

Chapter Eleven

What must defense counsel ethically do when she learns that her client intends to testify falsely at trial?

Chapter Twelve

During a confidential discussion with her client, a public defender learns information about her client that suggests the client may have provided false information to qualify for appointed/assigned counsel. What obligation, if any, does a public defender have to investigate or to reveal information relating to client eligibility or fraud in obtaining court-appointed counsel? Is that obligation affected by the fact that the defender and her office are burdened by high caseloads that limit the number of indigent clients who can be served?

Chapter Thirteen

Does defense counsel have an ethical duty to advise the trial judge that she is relying on a misunderstanding of the law or overlooking settled law in handling her client's case?

Chapter Fourteen

Must defense counsel correct a trial judge who, in sentencing the defendant, indicates he is relying on the prosecutor's statement that the client has no prior record when counsel knows the defendant has a prior record? If at a sentencing hearing, a defendant is asked by the court about a prior criminal record and denies having any record, does defense counsel have a duty to inform the court about the true state of the defendant's record? Must defense counsel divulge her client's criminal record if the judge specifically asks counsel whether her client has a criminal record?

Chapter Fifteen

May defense counsel who learns that her client has been charged under a false name continue to represent that client without disclosing the client's true identity?

Chapter Sixteen

Should two lawyers from the same public defender office represent co-defendants? To what extent is it ethically proper for a public defender to provide some representation to both codefendants before and at the initial appearance knowing that one codefendant will be assigned outside counsel?

Chapter Seventeen

May a public defender represent an indigent client when her husband is employed by the prosecutor's office? What if her husband is prosecuting a case she is defending? If she is disqualified, is her entire office disqualified? May the conflict be waived?

Chapter Eighteen

Is it ethically proper for a public defender to represent a defendant when that public defender previously prosecuted the defendant on an unrelated case?

Chapter Nineteen

What is the proper ethical response for a public defender when a client (Mr. Jones) discloses to that defender that he committed a crime for which another one of the defender's clients (Mr. Smith) has been charged? Can any other lawyer in the public defender office represent Mr. Smith?

Chapter Twenty

Does criminal defense counsel's ongoing sexual relationship with a police officer, prosecutor, or judge ethically bar counsel from handling cases involving that police officer, prosecutor, or judge? If she is disqualified, is her entire office disqualified? Must defense counsel advise the client if he is sexually involved with a prosecutor, police officer, or judge?

Chapter Twenty-One

Is it ethically proper for an appointed criminal defense lawyer to be sexually involved with a client? Is it ethically proper for such a lawyer to begin a sexual relationship with a client after the client's criminal case has been completed?

Chapter Twenty-Two

Is it ethically proper for a public defender or a public defender agency to compensate a lay witness or to advance funds to cover the expenses incurred by a lay witness? Is it ethically proper for a public defender or a public defender agency to compensate an expert witness or to retain an expert witness on a contingent basis?

Chapter Twenty-Three

What must a full-time public defender or appointed counsel do if the defender believes that she cannot competently handle any larger workload if assigned more cases or other work by a supervisor or if appointed to more cases by a judge? What must a defender do if she has more work than she can handle in a competent, quality manner? What must a public defender supervisor do when a subordinate lawyer refuses additional cases or other work because of an inability to do any additional work competently? If there is disagreement between the supervisor and subordinate about the ability of the subordinate to assume additional work, how is that difference of opinion resolved? Who, the supervisor or subordinate, is responsible if incompetent representation by the subordinate is afforded a client because of too large of a workload? What must the chief defender do with additional cases coming into the office if the defender's staff cannot handle additional work in a competent, quality manner?